Pablo Picasso's "Guernica" (1937)

MILESTONES
of the
20th CENTURY

Ronald Reagan and Mikhail Gorbachev

The funeral of U.S. President John F. Kennedy, Nov. 25, 1963

Henry Ford and a 1907 Ford

Kuwaiti oil field following 1991 Persian Gulf war

"Breitling Orbiter 3," March 1999

MILESTONES
of the
20th CENTURY

GROLIER

Danbury, Connecticut

Cover Photos: Front: Stalin, Roosevelt and Churchill—Courtesy, Franklin D. Roosevelt Library; Berlin Wall—© Reuters/David
Brauchli/Archive Photos; Elvis Presley—Courtesy, RCA Records and Tapes; hula hoop—© FPG International; Harry S. Truman—©
"St. Louis Globe Democrat"; astronaut—NASA; bomb blast—National Archives Photo/AP/Wide World Photos; Mother Teresa—©
Sygma; cellular telephone and computer—© Mel Lindstrom/Tony Stone Images; Martin Luther King, Jr.—© AP/Wide World Photos; family watching television—© Archive Photos. Spine: NASA. Back: Dwight Eisenhower—© AP/Wide World Photos; Vietnam
war—© Gilles Caron/Gamma; Muhammad Ali—© Ken Regan/Camera 5; the Kennedys—© UPI/Corbis-Bettmann; Nehru and Gandhi—© UPI/Corbis-Bettmann; Victrola—Courtesy, Henry Ford Museum and Greenfield Village; typewriter—© Archive Photos; telephone—Courtesy, AT&T Company Photo Center; mobile telephone—Courtesy, Siemens; women's-rights march—© UPI/Corbis-
Bettmann; 1928 Ford—Courtesy, Ford Motor Company; New York City's World Trade Center—© Pictor/Uniphoto; Bill Clinton and
Middle East leaders—© Brad Markel/Liaison Agency

CONTENTS

Mohandas Gandhi

Microsoft's Bill Gates

20TH CENTURY TIME LINE 1900–1999   10

GIANTS OF THE 20TH CENTURY   38

Gen. Douglas MacArthur, the Philippines, Oct. 20, 1944

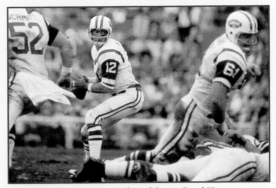

New York Jets' Joe Namath and Super Bowl III

CENTENNIAL REVIEW 90

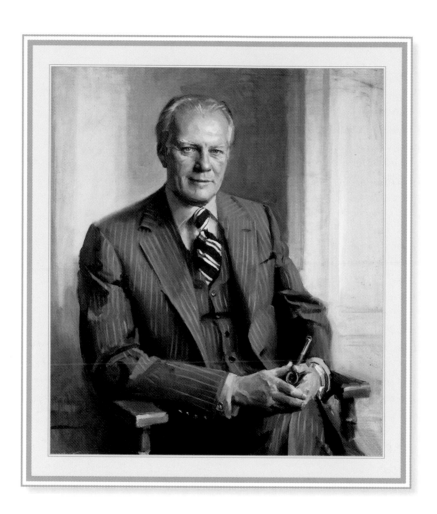

GERALD R. FORD

In many ways, the world into which I was born in July 1913 seems almost impossibly remote. Woodrow Wilson had been inaugurated president of the United States a few months before, carrying with him a brisk northwest wind of political reform. Soon the Constitution was amended to permit the first popular election of United States senators and a graduated income tax. The Federal Reserve System was created to give Washington a measure of control over the world's largest economy. Suffragettes marched up Pennsylvania Avenue carrying banners reading "Tell Your Troubles to Woodrow."

The world gave Wilson troubles enough. As a 5-year-old, I witnessed the celebration staged by my Grand Rapids, MI, neighbors over the end of World War I. The Armistice signed in November 1918 ushered in a provisional peace. Like many of my generation, I regarded American isolation as an article of faith. It took a second world war to change my outlook. I returned from service in the South Pacific believing that if this war, unlike its ghastly predecessor, was to be historically vindicated, then the United States must accept the obligations of leadership and stop thinking itself divinely sheltered behind two oceans.

These convictions led me into politics, beginning with a successful challenge of an isolationist congressman in the 1948 Republican primary. A few months later, I stood in the Oval Office for the first time as Harry Truman outlined the most constructive, creative, and generous chapter in the history of modern foreign policy. Because our offices were across the hall from each other, I often walked to the floor of the House with another young war veteran named John F. Kennedy. Jack and I came from vastly different backgrounds. More often than not, our votes canceled each other out, especially on domestic issues. Yet we reserved our disagreements for the legislative arena. To be sure, we might question one another's ideas, but rarely one another's motives, and never one another's patriotism. It may seem hard to believe, but politics really was more civil in those days before Vietnam and Watergate—events with which I am all too familiar. Yet I remain an optimist, and why not? In the course of my 86 years I have seen more than my share of miracles. I have witnessed the defeat of Nazi tyranny, the elimination of polio, the belated recognition of women and other groups too long condemned to the political and economic sidelines. I have watched as humankind soared into the heavens, and said a prayer of gratitude as the nuclear nightmare that haunted three generations of the world's children was relegated to the history books.

All this was once part of an uncertain future. All this should be a source of inspiration to Americans in the 21st century. To young readers, in particular, I would say: Outwardly, your world may not look the same as mine. New technologies, new industries, new forms of communications, and new medical breakthroughs promise to expand the frontiers of life in years to come. But amid all that is new, may I suggest that you should never lose the old faith in an America that is bolder, better, and fairer with each passing generation. Precisely because I have witnessed so much of America's past, I have no fears for its future.

20TH CENTURY TIME LINE

1900–1999

"Time has no divisions to mark its passage, there is never a thunderstorm or blare of trumpets to announce the beginning of a new month or year. Even when a new century begins, it is only we mortals who ring bells and fire off pistols."

THOMAS MANN

The 100th anniversary of the modern Olympic movement was marked during the opening ceremonies of the XXVI Summer Games in Atlanta, GA, on July 19, 1996, *left*.

20TH-CENTURY TIME LINE

1900

June 14. Hawaii becomes a U.S. territory.
Aug. 14. An eight-nation military force lifts the siege of Peking, ending the Boxer uprising by anti-foreign Chinese nationalists.
Nov. 6. Republican William McKinley is reelected president of the United States.
Also in 1900. German physicist Max Planck formulates the quantum theory.

1901

Jan. 1. The Commonwealth of Australia is founded.
Jan. 22. Queen Victoria of England dies after a reign of nearly 64 years; she is succeeded by her son, who will reign as Edward VII.
Sept. 14. Vice-President Theodore Roosevelt is installed as U.S. president following the assassination of President McKinley.
Also in 1901. American surgeon Walter Reed proves that yellow fever is transmitted by mosquitoes....The first Nobel Prizes are awarded.

1902

May 31. The Boer War (1899–1902) between Great Britain and the Afrikaners in South Africa comes to an end.
Also in 1902. The U.S. occupation of Cuba ends....Arthur Conan Doyle writes the Sherlock Holmes adventure *The Hound of the Baskervilles.*

1903

Nov. 18. The United States acquires the Panama Canal Zone through a treaty with Panama.
Dec. 17. Orville and Wilbur Wright make the first successful flight in a gasoline-powered airplane.
Also in 1903. Marie and Pierre Curie win the Nobel Prize in physics for their work on radioactivity....In baseball's first World Series, the American League's Boston Red Sox defeat the National League's Pittsburgh Pirates, five games to three....The pioneering Western film *The Great Train Robbery* opens in movie theaters.

1904

Feb. 8. Japan attacks Russian forces in Manchuria, initiating the Russo-Japanese War.
Nov. 8. President Roosevelt is elected to a full term.
Also in 1904. Russian physiologist Ivan Pavlov is awarded the Nobel Prize in medicine for his work on digestion in laboratory animals.

1905

Sept. 5. Japan and Russia sign the Treaty of Portsmouth, ending the Russo-Japanese War.

April 18, 1906

Oct. 26. Norway gains independence from Sweden.

Also in 1905. Civil disturbances known as the Revolution of 1905 take place in Russia, forcing Czar Nicholas II to grant some civil rights....German physicist Albert Einstein proposes his Special Theory of Relativity....W.E.B. Du Bois forms the Niagara Movement to fight for civil rights for African-Americans.

April 6, 1909

1906

April 18. Most of the city of San Francisco, CA, is destroyed by an earthquake and fire.

Also in 1906. William Sidney Porter (O. Henry) publishes his first collection of short stories....Upton Sinclair publishes *The Jungle,* leading to the passage of U.S. federal food and drug laws....Lee De Forest invents the triode, a key component for amplifying radio signals.

1907

July 25. Korea becomes a protectorate of Japan.
Nov. 16. Oklahoma becomes the 46th state.

1908

Nov. 3. Republican William Howard Taft is elected president of the United States.

Also in 1908. The Model T Ford is introduced....Jack Johnson becomes the first African-American heavyweight boxing champion....Robert Baden-Powell of Great Britain founds the Boy Scout movement.

1909

April 6. American Arctic explorer Robert E. Peary claims to be the first to have reached the North Pole.

Also in 1909. The National Association for the Advancement of Colored People (NAACP) is founded.

1910

Feb. 8. The Boy Scouts of America are founded.
May 6. King Edward VII of Great Britain dies and is succeeded by his second son, who will reign as George V.

May 31. The Union of South Africa is established.

Aug. 22. Japan formally annexes Korea.

Also in 1910. French sculptor Auguste Rodin creates the bronze figure "The Thinker."

"The Thinker," 1910

1911

Sept. 9. Italy declares war on the Ottoman Turks and annexes Libya, Tripolitania, and Cyrenaica.

Dec. 14. Norwegian explorer Roald Amundsen becomes the first man to reach the South Pole.

Also in 1911. Sir Ernest Rutherford formulates his theory of atomic structure....The first film studio is established at Hollywood in California....The first Indianapolis 500 auto race is held.

1912

Jan. 6. New Mexico becomes the 47th state.
Feb. 14. Arizona becomes the 48th state.
March 10. After the overthrow of the Manchu Ch'ing Dynasty, China becomes a republic.
March 12. The Girl Scouts of America are established.
April 14–15. On its maiden voyage, the British ocean liner *Titanic* strikes an iceberg and sinks off the coast of Newfoundland, killing more than 1,500 people.
Nov. 5. Democrat Woodrow Wilson is elected president of the United States.
Also in 1912. Swiss psychiatrist Carl Jung publishes *The Psychology of the Unconscious*....French Dada artist Marcel Duchamp paints "Nude Descend-

ing a Staircase No. 2"....Native American Jim Thorpe wins the Olympic decathlon and pentathlon.

1913

Feb. 1. Grand Central Station, the world's largest railway station, opens in New York City.

May 31. The 17th Amendment to the Constitution, establishing direct election of senators, is ratified. (The 16th Amendment, calling for a graduated income tax, was approved on Feb. 25, 1913.)

Dec. 23. The Federal Reserve Bill, a basic reform of the U.S. banking system, is signed into law by President Wilson.

Also in 1913. Albert Schweitzer opens his hospital in Africa....The Armory Show, a full-scale exhibition of contemporary painting, opens at the 69th Regiment Armory in New York City.

1914

June 28. Archduke Franz Ferdinand, heir to the Austro-Hungarian throne, is assassinated in Sarajevo, Bosnia, precipitating World War I.

July 28. World War I starts when Austria-Hungary declares war on Serbia.

Aug. 1–4. Germany declares war on Russia and France and invades Belgium; Britain declares war on Germany; President Wilson proclaims U.S. neutrality.

Aug. 7. Germany invades France.

Aug. 10. Austria-Hungary invades Russia.

Aug. 15. The newly constructed Panama Canal, across the isthmus of Panama, is opened.

Sept. 12. The First Battle of the Marne concludes, with the Allies halting the German offensive in France.

Oct. 31. The Ottoman Empire (Turkey) joins the Central Powers (Germany, Austria-Hungary, and Bulgaria).

Also in 1914. Charlie Chaplin develops his "little tramp" character in a series of slapstick films.

1915

April 22. At the Second Battle of Ypres, Germany becomes the first nation to use poison gas.

May 7. A German submarine sinks the British passenger ship *Lusitania*, killing 1,198 passengers, including 128 Americans.

May 23. Italy joins the Allies, declaring war on Austria-Hungary.

Also in 1915. U.S. Marines land in Haiti, beginning a 20-year period of mili-

Aug. 15, 1914

tary occupation....English author Somerset Maugham publishes *Of Human Bondage*....D.W. Griffith's controversial movie *The Birth of a Nation* is shown for the first time....Bayer introduces aspirin in tablet form.

1916

March 15. Gen. John J. Pershing leads U.S. troops into Mexico to punish revolutionary Pancho Villa, who earlier had raided New Mexico.

Nov. 7. Wilson is reelected president of the United States.

Dec. 18. The ten-month-long Battle of Verdun ends.

Also in 1916. U.S. Marines land in Santo Domingo (the Dominican Republic) to restore order; they will occupy the island until 1924....The Easter Rebellion in Dublin, Ireland, is put down by the British....Jeanette Rankin is the first woman to be elected to the U.S. House of Representatives....American poet Carl Sandburg publishes his first book, *Chicago Poems.*

June 28, 1919

March 2. The Russian Revolution begins; Czar Nicholas II abdicates....In the United States the Jones Act, making Puerto Rico a U.S. territory, is enacted.
March 31. The United States purchases the Virgin Islands from Denmark.
April 6. The United States declares war on Germany.
June 25. The first American fighting troops land in France.
July 7. Aleksandr Kerensky forms a provisional government in Russia.
Oct. 25. The Bolsheviks (Communists) under V.I. Lenin seize power in Russia.
Nov. 2. The British Balfour Declaration endorses "the establishment in Palestine of a national home for the Jewish people."
Dec. 2. Hostilities are suspended on the eastern front.
Also in 1917. British Col. T.E. Lawrence (Lawrence of Arabia) leads the Arab revolt against the Turks.

Jan. 8. President Wilson announces his Fourteen Points as the basis for peace after the end of World War I.
July 16. The Bolsheviks execute Czar Nicholas II of Russia and his family.
Sept. 26. The Allies begin their final offensive on the western front.
Nov. 11. Germany and the Allies sign an armistice, ending World War I.
Also in 1918. Austria, Poland, and Czechoslovakia become republics....Civil war breaks out in Russia between Communist and anti-Communist forces....An influenza pandemic that begins to sweep through Europe, Asia, and the Americas will kill more than 21 million people in two years.

Jan. 16. The 18th Amendment to the U.S. Constitution, which prohibits the transportation and sale of alcoholic beverages, is ratified; Prohibition will go into effect on Jan. 16, 1920.
June 28. Germany and the Allies sign the Treaty of Versailles, ending World War I and establishing the League of Nations. Leaders of the victorious "Big Four" had spent some six months in Paris negotiating the terms of the treaty.
Sept. 10. Austria and the Allies sign the Treaty of St.-Germain-en-Laye; Austria recognizes the independence of Czechoslovakia, Poland, Hungary, and Yugoslavia.
Also in 1919. The U.S. Senate rejects the Treaty of Versailles, as well as membership in the League of Nations....Walter Gropius founds the Bauhaus school of design in Germany.

Nov. 2. Republican Warren G. Harding is elected president of the United States.
Also in 1920. The League of Nations, with headquarters in Geneva, Switzerland, meets for the first time....The Reds (Communists) defeat the Whites (anti-Communists), ending Russia's civil war....Adolf Hitler forms the National Socialist German Workers' (Nazi) Party....American novelist Sinclair Lewis publishes *Main Street.*

Dec. 26. The Catholic Irish Free State becomes a self-governing dominion of Great Britain.
Also in 1921. Mexican artist Diego Rivera begins painting murals depicting contemporary Mexican life.

Feb. 27. The U.S. Supreme Court declares the 19th Amendment to the Constitution, which gives women the right to vote, to be constitutional; it was ratified in 1920.
Oct. 28. Fascist Benito Mussolini becomes prime minister of Italy.
Also in 1922. Egypt gains its independence....English Egyptologist Howard

The first "Time," March 3, 1923   July 21, 1925

Carter excavates the tomb of ancient Egypt's King Tutankhamen....Irish novelist James Joyce publishes *Ulysses*....*Readers Digest* is founded.

July 6. The Union of Soviet Socialist Republics is established.
Aug. 3. Vice-President Calvin Coolidge is inaugurated as the 30th U.S. president after the sudden death of President Harding.
Sept. 1. An earthquake and fire destroy Tokyo and Yokohama, killing some 100,000 Japanese.
Oct. 29. Turkey is declared a republic; Mustafa Ataturk becomes the nation's first president.
Also in 1923. Vladimir Zworykin patents the iconoscope, the first television transmission tube....*Time* magazine is founded.

Jan. 21. Soviet leader Lenin dies; Joseph Stalin begins a purge of his rivals for the leadership of the Soviet Union.
Nov. 4. President Coolidge is elected to a full term.

July 21. John T. Scopes is found guilty of teaching the theory of evolution in a Tennessee school.
Dec. 1. The Locarno Pact finalizes the treaties between the World War I protagonists.
Also in 1925. American writer F. Scott Fitzgerald publishes *The Great Gatsby*.

March 16. American physicist Robert Goddard launches the first liquid-fuel rocket.
May 2. U.S. Marines land in Nicaragua to put down a revolt and protect U.S. interests. (They will depart in 1933.)
Dec. 25. Japan's Taisho emperor dies; his son will reign as Emperor Hirohito until his death in 1989.
Also in 1926. U.S. Navy explorer Richard E. Byrd and pilot Floyd Bennett make the first airplane flight over the North Pole....English author A.A. Milne writes the children's book *Winnie-the-Pooh*.

May 21. Charles Lindbergh completes the first solo nonstop transatlantic flight.
Sept. 30. New York Yankee Babe Ruth hits his 60th home run of the season.
Also in 1927. The first sound motion picture, *The Jazz Singer*, starring singer Al Jolson, is released.

Aug. 27. The Kellogg-Briand Pact outlawing war is signed by 15 nations; 47 other nations later will sign the pact.

"The Jazz Singer," 1927

Nov. 6. Republican Herbert Hoover is elected the 31st president of the United States.
Also in 1928. Chiang Kai-shek becomes president of China....British bacteriologist Alexander Fleming discovers penicillin....Walt Disney's Mickey Mouse appears in *Steamboat Willie*, the first sound cartoon.

May 16. The first Academy Awards are presented; *Wings* wins the best-picture Oscar.
Oct. 29. The Wall Street stock market crashes, precipitating a worldwide economic depression.
Nov. 29. Richard E. Byrd becomes the first to fly over the South Pole.
Also in 1929. The Lateran Treaty creates the independent state of Vatican City....The Museum of Modern Art is founded in New York City....Erich Maria Remarque publishes *All Quiet On the Western Front*....Ernest Hemingway writes *A Farewell to Arms*.

Nov. 2. Haile Selassie is crowned emperor of Ethiopia.
Also in 1930. The planet Pluto is discovered....Vannevar Bush develops an early type of analog computer.

March 4, 1933

April 14. King Alfonso XIII leaves Spain after a 45-year reign, and Spain is declared a republic.
May 1. New York City's 102-story Empire State Building opens and becomes the world's tallest building.
Also in 1931. Japan occupies Manchuria, China's northeast territory....American writer Pearl Buck publishes *The Good Earth*.

March 1. Charles A. Lindbergh's infant son is kidnapped and later found dead.
May 20. Amelia Earhart becomes the first woman to fly solo across the Atlantic Ocean.
Sept. 22. Arab leader Ibn Saud founds the Kingdom of Saudi Arabia.
Nov. 8. Democrat Franklin D. Roosevelt is elected the 32d president of the United States.
Also in 1932. Eamon de Valera is elected president of the Republic of Ireland....The first particle accelerator is built at the Cavendish Laboratory in England....English physicist James Chadwick confirms the existence of the neutron....The Royal Shakespeare Theatre opens at Stratford-upon-Avon, England....Radio City Music Hall opens in New York City's Rockefeller Center.

Jan. 30. Adolf Hitler becomes chancellor of Germany.
March 4. Franklin D. Roosevelt is inaugurated as president of the United States.
Nov. 16. The United States and the Soviet Union establish relations for the first time.

Dec. 5. The 21st Amendment to the U.S. Constitution, ending Prohibition, is ratified.

May 11. A severe two-day dust storm, one of many, strips topsoil from the Great Plains and creates a "Dust Bowl."
May 25. The Dionnes, the first quintuplets to survive infancy, are born in Callander, Ont.
Aug. 2. Hitler assumes the title of Führer (leader) of Germany.
Also in 1934. George Balanchine and Lincoln Kirstein found the School of American Ballet....Nylon, the first successful synthetic fiber, is invented.

Aug. 14. The U.S. Social Security System is established.
Sept. 8. Louisiana Gov. Huey P. Long is assassinated.
Sept. 15. The Nuremberg Laws deprive German Jews of their citizenship.
Oct. 3. Italy invades Ethiopia.
Also in 1935. Hitler announces German rearmament in violation of the Treaty of Versailles....George Gershwin composes the American opera *Porgy and Bess.*

March 7. Germany reoccupies the Rhineland in violation of the Versailles Treaty.
July 18. The Spanish Civil War begins.
Nov. 3. Roosevelt is reelected president of the United States.
Dec. 11. Britain's King Edward VIII abdicates to marry American divorcée Wallis Warfield Simpson; he becomes the duke of Windsor.
Also in 1936. Joseph Stalin begins a purge of the Soviet Union's political and military leadership that will take as many as 10 million lives....African-American athlete Jesse Owens wins four gold medals at the Berlin Olympic Games....Henry R. Luce begins publishing *Life* magazine....Margaret Mitchell publishes the novel *Gone With the Wind.*

Dec. 11, 1936

July 2. Aviatrix Amelia Earhart disappears during a flight across the Pacific Ocean.
July 7. Japanese forces invade China.
Also in 1937. The German airship *Hindenburg* is destroyed by fire at Lakehurst, NJ....The Golden Gate Bridge is opened in San Francisco....Walt Disney's feature-length cartoon *Snow White and the Seven Dwarfs* is shown....Joe Louis wins the heavyweight-boxing championship.

March 14. Germany invades Austria; a union (Anschluss) of Austria and Germany is proclaimed.
Sept. 30. French and British appeasement of Hitler at the Munich Conference leads to the German occupation of the Sudetenland in western Czechoslovakia.
Also in 1938. Germany's Otto Hahn and Fritz Strassmann produce the first nuclear fission of uranium....Don Budge becomes the first to win tennis' Grand Slam.

March 15. German forces occupy the rest of Czechoslovakia.
March 28. The Spanish Civil War ends.
Aug. 23. Germany and the Soviet Union sign a nonaggression pact.
Sept. 1. Germany invades Poland, beginning World War II.
Sept. 3. Britain and France declare war on Germany.
Sept. 17. Soviet forces invade Poland; Germany and the Soviet Union partition Poland.
Also in 1939. The first jet airplane is flown in Germany....Igor Sikorsky develops America's first successful helicopter....American novelist John Steinbeck publishes *The Grapes of Wrath.*

March 12. Finland surrenders to Russia, ending the Russo-Finnish War.
April 9. Germany invades Denmark and Norway.
May 7. Winston Churchill becomes British prime minister.

May 10. Germany invades Belgium, France, the Netherlands, and Luxembourg.
June 4. British forces evacuate Dunkirk, on the coast of France.
June 10. Italy declares war on France and Britain.
June 22. A defeated France signs an armistice with Germany.
Sept. 16. The first U.S. peacetime draft is enacted by Congress.
Oct. 31. The British air victory in the Battle of Britain prevents a German invasion of Britain.
Nov. 5. President Roosevelt is reelected to a third term.
Also in 1940. The Soviet Union annexes the Baltic states of Lithuania, Estonia, and Latvia....Prehistoric cave paintings are discovered at Lascaux in France.

March 11. President Roosevelt signs the Lend-Lease Bill, allowing the transfer of U.S. war materiel to Britain.
June 22. Germany invades the Soviet Union.
Dec. 7. The Japanese bomb U.S. military bases at Pearl Harbor, Hawaii.
Dec. 8. The United States, Great Britain, and Canada declare war on Japan.
Dec. 10. Japan invades the Philippines.
Dec. 11. Germany and Italy declare war on the United States.
Also in 1941. The German Blitz, the nighttime bombing of London, is at its height....Orson Welles directs and stars in the film *Citizen Kane*.

Feb. 19. The U.S. government orders the internment of 110,000 West Coast Japanese-Americans.

Dec. 7, 1941

May 10. U.S. forces in the Philippines begin to surrender to the Japanese.
June 4–6. A U.S. fleet defeats a Japanese fleet at the Battle of Midway, ending Japanese expansion in the Pacific.
Nov. 8. U.S. forces invade Morocco and Algeria.
Nov. 22. The Battle of Stalingrad begins.
Also in 1942. Hitler proposes the Final Solution of the Jewish Question; the Holocaust begins....Physicist Enrico Fermi achieves the first nuclear chain reaction....American singer Bing Crosby records "White Christmas"....French writer Albert Camus publishes *The Stranger*....Humphrey Bogart and Ingrid Bergman star in the film *Casablanca*.

Feb. 2. The German siege of Stalingrad ends, marking a turning point in the German invasion of the Soviet Union.
May 8. The Germans suppress a revolt by Polish Jews and destroy the Warsaw ghetto.
May 13. Allied forces defeat the Axis powers in North Africa.
Sept. 3. Allied forces invade southern Italy after capturing Sicily.
Oct. 13. Italy signs an armistice with the Allies and declares war on Germany.
Also in 1943. French existentialist writer Jean-Paul Sartre publishes *Being and Nothingness*....The Richard Rodgers and Oscar Hammerstein musical *Oklahoma* opens on Broadway.

June 6, 1944

June 4. American forces enter Rome.
June 6. On D-Day, Allied invasion forces land at Normandy in northern France.
July 20. German officers fail in their attempt to assassinate Hitler.
Aug. 25. Allied forces liberate Paris.
Oct. 20. Allied forces invade the Philippines.
Nov. 7. With Harry S. Truman as his running mate, President Roosevelt is reelected for an unprecedented fourth term.
Dec. 16. The German army launches the Battle of the Bulge, its last counteroffensive.
Also in 1944. U.S. Marines invade Guam and Saipan in the Marianas....Iceland becomes independent of Denmark....Oswald Avery determines that DNA is the hereditary material of the cell.

Feb. 4–11. At the Yalta Conference, President Roosevelt, British Prime Minister Churchill, and Soviet Prime Minister Joseph Stalin outline plans for Germany's defeat.
March 16. U.S. Marines capture Iwo Jima.

April 15, 1945

April 12. President Roosevelt dies; Truman is inaugurated as the 33d U.S. president.
April 15. Following funeral services in Washington, DC, Franklin D. Roosevelt is buried in Hyde Park, NY.
April 30. Hitler commits suicide.
May 7. Germany surrenders to the Allies.
June 21. Allied forces capture Okinawa.
Aug. 2. President Truman, British Prime Minister Clement Attlee, and Soviet Premier Stalin conclude the Potsdam Conference.
Aug. 6. The United States drops an atomic bomb on the Japanese city of Hiroshima.
Aug. 8. The Soviet Union declares war on Japan.
Aug. 9. The United States drops an atomic bomb on the Japanese city of Nagasaki.
Aug. 14. Japan surrenders.
Also in 1945. The United Nations (UN) is established....Germany and Austria are divided into four Allied zones of occupation....Korea is divided between U.S. and Soviet occupation forces along the 38th parallel....The Arab League is founded.

Feb. 24. Juan Perón is elected president of Argentina.
April 14. The civil war between Communists and nationalists resumes in China.
July 4. The Philippines gains its independence from the United States.
Oct. 1. The Nuremberg Tribunal sentences 12 leading Nazis to death.
Also in 1946. The Viet Minh Communists begin a guerrilla war against the French in Indochina (Vietnam)....Transjordan (Jordan) becomes independent....ENIAC, the first successful electronic digital computer, becomes operational....Frances Xavier Cabrini becomes the first U.S. citizen to be can-

onized....Dr. Benjamin Spock publishes *The Common Sense Book of Baby and Child Care.*

March 12. President Truman outlines the Truman Doctrine, a plan to aid Greece and Turkey and to help them resist Communist takeovers.
May 31. Communists seize control of Hungary.
June 5. The U.S. Marshall Plan for economic recovery in Europe is proposed.
Aug. 15. India becomes independent of Great Britain and is divided into the nations of India and Pakistan.
Nov. 29. The UN General Assembly approves the partition of Palestine into Arab and Jewish states.
Also in 1947. The first India-Pakistan War begins over the disputed territory of Kashmir....The Dead Sea Scrolls, a collection of ancient Hebrew documents, are discovered....Jackie Robinson becomes the first African-American to play in modern major-league baseball....U.S. Air Force pilot Chuck Yeager breaks the sound barrier in an X-1 rocket plane.

Feb. 12, 1948

Jan. 30. Indian leader Mohandas Gandhi is assassinated.
Feb. 12. Following a religious ceremony, the ashes of India's Mohandas Gandhi are poured into the Ganges River.

Nov. 2, 1948

Feb. 25. Communists take over Czechoslovakia.
May 14. The independent state of Israel is proclaimed.
May 15. Arab armies invade Israel.
July 24. Soviet occupation forces in Germany blockade West Berlin; a U.S.-British airlift begins the following day.
Aug. 15. The Republic of Korea (South Korea) is proclaimed.
Sept. 9. The People's Republic of Korea (North Korea) is established.
Nov. 2. Surprising many polls and newspapers, President Truman defeats New York's Gov. Thomas Dewey to win a full term in the White House.
Also in 1948. Burma becomes independent....The Organization of American States (OAS) is founded...The transistor is invented at Bell Laboratories in the United States.

April 4. The North Atlantic Treaty Organization (NATO) is formed.
April 18. The Republic of Ireland is established.
May 12. The Berlin blockade is lifted.
May 23. The Republic of Germany (West Germany) is established.
Oct. 1. Communist forces defeat the Nationalists and form the People's Republic of China; Nationalist forces flee to the island of Taiwan.
Oct. 7. The German Democratic Republic (East Germany) is established.
Also in 1949. The Arab-Israeli war comes to an end....Indonesia (formerly

the Dutch East Indies) gains its independence....The Soviet Union detonates its first atomic bomb....British author George Orwell publishes *1984*.

June 25, 1950

1950

June 25. North Korea invades South Korea, initiating the Korean War.
July 7. The UN Security Council authorizes military aid for South Korea.
Sept. 15. U.S. and other UN forces land at Inchon and drive the North Koreans out of South Korea.
Oct. 8. UN forces cross into North Korea.
Oct. 21. Chinese forces invade Tibet.
Nov. 26. Chinese forces enter the Korean War, forcing UN forces to retreat.
Also in 1950. Cartoonist Charles Schulz introduces the "Peanuts" comic strip.

1951

Feb. 26. The 22d Amendment to the U.S. Constitution, restricting U.S. presidents to two terms, goes into effect.
April 11. After Gen. Douglas MacArthur calls for attacks on Chinese cities, President Truman dismisses him from all of his posts, including that of supreme commander in Korea.
Also in 1951. The first commercial broadcast of color television is made....American writer J.D. Salinger publishes *The Catcher in the Rye*.

1952

Feb. 8. Queen Elizabeth II ascends to the British throne upon the death of her father, George VI.
April 28. The U.S. occupation of Japan ends.
July 25. The U.S. Commonwealth of Puerto Rico is established.
Oct. 20. The Mau Mau uprising against white settlers begins in Kenya.
Nov. 1. The United States tests the first hydrogen bomb.
Nov. 4. Dwight D. Eisenhower, running with Sen. Richard M. Nixon of California, is elected U.S. president.
Also in 1952. Sony introduces the first pocket-size transistor radios.

1953

March 5. Soviet dictator Joseph Stalin dies.
May 29. Edmund Hillary and Tenzing Norgay become the first to climb Mount Everest.
June 17. Anti-Communist rioting in East Germany is put down by Soviet tanks.
June 19. Julius and Ethel Rosenberg are executed for atomic espionage.
July 27. The Korean War ends.
Aug. 12. The Soviet Union explodes a hydrogen bomb.
Also in 1953. Laos becomes independent....James Watson and Francis Crick propose the double-helix structure of DNA....African-American writer James Baldwin publishes his first novel, *Go Tell It on the Mountain*....American tennis player Maureen Connolly wins the Grand Slam.

Nov. 4, 1952

1954

Jan. 21. The USS *Nautilus*, the first nuclear submarine, is launched.
April 18. Col. Gamal Abdel Nasser takes over as premier of Egypt.
May 7. French forces are defeated at the Battle of Dien Bien Phu in North Vietnam.
May 17. Racial segregation in public schools is declared unconstitutional by the U.S. Supreme Court.
July 21. The Geneva Conference partitions Vietnam into North Vietnam and South Vietnam.

Oct. 31. The Algerian National Liberation Front (FLN) begins a revolt against French rule.

Dec. 2. U.S. Sen. Joseph R. McCarthy (R-WI) is condemned by the Senate for his abuse of the Senate.

Also in 1954. English runner Roger Bannister is the first to run the mile in under four minutes.

May 5. The Federal Republic of Germany (West Germany) attains sovereignty.

May 9. West Germany joins NATO.

May 14. The Eastern European Communist-bloc mutual-defense treaty, the Warsaw Pact, comes into effect.

July 17. Disneyland Park opens in Anaheim, CA.

July 27. The Allied occupation of Austria ends, and Austria regains its sovereignty.

Sept. 19. A military coup ousts Argentine President Juan Perón.

Nov. 25. The Interstate Commerce Commission bans racial segregation on interstate trains and buses.

Also in 1955. Jonas Salk's vaccine against polio comes into widespread use....Marian Anderson becomes the first African-American to perform at the Metropolitan Opera House.

July 26. Egypt's newly elected President Nasser nationalizes the Suez Canal.

Oct. 29. Israeli forces invade Egypt's Sinai Peninsula.

Nov. 5. Anglo-French forces invade Egypt.

Nov. 6. The Eisenhower-Nixon ticket wins a second term.

Jan. 21, 1954

Nov. 14. The USSR crushes the Hungarian uprising.

Dec. 22. The last British and French forces evacuate Egypt.

Also in 1956. Sudan, Morocco, and Tunisia become independent....Film actress Grace Kelly marries Prince Rainier III of Monaco.

Jan. 22. The Israeli army withdraws from the Sinai.

Sept. 24. President Eisenhower sends federal troops to Little Rock, AR, to enforce school integration.

July 17, 1955

Oct. 4. The Soviet Union launches Sputnik I, the first artificial Earth satellite.

Also in 1957. Ghana becomes independent....The Jerome Robbins musical *West Side Story* opens on Broadway.

Jan. 1. The European Economic Community (EEC) is established.

Jan. 31. Explorer I, the first U.S. satellite, is launched.

March 27. Nikita Khrushchev is designated chairman of the Soviet Council of Ministers.

July 15. U.S. Marines land in Beirut, Lebanon, to protect the nation's pro-Western government; they will withdraw on October 25.

Oct. 28. Angelo Giuseppe Cardinal Roncalli is elected supreme pontiff of the Roman Catholic Church and chooses the name Pope John XXIII.

Also in 1958. Charles de Gaulle is elected premier of France....The United States launches an intercontinental ballistic missile (ICBM)....Russian writer Boris Pasternak publishes the novel *Doctor Zhivago*.

1959

Jan. 3. Alaska becomes the 49th state of the Union.
Feb. 16. Fidel Castro seizes power in Cuba after ousting President Fulgencio Batista.
March 31. The Dalai Lama flees to India after China crushes an uprising in Tibet.
April 25. The St. Lawrence Seaway is opened to traffic.
Aug. 21. Hawaii becomes the 50th state of the Union.

1960

May 1. An American U-2 spy plane is shot down over the Soviet Union.
June 30. Upon the independence of the Congo from Belgium, the African nation falls into chaos as its Katanga province secedes.
Nov. 8. Democratic Sen. John F. Kennedy wins the U.S. presidential election, defeating Vice-President Nixon.
Also in 1960. Independence is granted to Cameroon, Togo, Madagascar, the two Congos, Somalia, Dahomey (now Benin), Upper Volta (now Burkina Faso), Ivory Coast, Chad, Central African Republic, Cyprus, Gabon, Mali, Niger, Senegal, Nigeria, and Mauritania....American physicist Theodore H. Maiman demonstrates the first successful laser....U.S. track star Wilma Rudolph wins three gold medals at the Rome Olympic Games.

1961

Jan. 3. The United States severs relations with Communist Cuba.
March 1. President Kennedy establishes the Peace Corps.
April 12. Soviet cosmonaut Yuri Gagarin becomes the first person to orbit Earth.

March 1, 1961

April 17. U.S.-aided Cuban exiles attempt the unsuccessful Bay of Pigs invasion.
May 5. Astronaut Alan B. Shepard, Jr., makes the first U.S. suborbital spaceflight.
Aug. 17. The Communist East German government completes the construction of the Berlin Wall.
Also in 1961. Tanganyika and Sierra Leone become independent....Baseball's Roger Maris breaks Babe Ruth's home-run record, with a season total of 61.

1962

Feb. 20. Astronaut John Glenn, Jr., becomes the first American to orbit Earth.
July 10. Telstar I, the first communications satellite, is launched.
Sept. 30. The University of Mississippi is forced to admit African-American student James Meredith.
Nov. 20. The monthlong Cuban missile crisis ends, as Soviet missiles and bombers are withdrawn from Cuba and the United States ends its blockade of the island.
Also in 1962. Algeria, Burundi, Rwanda, Jamaica, Trinidad and Tobago, Uganda, and Western Samoa (now Samoa) become independent....The British pop group the Beatles make their first recordings....Basketball's Wilt Chamberlain scores a record 100 points in one game.

1963

June 12. Civil-rights leader Medgar Evers is murdered in Jackson, MS.
Nov. 22. President Kennedy is assassinated in Dallas, TX; Vice-President Lyndon B. Johnson is inaugurated as the 36th president.
Dec. 4. The second session of Ecumenical Council Vatican II ends.

Nov. 22, 1963

Also in 1963. Kenya becomes independent....The Organization of African Unity (OAU) is established....A limited Nuclear Test Ban Treaty is signed by Britain, the United States, and the USSR.

Jan. 23. The 24th Amendment to the U.S. Constitution, prohibiting poll taxes in federal elections, is ratified.

May 27. Indian Prime Minister Jawaharlal Nehru dies.

June 30. The last UN troops leave Congo after a four-year effort to bring stability to the country.

July 2. President Johnson signs into law a civil-rights bill, outlawing discrimination in public accommodations, public facilities, public schools, voting qualifications, federally aided programs, employment, and union membership.

Aug. 5. U.S. aircraft bomb North Vietnam after North Vietnamese boats attack U.S. destroyers in the Gulf of Tonkin.

Oct. 14. Civil-rights leader Martin Luther King, Jr., is named winner of the Nobel Peace Prize.

Oct. 15. Nikita Khrushchev is ousted as leader of the Soviet Union.

Oct. 16. Communist China explodes an atomic bomb.

Nov. 3. President Johnson is elected to a full term.

Also in 1964. Fighting breaks out on Cyprus between Greek and Turkish Cypriots....Malawi, Zambia, and Malta gain their independence....Tanganyika and Zanzibar merge and later adopt the name Tanzania....The Palestine Liberation Organization (PLO) is formed.

Jan. 24. Sir Winston Churchill dies at the age of 90.

March 9. The first U.S. combat forces arrive in South Vietnam.

Aug. 11–16. Race riots in the Watts section of Los Angeles leave 34 dead.

Nov. 11. Rhodesia unilaterally declares its independence from Britain.

Also in 1965. An attempted Communist coup leads to military rule in Indonesia under Suharto....The Gambia and the Maldives gain their independence....The Houston Astrodome, the first covered baseball stadium, is completed in Texas.

Jan. 19. Indira Nehru Gandhi becomes prime minister of India.

June 2. The U.S. Surveyor 1 spacecraft achieves the first soft landing on the Moon.

Also in 1966. The Cultural Revolution begins in China....Barbados, Guyana, Botswana, and Lesotho become independent....The National Organization for Women (NOW) is founded.

Jan. 27. A fire kills U.S. astronauts Edward White II, Virgil ("Gus") Grissom, and Roger Chaffee during a launch test.

May 30. The state of Biafra secedes from Nigeria, and civil war erupts.

June 5–10. The Six-Day War between Israel and the Arab states is fought; a victorious Israel seizes Arab Jerusalem, the West Bank, and the Golan Heights.

Oct. 2. Thurgood Marshall becomes the first African-American member of the U.S. Supreme Court.

June 5, 1967

Aug. 20, 1968

Oct. 9. Bolivian soldiers kill Latin American guerrilla leader Che Guevara.
Dec. 3. Dr. Christiaan Barnard of South Africa performs the first successful human heart transplant.
Also in 1967. Race riots erupt in Newark, NJ, and Detroit....Anti–Vietnam war demonstrations take place in U.S. cities....The British colony of Aden and South Arabia becomes independent as the People's Republic of Southern Yemen.

1968

Jan. 30. The Viet Cong and North Vietnamese forces launch the Tet Offensive in Vietnam.
April 4. Civil-rights leader Martin Luther King, Jr., is assassinated.
June 6. U.S. Sen. Robert F. Kennedy dies after being shot while campaigning for the Democratic presidential nomination.
Aug. 20. Warsaw Pact forces invade Czechoslovakia to end increasing liberalization.
Nov. 5. Richard M. Nixon is elected U.S. president.
Also in 1968. Swaziland, Nauru, Mauritius, and Equatorial Guinea become independent.

1969

June 8. President Nixon announces the start of U.S. troop withdrawals from Vietnam.
June 23. Warren E. Burger succeeds Earl Warren as chief justice of the U.S. Supreme Court.
July 20. *Apollo 11* astronauts Neil Armstrong and Edwin E. Aldrin, Jr., become the first men to walk on the Moon.
Also in 1969. The Anglo-French supersonic transport Concorde makes its first flight....A rock-music festival at Woodstock, NY, attracts a crowd of some 400,000.

1970

Jan. 12. The breakaway state of Biafra capitulates, and Nigeria's civil war ends.
Jan. 16. Col. Muammar el-Qaddafi becomes premier of Libya.
May 4. Ohio National Guardsmen kill four Kent State students during an anti–Vietnam war protest.
Oct. 17. Anwar el-Sadat becomes president of Egypt following the death of Nasser.
Nov. 19. Hafiz al-Assad seizes power in Syria.
Also in 1970. Fiji and Tonga gain their independence....An earthquake in Peru kills 70,000 people and leaves 700,000 homeless....Egypt's Aswan High Dam is completed.

1971

Jan. 25. Maj. Gen. Idi Amin Dada seizes control of Uganda.
Feb. 13. South Vietnamese troops, backed by U.S. air and artillery support, invade Laos.
April 21. Haitian dictator François Duvalier dies and is succeeded by his son, Jean-Claude.

Feb. 20, 1972

June 10. The United States ends its 21-year trade embargo of China.

June 30. The 26th Amendment to the U.S. Constitution, lowering the voting age to 18, is ratified.

Sept. 9–13. Forty-three people, including 11 prison guards and 32 prisoners and civilian prison employees, are killed in a revolt at Attica state prison in New York.

Oct. 23. The UN General Assembly votes to expel Taiwan and seat Communist China.

Also in 1971. East Pakistan declares its independence from West Pakistan as Bangladesh, beginning a civil war....Six Persian Gulf sheikhdoms form the United Arab Emirates....Bahrain and Qatar gain their independence.

Feb. 20. President Nixon travels to Beijing to meet with Chinese leader Mao Zedong.

March 30. The British government assumes direct rule over Northern Ireland.

April 1. North Vietnamese and Viet Cong troops renew their offensive in South Vietnam.

May 15. Alabama Gov. George Wallace is shot and paralyzed.

June 17. Five burglars are arrested at the Democratic Party headquarters in Washington, DC, beginning what would become known as the Watergate affair.

Sept. 5. Arab terrorists kill 11 members of the Israeli team at the Munich Olympics.

Nov. 7. Nixon is reelected U.S. president.

Also in 1972. The United States returns Okinawa to Japan....The pesticide DDT is banned in the United States....Bobby Fischer defeats Boris Spassky of the USSR to become the first American world chess champion....American swimmer Mark Spitz wins a record seven Olympic gold medals.

Sept. 5, 1972

Jan. 1. Britain, Ireland, Denmark, and Norway join the EEC.

March 29. The last U.S. troops are withdrawn from South Vietnam.

Sept. 11. A right-wing military coup in Chile overthrows President Salvador Allende's Marxist government.

Sept. 23. Juan Perón is returned to power as president of Argentina.

Oct. 6. Egypt and Syria attack Israel, beginning a two-week war.

Oct. 10. U.S. Vice-President Spiro Agnew resigns after he is charged with income-tax evasion.

Dec. 6. In accordance with the 25th Amendment to the U.S. Constitution—which was ratified on Feb. 10, 1967, and calls for the appointment of a vice-president when that office becomes vacant—Republican House of Representatives leader Gerald R. Ford becomes vice-president.

Also in 1973. The Bahamas becomes independent.

March 18. A five-month Arab oil embargo against Europe, the United States, and Japan is lifted.

April 25. A military coup in Portugal leads to democratic reforms.

July 1. Isabel Perón becomes president of Argentina after the death of her husband, Juan.

July 20. Turkish forces invade Cyprus.

July 30. The House of Representatives Judiciary Committee votes to impeach Nixon for blocking the Watergate investigation and for abuse of power.

Aug. 9. Nixon resigns; Ford becomes the 38th U.S. president.

Sept. 12. Ethiopian Emperor Haile Selassie is deposed in a military coup.

Also in 1974. Grenada and Guinea-Bissau become independent....Soviet ballet dancer Mikhail Baryshnikov defects to the West....Hank Aaron breaks

Babe Ruth's record of 714 home runs....Nelson A. Rockefeller takes office as U.S. vice-president.

July 4, 1976

April 5. Nationalist Chinese leader Chiang Kai-shek dies.

April 16. The Khmer Rouge rebels win control of Cambodia after a five-year civil war; they rename the country Kampuchea and begin a reign of terror.

July 17. U.S. astronauts and Soviet cosmonauts link up for the first time.

Aug. 1. The Helsinki accords pledge the signatory nations to respect human rights.

Nov. 11. Angola gains its independence from Portugal, and civil war breaks out.

Nov. 22. Juan Carlos I becomes king of Spain following the death of Gen. Francisco Franco.

Also in 1975. Cyprus is partitioned into Greek and Turkish zones....Civil war between Muslims and Christians erupts in Lebanon....In addition to Angola, Suriname (Dutch Guiana), Mozambique, Cape Verde, Papua–New Guinea, the Comoros, and São Tomé and Príncipe also become independent....Microsoft is founded by Bill Gates and Paul Allen.

June 19. During three days of violence, black student protesters are massacred at Soweto in South Africa.

July 2. North Vietnam and South Vietnam are reunited.

July 3. Israeli commandos land at Entebbe Airport, Uganda, and rescue passengers and crew members of an Air France plane hijacked by pro-Palestinian terrorists.

July 4. The United States celebrates its Bicentennial.

Nov. 2. Democrat James Earl ("Jimmy") Carter is elected U.S. president.

Also in 1976. Chinese leaders Mao Zedong and Zhou Enlai die; Hua Guofeng assumes power....The Seychelles becomes independent....The U.S. Viking I and Viking II spacecraft land on Mars.

Sept. 7. Two treaties that will transfer the Panama Canal to Panama in 2000 are signed.

Also in 1977. The French Territory of the Afars and the Issas becomes independent as Djibouti....The Trans-Alaska Pipeline begins operation....George Lucas directs the first *Star Wars* space fantasy film.

April 27. Pro-Soviet Marxists seize control of Afghanistan.

September. President Carter oversees the Camp David peace accords between Egyptian President Anwar el-Sadat and Israeli Prime Minister Menahem Begin.

Oct. 16. Cardinal Karol Wojtyla of Poland is the first non-Italian in nearly 500 years to be elected pope, becoming Pope John Paul II.

Nov. 18. More than 900 members of a religious cult led by Jim Jones commit suicide at Jonestown, Guyana.

Also in 1978. The Northern Mariana Islands become a self-governing commonwealth of the United States....Tuvalu, Dominica, and the Solomon Islands become independent....Yiddish-language writer Isaac Bashevis Singer wins the Nobel Prize for literature....The first test-tube baby is born.

May 4, 1979

Jan. 1. The United States and Communist China establish diplomatic relations.

Jan. 7. Vietnamese forces seize Phnom Penh after invading Cambodia.

March 26. Israel and Egypt sign a treaty ending the 31-year state of war between them.

March 28. An accident at the Three Mile Island nuclear-power plant causes a near disaster.

April 1. Ayatollah Ruhollah Khomeini proclaims Iran an Islamic republic.

April 11. Tanzanians and Ugandan exiles invade Uganda; dictator Idi Amin Dada flees.

May 4. Conservative Party leader Margaret Thatcher becomes Britain's first woman prime minister.

July 16. Gen. Saddam Hussein becomes president of Iraq.

July 19. The Marxist Sandinistas seize control in Nicaragua.

Nov. 4. Iranian students take people hostage at the U.S. embassy in Tehran.

Dec. 24. Soviet troops occupy Afghanistan in support of the country's Marxist government, precipitating a guerrilla war by Islamic *mujahidin*.

Also in 1979. Kiribati (the Gilbert Islands), St. Lucia, and St. Vincent and the Grenadines become independent....Morocco annexes Western Sahara....Mother Teresa of Calcutta is awarded the Nobel Peace Prize.

Nov. 4, 1980

April 2, 1982

April 18. Rhodesia becomes the independent nation of Zimbabwe.

Sept. 22. A border dispute between Iran and Iraq erupts into open warfare.

Nov. 4. Republican Ronald Reagan is elected U.S. president; George W. Bush is elected vice-president.

Also in 1980. Vanuatu (the New Hebrides) becomes independent....Poland's Solidarity, led by Lech Walesa, becomes the first independent union in a Communist country.

Jan. 1. Greece joins the European Community (EC)—formerly the EEC.

Jan. 20. The U.S. hostages in Iran are released.

March 30. President Reagan is wounded in an assassination attempt.

April 14. *Columbia*, the first U.S. space shuttle, completes a 36-orbit mission around Earth.

May 13. Pope John Paul II is shot and wounded by a Turkish gunman.

June 7. Israeli fighter planes destroy Iraq's Osirak nuclear reactor.

Sept. 25. Sandra Day O'Connor becomes the first woman member of the U.S. Supreme Court.

Oct. 6. Egyptian President Anwar el-Sadat is assassinated; Hosni Mubarak becomes president.

Also in 1981. Antigua and Barbuda and Belize both gain their independence.

April 2. Argentina invades the British-held Falkland Islands.

May 30. Spain joins NATO.

June 6. The Israeli army invades Lebanon in order to drive PLO guerrillas out of Beirut.
June 14. British troops recapture the Falkland Islands from Argentina.
Also in 1982. The Voyager 2 spacecraft transmits pictures to Earth of the planet Saturn....*USA Today*, the first daily newspaper aimed at readers throughout the United States, is launched.

Sept. 1. A Soviet jet fighter shoots down a Korean Air Lines Boeing 747, killing 269 passengers and crew members.
Oct. 25. U.S. forces invade the Caribbean island of Grenada to oust a pro-Cuban regime.
Also in 1983. Car bombs destroy the U.S. embassy and U.S. Marine headquarters in Beirut, Lebanon....St. Kitts and Nevis becomes independent....Sally K. Ride becomes the first U.S. woman astronaut to travel in space, and Guion S. Bluford, Jr., becomes the first African-American astronaut to do the same....The compact disc is introduced for recorded music.

March 11, 1985

Feb. 26, 1986

Oct. 31. India's Prime Minister Indira Gandhi is assassinated.
Nov. 6. Reagan and Bush win reelection.
Dec. 3. A toxic-gas leak at a pesticide plant in Bhopal, India, kills more than 2,000 people.
Also in 1984. Brunei becomes independent....Bishop Desmond Tutu, opponent of apartheid in South Africa, is awarded the Nobel Peace Prize....American track athlete Carl Lewis wins four gold medals at the Los Angeles Olympics.

March 11. Mikhail Gorbachev is named chairman of the Soviet Communist Party.
Oct. 7. Palestinian terrorists hijack the Italian cruise ship *Achille Lauro*.

Also in 1985. Walter Payton sets an all-time National Football League record for rushes of 14,860 yards....Pete Rose beats Ty Cobb's 57-year-old record of 4,191 base hits.

Jan. 1. Spain and Portugal join the EC.
Jan. 28. The U.S. space shuttle *Challenger* explodes after launch, killing a crew of seven.
Feb. 7. Haitian President Jean-Claude Duvalier flees the country.
Feb. 19. The Soviet Union launches the *Mir* space station.
Feb. 26. Corazon Aquino is inaugurated president of the Philippines; long-time President Ferdinand Marcos goes into exile.
Feb. 28. Swedish Prime Minister Olof Palme is assassinated.
April 14. U.S. aircraft bomb military and terrorist-related targets in Libya.
April 26. A nuclear-reactor disaster takes place at the Chernobyl power plant in the Ukraine.
Sept. 26. William H. Rehnquist becomes U.S. chief justice.
Also in 1986. Micronesia and the Marshall Islands become independent....Human-rights activist Elie Wiesel is awarded the Nobel Prize for peace....Cyclist Greg LeMond is the first American to win the Tour de France.

Oct. 19. A Wall Street stock-market crisis—a plunge of 508 points in the Dow Jones industrial average—spreads to Tokyo and London.

Nov. 7. Habib Bourguiba, Tunisia's president since its independence in 1956, is overthrown.

Dec. 8. President Reagan and Soviet leader Gorbachev sign a treaty on the global elimination of intermediate-range nuclear forces.

Dec. 9. West Bank Palestinians launch an *intifada* (uprising) against Israeli occupation.

March 11. A cease-fire is declared in the war between Iran and Iraq.

March 27. The U.S. Senate ratifies the Intermediate-Range Nuclear Forces Treaty.

Oct. 1. Gorbachev assumes the Soviet presidency.

Nov. 8. George W. Bush is elected president of the United States.

Dec. 21. A terrorist's bomb blows apart Pan Am flight 747 over the Scottish village of Lockerbie.

Also in 1988. Vice Adm. John M. Poindexter and Marine Lt. Col. Oliver North are indicted in the Iran-contra affair—the illegal sale of arms to Iran and the use of the proceeds to support the contras in their fight against Nicaragua's Marxist government....German tennis player Steffi Graf becomes the third woman to win the Grand Slam.

Jan. 7. Crown Prince Akihito becomes emperor of Japan following the death of his father, Emperor Hirohito.

March 24. The oil tanker *Exxon Valdez* runs aground in the Gulf of Alaska, causing a massive oil spill.

June 3. Iran's Ayatollah Ruhollah Khomeini dies.

June 4. Hundreds of Chinese pro-democracy demonstrators are killed by troops in Beijing's Tiananmen Square.

Nov. 9, 1989

Nov. 9. East Germany opens its borders with West Germany. The action leads to the tearing down of the wall that divides East and West Berlin.

Dec. 20. U.S. forces invade Panama; Gen. Manuel Antonio Noriega is deposed.

Also in 1989. Communism collapses in Hungary, Romania, and Poland....Soviet troops completely withdraw from Afghanistan, but the civil war continues....Vietnamese troops leave Cambodia....San Francisco's Marina district is damaged by a severe earthquake.

March 21. Namibia, Africa's last territory, becomes an independent nation.

April 25. Sandinista rule ends in Nicaragua.

May 29. Boris Yeltsin becomes president of the Russian Federation.

Aug. 2. Iraq invades Kuwait.

Aug. 6. The UN authorizes an economic blockade of Iraq.

Oct. 3. East and West Germany are reunited.

Dec. 9. Lech Walesa, leader of the Solidarity movement, wins the first direct presidential elections in Poland's history.

Dec. 16. Jean-Bertrand Aristide is elected president in Haiti's first free elections.

Also in 1990. Communism continues to collapse in East Europe....Lithuania, Estonia, and Latvia declare their independence from the Soviet Union....North Yemen and South Yemen unite as the Republic of Yemen....The Hubble Space Telescope is deployed.

Gen. H. Norman Schwarzkopf

Feb. 15. The leaders of Czechoslovakia, Hungary, and Poland sign the so-called Visegard agreement, in which they pledge to cooperate in transforming their nations to free-market economies.

March 3. U.S. Gen. H. Norman Schwarzkopf announces that Iraqi military leaders have accepted allied terms for ending the Persian Gulf war. Following the failure of diplomatic initiatives, a U.S.-led international force had begun military action against Iraq in mid-January 1991, in an effort to liberate Iraqi-held Kuwait. General Schwarzkopf had given frequent briefings during the conflict.

March 24. The African nation of Benin holds its first presidential election in some 30 years.

March 26. The presidents of Argentina, Brazil, Paraguay, and Uruguay sign an agreement establishing the Southern Cone Common Market, a free-trade zone, by Jan. 1, 1995.

April 20. Mikhail Gorbachev becomes the first Soviet head of state to visit South Korea.

May 16. Queen Elizabeth II is the first British monarch to address the U.S. Congress.

May 21. India's former Prime Minister Rajiv Gandhi is assassinated while campaigning in parliamentary elections.

June 12. Boris Yeltsin is elected by popular vote as president of the Russian Republic.

July 31. U.S. President George

May 3, 1992

Oct. 24, 1992

Bush and Soviet President Mikhail Gorbachev sign the Strategic Arms Reduction Treaty.

Dec. 8. Leaders of Russia, Ukraine, and Byelorussia (later Belarus) establish the Commonwealth of Independent States.

Dec. 25. Mikhail Gorbachev gives up the presidency of the USSR; the Soviet system will collapse by year's end.

Also in 1991. Macedonia, Croatia, and Slovenia declare independence from Yugoslavia....The Warsaw Pact nations disband the alliance's military structure.

Jan. 1. Egypt's Boutros Boutros-Ghali begins a five-year term as secretary-general of the United Nations.

Jan. 16. El Salvador's 12-year-old civil war ends.

April 4. Sali Berisha is the first non-Marxist to become president of Albania since World War II.

April 20. Expo '92, the largest world's fair ever, opens in Seville, Spain.

May 3. Five days of rioting and looting end in Los Angeles, following the acquittal of four white police officers in the beating of an African-American Los Angeles motorist; 53 people have been killed.

May 24, 1993

May 7. The 27th Amendment to the U.S. Constitution, barring Congress from enacting midterm pay increases, is approved.

Aug. 24. China and South Korea establish diplomatic relations.

Sept. 22. Yugoslavia is expelled from the UN because of its role in the war in Bosnia and Herzegovina.

Oct. 4. The 16-year-long civil war in Mozambique ends with the signing of a peace treaty.

Oct. 23. Emperor Akihito is the first Japanese head of state to visit China.

Oct. 24. Canada's Toronto Blue Jays become the first non-U.S. team to win baseball's World Series.

Nov. 3. Democrat Bill Clinton, the governor of Arkansas, defeats Republican President George Bush and third-party candidate Ross Perot in U.S. presidential elections.

Dec. 9. U.S. Marines land in Mogadishu, Somalia, as part of UN-sanctioned efforts to provide famine relief for the African nation, which has descended into lawless violence.

Dec. 17. The United States, Canada, and Mexico sign the North American Free Trade Agreement.

1993

Jan. 1. Czechoslovakia splits into two separate countries, the Czech Republic and Slovakia.

Jan. 3. U.S. President George Bush and Russian President Boris Yeltsin sign the second Strategic Arms Reduction Treaty.

Feb. 26. Six persons are killed when terrorists explode a bomb at New York City's World Trade Center.

April 19. More than 80 members of the Branch Davidian cult die in a mass suicide as their Waco, TX, compound burns down. The Branch Davidians had been involved in a 51-day standoff with law-enforcement officers.

April 22. The U.S. Holocaust Memorial Museum is dedicated in Washington, DC.

May 24. The Ethiopian province of Eritrea declares itself an independent nation.

June 6. Mongolia holds its first direct presidential elections.

Aug. 9. Prince Albert succeeds his late brother, Baudouin, as king of Belgium.

Sept. 13. Israeli and Palestinian leaders sign an agreement that will lead to Palestinian self-rule in the Gaza Strip and some parts of the West Bank.

Oct. 15. South Africa's President F.W. de Klerk and African National Congress President Nelson Mandela are named winners of the Nobel Peace Prize for their efforts to end South Africa's apartheid system.

Aug. 9, 1993

Nov. 1. The European Community's treaty on European unity takes effect.
Dec. 30. Israel and the Vatican establish diplomatic relations.

1994

May 2. Nelson Mandela is elected president of South Africa after winning that nation's first all-race elections.
July 8. North Korean President Kim Il Sung dies; his son Kim Jong Il is the apparent successor to the leadership post.
July 25. Israel and Jordan formally end the state of war that has existed between them since 1948.

Aug. 8. Representatives of China and Taiwan sign a cooperation agreement.
Aug. 15. The U.S. Social Security Administration, which has been part of the Department of Health and Human Services, becomes an independent government agency.
Nov. 8. In midterm U.S. elections, the Republican Party gains control of both houses of Congress for the first time since 1954.
Nov. 20. The Angolan government and the rebel National Union for the Total Independence of Angola (UNITA) agree to end the 19-year civil war.
Also in 1994. Palau, a U.S. trust territory in the Pacific Ocean, becomes independent....Civil war in Rwanda between Hutu and Tutsi claims 500,000 lives.

1995

May 2, 1994

Jan. 1. The World Trade Organization, a 125-nation global-trade-monitoring group, comes into existence.
March 3. A UN peacekeeping mission in Somalia ends.
March 13. The first United Nations World Summit on Social Development concludes in Copenhagen, Denmark.
March 20. In Tokyo, Japan, terrorists belonging to a religious cult release a deadly nerve gas in the city's subway system, killing 12 people and injuring 5,500 others.
April 19. A car bomb explodes outside a federal office building in Oklahoma City, OK, killing 168 people.
July 27. The Korean War Veterans Memorial is dedicated in Washington, DC.
Aug. 16. In a referendum, voters in Bermuda reject independence from Great Britain.

April 19, 1995

Oct. 3. Former football star O.J. Simpson is found not guilty of first-degree murder in the deaths of his former wife Nicole Brown Simpson and her friend Ronald L. Goldman.

Nov. 6. World leaders attend the funeral of Yitzhak Rabin, Israel's prime minister, who was assassinated on Nov. 4, 1995, by a Jewish extremist opposed to Rabin's plans to make peace with the Palestinians.

Dec. 14. The presidents of Bosnia and Herzegovina, Croatia, and Serbia sign the Dayton Accords to end the fighting in Bosnia.

1996

Jan. 20. Palestinian voters choose a new self-rule Palestinian National Authority government; Yasir Arafat of the Palestinian Liberation Organization (PLO) is elected president.

March 23. Taiwan holds its first democratic presidential elections.

Sept. 26, 1996

July 17. Trans World Airlines (TWA) flight 800 explodes and plunges into the Atlantic Ocean after takeoff from Kennedy International Airport in New York City; all 230 people on board are killed.

Aug. 22. President Clinton signs major welfare-reform legislation, ending "welfare as we know it."

Sept. 19. The government of Guatemala and leftist rebels sign a peace treaty, ending their long war.

Sept. 26. Shannon Lucid returns to Earth after spending 188 days in space—a record for a U.S. astronaut and for a woman. The 53-year-old biochemist had conducted various studies while in space.

Nov. 5. U.S. President Bill Clinton and Vice-President Al Gore are reelected to a second term. The Republican Party retains control of both houses of Congress.

Dec. 17. Ghana's Kofi Annan is elected to succeed Boutros Boutros-Ghali as secretary-general of the United Nations.

1997

April 13. Tiger Woods wins the 61st Masters Golf Tournament with a 72-hole, tournament-record score of 270—18 under par.

May 1. The British Labour Party, led by Tony Blair, is victorious in parliamentary

April 13, 1997

May 1, 1997

elections. Britain's Conservative Party had been in power since May 1979.

July 1. China resumes sovereignty over Hong Kong, ending 165 years of British rule.

July 23. Slobodan Milosevic, who is completing his second term as president of Serbia, takes office as president of Yugoslavia (Serbia and Montenegro).

Aug. 31. Diana, Britain's 36-year-old princess of Wales and former wife of Prince Charles, dies following a car crash in Paris, France.

Sept. 5. Mother Teresa, the 87-year-old Roman Catholic nun who won the 1979 Nobel Peace Prize, dies of a heart attack in Calcutta, India.

Sept. 18. Citizens of Wales vote to accept London's offer to establish an elected assembly. One week earlier, the Scottish electorate voted to establish Scotland's own legislature for the first time since 1707.

Also in 1997. Researchers in Scotland announce the creation of the first genetic clone of an adult animal—a sheep called Dolly....*Cats*, a Broadway musical that opened on Oct. 7, 1982, becomes the longest-running show in Broadway history.

1998

March 27. The Food and Drug Administration (FDA) approves the first pill for male impotence.

April 10. Leaders of Great Britain and Ireland and Protestant and Catholic groups reach an agreement designed to bring peace to Northern Ireland.

May 7. The merger of Chrysler Corporation and the German auto manufacturer Daimler-Benz AG is announced.

May 21. Suharto resigns as president of Indonesia, a post he had held for 32 years.

Aug. 7. Two bombs explode outside the U.S. embassies in Nairobi, Kenya, and Dar es Salaam, Tanzania, killing more than 200 people. Osama bin Laden, a Saudi-born millionaire believed to be living in Afghanistan, later is indicted by a U.S. federal grand jury in connection with the attacks.

Aug. 31, 1997

Sept. 27. Gerhard Schröder, a Social Democrat, defeats German Chancellor Helmut Kohl in national elections.

Oct. 23. Israel and the Palestinians sign an agreement on Israel's withdrawal from the West Bank.

Dec. 19. The U.S. House of Representatives votes to impeach President Bill Clinton for lying under oath and for obstructing justice. In August 1998 the

Dec. 19, 1998

1998 world financial crisis

president had testified before the office of independent counsel and a federal grand jury regarding his relationship with former White House intern Monica Lewinsky. The president also had admitted in a televised address that his earlier comments and silence on the matter "gave a false impression."

Also in 1998. A major financial crisis strikes nations of the Asia-Pacific rim and Russia....India and Pakistan detonate underground nuclear devices....Baseball's Mark McGwire of the St. Louis Cardinals and Sammy Sosa of the Chicago Cubs both break Roger Maris' single-season home-run record of 61.

March 21, 1999

1999

Jan. 1. The euro, the new common currency of the European Union (EU), comes into existence, with 11 EU nations participating.

Feb. 7. King Hussein of Jordan dies of cancer at the age of 63; he is succeeded as king by his eldest son, Abdullah, 37.

Feb. 12. The U.S. Senate acquits President Clinton of both articles of impeachment that were approved by the House of Representatives in December 1998.

Feb. 27. Nigeria returns to civilian rule as Gen. Olusegun Obasanjo, a former military ruler, becomes the nation's first elected president since August 1983.

March 21. Dr. Bertrand Piccard, a Swiss psychiatrist, and Britain's Brian Jones complete a historic 19-day, around-the-world trip in the balloon *Breitling Orbiter 3.* They are the first balloonists to circle the world nonstop.

March 24. The North Atlantic Treaty Organization begins a sustained campaign of air strikes against Yugoslavia (Serbia, Montenegro, and the former autonomous regions of Kosovo and Vojvodina). The bombings are in response to Serbia's refusal to sign a peace treaty with ethnic Albanians seeking independence for the

March 24, 1999

province of Kosovo. Meanwhile, hundreds of thousands of ethnic Albanians flee from their homes in Kosovo, leading to a refugee crisis.

March 29. On the New York Stock Exchange, the Dow Jones industrial average of 30 industrial stocks closes above the 10,000 mark for the first time in history.

April 20. In Littleton, CO, two students go on a shooting spree at a local high school, killing 12 other students, a teacher, and themselves.

March 24, 1999

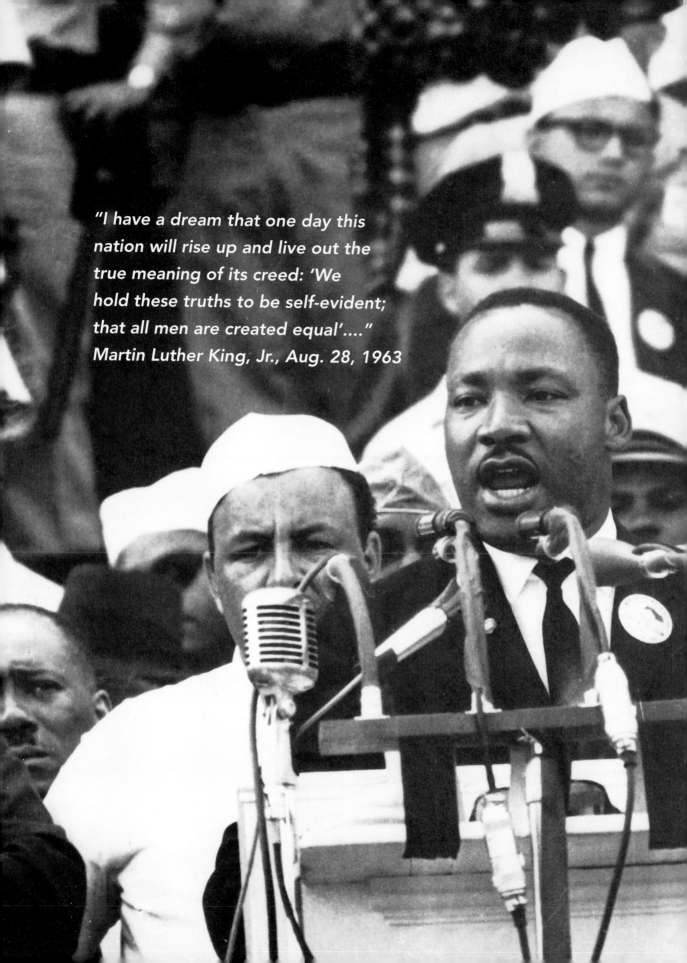

"I have a dream that one day this nation will rise up and live out the true meaning of its creed: 'We hold these truths to be self-evident; that all men are created equal'...."
Martin Luther King, Jr., Aug. 28, 1963

GIANTS OF THE 20TH CENTURY

Editor's note: Selecting 25 "Giants of the Century" was a difficult and controversial task. Accordingly, a survey of contributors, editors, and their colleagues was taken to decide those who merit inclusion. A cross section of those who had the greatest impact in all fields was the objective.

Winston Churchill

In a famous rectorial address—delivered as lord rector to the students of St. Andrews University in 1922—Sir J.M. Barrie, the playwright, said, "Courage is the thing. All goes if courage goes. . . 'Unless a man has that virtue, he has no security for preserving any other.'" That statement well might summarize the very essence of Sir Winston Churchill. Together with many triumphs, the British politician and statesman had many shattering failures—occasions that might have ended the career of a lesser man.

Churchill was pursuing high adventure well before the 20th century began, serving as a volunteer with the Spanish forces in Cuba in 1895. Three years as a war correspondent and a soldier during the Boer War were climaxed by his capture by the Boers and escape, and by his election to Parliament in December 1900 at the age of 26. He had entered upon the stage of history, which he never left for the remainder of his 90 years.

Having left the Conservative Party in 1904 for the Liberals, he was holding cabinet office by 1908, and in 1911 had the position of first lord of the admiralty. But he was near the first of his great reverses: Regarded, with some injustice, as responsible for the Dardanelles fiasco of World War I, he had to resign the post, and soon was in the trenches himself, in command of a regiment.

Churchill served as chancellor of the exchequer (1924–29), but from 1931 to 1939, though a member of Parliament, he held no office and was something of a pariah even in his own Conservative Party, which he had rejoined in 1924. He differed from the government on two major issues—limited self-rule for India and the necessity of rearming and facing the German threat. Today's wisdom is that he was wrong on the first of these issues and that he was right on the second. The frightened men who ran Britain in the 1930s did not like Churchill and were determined to keep him out of office.

In 1940, when Churchill became prime minister, the man found his hour, and the hour found its man. This was the high plateau of imperishable grandeur in his life, when Britain stood alone and he personified Britain as it faced a second world war. From 1940 until victory in 1945, he was an inexhaustible well of inspiration and courage for the whole free world.

Even before he died, much that Churchill cared deeply about had gone or was going—Britain's predominant place in the world, the

British Empire, the aristocratic structure of British society. What can be seen as his legacy? First, on the personal level, he was a matchless example of courage, determination, and industry. And of probity: No personal scandal ever touched him. In world politics, he was responsible more than any man for Britain's continued independent existence. His great dream was the closest possible Anglo-American cooperation, and he cared much for Europe. So today's world—in which Europe is progressing toward integration, and Britain and the United States see more eye to eye and cooperate more closely than any two other major powers—would not be altogether displeasing to him.

Arthur Campbell Turner

BIOGRAPHICAL HIGHLIGHTS

1874. Born on November 30 at Blenheim Palace in Oxfordshire, England.

1895. Joined the British army after being graduated from Royal Military College at Sandhurst.

1899. Was defeated in his first bid for a House of Commons seat. Served as a correspondent during the Boer War.

1901. Entered the House of Commons as a Conservative on January 23.

1904. Disagreed with the Conservatives and joined the Liberal Party.

1908. Married Clementine Hozier on September 12. Five children—one of whom died at the age of 3—were born of the union. Became president of the Board of Trade.

1910–11. Served as home secretary.

1911–15. Was first lord of the admiralty.

1916. Took up painting as a hobby. Volunteered for active army service.

1919–21. Was secretary of state for war and air.

1921–22. As secretary of state for air and colonies, took a leading part in establishing the new Arab states in the Middle East.

1924–29. Served as chancellor of the exchequer as a Conservative.

1929–39. During a period of political frustration, turned his attention to writing.

1939–40. Was first lord of the admiralty.

1940–45. During World War II, was Britain's prime minister and minister of defense.

1945. On July 26 the Labour Party's Clement Attlee succeeded Churchill as prime minister.

1948. The first of his eventual six volumes on World War II was published.

1951. Became prime minister on October 26.

1953. Was knighted by Queen Elizabeth II. Won the Nobel Prize in literature.

1955. Resigned the post of prime minister, but continued to sit in Commons until 1964.

1963. Was proclaimed an honorary U.S. citizen.

1965. Died in London on January 24.

Walt Disney

In the early days of Walt Disney's success, the world thought of him primarily as an animation genius, the creator of such delightful cartoon characters as Mickey Mouse and Donald Duck, and subsequently of popular full-length animated features like the groundbreaking *Snow White and the Seven Dwarfs* (1937). Yet that was only the beginning. By century's end, the extent to which Disney ultimately influenced popular culture had earned him a special niche among the important figures of the age.

Innovation was a Disney hallmark from the early days of his career. A midwesterner, Disney was born in Chicago in 1901 and spent part of his childhood in Marceline, MO. His artistic career, however, began in Kansas City, MO, where a critical teaming took place with another inventive artist, Ub Iwerks, with whom he eventually set up shop in Hollywood. Iwerks did the drawings to produce Mickey Mouse, a character that first was launched in silent films, then starred

in *Steamboat Willie* (1928), the first cartoon featuring sound. Disney also was among the early users of color.

His bold 1940 film *Fantasia* imaginatively combined symphonic music and animation and pioneered new sound techniques using special equipment installed in theaters. Disney, who won some 30 Oscars during his career, later expanded into the production of live-action family features, with one of the best of these being *Mary Poppins* (1964). At the 1964 World's Fair, Disney's puppet figures, which moved and spoke with recorded voices, proved yet another popular innovation hinting at a future mix of animatronics and special effects that others would master during the computer age.

Disney's influence also extended in other directions. The process of marketing and licensing products in connection with *Snow White and the Seven Dwarfs* was an early harbinger of the sophisticated tie-in marketing that escalated later in the century. But nothing was as far-reaching in cultural impact as the opening of Disneyland Park in California in 1955, followed by Walt Disney World Resort in Florida in 1971; the ventures expanded and solidified Disney's vision. In 1983 a Disneyland opened in Japan, followed by one in France (1992).

The company that Disney founded had its share of problems, including labor disputes, during his lifetime. After the force of his personality was lost to the company upon his death in 1966, there was a need for reorientation. Eventually, new leadership honed the company into an even greater force in tune with the times, building upon such interests as television programming, the nature series, theatrical family films, videos, publications, corporate acquisitions—resulting in the ownership of Miramax and Capital Cities/ABC Television—and a network of Disney souvenir stores trading upon the universal popularity of trademark Disney characters. The 1990s marked an expansion of the company's investment and influence on

Broadway with the shows *Beauty and the Beast* and *The Lion King*; and the Disney product image gained a prominent place in New York City's revitalized Times Square area.

The very name "Disney" remains, for many, symbolic of family entertainment. Yet the Disney legacy has met with criticism from those who feel the studio's bland pop approach represents a pervasive "dumbing down" of culture. Conversely, when the company attempts to present more adult films, there is criticism from those who see these movies as tarnishing the family-entertainment image they associate with the Disney name. However, in an entertainment world replete with violence and anything-goes sex, millions still look to the Disney label to symbolize fare that they regard as wholesome for the entire family. That is the ultimate legacy that this determined, foresighted Midwesterner left for the world.

William Wolf

BIOGRAPHICAL HIGHLIGHTS

1901. Walter Elias Disney was born in Chicago, IL, on December 5.

1915. Enrolled in art classes at the Kansas City Art Institute.

1918. Joined the Red Cross and was sent overseas to France as an ambulance driver at the end of World War I.

1919. Returned to Kansas City, MO, and took a position as art director with a commercial studio.

1923. Left for Hollywood, CA, and began Walt Disney Productions in partnership with his brother Roy.

1925. Married Lillian Bounds in Lewiston, ID. They had two daughters.

1928. Mickey Mouse made his first sound appearance onscreen in *Steamboat Willie*, the world's first fully synchronized sound cartoon.

1932. First used color in the film series *Silly Symphonies*. Won his first Academy Award for the film *Flowers and Trees*.

1937. The first full-length animated musical, *Snow White and the Seven Dwarfs* (photo above), made its debut.

1941. Disney's *The Reluctant Dragon* was the first film to use both cartoon characters and live actors.

1961. Produced Disney's first color TV series, *Walt Disney's Wonderful World of Color*.

1966. Died in Los Angeles on Dec. 15, 1966.

Albert Einstein

Albert Einstein was one of the greatest physicists of all time and one of the most important humanists of the 20th century. Born in Ulm, Germany, in 1879, he died in Princeton, NJ, on April 18, 1955. Three events during the last week of his life underscored his legacy to the world. On April 11, Einstein agreed to sign an influential manifesto urging the nations of the world to settle their differences and thereby avoid another major war and the inevitable use of nuclear weapons. On the same day, Einstein received the Israeli ambassador to the United States and agreed to prepare a statement in defense of Israel. And beside his hospital bed, Einstein left the last calcula-tions in his long quest for a unified theory of gravitation and electromagnetism.

Einstein's scientific legacy rests upon his development of the special and general theo-ries of relativity, his fundamental contribu-tions to quantum theory and statistical physics, and his search for a unified theory. The special theory introduced into physics fundamental changes in our basic concepts of space, time, and mass for events occurring at or near the speed of light (186,000 miles, or 299,792 kilometers, per second). While also inspiring new directions in philosophical re-search and cultural expression, this theory introduced the century's most famous equa-tion, $E=mc^2$ (where m is mass, E is the equiva-

(1879-1955)

lent amount of energy, and *c* is the speed of light). This equation's most striking application occurred in the unleashing of nuclear energy in the century's most horrific invention, the atomic bomb, as well as in the peaceful production of electricity. At the same time, Einstein's general theory of relativity, a theory linking gravitation and the curvature of space, continues to open startling new vistas in the study of the origin, structure, and fate of the universe.

Einstein provided major contributions to the search for a unified theory and to the development of quantum mechanics, including the quantum ideas underlying the invention of the laser. Nevertheless, his legacy in these fields, at present, is less pronounced. The search for unification was not successful, and Einstein's opposition to the use of probabilistic laws in quantum mechanics, summed up in his statement "God does not play dice," remained a minority position. Major research efforts continue in both of these areas.

After settling in the United States in 1932, Einstein worked largely alone, having no students and few assistants. Perhaps his greatest impact on U.S. science was in helping to establish a professional role and public image for the theoretical physicist. In a century of world wars, genocide, and weapons of mass destruction, Einstein helped to raise and define the issues surrounding the social responsibility of the scientist. Einstein's profound aversion to war and militarism, his support of the scientists' movement against nuclear weapons after World War II, his advocacy for the state of Israel, his promotion of social justice, and his determined opposition to demagoguery—whether in Germany or during the McCarthy era in the United States—were widely influential then and continue to inspire many today.

David C. Cassidy

BIOGRAPHICAL HIGHLIGHTS

1879. Born in Ulm, Baden-Württemberg, Germany, on March 14.

1896. Entered the Swiss Federal Polytechnic Institute in Zurich, Switzerland.

1900. Was graduated from the Institute as a teacher of mathematics and physics.

1902. Took a position as an examiner in the Swiss patent office in Bern.

1903. Married his former classmate at the Institute, Mileva Mariç, with whom he had two sons.

1905. Published a series of articles that included his theory of relativity; his doctoral thesis was accepted at the University of Zurich.

1909. Was appointed an associate professor at the University of Zurich.

1911. Was appointed a full professor at the Karl-Ferdinand University in Prague.

1912. Was appointed a professor at the Federal Polytechnic Institute.

1914. Moved to Berlin and separated from his wife, whom he eventually divorced.

1919. Married his cousin, Elsa, a widow with two grown daughters.

1921. Won the Nobel Prize for physics.

1932. Moved from Germany in December and accepted a position at the Institute for Advanced Study in Princeton, NJ.

1939. Collaborated with other physicists in writing a letter to President Franklin D. Roosevelt pointing out the need for the development of an atomic bomb.

1940. Became a U.S. citizen.

1952. Declined the position of president of Israel.

1955. Died on April 18 at Princeton, NJ.

Henry Ford

O f all the century's hero giants, none did more to elevate the quality of life of the underprivileged classes than a Michigan farm boy turned mechanic—Henry Ford.

Born to a poor family in Dearborn midway through the Civil War, Ford lacked a formal education and seemed the most unlikely prospect for the accomplishments of his adult life. But he was nothing if not dedicated. Overcoming opposition with his blunt style of interaction, Ford almost single-handedly achieved numerous breakthroughs in the opening years of the 1900s, including a mass-production system that transformed industry and a mass-consumption economy

that put the "world on wheels" by enabling the working classes to buy cars and comparable products previously sold only to the rich. And in 1914, Ford's establishment of a $5-a-day minimum worker wage for an eight-hour shift more than doubled the industry's previous $2.34-a-day wage for a nine-hour shift, making entry-level cars like Ford's Model T affordable for the workers themselves.

By 1914, 11 years after Ford Motor Company was founded and 18 years after Ford built his first car, the Model T had made the company a success, and some 50 competitors were eager to tap into a start-up industry with such obvious growth potential. Two "aftershocks" of the automaking eruption were the franchised dealer system and the popularization of gasoline stations on nearby corners instead of at distant garages.

Calling mass output "the new Messiah" that would keep reducing prices while raising wages and profits, Ford spared no expense in modernizing the Rouge plant in Dearborn. The Model T car he introduced in 1908, in black only, was not to be changed, however; this proved to be a near-fatal flaw of his stubborn character, which allowed GM's Chevrolet to overtake Ford by the late 1920s.

When the Model T was introduced, it took 12 hours to build one. By 1920 production time had been reduced to Ford's goal of one car every 60 seconds. In 1925 a car could be produced every ten seconds. All told, by the time the updated Model A finally replaced the Model T in 1927, 15,456,868 Model Ts had been built. Ford's dream had been realized in less than 20 years, and the birth of the first "people's car" had made him the world's richest man.

As undisputed ruler of Ford Motor Company for 44 years, Ford was a true patriarch who trusted few outside his family. His opposition to the new United Auto Workers

(UAW), even after GM and Chrysler Corporation recognized the union, sparked the 1937 "Battle of the Overpass," when company goons bloodied organizers led by future UAW President Walter P. Reuther. Ford did not accept the UAW until 1941. Similarly, the company did not go public with a stock issue until 1956, as a result of its founder's distrust of "Wall Street bankers."

Henry Ford's legacy transcends the cars and plants he built. He himself declared: "I invented the modern age."

Maynard M. Gordon

BIOGRAPHICAL HIGHLIGHTS

1863. Born on a farm near Dearborn, MI, on July 30.

1879. Became a highly skilled machinist in Detroit, eventually becoming chief engineer for the Edison Illuminating Company.

1888. Married Clara Bryant on April 11; they had one son, Edsel.

1896. Completed his first car, the Quadricycle.

1903. Started the Ford Motor Company.

1908. Created the Model T or "Tin Lizzie," which was manufactured for 19 years.

1913. Introduced the first assembly line, which reduced production time drastically.

1918. Ran as a Democrat for a Senate seat from Michigan, but lost the election. In December, turned the presidency of the Ford Motor Company over to his son.

1926. Began losing sales to GM because the Model T was outdated.

1927. Model T discontinued; Model A introduced to meet growing competition.

1932. Produced the powerful V-8 engine.

1936. Set up the Ford Foundation with his son.

1941. Signed a contract with the United Automobile Workers (UAW).

1943. Upon his son's death, resumed the presidency.

1945. Retired; his grandson, Henry Ford II, became company president.

1947. Died at his Dearborn home on April 7.

Sigmund Freud

Sigmund Freud, a Jewish neurologist in Vienna, shaped a provocative image of man for thousands of intellectuals, physicians, and ordinary people in the 20th century. If we believe dreams and slips of the tongue reveal our unconscious sexual and aggressive drives, hold early childhood to be determinative of human development, or consult a listening psychotherapist, we are reflecting the legacy of Sigmund Freud. He was a pioneer in the study of sexuality and the modern psychological understanding and treatment of nervous and mental disorder.

Inspired by a Viennese colleague, Joseph Breuer, Freud elaborated a "talking cure"—patients had to say everything that came to mind. These "free associations," the essence of his psychoanalysis, would lead to forgotten traumatic experiences that determined symptoms. Although he believed that sexual abuse in early childhood was traumatic, he concluded that his patients' memories expressed unconscious sexual wishes and fantasies. Their emergence, however, was blocked, repressed by his patients' equally powerful internalized anxieties and moral standards. Freud's therapy sought to discover and resolve such conflicts between impulse and control. Arguing that sexuality began in infancy, Freud believed that the child's first sensual contacts with caregivers set lifelong patterns of character.

Disillusioned by the barbarity of World War I, Freud judged aggression as central a human motive as sexuality and, partly for this reason, rejected facile sexual liberation for ignoring social needs. He advanced theories of art, religion, and society on the basis of his clinical findings and believed these were confirmed by common folk beliefs, jokes, dreams, and imaginative literature. The dreams and fantasies of neurotics and ordinary people resembled those of the mentally ill, demonstrating continuity between normal and abnormal.

A brilliant student, Freud read widely and received a rigorous classical education. He saw patients ten or 12 hours a day and wrote thousands of letters to correspondents around the world; his collected works run to 24 volumes in English. A consummate stylist, he remains one of the century's great writers. His views influenced psychiatry, child raising, the humanities, and social sciences and were popularized widely in movies, novels, and the press. His conceptions of trauma; catharsis; infantile sexuality; the unconscious; the id, ego, and superego; and defenses such as repression have become common coin.

Freud and his followers founded organizations, chiefly in Western Europe and the Americas, to develop his theory and therapy. Freud's opponents claim his theories, controversial from their inception, are unscientific and immoral; feminists dispute his views of women. Freud's defenders believe objective studies confirm his findings about unconscious processes and character. His theory of dreams as invariably wish fulfillments and claims for the superiority of psychoanalysis to other psychotherapies have not been demonstrated. Aware of the limits imposed by heredity and constitution, Freud envisioned the possibility of advances in somatic treatment for illness psychological methods could not reach.

Nathan G. Hale, Jr.

BIOGRAPHICAL HIGHLIGHTS

1856. Born on May 6 in Freiberg, Moravia (Czech Republic).

1881. Was graduated as a doctor of medicine from the medical school of the University of Vienna.

1886. Opened a neurology practice and married Martha Bernays. The Freuds had six children together.

1891. In September, moved to 19 Berggasse in Vienna, where he lived and worked for the next 47 years.

1895. With Joseph Breuer, published a collection of essays, "Studies in Hysteria."

1896. Used the term "psychoanalysis" for the first time.

1900. Published *The Interpretation of Dreams*.

1902. Was appointed a professor at the University of Vienna; founded what became the Vienna Psychoanalytic Society.

1905. Published *Three Essays on the Theory of Sexuality*.

1906. Began to exchange letters with the Swiss psychologist Carl Jung.

1908. First International Congress of Psychoanalysis held in Salzburg.

1910. Formed the International Psychoanalytical Association with Jung.

1912. Started the psychoanalytical journal *Imago*.

1913. Ended his association with Jung.

1920. The *International Journal of Psycho-Analysis* was founded.

1923. First signs of Freud's oral cancer were detected.

1932. Wrote the *New Introductory Lectures on Psycho-Analysis* to ease the financial situation of the International Psychoanalytical Press.

1935. Was elected an honorary member of the British Royal Society of Medicine.

1938. The Freuds moved to London as Austria was annexed to the German Reich.

1939. Died in London on September 23.

Mohandas Gandhi

It would be difficult today to find any apparent legacy left by Mohandas Gandhi in South Africa—where he honed his nonviolent strategy—India, or even the world as a whole. Yet he remains a giant of the 20th century for his accomplishments, and, if one looks beyond the turmoil of Indian politics or apartheid in South Africa, the proliferation of nuclear weapons, and ethnic conflict worldwide, there is a glimmer of a positive Gandhian legacy.

In South Africa apartheid was not ended by nonviolence—rather, increased domestic violence and international pressure brought it down. Violence between different ethnic groups continues. Yet leaders such as South Africa's Nelson Mandela have carried on the tasks of nation-building and ethnic reconciliation, believing firmly in the possibility of true tolerance as preached by Gandhi.

In India the politics of religion and caste conflict belie Gandhi's vision of a peaceful India where all groups could coexist freely. Part of his dream died before he did with the partition of British India into Muslim Pakistan and predominantly Hindu India. Pakistan itself was to break up in 1971 through a violent ethnic civil war. Wars between Pakistan and India further have poisoned relations between Hindus and Muslims in both countries. Within India, parties such as the Shiv Sena and Bharatiya Janata Party openly espouse Hindu nationalism. Elements of each have destroyed Muslim and Christian places of worship, opposed protective legislation for low castes and minority communities, and instigated violence against both low castes and religious minorities. Caste and religion are used routinely to appeal to voters. Even elements of the low-caste Dalit communities question Gandhi's antidiscrimination stance.

Nonviolence—used so effectively against the might of the British Empire—has given way to increasing civic violence inflicted by citizens upon each other and by the state upon citizens; intolerance and corruption also have increased. Rather than living simply, as Gandhi advocated and exemplified, expanding middle and wealthy classes pursue material wealth while India's poverty rate shows little decline below 45%.

The spread of nuclear weapons, including on the Indian subcontinent, would upset Gandhi greatly. Especially painful for him would be India's nuclear-weapons program. Though Gandhi recognized the need for strength and defense, such a program in the absence of any real threat would be indicative of a loss of moral leadership.

Perhaps a Gandhian legacy can be found in two places. The U.S. civil-rights movement under Martin Luther King, Jr., in the 1950s and 1960s retained the nonviolent character of India's own independence movement under Gandhi. Although both were checkered with some violence, it was at least partially state violence against unarmed "fighters" that led to reinterpretation of laws in the United States and independence for India. Secondly, nonviolence required the political mobilization of ordinary people who refused to obey "illegitimate" authority. It also required political education about peaceful conflict resolution. India probably can thank that mobilization and education for the continuation of its democracy. An extraordinarily high percentage of the nation's population votes, and those voters time and again have rejected extremism and violence in favor of moderation and peace.

Aruna Nayyar Michie

BIOGRAPHICAL HIGHLIGHTS

1869. Born in Porbandar, Gujarat, India, on October 2.

1882. Was married to Kasturba Makanji. Together they had four children.

1891. Was admitted to bar and practiced law in Bombay.

1893–1914. Worked for an Indian firm in South Africa. Developed his technique for nonviolent resistance, *satyagraha*.

1915. Returned to India in January.

1919. Turned to direct political protest after troops fired on an unarmed crowd in Amritsar.

1920–22. Launched a policy of noncooperation with the British.

1924. Supported a *satyagraha* movement to give "untouchables" more rights.

1930. In April, inaugurated a campaign against the government's monopoly on the manufacturing of salt, and was interned.

1931. Was released from prison.

1939–45. During World War II, continued his struggle for India's independence through nonviolent disobedience of British rule.

1942–44. Was imprisoned after demanding total withdrawal of the British from India.

1947. Was the principal participant in negotiations when India gained independence.

1948. Was assassinated in Delhi on January 30 by a Hindu fanatic.

William Henry Gates III

As the personal-computer (PC) revolution engulfed the last two decades of the 20th century, a young college dropout named Bill Gates took command, helping change indelibly the way people work and play. The explosive growth of his Microsoft software empire made Gates the world's richest man—with a personal fortune exceeding $50 billion—and created an icon of the Information Age who is at once admired, feared, and, in some quarters, loathed.

In 1975 the 20-year-old Gates and his childhood friend Paul Allen founded Microsoft after developing a computer language for the Altair, the first PC. Five years later, IBM, which was creating its first PC, selected Microsoft to create an operating system—the software that runs basic computer functions. Microsoft quickly became an international company.

Meanwhile, upstart Apple Computer was developing the Macintosh, a PC with point-and-click technology that took the mystery out of home computing. The Mac set the standard for the future of PCs, and Gates responded. In 1985, Microsoft introduced Windows, its first operating system with graphics, to counter the Mac. Newer versions became easier to use during the following years, and—helped by Gates' aggressive sales tactics—Windows was running most of the world's PCs by the end of the 1990s. Microsoft's array of software products for home and business computers also dominated the competition, generating huge profits that made the company a Wall Street darling. The growing ranks of "Microsoft millionaires," led by Gates, became symbols of high technology's increasing role in the United States' economy and society.

Microsoft's success has made Gates one of the business world's most renowned and unlikely leaders—a bookish young "computer nerd" whose fortune quickly exceeded those of the slick, graying executives in pinstriped power suits who for so long had represented corporate America. But behind Gates' boyish appearance is a shrewd businessman whose pursuit of power has angered rivals and attracted government scrutiny.

In 1988, Apple sued Microsoft for copyright infringement, claiming Windows was patterned after the Macintosh system. Six years later, Microsoft settled a federal antitrust investigation by promising to stop

discouraging computer makers from buying rival operating systems. But competitive concerns remained. As the decade drew to a close, Gates again was fighting the government, which sued Microsoft for unfairly trying to dominate the young market for Internet software.

Like the great industrialists of the early 20th century, Gates inspires both awe and dread in those who observe his role in shaping a business that has altered everyday lives. The personal computer, Gates says, "is about solving problems, letting you learn, letting you take something you believe in and advance your cause, letting you express your creativity, letting you have an impact on the world by reaching out and using it as a tool to change things." Gates was not the first to envision computers and the Internet emerging as television, newspaper, library, and telephone all in one, but he has made sure the Microsoft name is stamped permanently across this new era of communication.

Eric Quiñones

BIOGRAPHICAL HIGHLIGHTS

1955. Born on October 28 in Seattle, WA.

1967. Began attending Lakeside School, a private school known for its intense academic environment.

1968. Became extremely interested in computers when Lakeside School invested in computer time for its students.

1969. Teamed up with fellow student Paul Allen and two other classmates to form the Lakeside Programmers Group.

1973. Entered Harvard University as a prelaw major; he would drop out in his junior year.

1975. With Allen, created a form of the computer language BASIC that could be used with the Altair 8800—a home-computer kit sold by Micro Instrumentation and Telemetry Systems (MITS)—and signed a deal with MITS in February. Later that year, again with Allen, established Microsoft in Albuquerque, NM.

1979. Microsoft moved to Bellevue, WA.

1981. Devised the Microsoft Disk Operating System (MS-DOS) for IBM.

1986. Became an instant millionaire after Microsoft's stock went public on the Nasdaq Stock Market.

1990. In July, Microsoft became the first personal-computer-software company to exceed $1 billion in sales in a single year.

1992. Was awarded the National Medal of Technology.

1994. Married Melinda French on January 1 and established the William H. Gates Foundation.

1995. Wrote *The Road Ahead*, his vision of where information technology will take society.

1999. His book *Business @ the Speed of Thought: Using a Digital Nervous System* was published.

Adolf Hitler

Despite the fact that Adolf Hitler died less than halfway through the 20th century, the former German chancellor left a legacy in Germany, Europe, and the world that has remained pervasive for the 55 years following his death and that doubtless will continue well into the 21st century. Hardly a day has passed since Hitler's death without some event somewhere in the world being connected to his catastrophic 12-year reign as the absolute ruler, or Führer, of the German Reich. These events range from the important to the trivial. Germans agonize over the architecture of Berlin, which soon is to become Germany's capital once again. Can any Nazi influence be seen in any of the buildings? What kind of Holocaust memorial should be built in the capital? Although Germany in the past half century has paid billions of dollars in reparations for Hitler's crimes, German political leaders still must face the damage claims of 12 million forced laborers and their survivors. German companies, banks, and insurance firms still wrestle with issues arising from Hitler's Reich. A latent pacifism among many Germans is another legacy of Hitler, which hinders the attempts of the country to carry its share of peacekeeping responsibilities in the United Nations and the North Atlantic Treaty Organization (NATO). When Germany today asks to be treated as a "normal" country, it in fact is asking the world to free it from the Hitler legacy.

In Europe the Hitler legacy can be seen in the determination of postwar Europeans to create a peaceful, united continent of democratic societies. The attempt since 1945 to overcome the heritage of nationalism and militarism and create a single European economy and political order was motivated in essence by the trauma of World War II.

Following the war, Europe no longer was at the epicenter of world politics. Its hegemony passed to Hitler's conquerors—the United States and the Soviet Union—and, since the collapse of Communism, to the United States alone.

Hitler's legacy also can be seen in contemporary world politics. The establishment of

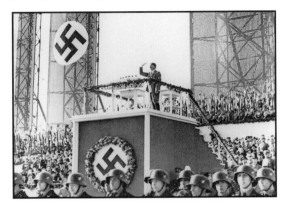

the state of Israel in 1948 was a direct result of the Nazi Holocaust. The major Western nations, above all the United States, would not have been as decisive in their support for this bold move were it not for Hitler's attempt to exterminate the Jewish people. The subsequent half century of tensions and wars in the Middle East is another example of the Hitler legacy.

Throughout the world, Hitler has provided artists, writers, filmmakers, and journalists with a symbol of pure evil unmatched by any other historical figure. The scholarly works about him number in the tens of thousands. Many have achieved best-seller status. Even "everyday people" far removed by time and space from Hitler still find their lives intersecting with his legacy, as with the high-school student who is suspended because he compared his band teacher to Hitler, the baseball-team owner who loses her team for an ill-informed remark about Hitler's "positive accomplishments," or the former sports star who must retract some ill-advised reference to the Führer. Hitler has redefined the meaning of evil perhaps forever.

David P. Conradt

BIOGRAPHICAL HIGHLIGHTS

1889. Born on April 20 at Braunau-am-Inn, Austria.

1907. Left Austria to study art in Vienna.

1913. Moved to Munich, Germany, to evade Austrian military service.

1914. At the outbreak of World War I, served as a volunteer in a Bavarian infantry regiment.

1920. Took an active role in organizing the National Socialist German Workers' Party, or the Nazi Party.

1923. On November 9, led a march of about 3,000 Nazi storm troopers to the center of Munich. Was arrested three days later and was convicted of treason. Served less than nine months, during which time he wrote *Mein Kampf*.

1924. Reorganized the Nazi Party after his release from prison.

1930. Nazi seats in the Reichstag increased from 12 to 107 after elections.

1933. Was appointed chancellor of a coalition government of Nazis and conservative nationalists by President Paul von Hindenburg on January 30. Withdrew Germany from both the disarmament conference and the League of Nations.

1934. On June 30, instigated a bloody purge within the Nazi Party. Assumed title of Führer, supreme head of Germany, with Hindenburg's death on August 2.

1935. Escalated the persecution of Jews through the Nuremberg Laws.

1939. Signed a military alliance with Italy in May; in August, signed a ten-year nonaggression pact with the Soviet Union. On September 1, ordered his troops to invade Poland, thus beginning World War II.

1943. The German defeat at Stalingrad and the Allied reconquest of North Africa signaled the eventual loss of the war.

1944. Survived an assassination attempt.

1945. Committed suicide with Eva Braun, his former mistress and wife of one day, on April 30.

John Paul II

As John Paul II completed the 20th year of his pontificate in October 1998, speculation mounted that history would acclaim him as "John Paul the Great," much as we speak of the 5th- and 6th-century popes, Leo the Great and Gregory the Great. Some see John Paul's greatness chiefly in the part he played in the collapse of the Soviet Communist empire. Cautioned about incurring the displeasure of Pope Pius XII, Soviet leader Joseph Stalin dismissively asked, "How many divisions does the pope have?" John Paul II marshaled divisions of the human spirit, first in Poland and then throughout Eastern Europe,

emboldening millions of people to stand up and declare their determination to "live in the truth." This was at least as important, if not more important, than the economic, military, and other factors that brought an end to the cruel lie of totalitarianism.

While the political consequences of his pontificate are monumental, John Paul should not be viewed as a political figure in any ordinary sense of the term. He is a priest, a philosopher-theologian, a bishop, and successor to the Apostle Peter in the See of Rome. Among his chief titles is that of *Servus servorum Dei* ("Servant of the servants of God"). He is servant to the more than 1 billion Roman Catholics in the world, but also to the entire human family—all of whom he sees as being called to be servants of God and of one another. The theme of his pontificate, first declared at his installation in October 1978, has been "Be not afraid!" That means, he has explained, that—despite all the perils facing the human project—the project itself cannot fail, because God has invested himself in the human project by becoming one of us in Jesus Christ, and Christ already has overcome sin, evil, and every threat to human existence.

For all the pope's travels and many achievements, especially his rallying of millions of young people to a vision of moral greatness, the service of John Paul chiefly has been that of a teacher. His is possibly the most assertive teaching pontificate in the 2,000 years of the Catholic Church's history. He has taught through literally thousands of homilies, speeches, and official documents, but perhaps most influentially through 13 encyclical letters. Four major encyclicals may be singled out for special attention. In 1991, *Centesimus Annus* (The Hundredth Year) set forth the moral basis of a free and just social order. *Evangelium Vitae* (The Gospel of Life [1995]) explains why the protection of unborn children and other vulnerable human lives is essential to the defense of human rights against "the culture of death." *Veritatis Splendor* (The Splendor of Truth [1993]) makes the argument for the objectivity of moral truth, in opposition to every form of relativism and nihilism, while the 1998 encyclical *Fides et Ratio* (Faith and Reason) highlights the unity of science, religion, and philosophy in knowing the truth. The arguments made in these and other teaching initiatives likely will be studied and debated for centuries to come.

At the beginning of a new millennium, it generally is agreed that there is on the stage of world history no figure of combined moral, intellectual, and spiritual stature comparable to that of John Paul II. It will be no surprise if future generations refer to him as John Paul the Great.

Rev. Richard John Neuhaus

BIOGRAPHICAL HIGHLIGHTS

1920. Born on May 18 in Wadowice, Poland, and named Karol Wojtyla.

1942. With Germany occupying Poland, entered an "underground" seminary.

1946. Was ordained to the priesthood on November 1.

1948. Earned a doctorate in theology at the Angelicum in Rome.

1948–51. Served as a parish priest in the Kraków, Poland, diocese.

1952–58. Taught social ethics at the Kraków Seminary.

1956. Was appointed a professor of ethics at the Catholic University of Lublin.

1958. Was named an auxiliary bishop in Kraków by Pope Pius XII on July 4.

1960. Published *Love and Responsibility*.

1963. Was named archbishop of Kraków by Pope Paul VI on December 30.

1967. Was elevated to cardinal in June.

1978. On October 16, became the first non-Italian to be chosen pope since Hadrian VI (1522–23).

1981. Survived an almost-fatal assassination attack in St. Peter's Square on May 13.

1994. His new book, *Crossing the Threshold of Hope*, became a best-seller.

1998. Met with President Fidel Castro (*photo above*) during a much-publicized trip to Cuba.

Michael Jordan

If Michael Jordan's legacy rested strictly on his abilities as a basketball player, he would have an elite place in the history of sports. But Jordan's impact extended far beyond the playing court that he dominated for 13 seasons with the Chicago Bulls of the National Basketball Association (NBA). His charisma and engaging personality helped him become a worldwide celebrity, easily the most famous athlete of his generation, and, just as important, the breakthrough figure among his peers in terms of athletic endorsement dollars.

Jordan became the first athletic megabusinessman. His role as spokesperson for Nike turned that athletic-shoe and -apparel company into the world leader, earning both him and Nike millions of dollars. During his career, Jordan became the spokesperson for numerous other companies, all of which could measure through increased sales the positive effect he had on their bottom line. He also started his own businesses, ranging from a restaurant to a very successful clothing line. In the process, he became fabulously wealthy. Besides being the highest-paid basketball player ever—he was earning $30 million a year when he retired after the 1997–98 season—he earned another $35 million-plus annually through endorsements (*photo, page 59*) and his private business ventures.

All his off-court success stemmed from his on-court prowess. As a young player with the Bulls, he established new levels for spellbinding, acrobatic plays and seemingly new levels for jumping ability. His soaring dunks and body-twisting baskets quickly made him the most popular player in the league. No one ever had seen anyone quite like this 6'6" (1.98-meter), 216-pound (98-kilogram) native of Wilmington, NC, who once had been college player of the year with the University of North Carolina, leading the Tar Heels to one national title. As he matured in the NBA, he also became an on-court leader, guiding the Bulls to six championships in eight years, a string interrupted when he retired in 1993 for nearly two seasons to pursue an ill-fated baseball career.

At his best, Jordan was unstoppable. He led the league in scoring a record ten times. He was the regular-season most valuable player (MVP) five times and the championship-round MVP six times. But he was not a one-dimensional player. He made the league's all-defensive team nine times and was considered one of the premier defensive guards ever to play the game. His last basket as a pro was vintage Jordan: In the final seconds against the Utah Jazz in the sixth game of the 1997–98 championship round, he stole the ball and drove the length of the court, pulling up for a magnificent foul-line jump shot. Of course, it went in, and the Bulls won their sixth title.

Jordan was the perfect athlete for his generation, during which television—particularly

with the blossoming of cable sports networks—emerged as the dominant media force. His humor and thoughtful ways with the media resulted in unprecedented coverage. He played to the camera well, and he relished the spotlight. In an era where many of his peers turned off the public with their behavior, Jordan was refreshingly real and warm. Everyone—particularly the fans, who bought his merchandise and mobbed him wherever he went, so much so that he required bodyguards in public—found him charming. He appeared in a hit movie and was the center of incredible adulation when he played on the Dream Team, the 1992 U.S. Olympic basketball team comprised of NBA stars that won a gold medal in Barcelona. He retired as a player not because of diminished skills, but because he had lost that burning desire to win yet more titles.

Paul Attner

BIOGRAPHICAL HIGHLIGHTS

1963. Born in Brooklyn, NY, on February 17.

1982. While a freshman at the University of North Carolina, made the winning shot in the championship game of the National Collegiate Athletic Association (NCAA) basketball tournament.

1984. Was chosen college player of the year. Played on the U.S. men's basketball team that won a gold medal at the Summer Olympics.

1985. After being drafted by the Chicago Bulls, was named the National Basketball Association's (NBA's) rookie of the year. Agreed to become a spokesperson for Nike.

1988. Was voted the most valuable player and the defensive player of the year—the first in NBA annals to receive both of these awards in the same season.

1989. Married Juanita Vanoy in September. The couple would have two sons and one daughter.

1993. His father was murdered in South Carolina. Retired from the Chicago Bulls in October.

1994. Signed a minor-league-baseball contract with the White Sox in February.

1995. After a mediocre baseball career, returned to the Chicago Bulls in March.

1996. Appeared in the motion picture *Space Jam*.

1998. Became the third player in NBA history to score 29,000 points.

1999. Announced his retirement from pro basketball on January 13.

James Joyce

Considered one of the greatest and most challenging writers of the 20th century, James Joyce is known for his experimental use of language and revolutionary narrative techniques. He is also famous for his detailed representation of Dublin life, epiphanies, stream-of-consciousness narratives, and probing insights into the human condition. A leader in the literary movement known as Modernism, Joyce had a profound impact on the form of the novel, influencing almost every modern writer who came after and keeping critics busy for the better part of the century.

Born James Augustine Aloysius Joyce on Feb. 2, 1882, in Rathgar, a suburb of Dublin, Ireland, Joyce spent much of his early life moving from place to place as his family's wealth and middle-class status steadily declined, due in large part to the spendthrift habits of his father, John Stanislaus Joyce. Despite his family's dwindling fortune, Joyce was educated at some of the finest Jesuit preparatory schools in Ireland, including Clongowes Wood College, where he received a strict Catholic education and instruction in languages and literature. Ireland in the late 19th century was a country in conflict, struggling with the omnipresent force of the Catholic Church and the desire for independence from Great Britain. These factors had a profound effect on Joyce and his work. His rebellion against the Catholic Church, concerns about Irish nationalism, and views on the role of art in life were topics Joyce struggled with throughout his fiction; they are chronicled in his largely autobiographical novel *A Portrait of the Artist as a Young Man* (1916).

In 1904, Joyce met and fell in love with Nora Barnacle. A few months after meeting, Joyce and Nora left Ireland together for Trieste, Italy. With the exception of a few short visits to Ireland, they lived the rest of their lives in Trieste, Rome, Paris, and Zurich. Their lives together early on often were difficult, as Joyce struggled to make ends meet by teaching English. Despite financial difficulties and deteriorating eyesight that left him at times almost completely blind, Joyce wrote diligently in the evenings.

From 1914 to 1921, Joyce composed his most controversial novel, *Ulysses* (1922), which—in spite of initially being banned as obscene by censors in the United States and elsewhere—is believed by many to be the greatest novel of the 20th century. *Ulysses* takes place on one day, June 16, 1904—the day Joyce and Nora had their first date—and introduces many of the innovative fictional techniques, such as stream of consciousness and complex rhetorical structures, for which Joyce became famous. The novel follows the doings of Leopold Bloom; his wife, Molly Bloom; and Stephen Dedalus, the hero of *A Portrait of the Artist as a Young Man*, who returns to Ireland unsuccessful in his attempt at the end of *A Portrait* to "to forge in the smithy of [his] soul the uncreated conscious of [his] race." In the years since its publication, *Ulysses* has become one of the most discussed novels ever written.

Even though Joyce lived in exile from Ireland for the majority of his adult life, Dublin remained the source and setting of all of his works. From his earliest short stories in *Dubliners* (1914), which record the "paralysis" that Joyce found so vivid in the city, to his experimental use of puns, neologisms, and Irish myth in *Finnegans Wake* (1939), Ireland was the center of Joyce's fiction. Like Catholicism and his family, Joyce's native land had a profound influence on his life and work.

Edward Maloney

BIOGRAPHICAL HIGHLIGHTS

1882. Born on February 2 in Rathgar, a suburb of Dublin, Ireland.

1888–91. Attended Clongowes Wood College, a Jesuit boarding school.

1893–98. Was a student at another Jesuit school, Belvedere College in Dublin.

1902. Was graduated from University College, Dublin, with a degree in modern languages, and subsequently went to Paris.

1903. Was recalled to Dublin in April by his mother's illness; she died in August.

1904. In June, met Nora Barnacle, who remained his lifelong companion. They were married in 1931.

1905. Moved to Trieste, Italy, after the birth of a son.

1907. *Chamber Music* was published; a daughter was born.

1913. Was contacted by Ezra Pound, who helped organize financial payments to keep Joyce writing.

1914. *Dubliners* was published.

1915. Moved to Zurich and received various subsidies from his chief benefactor, Harriet Shaw Weaver.

1916. *A Portrait of the Artist as a Young Man* was published in the United States. It had appeared in serial form in 1914.

1917. Eyesight problems began.

1918. *Exiles*, his only play, was published.

1919. Returned to Trieste, but moved to Paris after a few months.

1922. *Ulysses* was published in Paris on February 2. A serialization of the work began in 1918.

1930. His daughter showed increasing signs of schizophrenia; his father died.

1939. *Finnegans Wake* was published in May; moved to a village near Vichy, France, in December.

1940. Moved to Zurich, Switzerland.

1941. Died on January 13 in Zurich.

Martin Luther King, Jr.

For roughly a dozen years, Dr. Martin Luther King, Jr., moved the United States through speeches, mass marches, and boycotts to undo Jim Crow and accept the moral imperative of civil rights. King first gained national recognition as a leader in the Montgomery bus boycott of 1955–56. His eloquence and his book, *Stride Toward Freedom* (1958), describing the boycott and his philosophy of nonviolent direct action based on Christian brotherhood and the tactics of Mohandas Gandhi, among others, established him as the voice and conscience of the emerging civil-rights movement. King's early leadership in the movement rested largely on his ability to mobilize poor blacks through the church and his emphasis on building a "beloved community" rather than demanding retribution. His Atlanta-based Southern Christian Leadership Conference (SCLC),

organized in 1957, was an important vehicle for such mobilization.

King was sometimes uncomfortable with the more aggressive direct-action tactics of sit-ins and confrontation practiced by younger civil-rights activists, and he lost influence among "black power" advocates for his willingness to negotiate with whites. But King hardly stood still in either tactics or criticism of racism. He understood the importance of winning mass public support for civil rights and staged demonstrations to gain maximum news coverage. He sought means that would expose injustices and appeal to Americans' conscience and respect for constitutional principles. Some of the most indelible images of the wrongs of racism and the power of nonviolence were scenes from King-led protests in Birmingham (1963) and Selma, AL (1965). His greatest moment

(1929-1968)

came at the 1963 March on Washington, when his "I Have a Dream" speech rang out the great hopes of a civil society.

King's speeches and marches did not by themselves get the federal civil-rights legislation he so desperately wanted, but they helped shift opinion enough to make passage of the civil-rights bill that President Lyndon B. Johnson signed on July 2, 1964 (*photo, right*) possible, and put racial discrimination forever on the defensive. King's legacy must include his recognition that civil rights demanded federal protection in law. Thus, he had pressed for a wide-ranging civil-rights bill to end segregation and open opportunities for blacks and others in education, employment, entertainment, and more. His insistence on a voting-rights bill as the only security for blacks was realized after the march on Selma. So, too, King's insistence that poverty was the root of racism led to passage of the Civil Rights Act of 1968, prohibiting discrimination in housing. King and his allies had secured three legislative triumphs and won many court battles to enforce desegregation and ensure enfranchisement—the foundation for civil-rights protections.

After 1965, King moved northward to attack de facto segregation in housing, employment, and use of public facilities. He met physical abuse and suffered defeats. By 1965, too, the civil-rights movement was coming apart, as black "militants" eschewed nonviolence for "black power." As King's generation of civil-rights activists lost its monopoly on public attention, King broke with many in the movement and with his putative white allies. He began to criticize the Vietnam war for its immorality and costs to social change at home and launched his "Poor People's Campaign" for economic justice.

Over time, King's message of brotherhood and ending any discrimination became so universally accepted that public figures of all stripes invoked King's name to justify their stands on any number of issues.

Randall M. Miller

BIOGRAPHICAL HIGHLIGHTS

1929. Born on January 15 in Atlanta, GA.

1948. Was ordained a minister in February; four months later, was graduated from Atlanta's Morehouse College.

1951. As the class valedictorian, was graduated from Crozer Theological Seminary in Chester, PA. He continued his doctoral studies at Boston University.

1953. Married Coretta Scott in June. They had four children.

1954. Assumed the pastorship of Dexter Avenue Baptist Church in Montgomery, AL.

1955. Boston University's School of Theology awarded him a doctorate in June. In December, was drafted as president and principal spokesperson for the Montgomery Improvement Association (MIA) by the city's black community as a result of Rosa Parks' arrest for refusing to surrender her seat on a bus in the city.

1957. Southern Christian Leadership Conference (SCLC) officially founded by King and several supporters.

1963. At the August 28 March on Washington, a multiracial crowd supported antidiscrimination legislation in a massive rally highlighted by King's "I Have a Dream" oration.

1964. Was awarded the Nobel Peace Prize.

1968. Was assassinated on April 4 at a Memphis, TN, motel.

Nelson Rolihlahla Mandela

When South Africa's Nelson Mandela—perhaps the world's most famous political prisoner for more than 30 years—was released from prison in 1990, many were seeing him for the first time. Mandela became an instant presence on the international political scene, and millions waited to hear his first public statement since his imprisonment. After years of hardship, Mandela did not seek vengeance or retribution; rather, he reaffirmed the basic principles of peace, freedom, and democracy. He did not waver from these beliefs as president of South Africa (1994–99).

In his 1994 inaugural address as president, Mandela promised to tackle the challenges of "building peace, prosperity, nonsexism, nonracialism, and democracy." Under his leadership, the South African government instituted policies of racial reconciliation and of reconstruction and development. Mandela pledged that there would be a redistribution of land, access to running water and electricity for households, and better nutrition, health care, housing, and education. He was instrumental in the creation of the Truth and Reconciliation Commission that held hearings on gross violations of human rights by the white government, as well as by Mandela's own African National Congress (ANC), during the apartheid era. His integrity, dignity, grace, and humor allayed many

(1918-)

white fears. His evenhanded approach, fiscal conservatism, recognition of the importance of private enterprise, and ability to reach out to all races proved to be an inspiration for a bitterly divided country. While there were substantial achievements, many social programs remained unfulfilled because of the magnitude of the nation's needs, limited resources, increasing violence (in part, a legacy of the inequities of apartheid), and the continuing hesitancy of foreign investors.

Mandela personified the peaceful transition of South Africa from the atrocities of apartheid to a nation seeking reconciliation. In 1993 he was awarded the Nobel Peace Prize jointly with President F.W. de Klerk. Mandela received worldwide recognition as an outstanding statesman. He showed his gratitude

to governments that had supported the African National Congress (ANC) during the liberation struggle by paying state visits—including a controversial one to Libya for a meeting with Muammar el-Qaddafi (*photo above*).

While Mandela became an inspiration for all who suffered from oppression, he chose not to attempt to resolve crises on the African continent, so that he could save his energies for the needs of South Africa. Mandela's greatest legacy will be the solid democratic foundations that have been established and the fostering of a tolerant and open political culture in South Africa.

Patrick O'Meara

BIOGRAPHICAL HIGHLIGHTS

1918. Born in the Transkei region of South Africa on July 18.

1938. Began his studies at Fort Hare University. Expelled during his second year for leading a student demonstration.

1942. Earned a bachelor's degree by correspondence through the University of South Africa and then pursued a law degree at the University of the Witwatersrand.

1944. Joined the African National Congress (ANC) and participated in the founding of the ANC Youth League.

1950. Became national president of the Youth League.

1952. Was given a suspended sentence for organizing the nonviolent defiance campaign against the government's racial policies. With Oliver Tambo, formed the first black law partnership in South Africa.

1956. Was indicted by the South African government for treason. Five years later, was found not guilty.

1958. Married Winnie Nomzamo, with whom he had two daughters.

1959. Was elected provincial president of the ANC's Transvaal region.

1961. Formed Umkhonto we Sizwe (Spear of the Nation) as a military organization independent of the now-outlawed ANC.

1963. Was convicted of sabotage and conspiracy to overthrow the government.

1964. Was sentenced to life imprisonment.

1990. On February 11, was released from prison.

1991. Was elected president of the ANC.

1993. Shared the Nobel Peace Prize with F.W. de Klerk for dismantling apartheid.

1994. Following the ANC's decisive victory in nonracial elections in April, was sworn in as president of South Africa on May 10.

1998. After receiving a divorce from his wife, married Graça Machel, the widow of the president of Mozambique.

Mao Zedong

Converted as a young intellectual to a belief in Marxism-Leninism, Mao Zedong first went about transforming it to serve as a tool for analyzing the problems that long had plagued Chinese society and for carrying out a revolution to address those problems. He realized early on that the Chinese peasants, not the proletariat, must serve as the main force in such a revolution. His strategy of a revolution that begins by seizing control of the countryside and only as a last step takes control of the cities served as a starting point for other Third World revolutionary leaders.

After a nearly three-decade-long struggle against the Kuomintang (Nationalist Party) and the invading Japanese, Mao and his Chinese Communist Party (CCP) colleagues set up a highly authoritarian government in Beijing in 1949. In its early years, it was known and admired for its honesty and dedication, for its concern for the interests of poor working people, and for its success in uniting China for the first time in nearly a century. Mao immediately launched a massive program of land reform and collectivization in the countryside and nationalization of industry and commerce in the cities. The Chinese economy not only recovered from the ravages of corruption and war, but actually began to grow for the first time in decades.

Mao's relationship with Soviet leader Joseph Stalin was a troubled one. Early on he split with the Moscow-controlled wing of the CCP. Following the CCP victory in 1949, he traveled to Moscow but returned home deeply disappointed with the scanty assistance Stalin was prepared to offer China. After Stalin's death in 1953, Mao saw himself as the logical heir to the mantle of leadership in the world revolution. When Nikita Khrushchev claimed that mantle for himself, there began a growing rivalry between him and Mao—and, by extension, between the Soviet Union and China. The "socialist camp" no longer spoke with a single voice.

The competition took the form, for Mao, of a drive to insure that China "reached communism"— the ultimate of Marx's developmental stages— before the Soviet Union did. Impelled by this drive, and increasingly out of touch with the needs and interests of the Chinese people, Mao undertook a series of misguided national campaigns that caused great social and political dislocation, and—in the case of the Great Leap Forward—widespread famine. The last of these campaigns, the Great Proletarian Cultural Revolution, was Mao's attempt to seize back power from party leaders whom he accused of having become a new bourgeoisie seeking to restore capitalism. It was a campaign that cost China more than a decade of economic development, but one that resonated widely among disaffected young people in the United States and Europe.

Among Mao's last achievements was to mend the rift with the United States that had occurred with the defeat of the Nationalists in 1949— a rift he had hoped could be avoided in the first place. The common ground he found and shared with President Richard Nixon in 1972 was the belief that a Sino-American rapprochement would weaken the position of the Soviet Union.

Only after Mao's death in 1976 did it prove possible to launch the reforms that have enabled China, during the last two decades of the century, to make such extraordinary economic progress. If Mao is missed by the Chinese people in the midst of their newfound prosperity, it is because of their nostalgia for the honesty, dedication, and patriotism for which he was known in the later days of the revolution.

John Bryan Starr

BIOGRAPHICAL HIGHLIGHTS

1893. Born on December 26 in a small village in Hunan province.

1911. Joined the revolution against the Ch'ing dynasty.

1918. Graduated from the Hunan First Normal School and went to Beijing.

1920. Became a Marxist and married Yang Kaihui, who was executed by the Kuomintang in 1930.

1921. Helped found the Chinese Communist Party (CCP) in Shanghai.

1928–31. Established rural soviets and built up the Red Army.

1931. Was elected chairman of the Soviet Republic of China, based in Jiangxi province.

1934–35. Fleeing attacks led by Chiang Kaishek, led the Red Army on the Long March from Jiangxi north to Shaanxi province, establishing a base there.

1939. Married Jiang Qing. In 1937 he had divorced his second wife, Ho Zizhen, whom he had married in 1930.

1949. Proclaimed the People's Republic of China and became its first leader.

1958. Launched the Great Leap Forward, a disastrous effort to modernize China rapidly.

1966. Began the Cultural Revolution, directed against party leadership. Took a much-publicized swim in the Chang (Yangtze) River (*photo above*).

1969. Served as chairman of the Ninth Communist Party Congress.

1970. Was named supreme commander of the nation and army.

1972. Met with U.S. President Richard Nixon.

1976. Died of a heart attack in Beijing on September 9.

Margaret Mead

Margaret Mead, renowned American anthropologist and author, began her anthropological fieldwork in Pago Pago, American Samoa, on Aug. 31, 1925. Under the tutelage of Franz Boas, her professor at Columbia University, she investigated the lives of adolescent girls in Samoa to determine whether rebellion and psychobiological upheaval in adolescence was culturally or biologically determined. Mead suspected that the stress experienced by adolescents in the United States resulted from the American cultural environment. If she found that the behavior of Samoan girls differed from that of American girls, she could use her studies to challenge the claims of a physiological determinant for adolescent behavior. Indeed, by examining the lives of Samoan adolescent girls, Mead found that they did not suffer the emotional turmoil experienced by their American counterparts.

Nineteenth-century evolutionary racialism in the fields of eugenics and genetics had exerted a powerful influence on anthropology, and Mead's mentor, Boas, sought to sort out the effects of biological and cultural influence on human behavior. In the foreword to Mead's first book, *Coming of Age in Samoa*, Boas wrote that Mead's investigation in Samoa confirmed that "much of what we ascribe to human nature is no more than a reaction to the restraints put upon us by our civilization." Mead's work derived from Boas' struggle to wipe out racist concepts in anthropology. Boas had provided the seeds for the school of anthropology called "Personality and Culture," which rejected the idea that an organism could be studied in isolation from its environment. Mead became one of the school's most famous spokespersons.

During the 1940s, Mead and her colleague, Rhoda Métraux, devoted their work to wartime problems. They developed the discipline called "national character studies," creating typologies to describe the basic characteristics of countries that U.S. military leaders and diplomats dealt with as allies or enemies. Under the influence of Ruth Benedict, Mead fashioned her research on the idea that clear and consistent patterns of behavior could be revealed through the study of any culture.

Western culture during the 19th and 20th centuries was dominated by the paradigm of progress and science. Mead, a true citizen of Western civilization, was not immune to the belief that progress and Westernization went hand in hand, and that the United States, with its more advanced technology, would lead the Pacific people into the future. Working under this assumption, she returned to Manus Island in 1953 to observe and record the effects of World War II on the community she had studied in 1929. The results of her 1953 fieldwork were presented in the book *New Lives for Old* (1956). In 1965 and 1966 she did further fieldwork in Manus, and a 1967 film by National Educational Television, titled *Margaret Mead's New Guinea Journal*, documented her work there.

During her many years of fieldwork, Mead was able to follow the children she studied into their adulthood in Manus, Bali, and New Guinea. In turn, she has been criticized by the subjects of her fieldwork, the very adults she studied as children. Many felt that her work did not always present an accurate or in-depth picture of the people under study. Some anthropologists also have expressed suspicion that her data had been "tailored or selected to fit a preconceived case."

Despite the criticism, Margaret Mead received many honors and great recognition. Her contribution to anthropology has earned her a permanent place in American scholarship.

Lenora Foerstel

BIOGRAPHICAL HIGHLIGHTS

1901. The future anthropologist was born on December 16 in Philadelphia, PA.

1923. Received a bachelor's degree from Barnard College; married Luther Cressman.

1926. Was appointed curator of ethnology at the American Museum of Natural History in New York City.

1928. Fieldwork in the South Pacific resulted in the publication of her dissertation, *Coming of Age in Samoa.*

1929. Received a doctorate degree from Columbia University, where she studied anthropology under Ruth Benedict and Franz Boas.

1930. *Growing Up in New Guinea* was published.

1935. Wrote and published *Sex and Temperament in Three Primitive Societies*, about her studies of the Arapesh, Mundugumor, and Tchambuli peoples of New Guinea.

1936. Went to Bali, an Indonesian island, with Gregory Bateson, her third husband.

1939. Gave birth to a daughter, Mary Catherine Bateson.

1942. Her book *Balinese Character: A Photographic Analysis*, written following research work in Bali (*photo, above*), was published. Another book, *And Keep Your Powder Dry: An Anthropologist Looks at America*, attempting to explain the American character to the world, was published.

1954. Was named an adjunct professor of anthropology at Columbia University.

1961. Started writing a monthly column for *Redbook* magazine.

1969. Was appointed curator emeritus of ethnology at the American Museum of Natural History; was named "mother of the year" by *Time* magazine.

1970. *Culture and Commitment: A Study of the Generation Gap* was published.

1978. Died in New York City on November 15.

Pablo Picasso

LA VILLE D'ANTIBES
DESIRANT MANIFESTER
SA RECONNAISSANCE
ET SON ADMIRATION A

PABLO PICASSO

By 1900, when Spanish artist Pablo Picasso first visited Paris, the rise of Impressionism had identified modern painting with a purely optical play of light and color, divorced from the actual three-dimensional forms of things. This created a hunger for a simpler, cruder art that would evoke the presence of bodies and objects more powerfully than either Impressionism or academic painting. Several years later, Picasso set out to reconcile these contradictory goals by using geometric facets to describe both the human figure and the space surrounding it. His first experiments culminated in "Les Demoiselles d'Avignon" (1907) and "Three Women" (1908), which

established him as a leader of the Parisian avant-garde. Within a few years, the influence of this new "Cubist" style extended to Italy, Germany, Russia, and the United States.

After 1909 the figures and objects in Picasso's pictures broke apart into discontinuous planes, held in place by vertical and horizontal lines. Recognizable colors and textures were banished from 1910 through 1911, but then reappeared in the interstices of this abstract "grid." In 1912, Picasso began gluing found images and objects to his pictures—a technique known as collage. Although Picasso remained committed to figuration, artists like Piet Mondrian and Kasimir Malevich saw his new pictures as announcing an art of rigorous geometric abstraction. For Marcel Duchamp and the various Dadaists, on the other hand, Picasso's geometric, seemingly mechanical drawing and his new technique of collage suggested that "art" itself was now obsolete.

By 1925, Cubism had emerged as the classical style of modern art. Picasso continued to broaden its scope, exploring compositions of broad, flat planes and interlacing curves, austere harmonies and clashing rhythms. His images seemed to metamorphose between abstract and figurative, human and animal. He now emerged as one of the leaders of a new school of Surrealist artists who made abstract forms into powerful symbols of sexuality and violence. Later, in the 1940s, this work provided an essential inspiration for Jackson Pollock and the Abstract Expressionists. Picasso's experiments with sculpture—from his first cardboard constructions of 1912 through his welded metal works of 1928–31—played a similar role in creating a new vocabulary for modern sculpture.

At other moments in his career, however, Picasso contributed equally to the renewal of figurative art. His "neoclassical" style of 1918–24 anticipated a broader European "Return to Order." In his etchings of the mid-1930s, he reinvented Greek mythology as an allegory of the modern condition. His combination of lyrical realism and expressive liberty had a far-reaching effect on printmakers and illustrators of the following decades.

After the end of World War II, Picasso became a celebrity, but his new work exerted little influence on the avant-garde. His extraordinary imagination—his ability to reinvent constantly the world around him—seemed irrelevant to younger artists torn between abstraction and appropriation. Nonetheless, Picasso's technical innovations have continued to provide a lingua franca for contemporary art.

Pepe Karmel

BIOGRAPHICAL HIGHLIGHTS

1881. Born on October 25 in Málaga, Spain.

1895. Enrolled at the School of Fine Arts in Barcelona, Spain.

1897. Went to Madrid to study at the Royal Academy.

1901–04. During his "Blue Period," painted prevalently in shades of blue. Settled permanently in Paris after 1904.

1904–06. Began his "Rose Period," during which predominantly earthen, brown, and pink hues were used in his paintings.

1906. Completed a self-portrait (*left*).

1908. His "Three Women" heralded the advent of Cubism. With Georges Braque, invented and developed Cubism as well as the new technique of collage.

1918. Married a young Russian dancer, Olga Koklova; a son, Paulo, was born in 1921. Collaborated on several ballets over the next years.

1921–22. Depicted monumental and classically modeled figures.

1926. Began a relationship with Marie-Thérèse Walter, who would inspire much of his work.

1935. Separated from his wife; Marie-Thérèse Walter gave birth to a daughter.

1937. Created "Guernica," an allegorical mural portraying the Spanish town bombed by Franco's forces.

1944. Joined the Communist Party.

1946. Began living with Françoise Gilot, with whom he would have a son, Claude, and a daughter, Paloma.

1961. Married Jacqueline Roque and moved to Mougins.

1973. Died on April 8 in Mougins.

Elvis Presley

Elvis Presley was the first rock 'n' roll star, and his debut single for Sun Records displayed the stylistic alchemy that defined his best work. One side featured a rockabilly-styled version of "That's All Right," a tune originally recorded by black bluesman Arthur Crudup. The flip side was an equally rollicking take on "Blue Moon of Kentucky," a country song drawn from the repertoire of bluegrass pioneer Bill Monroe. Presley's artistic muscle was derived from his instinctive mix of black and white musical styles. For Sam Phillips, who had signed him to Sun Records and produced his first sides, Presley was just the talent he had been thirsting to discover—"a white man with the Negro sound and the Negro feel."

Three figures define distinct stages in the history of the 20th century pop-music celebrity—Frank Sinatra in the 1940s, Elvis Presley in the 1950s, and the Beatles in the 1960s. Sinatra's bobby-soxer popularity was derived from radio exposure and concert appearances, and this was the case for Presley when his Sun records made him a regional attraction in the South and a star in his hometown of Memphis. In 1955 his manager, Colonel Tom Parker, arranged to have RCA Records buy out his Sun contract for $35,000.

Presley became the king of rock 'n' roll in 1956, and his massive celebrity was stoked through multiple appearances on television variety shows, performing such newly recorded hits as "Heartbreak Hotel," "Don't Be Cruel," and "Hound Dog." Onstage, Presley would shake his hips in a way that caused a sensation, and TV host Ed Sullivan instructed his crew to shoot Presley from the waist up. But it did not matter, because Presley could make the girls squeal by raising an eyebrow.

Presley was drafted into the army in 1958, and served in Germany, where he met his future wife, Priscilla, when she was 14 years old. Before the army, Presley was a rock 'n' roll star who had done well in a few movies. After his service, he became a profitable star of B movies who also made records. Some of the movies were good, but most were not. By 1964, when Britain's Beatles invaded the United States (via Ed Sullivan's TV stage), Presley was seen increasingly as an out-of-touch musician who made bad movies.

Presley mounted a brief second act after a 1968 television special featured a lithe and lively Elvis singing before his first live audience in seven years. He suddenly attacked his recordings with gusto, creating classics like "Suspicious Minds" and "Burning Love," but the flame quickly expired. The mediocre movies were replaced with indifferent concert performances. Years of pills—amphetamines to face the day, and tranquilizers to get some sleep—had taken a toll on his body, which now was puffy in his karate-style stage outfits.

In 1977, Presley died in Memphis at the age of 42. Then—behaving like a true pop icon—he became an even larger legend in death. Part of his legacy is as a joke; Elvis sightings have became akin to spotting the Loch Ness monster. However, the reason he will not be forgotten is that in his most singular moments, Elvis Presley mixed strains of country and blues into a new music that forevermore would be known as rock 'n' roll.

John Milward

BIOGRAPHICAL HIGHLIGHTS

1935. Elvis Aron Presley was born on January 8 in Tupelo, MS.

1954. Recorded his first singles, "That's All Right" and "Blue Moon of Kentucky," at Sun Studios in Memphis, TN.

1955. RCA paid Sun Records $35,000 for Presley's contract.

1956. At his first session for RCA in January, Presley recorded "Heartbreak Hotel," which became his first Number 1 hit.

1957. Bought the Memphis mansion called Graceland; "All Shook Up" spent eight weeks at Number 1.

1958–60. Was in the U.S. Army. Previously recorded tunes became hits during this period.

1961. Presley's last concert until 1969 was given on March 25. By mid-decade, his movie salary was about $1 million per picture, including a share of the profits.

1967. Married Priscilla Beaulieu on May 1.

1968. Presley's daughter, Lisa Marie, was born on February 1. The *Elvis* "comeback" TV special was broadcast on December 3.

1969. Opened a monthlong concert engagement in Las Vegas on July 29, and soon returned to concert touring.

1972. Filed for divorce from Priscilla in August.

1977. Gave his last concert in Indianapolis, IN, on June 26. Died at Graceland on August 16.

Eleanor Roosevelt

One of the most admired U.S. first ladies, Eleanor Roosevelt earned recognition nationally and internationally for her humanitarian efforts, and is regarded widely as one of the most significant women in 20th-century America.

Born in New York City and orphaned by age 10, Eleanor was raised by relatives, who enrolled her at age 15 at a private girls' school outside London. Three years later, she returned to New York and followed family tradition: She made her debut in society at age 18; married her distant cousin, Franklin Delano Roosevelt, at the age of 20, on March 17, 1905; and gave birth to six children, including one who died in infancy.

Family tradition on her father's side—her uncle was President Theodore Roosevelt—emphasized community and public service, and Eleanor began this work while still young. But it was not until after 1913, when her husband's work took the entire family to live in Washington, DC, that she began her metamorphosis into a leader. After the United States entered World War I in 1917, she volunteered at soldiers' canteens, organized other women workers, and helped with various Red Cross activities.

She increased her public role after 1920. FDR's nomination for U.S. vice-president on the Democratic ticket in 1920 drew Eleanor into involvement in national social issues. Inspired by women who took active roles in the Democratic Party, the League of Women Voters, and the Women's Trade Union League, she joined their efforts to improve working and living conditions and to win equal rights for all Americans.

As wife of the governor of New York (1929–33) and then of the president of the United States (1933–45), Eleanor Roosevelt broke new ground. She scheduled regular press conferences for women journalists at the White House, thus prompting some of the wire services to hire women for the first time. Her prominence in the Democratic Party expanded as she helped organize campaigns, put forward the names of qualified people—including women and minorities—for appointments to powerful posts, and toured the country, investigating and reporting to her husband, the president.

Reaching out to a wide variety of Americans, she accepted countless invitations to speak on radio and in person. In 1936 she began writing a syndicated newspaper column, "My Day," that continued until a few weeks before her death. She championed the causes of African-Americans, young people, and women—many of whom had felt isolated from the political process—helping to improve their status and draw them into involvement with government.

After FDR's death in 1945, President Harry Truman nominated Eleanor as a U.S. delegate to the United Nations, where she spearheaded the campaign for a Universal

Declaration of Human Rights, adopted in 1948. Through the 1950s, she traveled widely, wrote books and articles, spoke out on civil rights and human concerns, and worked actively for Democratic Party candidates. In 1961, President John F. Kennedy named her chair of the President's Commission on the Status of Women.

By the time of her death, Eleanor Roosevelt's life and work had earned her international recognition, partly captured in President Truman's description of her as "First Lady of the World."

Betty Boyd Caroli

BIOGRAPHICAL HIGHLIGHTS

1884. Born Anna Eleanor Roosevelt in New York City on October 11.

1902. Made her society debut.

1905. Married a distant cousin, Franklin D. Roosevelt, on March 17. A daughter and five sons would result from the union.

1918. Was devastated by her discovery of FDR's affair with Lucy Mercer.

1921. Became her husband's political stand-in when he was stricken with polio.

1933. Assumed the role of first lady with FDR's election to the U.S. presidency.

1941. Held her first public office, as codirector of the Office of Civilian Defense.

1945. FDR died in April; she was appointed a member of the U.S. delegation to the United Nations by President Harry Truman in December.

1948. Helped secure passage of the UN's Universal Declaration of Human Rights.

1952. Resigned from the United Nations.

1961. Was reappointed to the United Nations by President John F. Kennedy.

1962. Died on November 7 in New York City.

Franklin Delano Roosevelt

Along with George Washington and Abraham Lincoln, historians consider Franklin D. Roosevelt one of the greatest presidents in U.S. history. Few would dispute that he is the greatest American political leader of the 20th century. FDR's high standing rests on his mastery of two of the greatest crises in the national experience—the Great Depression of the 1930s and the Second World War of 1939–45.

When Roosevelt entered the White House in March 1933, the country's economy had all but collapsed. One quarter of the workforce—some 13 million Americans—were without jobs, and middle-class families were losing their homes and farms. Many of the country's banks had closed their doors, barring depositors from withdrawing desperately needed cash.

FDR initiated a series of steps to meet the crisis. He gave a radio talk—the first of what came to be called Fireside Chats—in which he declared a bank "holiday" and began the process of restoring confidence in the national banking system. He then launched a 100 days' war on the Depression, winning congressional passage of 15 major laws that provided for relief and recovery, and instituted reforms that would prevent recurrences of so severe an economic downturn. In 1935 he won enactment of Social Security, a federal system of old-age pensions, and of the National Labor Relations Act, legalizing labor unions and the right to strike. His New Deal measures, creating a welfare state, made him uncommonly popular and assured his reelection to a second term by a landslide in 1936.

A number of problems troubled Roosevelt's next four years, including an abortive attempt to "pack" the U.S. Supreme Court with liberal justices who would reverse court decisions barring New Deal measures. A major recession in 1937–38 also undermined his influence and cost the Democrats seats in the 1938 congressional elections.

Beginning in 1939, the outbreak of World War II forced him to shift his focus to foreign affairs. Between 1939 and 1941, he struggled to convince an isolationist Congress and country that German and Japanese aggression posed a vital threat to the national security. A destroyers-for-bases agreement with Britain and a peacetime draft helped Britain combat Nazi advances and improved American defenses in 1940. But it was Roosevelt's promise to keep America out of war that largely made his reelection to a third term possible that year.

In 1941, Lend-Lease, an Atlantic conference with Winston Churchill in August, and the convoying of essential supplies to Britain brought the United States closer to involvement in the war. But it was the Japanese surprise attack on Pearl Harbor on Dec. 7, 1941, that finally led the country into the fighting. A Europe First strategy, making the defeat of Nazi Germany in conjunction with Britain and the Soviet Union the United States' first priority, brought victory over Germany in May 1945. Successful sea battles and an island-hopping campaign in the Pacific forced Japan's surrender in August. FDR, however, had died in April, before either victory was achieved.

FDR's three greatest achievements were the reform of the U.S. industrial system to prevent future depressions and create a humane safety net for needy citizens; the defeat of Nazism, fascism, and Japanese militarism; and the transformation of the United States from an isolationist to an internationalist nation committed to combating aggression and fostering world peace.

Robert Dallek

BIOGRAPHICAL HIGHLIGHTS

1882. Born on January 30 at the family estate in Hyde Park, NY.

1904. Was graduated from Harvard University with a B.A. degree.

1905. On March 17, married a distant cousin, Anna Eleanor Roosevelt. Within 11 years, six children were born to the Roosevelts; one died in infancy.

1907. Passed the New York State Bar examination. Was hired by a Wall Street law firm.

1911–13. Served as a Democratic New York state senator.

1913–20. Was assistant secretary of the U.S. Navy.

1920. The James Cox and F.D. Roosevelt presidential ticket was defeated.

1921. Was stricken with polio in August. He never regained the use of his legs.

1928. Was elected to the first of two terms as governor of New York.

1932. Was elected U.S. president. Was reelected in 1936, 1940, and 1944.

1941. Following the bombing of Pearl Harbor, the United States entered World War II.

1943. Attended the Teheran Conference with Soviet Prime Minister Joseph Stalin and British Prime Minister Winston Churchill (*photo above*).

1945. Attended the Yalta Conference. Died at Warm Springs, GA, on April 12.

Babe Ruth

When Babe Ruth's baseball career began, it was hard to envision him—or anyone else—as a great slugger. Early teams relied on pitching, defense, and speed rather than the long hits that eventually would make Ruth the game's greatest star. In fact, Ruth himself first found fame as a talented left-handed pitcher. A schoolboy star at St. Mary's Industrial School in Baltimore—where he was confined at age 7 for repeated petty theft—the future star was loaned to the Baltimore Orioles, an independent team in the International League, and eventually was purchased by the Boston Red Sox. He pitched briefly for Providence, a farm club for Boston, before breaking in as a pitcher for the 1914 Red Sox, with baseball still in the throes of the "dead-ball era." Two years later, Ruth led the American League with a 1.75 earned run average (ERA) and nine shutouts, and posted a 23–12 record for the world-champion Red Sox. He won a career-best 24 games a year later. At his best under pressure, Ruth recorded 29 consecutive innings pitched in World Series play. That record stood for 42 years.

Not until 1918, when Ruth appeared in 72 games as an outfielder–first baseman, did he move off the mound. He became a full-time outfielder only after Red Sox owner Harry Frazee sold him to the New York Yankees for $125,000—a staggering sum at the time—in 1920. The sale, which changed the balance of power in the American League, stunned Boston fans, who had watched the 24-year-old Ruth hit .322 with 29 homers, 114 runs batted in, and a 9–5 pitching record the previous year. No previous player transaction had involved so much money or impacted the game so hard. The Yankees, who never had won a pennant before Ruth arrived, suddenly became the powerhouse of baseball. They finished first 14 times before the Red Sox won another flag—leading writers to dub the Boston drought "the Curse of the Bambino." The Bosox have not won a World Series in the 80 years since the Babe left—a record of futility that is exceeded only by the Chicago Cubs, winless since 1908.

The Yankees, on the other hand, made the World Series for the 35th time in 1998. Getting Babe Ruth started the ball rolling. In his first two years in New York, he pounded 54 and 59 home runs, respectively, ending the dead-ball era by convincing teams that home runs—with their instant run-making potential—had more appeal to fans than did bunts and hit-and-run plays. Ruth's heroics were especially timely because the game needed something new to offset public disenchantment prompted by the 1919 "Black Sox" scandal.

Ruth, a larger-than-life character who craved attention, befriended members of the media and made no secret of his affection for women and children. His off-the-field antics, carousing, and training violations made Ruth a controversial as well as a colorful figure. His baseball ability, however, could not be questioned. The Yankees derived so much revenue from Ruth's performance that they left the Polo Grounds, which they had shared with the New York Giants, to build their own ballpark on the opposite side of the Harlem River. Even before its opening in 1923, it was dubbed "the House That Ruth Built."

During his heyday, the 6-foot 2-inch (1.9-meter), 215-pound (97.5-kilogram) slugger teamed with Lou Gehrig, another left-handed hitter, to form one of the most potent 1-2 punches in baseball history. Together, they served as the anchors of the famous "Murderer's Row" Yankee lineup of 1927.

Ruth hit the game-winning home run in the first All-Star Game, in 1933, then retired after playing 28 games for the Boston Braves two years later. He finished with a lifetime .342 batting average and both single-season (60) and career (714) home-run records that stood for more than 30 years. He also had a 94–46 record and 2.28 earned run average as a pitcher. Ruth won a dozen home-run titles, led six times in runs batted in, and compiled record slugging percentages for a season

(.847 in 1920) and career (.690). He also had a record 457 total bases in 1921.

Ruth's No. 3 later became the first uniform retired by the Yankees. The team also honored Ruth with a plaque in Monument Park at Yankee Stadium. Babe Ruth became one of five charter members of the Baseball Hall of Fame in 1936.

Dan Schlossberg

BIOGRAPHICAL HIGHLIGHTS

1895. George Herman Ruth was born in a Baltimore, MD, row house on February 6.

1902. Was sent to St. Mary's Industrial School in Baltimore.

1914. Began his big-league career as a pitcher with the Boston Red Sox. Married Helen Woodford on October 17.

1920. Was sold to the Yankees; hit a record 54 home runs for New York.

1921. Ruth and his wife adopted a baby girl.

1923. Yankee Stadium, "the House That Ruth Built," opened.

1925. Was suspended and fined for training violations.

1926. Became the first man to hit four home runs in a World Series.

1927. Led the "Murderer's Row" team of sluggers with record 60 home runs.

1929. Ruth's wife died in a fire on January 11; on April 17, married Claire Hodgson.

1935. Finished his playing career with the Boston Braves.

1936. Was elected to the Baseball Hall of Fame.

1938. Served as coach for Brooklyn Dodgers.

1947. Established and endowed the Babe Ruth Foundation to aid underprivileged youngsters.

1948. Died in New York City on August 16.

Jonas Salk

Although he is best known as the developer of the first successful vaccine against paralytic poliomyelitis, Jonas Salk also made many other contributions in the fields of medicine and biology, philosophy, architecture, and the history of medicine. As a child, he was concerned about injustices in life; he hoped to study law and become a member of Congress. He became interested in science and medicine, however; after his medical training, he entered research rather than private practice, hoping to be able to help many people rather than a few. His earliest concerns still remained with him, but he expressed them through biology and medicine rather than through law.

Through his contributions to the development in the 1940s of the first successful inactivated vaccines against influenza and his subsequent development in the 1950s of an inactivated poliovirus vaccine, Salk established that noninfectious vaccines could protect against viral diseases. This idea ran counter to the prevailing belief that only vaccines containing live, infectious viruses could be effective. His work was the foundation for the modern array of vaccines made from noninfectious materials, including killed whole viruses or parts of viruses. He introduced the term "vaccinology" to describe the development of effective vaccines based on specific requirements for inducing immunity rather than on any preconceived notions of mechanism. Techniques developed by Salk for virus typing, virus culture, and principles of vaccine manufacture continue to be used today.

The inactivated poliovirus vaccine was released for general use in 1955. Within six years, the incidence of paralytic poliomyelitis in the United States was reduced by 95%. In countries where the inactivated vaccine continued to be used exclusively, paralytic poliomyelitis disappeared. What had been one of the most frightening epidemics of the 20th century was brought rapidly under control in the developed world.

In the late 1970s, Salk collaborated to standardize and produce an inactivated poliovirus vaccine that would be effective in a single dose and could be combined with other childhood immunizations. Such a combined vaccine would benefit the developing world, where live oral poliovirus vaccine has proven less effective than had been hoped. In 1977 he suggested that poliovirus could be eradicated, a goal formally adopted by the World Health Organization in the 1990s.

Throughout his life, Salk was active in various areas of research, always looking for ways to help as many people as possible. In 1961 he observed analogies between the development and function of the central nervous system and the immune system, and in this respect was one of the founders of the field of psychoneuroimmunology—the study of how mind, nervous system, and immune system work together. And in 1987 he proposed a novel "therapeutic" vaccine to control the acquired immune deficiency syndrome (AIDS) in persons already infected with the human immunodeficiency virus (HIV). This inactivated whole virus vaccine is being evaluated both as a therapeutic vaccine and as a preventive vaccine for individuals not yet exposed to HIV.

In 1960, Salk established the Salk Institute for Biological Studies in La Jolla, CA, now one of the preeminent biomedical-research centers in the world. Salk collaborated with architect Louis Kahn in the design of the Institute's buildings, renowned for their innovative laboratory design and architectural features. Salk published four books of essays, was the author of many short papers, and lectured widely on human life and the nature of evolution. He was deeply interested in the fulfillment of humans' biological potential and place in the metabiological world, and applied these intellectual concepts to practical social issues in many ways. As a director of the MacArthur Foundation, he helped create the MacArthur Fellowship Program and influenced the foundation's support of health-related issues. His personal archives, now housed at the University of California, San Diego, are one of the largest, most complete manuscript collections of a 20th-century scientist.

Darrell Salk, M.D.

BIOGRAPHICAL HIGHLIGHTS

1914. Born in New York City on October 28.

1939. Obtained medical degree from the New York University College of Medicine. Married Donna Lindsay on June 8; the couple had three children.

1942. Worked with Thomas Francis, Jr., a noted virologist, at the University of Michigan School of Public Health.

1947. Joined the faculty of the University of Pittsburgh's School of Medicine as director of the Virus Research Laboratory.

1953. Published the results of the first human studies with an inactivated poliovirus vaccine that could serve as an immunizing agent against the disease.

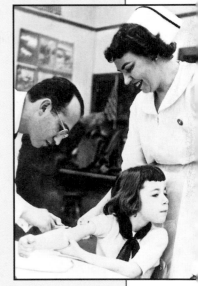

1955. Large-scale field trials of the poliovirus vaccine conducted in 1954 were declared successful; Salk received a presidential citation and was awarded a special Medal of Congress.

1960. Founded the Salk Institute for Biological Studies in La Jolla, CA.

1968. He and his wife were separated.

1970. Married painter Françoise Gilot on June 29.

1972. Published the first of three philosophical books.

1977. Was awarded the Presidential Medal of Freedom.

1986. Cofounded the Immune Response Corporation, where research on AIDS and other diseases is conducted.

1995. Died in La Jolla, CA, on June 23.

Joseph Stalin

Joseph Stalin, ruler of the Soviet Union (USSR) for more than three decades, transformed the country into a superpower rivaled only by the United States. A Georgian by birth, Stalin became the most powerful leader in Russian history, ruling the country with an iron fist from the late 1920s until the early 1950s. During his reign as the leader of the USSR's Communist Party, Stalin exercised unchecked power. History will remember him as a cruel despot, the industrializer of Russia, an architect of victory over Adolf Hitler's Germany, and the initiator of the Cold War that threatened the peace of the globe until the fall of the Soviet empire in 1991.

An early member of V.I. Lenin's underground Bolshevik Party, Stalin participated in the 1917 Bolshevik Revolution. He became the party's internal manager in Lenin's new party-government. When Lenin died in 1924, Stalin held a powerful position in the bureaucracy of the renamed Communist Party of the Soviet Union. During the ensuing succession struggle, Stalin became the leader of the regime.

Stalin inherited from Lenin an economically underdeveloped country. Beginning in 1928, he introduced the First Five-Year Plan, a blueprint for centrally administering the economy. The plan launched a program for rapid, heavy industrialization coupled with a policy of forcibly reorganizing agriculture by eliminating small peasant farming in favor of large, state-controlled farms. Ruthlessly crushing peasant resistance, Stalin also began purging the Communist Party and state bureaucracy of anyone deemed suspicious—policies that cut down millions of people, who perished in the inhumane forced-labor-camp system. By the outbreak of World War II, however, Stalin had transformed the USSR into a great military-industrial power.

In 1941 the USSR reeled in near defeat before the surprise Nazi German attack, but Stalin soon recovered, drew on the nation's deep reserves, and eventually defeated Hitler on the eastern front. In the course of victory, the USSR gained control over East Europe, upon which Stalin imposed the Soviet Communist model. Thus began the Cold War, a form of political warfare between the two victorious superpowers, and a world ideologically polarized into two armed camps.

Stalin modernized the USSR with impressive gains in longevity, literacy, and economic well-being, but at a staggering cost in human life and personal freedom. Yes, World War II in Europe could not have been won without the feats of Soviet arms, but for East Europe, victory meant Soviet tyranny.

Robert Sharlet

BIOGRAPHICAL HIGHLIGHTS

1879. Born on December 21 in the town of Gori, Georgia, as Iosif Vissarionovich Djugashvili (also spelled Dzhugashvili).

1894. Won a free scholarship to the Orthodox theological seminary in Tiflis but was expelled in 1899.

1901. Joined the Social Democratic Party of Georgia and worked full-time on revolutionary goals.

1905. Served as a delegate from the Caucasus to the first national conference of Bolsheviks in Finland, where he met V.I. Lenin.

1907. His wife, Yekaterina Svanidze, whom he married in June 1904, died, leaving a son.

1911. Was exiled to Vologda.

1912. Escaped from exile and arrived in St. Petersburg, where he helped set up *Pravda*, the Bolsheviks' newspaper.

1913. Joined Lenin in Vienna in order to write *Marxism and the National Problem*. Adopted the name Stalin, meaning "man of steel." Was arrested and deported to Siberia.

1917. Returned from exile and became editor of *Pravda*. After the Bolsheviks seized power, was appointed people's commissar for nationalities.

1919. On March 24, married his second wife, Nadezhda Alliluyeva, with whom he had two children. Was named to the newly formed inner directorate of the party, the Politburo.

1922. Was elected general secretary of the central committee of the party.

1924. After the death of Lenin, formed a triumvirate with L.B. Kamenev and G.E. Zinoviev allied against Leon Trotsky.

1925. Managed to oust Trotsky as commissar of war.

1926. Succeeded in removing Kamenev and Zinoviev from the power structure.

1932. The suicide of his wife, who left a letter indicting Stalin personally and politically, made him extremely suspicious of others.

1934–39. During a period of purging and terror, established his personal dictatorship over the party and the country.

1939. In August, concluded a bilateral nonaggression treaty with Germany's Adolf Hitler.

1941. Took command of the Soviet armed forces when the German armies attacked in June.

1953. Died on March 5 in Moscow.

Mother Teresa

By the time Mother Teresa died in 1997, the Congregation of the Missionaries of Charity she had set out to found 49 years previously had spread to more than 120 countries. It incorporated 4,000 Sisters, more than 400 Brothers, and Missionaries of Charity priests, as well as people of all nationalities and creeds throughout the world who were committed to living in Mother Teresa's spirit as lay Missionaries of Charity, volunteers, or "Co-Workers." She herself estimated the number of these last at more than 3 million.

Mother Teresa's less tangible legacy was a greater awareness of the nature of poverty. The work she began in Calcutta, India, with the provision of slum schools, homes for abandoned children, mobile and static leprosy clinics, and shelters for the dying spread in time to wherever a need was identified. Contact with rich Western societies brought Mother Teresa to the realization that the spiritual poverty, loneliness, and psychological consequences of disrupted family life experienced in those societies constituted a more complex problem than did the physical poverty of the Third World. The spiritual foundation for her work lay in the words of St. Matthew's Gospel (Matt: 25:40): "Whatsoever you did to the least of these my brethren, you did it to me." She and her Sisters saw Christ in the dying destitute of India and Africa, and in the drug addicts, isolated elderly, alcoholics, and AIDS sufferers of richer countries. She saw Christ furthermore in those whom others regarded as morally questionable, as dictators or abusers of power, for she believed that every human being contains the divine presence and should be given the opportunity to love and to be loved. Increasingly, her message to those seeking to support her was not to raise funds but to seek to help the poor of their own neighborhoods and homes, and to give "until it hurt" of those more precious commodities: time, energy, and love. She bequeathed to them the radical idea that not only could the rich save the poor; the poor also could save the rich.

Despite her personal reticence, Mother Teresa accepted media attention as well as numerous international awards, on behalf of the poor and in order that "God's work might be known." Criticized by some for concentrating on individual need rather than striving for collective change, she nevertheless was responsible for "conscientizing" millions. The controversially rigorous poverty of her congregation and its methods, intended to safeguard its openness to "divine providence" and accessibility to the poorest of the poor, was upheld by her successor. Yet the period following her death brought an upsurge in vocations. Although she was a conservative Roman Catholic—uncompromising on such issues as birth control, abortion, and the role of women—Mother Teresa's respect for the manner in which God was at work in every soul, the primacy she afforded to love, and the way she expressed her faith in action continued nonetheless to find resonance in people of all world views.

Kathryn Spink

BIOGRAPHICAL HIGHLIGHTS

1910. Born Agnes Gonxha Bojaxhiu on August 27 in Skopje, which was then part of Yugoslavia.

1928. Joined the Sisters of Loreto, who had missionary houses in India.

1931. Made first vows as a Sister of Loreto, changing her name to Teresa.

1931–48. Taught at the Loreto convent school, then at St. Mary's High School in Calcutta, India.

1946. Received "a call within a call" to leave the convent and help the poor while living among them. Two years later, she obtained permission from the Congregation for the Propagation of the Faith to follow this call.

1950. The order of the Missionaries of Charity, initiated two years earlier, was erected formally.

1952. Opened the Nirmal Hriday (Immaculate Heart) Home for Dying Destitutes in Calcutta.

1963. Male branch of the society, the Brothers of Charity, was formed on March 25.

1965. Society was recognized by the Vatican as a Congregation of Pontifical Right.

1969. A British television-documentary profile helped to make Mother Teresa a household name.

1971. Received the Pope John XXIII Peace Prize.

1979. Was awarded the Nobel Peace Prize and the Balzan Prize for promoting peace and brotherhood among the nations.

1996. Was given honorary citizenship by the United States.

1997. Died of a heart attack on September 5 at her convent in Calcutta.

Frank Lloyd Wright

Frank Lloyd Wright went to Chicago in 1887 to become "the world's greatest architect," which is exactly the way he identified himself when he later was booked for being in a speakeasy. There are many who believe that he earned that title, at least during his lifetime. And although he died in 1959, buildings he designed continue to be built by his successor firm, Taliesin Associated Architects (now Taliesin Architects).

While the list of buildings Wright designed has been impressive in illustrating the landmarks of a much-celebrated career, his most long-lasting impact on architecture came through his innovations. He was a pioneer in shunning symmetry, a cornerstone of then-prevailing Beaux Arts design. Instead he favored asymmetrical plans, which he found better able to blend into the landscape. An exception was Unity Temple (1906) in Oak Park, IL, where he displayed a second innovation, the use of economical and then-unusual building materials—in the temple's case, unfinished poured concrete, which lent itself to a square plan so that forms could be reused. He was an early user of concrete block, both plain and embossed, as a finish material. From the early 1930s to the 1950s, he developed two generations of his Usonian House, meant to be an affordable system of construction that owners themselves could build on a concrete slab on the ground. For the second version, he designed large load-bearing concrete-block units held together with grouted steel reinforcing rods.

Wright designed new air-handling systems; the Larkin Administration Building (1904), in a heavily polluted factory district of Buffalo, not only had a heating and cooling system, but air scrubbers as well. For the Usonian houses, he advocated the installation of heating coils directly in the concrete base slab, a system that has plagued installers ever since with failures. To solve earthquake-damage problems on a spongy site in Tokyo, he designed one of the great monuments of his career, the Imperial Hotel (1915–22). Another atypically symmetrical building, the hotel withstood a disastrous earthquake in 1923, but not commercial development. It was replaced by a high-rise in 1968.

(1867-1959)

A trademark of Wright's designs (*photo, right*) was the provision of interiors with maximum sunlight and outside views. Accordingly, he replaced Beaux Arts cornices with bands of windows and introduced windows on the corners of buildings. He also introduced casement windows from Europe to replace America's standard double-hung sash windows, which he referred to as "guillotines." He redesigned the casements to open outward instead of inward as in Europe, and replaced the traditional vertical shape with a horizontal one he considered better able to provide contact with nature. In fact, horizontality—emphasized by long low lines, wide roof overhangs, lateral windows, and elongated masonry-wall units—was the single most characteristic feature of Wright's residential work, as typified by his most famous house, Fallingwater (1936) in

Pennsylvania. Many of Wright's residential innovations were to become familiar in developers' suburban "ranches" built during the 1940s and through the 1960s.

Charles King Hoyt

BIOGRAPHICAL HIGHLIGHTS

1867. Born on June 8 in Richland Center, WI.

1885–86. Attended the University of Wisconsin at Madison for two terms, taking engineering courses since architecture was not offered.

1887. Took a job with the architectural firm of Dankmar Adler and Louis Sullivan in Chicago.

1889. Married Catherine Tobin in June. The family grew to include six children.

1902. Having become the chief practitioner of the "Prairie school" of architecture, built the first masterwork of the school, the home of the W.W. Willitses.

1904. Designed the Larkin Administration Building in Buffalo, NY.

1906. Created another major work, the Unity Temple, in Oak Park, IL.

1909. Separated from his wife and began a relationship with Mamah Cheney, the wife of his former client.

1911. Built his house, Taliesin, on his grandfather's Wisconsin farm, where he lived with Cheney.

1914. Cheney and her children were killed at Taliesin by an insane houseman.

1915. Went to Japan to make plans to design the Imperial Hotel there.

1922. The Imperial Hotel opened in Tokyo.

1923. After divorcing his wife in 1922, married Miriam Noel, who later divorced him.

1928. Married Olgivanna Hinzenberg.

1932. Wrote and published *An Autobiography*. Established the Taliesin Fellowship training program for architects.

1936. Designed Fallingwater, the Edgar Kaufman House, near Bear Run, PA. Designed the Johnson Wax Company Administration Building in Racine, WI.

1938. Began to plan Taliesin West in Scottsdale, AZ.

1939. Created the master plan, his first, for Florida Southern College in Lakeland, FL. Was awarded the gold medal of the Royal Institute of British Architects.

1956. Construction began on New York City's Guggenheim Museum, which he designed in 1943.

1959. Died on April 9 in Phoenix, AZ.

Babe Didrikson Zaharias

Mildred Ella ("Babe") Didrikson Zaharias left an unparalleled legacy as the best all-around athlete, male or female, in the first half of 20th-century America. In fact, her legacy is multifaceted: She excelled in numerous and diverse sports, and was named Woman Athlete of the Year six times by the Associated Press and Woman Athlete of the Half Century in 1950. She earned three Olympic medals; cofounded a professional women's sports association and served as its president; and was a pioneering role model for other female athletes.

Babe Didrikson was one of seven children born to Norwegian immigrant parents who settled in southeast Texas. She distinguished herself in early schoolyard competitions as a naturally gifted athlete who outhit, outran, and outjumped all others. In high school she dominated the Beaumont High Royal Purple girls' basketball and tennis teams. She also competed in softball, diving, and golf. Her basketball skills earned her a spot as a starting forward with the Employers Casualty Insurance Company (ECC) team in Dallas, TX. She led her team to two national championships in the Women's Industrial League (1930–31).

Didrikson was appointed a one-woman team to represent ECC at the 1932 Amateur Athletic Union track and field competition held in Evanston, IL. This meet doubled as the 1932 Olympic tryouts. In a single July afternoon, Didrikson placed first in six of the eight events she entered and set world and national/Olympic records in four of these. She outscored the nearest second-place *team*. At the 1932 Olympic Games, Didrikson won gold medals with world-record performances in the javelin throw and the 80-meter hurdles. A technicality denied her a third gold medal, in the high jump.

Alongside her astounding athletic prowess, the Olympian established herself as a fierce competitor and, at times, difficult teammate. She learned how to manipulate reporters so they reported her victories (and antics) to a widening fandom. Didrikson mastered self-promotion long before sports agents "created" athletes as commodities. She parlayed this fame into a short stint as a harmonica-playing stage entertainer in Chicago; she enacted mock athletic feats and bantered with the audience. She barnstormed with the House of David all-male traveling baseball team. These activities distinguish her as one of the first female athletes—not in a "beautiful sport" such as swimming or skating—to earn a post-Olympics living successfully.

Didrikson fostered public acclaim for her excellence in competitive, traditionally working-class team sports (e.g., basketball and track and field). She challenged traditional notions of femininity with her brash quips to the press, androgynous body form, and bawdy behavior. She expanded the acceptable limits of what a female athlete could and *should* be.

Didrikson's most-remembered athletic legacy hails from her golfing excellence. She cofounded the Ladies Professional Golf Association (LPGA) in the 1940s. During one stretch she won 13 consecutive tournaments. She was the first American woman to win the British Women's Amateur. She persuaded sponsors to increase the tours' purses. Her charismatic—though problematic—personality propelled the LPGA into prominence.

Babe Didrikson, who was married to pro wrestler George Zaharias, also created a singular legacy as a medical humanitarian. She was diagnosed with colon cancer in 1953. She went public with the disease when this rarely was done, and established a cancer fund-raising agency in her own name that aided low-income patients seeking care. She also appeared publicly as a self-help role model for others struggling against cancer.

Susan E. Cayleff

BIOGRAPHICAL HIGHLIGHTS

1911. Was born Mildred Ella Didrikson on June 26, in Port Arthur, TX.

1930. Began her sports career as a star basketball player.

1932. Gained national acclaim by winning six of eight events at the Amateur Athletic Union's (AAU's) national women's track and field championships. Later in the year, set two world records at the Olympic Games, winning two gold medals and a silver.

1938. Met and married George Zaharias, a professional wrestler.

1940. Started her championship record in golf.

1949. Became one of the founding members of the Ladies Professional Golf Association (LPGA).

1950. Was chosen by an Associated Press poll as the outstanding woman athlete of the first half of the 20th century.

1951. Was inducted into the LPGA Hall of Fame.

1953. Was stricken with cancer.

1954. Captured the U.S. Women's Open golf tournament and took the Vare Trophy for lowest scoring average.

1955. Published her autobiography, *This Life I've Led*.

1956. Died in Galveston, TX, on September 27.

1983. Was elected to U.S. Olympic Hall of Fame.

CENTENNIAL REVIEW

At Kitty Hawk, NC, on Dec. 17, 1903, Orville Wright completed the first successful trial of a heavier-than-air, engine-driven flyer, *below*. The historic achievement received little publicity. On a July day 66 years later, the world watched as Col. Edwin E. Aldrin, Jr., *left*, and Neil A. Armstrong walked on the Moon.

WORLD SCENE

The United Nations, New York City

A New Century, World War,

The Search for Peace

As the 19th century neared its end, there was a controversy, to be renewed in the later years of the 20th century, about when the new century would begin—on Jan. 1, 1900, or Jan. 1, 1901.

Historians are less interested in the rigidity of the number of years and more interested in the continuities, or the changes, that delimit historical eras. As the decades of the 20th century wore on, historians increasingly tended to regard the 19th century as lasting from 1815 to 1914. That was an epoch possessing specific characteristics marking it as different from what came before and what came after. After 1815 and Napoleon's defeat at the Battle of Waterloo, the 19th century was entirely, and thus unusually, free of major wars involving the Great Powers. The period also was characterized by great economic advances, the increasing power of the middle class, and an unprecedented inventiveness in many fields, notably transportation, communication, medicine, and military matters. These advances completely changed the way in which people in all the more advanced countries lived, and spread rapidly to most other parts of the world. In turn, the 20th century, a bloodstained one, began in 1914.

Life in 1900

The 20th century has seen quite extraordinary, indeed fantastic, advances and innovations in technology, so that what was science fiction only a few decades ago has become everyday fact. Observers, therefore, may be tempted to exaggerate the primitive character of life in the early 1900s. Actually, a great deal of novel technology that had improved the character of life already was in place or would be within a few years, especially in the cities. Railroads, perhaps the greatest of 19th-century innovations, had been flourishing for many decades. The U.S. transcontinental line was completed in 1869. Russia's Trans-Siberian Railway, begun in 1891, was completed in the early 1900s. Electricity was known and in wide use, although even in cities many homes still were lit by gas. Telephones also were in wide use, mostly for business. A profusion of telephone wires, not yet underground, darkened the skies in central areas of cities. The telegraph provided worldwide linkage: Messages could be transmitted anywhere in an hour or two. Radio ("wireless telegraphy") was known and was in use to a limited extent. The automobile had been invented and was being developed enthusiastically, mostly at first in continental Europe. Henry Ford began production of the Model T in 1908. The great, still eagerly awaited, breakthrough was flight. Various experiments involving models and unmanned craft had been made in the last years of the 19th century; but genuine heavier-than-air powered flight did not arrive until Orville and Wilbur Wright achieved it in December 1903. Thereafter development went forward at a gallop. France's Louis Blériot flew across the English Channel in 1909.

Optimism v. Apprehension

In 1900 countries either had, or seemed to be heading in the direction of, some form of representative government—either the presidential type, as in the United States, or the parliamentary type (the British style) that was found in Western Europe and Japan. In Russia the first *Duma* (parliament) met in 1905. In economics, liberal capitalism was clearly triumphant. It and representative government went together. Also, the world was overwhelmingly Europeanized. In the last decades of the 19th century, almost all of Africa had been brought under the rule of one or another European power; the European powers also had extensive possessions in the Pacific and Asia, and were nibbling at the coasts of China. This European dominance suffered its first blow in 1905, when Japan trounced the Russian giant.

The Great Power roster of 1900, or of 1914, was not substantially different from that of 1815. The Great Powers of 1815—Britain, France, Austria, Russia, Prussia—

Paris hosted the 1900 Exposition Universelle. Such future French landmarks as the Grand Palais and the Musée d'Orsay were built for the expo, which attracted 40 million visitors. For arbitrating the end of the Russo-Japanese War, President Theodore Roosevelt (below center) was awarded the 1906 Nobel Prize for peace.

were still Great Powers as the 20th century began, though Prussia had become Germany (1871), and Austria had become Austria-Hungary (1867). There had been three additions to the ranks—united Italy, the United States, and Japan. It was of great importance for the future that two of the new powers were non-European.

Indeed, at the end of the 19th century, attitudes differed from country to country. The United States faced the new century with a robust optimism that, in fact, was fully justified. A successful minor war with Spain in 1898 had launched the United States on its own version of imperial expansion, with new insular possessions in the Caribbean and the Pacific. In Britain and France the mood was less optimistic. In 1900, Britain was engaged in a mismanaged little war in South Africa, against the Boer Republics, that was not going well. Queen Victoria, who had reigned on the British throne since 1837, died on Jan. 22, 1901. Thinking people in Britain were concerned that the world's greatest imperial power—and the British Empire had not yet reached its greatest extent—was in relative decline. By 1900, British steel production—a significant index—had been passed not only by that of the United States but by that of Germany as well. By 1914, German steel production was twice that of Britain. Also, German industry was the more productive and inventive in many new fields. German industry was protected by tariffs, while Britain adhered to free trade until the early 1930s. The population of united Germany, at 67 million, far surpassed the British population of about 42 million. France, closer geographically to Germany than Britain and with more cause to be apprehensive, had a population about the same as that of Britain. Also, major internal conflicts on social and religious questions had undermined French national unity.

Alliances and Arms Races

There were voices in fiction and science fiction, and in serious discussion, prophesying war. It is hard to say if these represented a widespread fear. The cataclysm that led to the first world war of 1914–18 had a long fuse, stretching back to the Franco-Prussian War of 1870–71. The achievement of Otto von Bismarck, made possible by the successful war, was a united Germany. The king of Prussia also became the German emperor; Prussia was predominant within Germany;  and Germany was predominant in Europe. Bismarck's whole anxiety after that was to safeguard his achievements, not to make further advances. He was not interested in colonies; later, however, internal political pressures led him to acquire a few for Germany. In the Treaty of Frankfurt, ending the Franco-German war, Germany imposed on France the loss of Alsace-Lorraine. It was something that Bismarck had not favored, and a humiliation that France did not forget.

Bismarck was haunted by the possibility that some combination of European powers might arise to threaten the situation he had brought about. To avert the danger, he constructed his own complicated network of alliances, in which the keystone was the Dual Alliance (1879) with Austria-Hungary, a secret defense alliance whose general nature, however, was known widely. Immediately after the Franco-Prussian War, in 1873, he had concluded the Three Emperors' League of Germany, Austria-Hungary, and Russia—a rather vague commitment to consult together on matters of great common

Britain's Queen Victoria, above left, *who reigned for nearly 64 years, died on Jan. 22, 1901, causing widespread mourning among her subjects. Following a royal funeral,* top, *she was buried alongside her husband, Prince Albert, at Frogmore, near Windsor. At the beginning of the century, British military forces—some 450,000 strong—were engaged in a struggle of nearly three years against the Boers in South Africa,* above.

interest. The League was replaced by another treaty in more precise form in 1881. Russia refused to renew this treaty in 1887, and Bismarck produced another piece of diplomatic juggling, the Reinsurance Treaty of 1887. The great, irreparable defect in Bismarck's scheme of alliances was that there was no way of permanently reconciling the rivalries of Russia and Austria-Hungary in the Balkans. In 1882, Italy had been joined to the Dual Alliance of 1879, which thus became the Triple Alliance; but Italy's treaty was framed in defensive terms only, and Italy did not line up with the Central Powers in World War I in 1914, but with the Allies in 1915.

The accession of William II as emperor of Germany in 1888 inaugurated a more dangerous era. He was an erratic, ambitious, and unstable personality given to ill-considered words and actions. Bismarck was dismissed (1890), and the Reinsurance Treaty was dropped. The new emperor drummed up an interest in the Middle East (where Germany never had had any interest before). He visited Turkey, assured the Islamic world of his support (presumably against Britain and France), and planned a Berlin-Baghdad Railway (never completed). He also assured President Paul Kruger in South Africa of his support (1896)—another anti-British gesture. In Wilhelmine Germany a reckless and aggressive policy became the fashion. Russia turned, if reluctantly, to republican France, and the result was the Franco-Russian defense agreement of 1894. This completed the two-alliance system of 1914.

Inevitably, Anglo-German antagonism increased. An 1898 law that built up the German navy initiated naval rivalry. It was impossible for British opinion to accept any justification for Germany, possessor of Europe's most formidable army, to proceed to build a navy that rivaled the Royal Navy—a program accelerated in 1906.

There were many attempts on Britain's part to achieve a reconciliation with Germany, including the 1912 Haldane mission, which attempted to reach an agreement between the two nations on naval armaments. But Germany wanted a guarantee of British neutrality. Britain reformed its army, modernized its navy, and in 1906 built the first all-big-gun battleship, the *Dreadnought*.

Britain also turned to France and Russia, to clear up outstanding issues with them. The Entente Cordiale (1904) between Britain and France had as its core British acceptance of France's position in Morocco and French acceptance of Britain's dominant role in Egypt. A 1907 entente with Russia demarcated a Russian sphere of influence in north Persia and a British one in the south, adjacent to the Persian Gulf.

In the period 1900–14, there were three crises—and a fourth that proved disastrous. The first two crises occurred in 1905–06 and in 1911, and were provoked by Germany's

William II, above, became emperor of Germany in June 1888 at the age of 29 and served until his abdication in November 1918 at the conclusion of World War I. The assassinations of Archduke Franz Ferdinand, heir to the Habsburg empire, and his wife, right, on June 28, 1914, in the city of Sarajevo, was one of the factors that led to the hostilities.

unsuccessful attempts to lessen France's role in Morocco. A third crisis in 1908 resulted from Austria-Hungary's outright annexation of Bosnia and Herzegovina, nominally part of the Ottoman Empire, but which had been under Austrian administration since the Congress of Berlin of 1878.

The 1912–14 developments in the Balkans that led to a general war had their origins in the manifest decline of Turkey. In the First Balkan War (1912) and the Second (1913), a varying combination of Balkan states succeeded in reducing Turkey's holdings in Europe to a small remnant. The most important point was that Serbia doubled its territory, a development alarming to Austria. That was the third crisis. The fourth began on June 28, 1914, when the heir to the Habsburg empire, the Archduke Franz Ferdinand, and his wife were murdered in Sarajevo by Gavrilo Princip, a Bosnian Serb student. He was one of a group of conspirators determined to end Austrian rule in Bosnia and Herzegovina, and was supported by the Serbian terrorist group the Black Hand. The Austrian government had no proof of complicity by the Serbian government, but it is reasonably certain that some in government and high officers of the Serb military had a notion of what was planned. The Austrian government responded with an ultimatum that, in effect, would have placed the Serbian government under Austrian supervision. Upon its rejection, Austria, previously assured of unconditional support by Germany, declared war on Serbia on July 28. This, the beginning of the Third Balkan War, escalated rapidly into World War I.

The days of July and early August were a period of the most intense diplomatic activity. But the outcome was that the members of the two confronting blocs, except Italy, fell into their predetermined places. Russia, as it traditionally had done, supported its fellow Slavs and coreligionists, the Serbs. Germany declared war on Russia and on France. Britain, outraged by the German invasion of Belgium, declared war on Germany on August 4. Britain was bound—as, indeed, was Germany—by the 1839 Treaty of London to uphold Belgian independence.

The Great War

Apparently, all belligerents in World War I—the "Great War," as it was known to contem-

Newspapers throughout the European continent announced the beginning of the "Great War"—the first major conflict involving the Great Powers in nearly 100 years—in late July/early August 1914. Most observers thought the war would be a short one.

poraries—expected that their soldiers would be home in time for Christmas. Indeed, it is striking how very wrong all expectations were about what the first world war would be like. In terms of the Schlieffen Plan—Germany's military plan for offensive action—the first great German drive southwest was defeated by the French at the battle of the Marne in early September 1914. The race to the ports of the English Channel had produced by December a continuous line of trenches stretching from the Channel to the Swiss frontier. The two sides dug in, in ever more elaborate protective trench systems, and used barbed wire and machine guns for defense; stalemate, with a steady loss of life, was the result.

(Continued on page 100.)

The Russian Revolution

The Russian Revolution of 1917 was one of the most influential events of the 20th century, sending shock waves through Russia, and, after World War II, through many other countries as well. From the wreckage of the Imperial Russian Empire, the revolution produced the Soviet Union, one of history's mightiest states. The Soviet Union later went on to gain control over Eastern Europe; extend its ideology and influence to Asia, the Middle East, and Latin America; and engage the United States in a Cold War nearly 50 years in duration.

The Russian Revolution actually was a process of many months framed by two dramatic upheavals rather than a single moment in history. The revolutionary process began with the February Revolution, which brought down the Russian monarchy in early 1917, and culminated in the October Revolution, when the Bolshevik Party seized power in Russia. After October 1917 the Bolsheviks renamed themselves the Communist Party; they had a profound effect on the political life of the 20th century until the abrupt collapse of the Soviet Union in 1991.

To a great extent, the uprising that began in Petrograd (St. Petersburg), capital of the Russian Empire, was marked by the relatively spontaneous actions of tens of thousands of ordinary Russians. Russia had been in turmoil for more than a decade, since Czar Nicholas II's unsuccessful war against the Empire of Japan in 1904–05. Seeing opportunity in the government's disarray, a coalition of Marxist parties had attempted to seize power in the capital in 1905. The short-lived effort, put down by czarist forces, produced a number of martyrs but had the effect of raising political consciousness among Russia's relatively small, urban working class. The years leading up to the outbreak of World War I in 1914 witnessed many strikes—largely, but not all, in pursuit of economic issues. The war itself, which Russia was losing, put enormous strain on the already faltering autocracy, its bureaucracy, and the Russian economy. By 1917 economic and bureaucratic breakdowns were occurring, inflation was soaring, and food and fuel were in short supply in Petrograd (*photo at right, page 99*), a key manufacturing center for the war effort. It was in this environment that long-seething public discontent boiled over and, in little more than a week, swept away the Romanov dynasty.

The revolutionary events of February were a combination of grassroots action by Petrograd's workers' movement and the efforts of district- and factory-level revolutionary activists, especially Socialist Revolutionaries and Bolsheviks. Food shortages were the initial spark that brought women textile workers into the streets on February 23. They soon were joined by thousands of metalworkers. By the 25th a general strike was under way involving more than 200,000 workers, effectively paralyzing the capital. Violence broke out between demonstrators and police as the authorities tried to suppress the unrest, but as several garrison units revolted and joined the workers, power began to shift to the streets. By the time Czar Nicholas (*photo above*) was notified at front headquarters in Mogilev, it was too late for decisive military counteraction. Liberal and moderate factions quickly picked up power as it lay in the streets, forming a bourgeois provisional government and calling for the czar's abdication. On March 2, Nicholas II abdicated the throne, and power passed to the new Provisional Government. Hoping to save the war effort, the General Staff shifted allegiance to the new authority, but the calm was illusory, for the February Revolution was to be the prologue to more revolutionary violence.

The revolutionary process continued during the spring and summer of 1917 in what, retrospectively, was the interregnum between the end of autocracy and the rise of Soviet power. Vladimir Lenin (*photo below*), leader of the Bolsheviks, returned from exile in April, but the failure of a premature Bolshevik uprising in July forced him into hiding to avoid arrest. In August, Gen. Lavr Kornilov launched a counterrevolution, but troops loyal to the Provisional Government thwarted the attempt. Meanwhile, unrest had begun in the countryside, as peasants turned on landlords, seizing houses, land, and crops. By September, with workers further politicized by the abortive Kornilov putsch, peasant seizures driven by land hunger, and soldiers deserting the front, Lenin felt conditions had ripened for the Bolsheviks to seize power from Prime Minister Aleksandr Kerensky's weak government. Although two Central Committee comrades—chastened by the party's July failure—dissented, Lenin carried the majority as the Bolsheviks went forward to revolution under the banner of "land, peace, and bread."

detachments poised to strike. The Provisional Government was unable to mobilize effective resistance, and the railroad stations, post office, telegraph agency, and state bank easily fell into the hands of the insurgents. The Winter Palace, long the residence of the czars and now the seat of the government, offered only token resistance. It soon crumbled under threat of naval gunfire. The ministers were arrested, as the Provisional Government passed into history. The Bolsheviks had come to power in Russia.

The Bolshevik Revolution was to the 20th century what the French and American revolu-

The Petrograd Soviet's Military Revolutionary Committee, headed by Bolshevik Leon (Lev) Trotsky, played the key role in carrying out the final assault on the centers of power of the Kerensky government. On the morning of October 25, Red sailors from the Baltic Fleet bases headed for Petrograd in ships and trains to join rebel regiments, and armed workers'

tions had been to the 18th century—a watershed event. Coming to power with a Marxian utopian vision, Lenin's new party-government soon, however, became mired in the difficulties of governing backward Russia, as utopianism gave way to reality. Following Lenin's death in 1924, a succession struggle brought to power Joseph Stalin, who ruled despotically until his death in March 1953. Stalin left a harsh imprint on the Soviet system that his successors never overcame fully. Thus, unlike its French and American predecessors, the Bolshevik Revolution, which had begun with great promise, came to an end in disarray and disillusionment in the final decade of the 20th century.

Robert Sharlet

(Continued from page 97.)

It was a world war. It was fought on the western front; on the eastern front—where Russia faced Germany and Austria; in the Balkans—Romania and Greece entered the war on the Allied side in 1916 and 1917, respectively; in the Middle East—Turkey joined on the German side in 1914; and in the Far East and Africa. It also was fought on the high seas. A British defeat by the German fleet, of course, could have been disastrous. The sole major action between the British and German fleets was the Battle of Jutland (May 31–June 1, 1916). Although Britain lost more in tonnage, Jutland was a strategic victory for the British in that the German fleet did not make such a challenge again—relying, thenceforth, on submarine warfare.

Apart from the war at sea, it was the western front alone that was decisive. The appalling experience of trench warfare, especially attacks costly in life that achieved only minimal gains, was etched deeply on the consciousness of a generation. The French offensives of 1915 were costly failures. On the first day of the Battle of the Somme (July 1, 1916), the British sustained nearly 60,000 casualties, with 19,000 dead. The German attack on Verdun (1916) failed in the end.

Stalemate might have continued indefinitely, or Germany might have won the war, but for the entry of the United States. President Woodrow Wilson's early determined neutrality in the conflict, then a desire to mediate, changed only very gradually into a reluctant decision to intervene. The precipitating factor was submarine warfare. Unrestricted German submarine warfare near the British coasts, begun in 1915 and suspended in 1916, was resumed in early 1917. Wilson had warned that such a move would lead to

The trench, requiring a large number of troops, rapidly became the symbol of World War I. A continuous line of trenches was built from the English Channel to the Swiss frontier during the initial months of the conflict. When the trenches became difficult to defend, both sides adopted new military strategy.

Britain, France, and Germany all suffered heavy casualties at the Battle of the Somme, above left, which began in July 1916 and continued until mid-November 1916. The Battle of Jutland, right, May 31–June 1, 1916, was the sole major naval engagement of World War I between British and German forces.

U.S. intervention. However, Russia—embroiled in political change, then revolution (*see* page 98)—fell out of the war in 1917, enabling Germany to move large numbers of troops to the western front. The German calculation was that France and Britain could be defeated before American help became effective. So the risk was taken, and the United States declared war on April 6, 1917. The German decision was a colossal mistake.

The German offensives in the early summer of 1918, despite initial successes, failed; by autumn, Austria-Hungary, Bulgaria, and Turkey were collapsing. Revolution followed in Germany; Kaiser William II abdicated and fled to Holland. The Armistice of Nov. 11, 1918, ended the war. In round figures, 9 million soldiers had died, and 21 million had been wounded.

The question of responsibility for the war sparked a controversy that never has ceased entirely. However, there is considerable agreement that, while other countries made mistakes, Germany was primarily responsible for the hostilities. Two central points were that Germany was at fault in giving Austria-Hungary a free hand in its quarrel with Serbia, and that Germany was wrong to have a war plan that involved advancing through Belgium.

Following the Armistice of Nov. 11, 1918, bringing the first world war to an end, troops of the victorious Allies paraded under the Arc de Triomphe in Paris on Bastille Day, July 14, 1919.

Quest for Peace, 1919–29

The future of much of Europe, at least for the next 20 years, had been determined before the emissaries, including President Wilson, assembled in Paris in January 1919 to negotiate a peace agreement. In a unique combination of events, the collapse of the Russian Empire in 1917 had been followed in 1918 by the end of the Austro-Hungarian, Turkish, and German empires. Thus the powers that had shaped events in Eastern Europe for hundreds of years ceased to exist or were in a powerless phase, though two would recover. Poland reemerged as a sovereign nation, and many other nations appeared, reappeared, or enlarged their fron-

tiers. Two new composite states—Czechoslovakia and what later was called Yugoslavia—were created. Apart from minor frontier revisions, none of this could be altered or undone during the treaty negotiations.

What loosely is called "the Versailles settlement" or "the Versailles Treaty" consisted in fact of five treaties drafted over 18 months: the Treaty of Versailles, with Germany; St.-Germain-en-Laye, with Austria; Trianon, with Hungary; Neuilly, with Bulgaria; and Sèvres, with Turkey. The first four were carried out, after a fashion; Sèvres proved unenforceable in face of the Turkish national revival led by Kemal Ataturk. It was replaced by the Treaty of Lausanne (1923), which was more favorable to Turkey.

President Wilson arrived in Europe with immense prestige, determined to create a more idealistic settlement than the European victors wanted. He insisted that the first order of business should be the creation of a

League of Nations. The Covenant of the League was embodied in all five peace treaties. Whatever the League's merits or demerits, it was hamstrung from the beginning by the failure of the U.S. Senate to ratify the Versailles Treaty or to join the League. It was not the case either that Germany surrendered on the terms of Wilson's Fourteen Points, or that the Fourteen Points were disregarded flagrantly at Paris. The Fourteen Points had been a statement about Wilson's ideas on a desirable peace, delivered in an address to Congress in January 1918, without any prior consultation with the Allies. Before January 1918, some things called for in the Points already had happened. Wilson had issued some addenda, and the Allies had made clear to Wilson, and the Germans, what was acceptable and what was not. Some, like "open covenants of peace openly arrived at," did not have much connection with reality. Wilson did not follow such a procedure in Paris.

Arthur James Balfour (standing in photo below) *was Britain's chief representative at the postwar meetings of the League of Nations. The failure of the United States to join the League hindered its effectiveness.* **Ramsay MacDonald,** *poster above, was Britain's first Labour Party leader to serve as prime minister (1924; 1929–35).*

Eamon de Valera, a longtime leader for Irish independence, inspected Irish Republican Army troops during the 1919–21 Anglo-Irish War. A treaty ending the fighting and granting dominion status to the 26 counties of "southern Ireland"—the Irish Free State—was signed in December 1921.

The treatment of Germany was not unduly harsh. Germany lost about 13% of its 1914 territory as a result of the peace accord. The substantial parts of this territory were areas that should not have been German in the first place—Alsace-Lorraine and the western Polish areas annexed in the 18th-century Partitions. Nor was it surprising that reparations should be imposed on defeated Germany. Germany had fought the entire war on other states' territory and had surrendered as soon as it seemed possible the fighting would move onto German territory.

The extraordinary inflation that struck Germany in 1923 was not the result of reparations but of simple refusal to balance income and expenditures. When that was done, the inflation disappeared. Reparations were modified progressively—reduced—in the Dawes Plan (1924) and the Young Plan (1929), and, when the Great Depression hit, abandoned. Germany, in all, paid about one eighth of the sum fixed in 1920.

What determines the durability of treaty settlements is not their justice or other merits but the will to enforce them. This was lacking in the 1920s and 1930s. Both the United States and Britain refused the French plea to sign treaties of guarantee to uphold the settlement. The United States retreated into isolation, disclaiming all responsibility for Europe. Britain disclaimed responsibility for Eastern Europe. Thus victorious France could look for support only to its Eastern European allies: Poland and the "Little Entente"—Czechoslovakia, Romania, and Yugoslavia, the beneficiaries of the breakup of the Eastern European empires. "This," said France's Marshal Ferdinand Foch, "is not peace: It is an armistice for 20 years."

Nevertheless, the 1920s were, for the most part, a period of optimism about the prospects for peace. The Washington Naval Conference of 1922 stabilized, at least for a time, naval competition among Japan, the United States, and Britain. The great symbol of the decade of optimism, however, was the Locarno treaties of 1925. The fruit of the cooperation of Aristide Briand (France), Gustav Stresemann (Germany), and Austen Chamberlain (Britain), the series of treaties were signed by seven states, including Germany. They guaranteed the Western European frontiers of France, Belgium, and Germany. As a reward, Germany was permitted to join the League of Nations. But Britain refused to join France in an "Eastern Locarno" pact guaranteeing frontiers in Eastern Europe.

Arthur Campbell Turner

INSTABILITY AND A SECOND WORLD WAR

The 1919 Treaty of Versailles, which ended the first world war, laid the foundation for World War II. The treaty burdened Germany with repatriations it could not pay and essentially ignored the claims of Italy, which had helped to defeat Germany at a cost of more than 600,000 lives. In both nations, economic depression and political unrest led to the rise of Fascism. The treaty, however, did reward Japan, which fought Germany at little cost, by giving Japan control of German islands in the Pacific. The Japanese military saw the islands as part of a new Japanese empire. United as the Axis Powers, Germany, Italy, and Japan would become allies in a new world war. Opposing them would be the principal allies of World War I—Britain, France, and the United States.

A Period of Instability

For Japan and China, World War II began on Sept. 18, 1931, when Japan, claiming that Chinese troops were planning to sabotage a Japanese-controlled railway, seized the Chinese city of Mukden (now Shenyang). Japan responded to a League of Nations censure by resigning from the League and conquering northeastern China. In what had been Manchuria, Japan established the state of Manchukuo and installed a Chinese puppet administration. Japan launched a full-scale invasion of China in 1937, outraging the world with the bombing of civilians and the "rape of Nanking." In a rampage in the captured Chinese capital, Japanese soldiers slaughtered as many as 100,000 civilians and raped tens of thousands of women.

Italy, under dictator Benito Mussolini (*Il Duce*), got its first taste of war on Oct. 3, 1935, invading Ethiopia from Italy's African colonies, Somaliland and Eritrea. Using bombers and poison gas against the spears of Ethiopians, Italian troops won after seven months of ferocious fighting. The League of Nations condemned the aggression, but Italy ignored the consequent economic sanctions. Italy quit the League in 1937.

Both Italy and Germany helped military dictator Francisco Franco win the Spanish Civil War of 1936–39 (*see* page 106), which was a dress rehearsal for the full-scale war to come. Soviet dictator Joseph Stalin sent aid to the leftist Republicans fighting Franco. But Stalin and Adolf Hitler, leader (*Führer*) of the German National Socialist (Nazi) Party, soon found themselves on the same side. On Aug. 23, 1939, Germany and the Soviet Union announced a Nonaggression Pact, giving notice that the Third Reich was on the rise, demanding *Lebensraum* ("living space") and the rearming of Germany in defiance of the Versailles Treaty.

Germany's march of conquest had begun in March 1938, when Hitler took over Austria in a bloodless coup. Six months later, ignoring protests from Britain and France, Hitler threatened to invade the Sudetenland, claiming that the land and its 3.5 million ethnic Germans belonged to the new Germany, the Third Reich. The Sudetenland was part of Czechoslovakia, which had been cre-ated under the Ver-sailles Treaty. In negotiations in Munich in September 1938, British Prime Minister Neville Chamberlain won a promise from Hitler that he would not seize any more Czech territory. Chamberlain hailed the Munich Pact for accomplishing "peace in our time." But within six months, Germany had taken over all of Czechoslovakia; "Munich" had become a synonym for appeasement; and Hitler was bullying Poland. The British government pledged to support Poland against "any action" that threatened Poland. France already had a mutual-defense treaty with Poland.

Hitler, having neutralized the Soviet Union with the Nonaggression Pact, now prepared to conquer Poland. On August 31, German SS (*Schutzstaffel* or "protection detachment") troops in Polish-army uniforms staged an attack on a German radio station at Gleiwitz on the German-Polish border. They then fired into the bodies of German concentration-camp inmates who had been murdered and dressed in Polish uniforms. The next day, Hitler condemned "the attack by regular Polish troops on the Gleiwitz transmitter," and German forces crossed the Polish border, while German warplanes bombed Warsaw.

Britain and France simultaneously started mobilizing and urged Hitler to withdraw and begin peace negotiations. When Hitler did not respond, the two nations issued an ulti-matum that would expire on Sunday, Sep-

The mid- and late 1930s, the period leading up to World War II, was a time of great instability. In Germany, Adolf Hitler had assumed the title of Führer and was captivating the nation's youth, page 104; China was in the midst of a prolonged civil war, above, top, and faced an invasion from Japan; and Italy, under Benito Mussolini, was invading Ethiopia from its colonies of Eritrea and Somaliland, above.

The Spanish Civil War

On July 17–18, 1936, civil war broke out when a group of military and civilian conspirators launched a general rebellion against Spain's legitimate government. Though the war began as a domestic struggle, the direct intervention of foreign powers on both sides quickly led to the internationalization of the conflict. Because of this and because of the enormous impact the hostilities had on the subsequent course of Spanish history, the civil war is regarded widely as one of the key events of the 20th century.

The rebels' initial failure to overthrow completely the Republican government divided Spain into two mutually hostile blocs. The "Nationalist" or rebel side comprised not only antirepublican elements of the Spanish army but also industrialists, monarchists, fascists, and the Roman Catholic Church. The heterogeneous supporters of "Republican Spain" included traditional republicans, revolutionary anarchosyndicalists, Basque and Catalan separatists, and socialists and Communists of various stripes. In an effort to contain Spain's troubles, a formal policy of nonintervention was adopted in August 1936 by Great Britain, France, and 25 other countries. But the futility of this diplomatic strategy became apparent when flagrant violations of the policy by Germany, Italy, and the USSR went unpunished.

Out of the inner circle of military officers who were behind the rebellion, Gen. Francisco Franco emerged in the autumn of 1936 as the principal leader of the Nationalist forces. Soon after assuming command of the army and becoming head of state (*el caudillo*), Franco began building the institutional basis of a regime (*el nuevo estado*) that he intended to rule after the war. To this end, he orchestrated in April 1937 the merger of all right-wing factions into one party under his control, the *Falange Española Tradicionalista* (FET). In a similar fashion, trade unions and other social and economic institutions in the rebel zone were absorbed into a state structure organized along corporatist-fascist lines.

Parallel to these developments, the disparate republican factions were searching for ways to present a united front against their enemy. Some progress in this direction was made under the coalition Popular Front government that ruled from September 1936 until May 1937. Chief among its early accomplishments was the creation of an effective military force under a unified republican command (Popular Army). But as the war dragged on, republican unity was undermined fatally both by the incessant pull of regionalist movements and by the fierce competition between prorevolutionary and antirevolutionary groups. On the one side of this power struggle stood anarchosyndicalists, left socialists, and anti-Stalinist Marxists. They were opposed by a coalition of middle-class republicans, pro-Soviet Communists, and reformist socialists. With the material and political backing of the Communist International and the Soviet Union, the moderate forces on the left gained ascendancy after May 1937 and tended to dominate Republican affairs until the end of the war.

Throughout the civil war, the Nationalists maintained their supremacy on the battlefields. This was due in no small measure to the generous assistance provided by fascist Italy and Nazi Germany, both of which defied international law by supplying Franco's cause with military personnel and armaments. The Nationalists' ability to dominate both the ground and air war after 1937 enabled them to crush every major republican offense launched in the summers of 1937 (Brunete and Belchite) and 1938 (Ebro). The air war itself resulted in numerous bombings of civilian targets, including the highly publicized destruction of the Basque town of Guernica in April 1937.

The Nationalists captured Barcelona at the end of January 1939. Shortly afterward, both France and Great Britain extended official recognition to Franco's Spain. With the war grinding to a close, tens of thousands of civilians fearful of a Nationalist victory trekked across the Pyrenees. Meanwhile, further feuding among republican parties in Madrid and elsewhere paved the way for Franco's final offensive. At the end of March 1939, Nationalist troops occupied Madrid, thus ending Spain's costliest war in modern times.

George Esenwein

tember 3. Chamberlain announced that a state of war existed between Great Britain and Germany; France quickly followed suit. Later that same day, a German U-boat torpedoed a British liner bound for Montreal; 112 people, including 28 Americans, died.

War Begins

Led by panzer armor units, German forces rolled across Poland in a month; British newspapers dubbed the conquest a *blitzkrieg* ("lightning war"). The Soviet Union, under a secret clause in the Nonaggression Pact, swept into Poland from the east. The pact also secretly had handed over to the USSR the Baltic republics of Lithuania, Estonia, and Latvia. The Soviets next attempted to conquer Finland. The Finns' stubborn resistance won the admiration but not the aid of England and France. The Red Army finally defeated the Finns in March 1940.

In what was called "the phony war," for months there were no battles between German forces and either French troops or the British Expeditionary Force that began deploying in France in September. France

In 1938, Britain's Prime Minister Neville Chamberlain and Germany's Chancellor Adolf Hitler signed the Munich Pact, accepting Germany's claims to areas of Czechoslovakia. France also agreed to the pact.

put its faith in the Maginot Line, a string of steel-and-concrete pillboxes and underground forts along the German-French border. Then, in another blitzkrieg, in April 1940, Germany stunned the world with a swift and victorious invasion of Denmark and Norway. Vidkun Quisling ruled over Norway for the Germans; his name became synonymous with treason. On May 10, Ger-

Chancellor Hitler and his troops marched triumphantly into Paris following Germany's occupation of France in June 1940, below, left. Four years later, Gen. Charles de Gaulle, the leader of the French resistance movement, led the parade in the French capital following France's liberation by the Allies, right.

many launched a massive campaign against Belgium, France, the Netherlands, and Luxembourg. Chamberlain's government fell, and Winston Churchill replaced him as prime minister.

U.S. President Franklin D. Roosevelt had responded to the start of the European war by saying, "This nation will remain a neutral nation, but I cannot ask that every American remain neutral in thought as well." He won from Congress a new neutrality law that essentially legalized the sale of arms to Britain and France.

Germany's armored armies, aided by airborne troops and mastery of the air, crushed opposition in the Netherlands, Luxembourg, and Belgium. Skirting the Maginot Line, German forces poured through the wooded hills of the Ardennes, entered France at Sedan, and began an offensive toward the Channel ports. Only one French unit counterattacked— the 4th Armored Division, commanded by the youngest general in France's service, Charles de Gaulle.

The British—launching warships, barges, small boats, and yachts—carried out an epic evacuation at the port of Dunkirk, saving 338,226 men, including some 100,000 French troops. On June 14, ten days after the Dunkirk evacuation, German troops marched into Paris and negotiated the fall of France. Germany annexed the Alsace-Lorraine area and spread occupation troops across northern and western France. The rest of France and its colonies were administered by a collaborationist government known as Vichy France. Most French accepted their fate, but a French underground, the *Maquis*, badgered German occupation troops with sabotage and intelligence-gathering for the British.

As German forces invaded France and the Low Countries in the spring of 1940, British and French troops were evacuated to England from their entrapment at the French port of Dunkirk, above.

At sea, Britain was fighting the Battle of the Atlantic. By Churchill's estimate, each day the island kingdom needed the cargo of at least 20 ships—about 120,000 tons of food, weapons, and other supplies—for the country to survive and defeat Germany. Most of those vital goods were coming from America. But German U-boats were gnawing at that lifeline. Britain also was being attacked from the air in what became the Battle of Britain, a prelude to "Operation Sea Lion," Hitler's plan to invade England—a plan that depended upon the destruction of the Royal Air Force (RAF). The campaign began in earnest on Aug. 13, 1940, when the RAF Fighter Command's 909 first-line Spitfire and Hurricane fighters (plus 84 older aircraft) defended Britain against more than 2,800 German fighters and bombers. Day after day, German aircraft attacked RAF bases and radar stations. Then, suddenly, throughout the night of September 7, German bombers began a concentrated attack on London—the first of 57 consecutive nights of bombing. Although Hitler postponed Operation Sea Lion indefinitely, the air raids on London and other British cities continued through the winter of 1940–41 and into the spring. What the British called the Blitz cost more than 40,000 Londoners' lives.

The three members of the Axis Powers officially united on Sept. 27, 1940, when Germany, Italy, and Japan signed the Tripartite Pact. (Italy already had declared war on Britain and France.) The pact called on each nation to provide military aid if attacked by a nation not yet in the war—a clear warning to the United States. Germany and Italy also recognized Japan's empire, the "Greater East Asia Co-prosperity Sphere." The pact did not deter the United States. Bypassing congressional opposition, Roosevelt negotiated with Churchill the swap of 50 overage U.S. destroyers for the rights to several British bases in the Western Hemisphere. Roosevelt,

The Holocaust

Sworn in as chancellor of Germany on Jan. 30, 1933, Nazi Party leader Adolf Hitler took power pledging to end Jewish influence in Germany, and ultimately in all of Europe.

Building upon the legacy of Christian anti-Semitism, 19th-century racial theory, alleged Jewish control of Communism, and the charge that Jews were responsible for Germany losing World War I, Nazism insisted that the salvation of the German people—of the Western world—depended on the elimination of the Jewish "cancer." If Hitler was vague about how he would accomplish this, the result 12 years later could not have been clearer. At the end of World War II, some six million Jews, two thirds of European Jewry, were dead.

The first stage of the Nazi war against German Jews was the passage of laws that removed them from government service, the professions, the public schools, and the arts. The Nuremberg Laws of 1935 revoked Jews' German citizenship and forbade marriage or sexual relations between Germans and Jews. Three years later, Jewish-owned businesses were expropriated, and on Nov. 8, 9—known as Kristallnacht or "Night of Crystal"—and 10, 1938, synagogues and other buildings owned by Jews throughout Germany were burned. As the Nazi regime took over Austria and Czechoslovakia in 1938 and 1939, the anti-Jewish laws were applied in those nations as well.

World War II began in September 1939 as German troops swept into western Poland. Jews there were herded into ghettoes. In June 1941, Germany invaded Russian-controlled eastern Poland and then crossed into Russia proper. In the following months, special units called Einsatzgruppen, which traveled with the army units, rounded up the Jews in each captured area and shot them into open pits.

In the summer of 1941, work began on the construction of the death camps. All the camps—Chelmno, Belzec, Sobibor, Treblinka, Majdanek, and, by far the largest, Auschwitz-Birkenau—were located in occupied Poland. Jews were taken by train from the Polish ghettoes and from other occupied and allied countries of Europe to those sites. They then were killed through the inhalation of engine exhaust fumes or cyanide gas—called by its trade name, Zyklon B. The process of deportation and extermination was carried out with extraordinary efficiency, even after it was clear that Germany was losing the war.

The Holocaust marked a turning point in history. Postwar trials conducted by the victors punished Nazi leaders for "crimes against humanity," establishing the principle that perpetrators of mass murder bear international accountability. The evidence that racial hatred could have deadly consequences set the stage for the American civil-rights revolution and for the end of apartheid in South Africa. The vulnerability of European Jewry to the Nazi onslaught gave support to the Zionist thesis that Jews needed their own sovereign state, leading to the establishment of Israel in 1948.

The Holocaust dashed, once and for all, the optimistic assumption that scientific and technological progress was leading humanity toward peace and brotherhood.

Lawrence Grossman

after winning a third term in the White House in 1940, got from Congress a Lend-Lease law, authorizing him to aid any country "whose defense the president deems vital to the defense of the United States."

Japan, meanwhile, was on the verge of invading French Indochina, from which supplies had been flowing to China in its war against Japan. Indochina would give Japan a base for further expansion and acquisition of Southeast Asia's oil, rubber, tin, quinine, and timber. In August, Roosevelt and Churchill met and issued the Atlantic Charter, which declared that the two allies had joined together "to ensure life, liberty, independence, and religious freedom and to preserve the rights of man and justice." The charter's principles, which would be ratified by 26 Allied nations at the United Nations Conference of January 1942, laid the foundation for the UN. In September, Roosevelt responded to Japan's invasion of Indochina by freezing Japanese assets in the United States. In October he cut off all oil exports to Japan.

The war's battlefields steadily multiplied. The British, reacting to an Italian thrust into Egypt, attacked Tobruk in Libya in January 1941, taking the port and a large swath of Italian territory. In March, *Generalleutnant* Erwin Rommel landed in Libya, engaged the British, and besieged Tobruk, starting a tank duel that would churn the desert sands from Egypt to Tunisia for more than two years. Germany also sent troops into Greece to aid badly mauled Italian forces and went on to conquer Greece and Crete. At the same time, Germany invaded Yugoslavia, where guerrillas frustrated the conquerors in an underground war led by a resistance leader who took the name Marshal Tito. Then, on June 22, 1941, Hitler broke his Nonaggression Pact with Stalin and invaded the Soviet Union in Operation Barbarossa. This biggest blitzkrieg sent more than 3 million German troops streaming across the Soviet border along a 1,000-mile (1,600-kilometer) front from the Baltic to the Black Sea. By November, German combat engineers were within 20 miles (32 kilometers) of Moscow.

In the Atlantic an undeclared war against the United States had begun. During the autumn of 1941, German U-boats attacked two U.S. destroyers escorting Britain-bound convoys and sank a third, the *Reuben James*; of its 160-man crew, only 45 were saved. Roosevelt warned that German or Italian warships entering U.S.-patrolled waters would "do so at their own risk." War for America now also threatened from the East. Japanese military officers, urging a tougher stand against the United States, installed a "war party" leader, Gen. Hideki Tojo, as prime minister. At the same time, the Japanese Imperial Navy began planning an attack on the U.S. Pacific Fleet at Pearl Harbor, a major U.S. naval and air base in Hawaii.

Tojo reiterated demands that the United States end aid to China, accept the Japanese occupation of Indochina, and resume normal trade. While U.S.-Japanese talks dragged on in Washington, Tojo ordered an aircraft-carrier task force to attack Pearl Harbor on December 7. Caught unprepared, the fleet suffered grievous losses. In two air strikes, the Japanese destroyed or damaged eight battleships, three light cruisers, three destroyers, four smaller vessels, and 188

Britain suffered heavy losses as a result of German air attacks during the Battle of Britain, or the Blitz, which began in August 1940. Only the walls, tower, and spire remained at the 14th-century cathedral in Coventry following a bombing raid, left.

In the Battle of Midway in June 1942, four Japanese carriers were sunk, while the United States lost an aircraft carrier. The U.S. victory marked a turning point in the war, as it ended Japan's advance in the Pacific.

planes. The attack killed 2,403 people, most of them U.S. servicemen, and wounded 1,104 others. Spared were the fleet's aircraft carriers, which were not at Pearl Harbor.

The United States Enters the Hostilities

President Roosevelt, calling Dec. 7, 1941, "a date which will live in infamy," asked Congress for a declaration of war against Japan. The Senate and House responded with a single dissenting vote, cast by Rep. Jeannette Rankin of Montana, who also had voted against a declaration of war in 1917. President Roosevelt, despite his fear that Britain might fall to Hitler, had no way of justifying war against Germany. Then, on December 11, Germany and Italy solved his dilemma by declaring war against the United States.

Japan followed the attack on Pearl Harbor with a stunning sweep across the Pacific, seiz-

ing the Gilbert Islands and the U.S. island bases of Guam and Wake. Off Malaya, Japanese bombers sank the British battleship *Prince of Wales* and the battle cruiser *Repulse*, the first capital ships ever to be sunk by air attack at sea. In quick succession, Japanese troops invaded the Philippines, Hong Kong, Singapore, Malaya, Burma, and the Dutch East Indies. Singapore would fall in February with the surrender of 80,000 defenders.

By January 1942, the Japanese held Hong Kong and were driving U.S. and Filipino troops down the rugged, mountainous Bataan Peninsula, dooming them to annihilation or surrender. Under the command of U.S. Army Gen. Douglas MacArthur, the ill-supplied, malaria-plagued defenders stubbornly fought for every mile. In March, on orders from President Roosevelt, MacArthur left for Australia. Surrender of the Philippines finally came in May. But the ordeal continued for some 76,000 prisoners of war—12,000 of them Americans. Ordered to walk 65 miles (105 kilometers) to a railroad junction, about 5,200 Americans died on what became known as the "Bataan Death March." In the overcrowded prison camps, as many as 550 prisoners died in a day.

While the drumbeat of military defeats continued, American industrial might tri-

Germany's Sixth Army was annihilated by the Russians at the Battle of Stalingrad, the scene of harsh fighting from August 1942 until February 1943. Stalingrad (now Volgograd), a major industrial center, was of prime importance to the Russians.

In the final months of World War II, Japan resorted to "kamikaze" attacks, in which Japanese suicide pilots tried to crash their bomb-loaded planes onto the decks of U.S. warships in order to try to avoid total defeat.

umphed, sustaining the Allies' worldwide war effort. The Soviet Union, getting aid via U-boat–stalked convoys to Murmansk, was a major beneficiary; in one month the United States sent the Soviets 7,800 planes, 4,700 tanks and tank destroyers, 170,000 trucks, 2.25 tons of food, more than 1 million tons of steel, and millions of boots and shoes. In May 1941 there were 16 U.S. plants producing 100-octane aviation gasoline; by the end of 1941 there were 73 such plants. In peacetime, shipyards needed about three years to build an aircraft carrier. Now it took only 15 months to build a carrier. By war's end, the United States had produced 86,388 tanks, 71,060 ships, and 296,601 aircraft.

Another triumph, unacknowledged until long after the war, was the Allied ability to read German, Japanese, and Italian military and diplomatic codes. Both Japan and Germany relied upon "unbreakable" codes produced by electromechanical enciphering machines. Allied cryptanalysts figured out how the machines worked and duplicated them. Allied operatives intercepted, deciphered, and translated messages, then sent them, in great secrecy, to top commanders. The best example of the code-breakers' value came when they set the stage for the pivotal Battle of Midway. In May 1942 cryptanalysts at Pearl Harbor determined that the Japanese Imperial Navy was planning an invasion of Midway, a U.S. Navy base vital to the defense of Hawaii. The Japanese thought that the invasion would lure to

their doom the U.S. aircraft carriers that had not been at Pearl Harbor on December 7. Forewarned by the code-breakers, Adm. Chester W. Nimitz, commander of the Pacific Fleet, sent three carriers to a rendezvous point off Midway. On June 4, dive bombers sunk all four Japanese carriers in the Midway task force. The U.S. Navy lost an aircraft carrier but saved nearly all of its 2,270 men.

Midway became a turning point in the Pacific War during a year marked by other momentous events for the Allies. The RAF Bomber Command began extensive bombing of Germany; in May the first 1,000-plane raid devastated Cologne. On the Russian front, the Germans were losing men and momentum. Soviet counterattacks—and the bitter Russian winter—drove the invaders back from Moscow, never to return. In September 1942, Germans fought their way into Stalingrad (now Volgograd) and pounded the city to rubble. Undaunted, the Red Army defended the city, block by block, obeying Stalin's order: "Not a step back!" The Russian defenders of Stalingrad counterattacked in November 1942; a month later, the Red Army was on the offensive along the Don and on the Caucasus front. Of the 300,000 German, Romanian, and Italian troops who entered Stalingrad, about 150,000 had been killed by the time the remnants of the invading army surrendered in February 1943. The Russians put some 90,000 prisoners on a murderous march to Siberia. Only about 5,000 ever would see their homes again.

In Africa, 1942 began with a Rommel drive that took Tobruk and rolled into Egypt. The British stopped the Afrika Korps advance at El Alamein, a coastal village 60 miles (97 kilometers) west of Alexandria. In October, British forces, under Lt. Gen. Bernard L. Montgomery, drove the Germans back, beginning a 1,750-mile (2,816-kilometer) drive to join Allied forces that landed in French North Africa in November 1942. The landing, under the command of Lt. Gen. Dwight D. Eisenhower, would put British and American troops in control of North Africa in May 1943.

War in the Pacific and Air War in Europe

In the Pacific a growing web of air bases in the captured territories threatened to extend Japan's reach all the way to New Guinea and Australia. U.S. and Australian forces under MacArthur began a long campaign to take New Guinea as a prelude to his return to the Philippines. At the same time, U.S. Marines began to tear apart the Japanese airbase web on Aug. 7, 1942, with an amphibious landing on Guadalcanal, one of the Solomon Islands. There the Japanese were building an airfield in a campaign aimed at air strikes and possible landings in Australia. This first U.S. offensive of the war lasted until February 1943, when Emperor Hirohito allowed Japanese troops to evacuate.

More than 25,000 Japanese died on Guadalcanal, including about 9,000 from disease and starvation. U.S. forces suffered about 1,500 dead and 4,800 wounded. Such disproportionate losses would mark the U.S. island-hopping campaign as men were poured ashore in landings on Bougainville and Tarawa (November 1943), Kwajalein (late January–February 1944), Saipan (June

U.S. Gen. Dwight Eisenhower (above, left) and Britain's Gen. Sir Bernard Montgomery were supreme commander of Allied forces and commander of ground forces, respectively, for the successful D-day invasion of France in June 1944.

1944), Guam and Tinian (July 1944), Peleliu (September 1944), Iwo Jima (February 1945), and, finally, Okinawa (April 1945), 350 miles (563 kilometers) from Japan. Okinawa's defenders, often holed up in caves or pillboxes, fought fanatically. Choosing death over surrender, they forced U.S. soldiers and Marines to dislodge them with flamethrowers and high explosives.

Okinawa, seen by the Japanese as part of their homeland and by the Allies as an advanced staging base for the expected invasion of Japan, gave strategists a forecast of how bloody that invasion would be. On Okinawa, Americans suffered the highest casualties of any action against the Japanese: 7,163 killed or missing in action and 31,807 wounded in ground fighting. Japanese pilots, during *kamikaze* ("divine wind") suicide flights, plunged into U.S. Navy ships offshore, sinking or damaging 263 ships. The 1,900 kamikaze sorties left 4,907 navy men killed or missing and 4,874 wounded.

The kamikaze attacks revealed how desperate the air war had become for a Japan bereft of trained pilots. After Midway, Japan's air power steadily evaporated over the Pacific and ultimately over Japan. The air war between the Allies and the German *Luftwaffe* lasted longer. American bombers joined the RAF in 1943 in an RAF-by-night and U.S.-by-day strategic bombing campaign. When long-range fighters began escorting the U.S. bombers, losses dropped from 9.1% per raid in October 1943 to 3.5% in March 1944. By then, Germany clearly was losing the air war.

The bombing was part of the grand plan, code-named Overlord, for the Allied invasion of Europe in the spring of 1944, the epochal operation of the war. In history's mightiest invasion fleet there were more than 4,400 ships and landing craft. In the air over the invaders were 11,000 fighters, bombers, transports, and gliders. Of the 47 divisions used in the invasion, 21 were American; the rest were British, Canadian,

In August 1939, after meeting with other concerned physicists, Albert Einstein signed a letter to President Franklin D. Roosevelt. "Some recent work," the letter said, "...leads me to expect that the element uranium may be turned into a new and important source of energy in the immediate future...and it is conceivable...that extremely powerful bombs of a new type may thus be constructed." Roosevelt set up an advisory committee on uranium.

By 1939 physicists in both Germany and Japan also were exploring the possibility of using atomic energy to make a bomb. British atomic scientists were working toward production of weapons-grade fissionable material. One of the British physicists was Klaus Fuchs, a German refugee. He was also a spy, aiding Soviet scientists in their research, which focused on uranium.

In June 1942 a U.S. presidential science advisory group reported that an atomic weapon was feasible. In a rush to try all methods, new industrial complexes sprang up at Oak Ridge, TN, and Hanford, WA. The central laboratory for designing the bomb was in the wilderness of Los Alamos, NM. The lab designed two different bombs. "Little Boy" was essentially a gun with a U-235 bullet fired at a U-235 target; when the two U-235 components met, a rapid chain reaction would produce an explosion. The more complicated "Fat Man" involved two hemispheres containing plutonium. Conventional explosives, arranged to produce a tightly focused implosion, hurled the hemispheres together. This doubled the plutonium's density and created a "supercritical mass." The chain reaction that resulted would produce an atomic explosion.

and Polish. There were also French, Italian, Belgian, Czech, and Dutch troops. General Eisenhower was supreme commander, with British General Montgomery, the hero of El Alamein, in command of the ground forces.

D-day

Elaborate deception—fake radio traffic and dummy landing crafts and tanks—drew off German divisions to the Pas de Calais. But on D-day, June 6, 1944, the Allied invaders still faced a formidable defense: nine German infantry divisions and one panzer division arrayed along fortifications Hitler called the Atlantic Wall. Offshore, submerged obstacles threatened landing craft. The beaches bristled with antitank barriers; beneath the sands lay mine fields. Beyond the beach were more mine fields and weapons ranging from machine guns to railroad guns.

The invasion beaches stretched for 60 miles (97 kilometers), and each beach had a different fate. At Omaha Beach some 2,000 men fell; at Utah, about 200; about 15,000 invaders were killed or wounded on D-day. By the end of the day, nearly 150,000 troops and their vehicles, equipment, ammunition, and provisions had been landed. In a week, 500,000 men held a continuous beachhead as deep as 15 miles (24 kilometers). Day by day, week by week, the Allies advanced across a rejoicing France, liberating Paris on August 25. Gen. Charles de Gaulle entered the city triumphantly the next day.

Germany's revenge would rain down on London in the form of the *Vergeltungswaffe* ("reprisal weapon"), the V-1 guided missile Londoners called the buzz bomb. During an 80-day bombardment, the missiles' 1,870-pound (848-kilogram) warheads killed 6,184 people and seriously injured 17,981 others. In September the V-2s—rocket-propelled missiles with 2,145-pound (973-kilogram) warheads—began to hurtle out of the sky. There was no defense against them. They

In a test, code-named "Trinity," in the New Mexico wilderness on July 16, 1945, the Fat Man–type bomb produced an explosion equivalent to 18,600 tons of TNT. Convinced by the test and a scientific advisory committee, President Harry S. Truman authorized its use. The U.S. cruiser *Indianapolis* carried all the parts of a Little Boy–type bomb, except the U-235 target element, to Tinian Island, the Pacific base for the B-29 Superfortress bomber that would carry the bomb.

On August 6 a B-29 named the *Enola Gay*, after the pilot's mother, dropped a Little Boy bomb on Hiroshima. With a force equivalent to 12,500 tons of TNT, the bomb exploded, destroying the city. On August 9 another B-29 dropped a Fat Man–type bomb on Nagasaki. The bomb exploded 1,650 feet (503 meters) above the city with a force equivalent to about 22,000 tons of TNT. Japanese estimates later put the cities' combined death toll—either instantly or through the effects of radiation—at 240,000. On August 14, Japan surrendered.

Thomas B. Allen

killed 2,754 people and injured 6,523 others. More than 1,600 bombs fell on Antwerp, the key port for supplying Allied forces, killing 4,152 people.

Overshadowed by D-day and the Allied sweep across France was the liberation of Rome on June 4. Italy had surrendered in September 1943, and the new government had arrested Mussolini (who later was freed in a daring German rescue). But the Allied campaign in Italy, which had begun with the invasion of Sicily in July 1943, slogged on. After pulling out of Rome, the Germans established new defensive positions in the north and fought on.

On the Russian front, defeat in Stalingrad had marked the end of Germany's offensive. In July 1943 at Kursk, a railroad junction north of Kharkov, a German attempt to encircle Soviet forces led to the greatest tank battle of the war. Aided by guerrillas attacking in the German rear, the Soviets killed 70,000 Germans and destroyed 2,950 tanks.

After that battle, the Germans continually retreated, and the Russians continually advanced, surging across eastern Europe in a conquest that would end in Berlin.

In February 1945, Roosevelt, Churchill, and Stalin—the Big Three—met in Yalta. At the conference, Stalin secretly agreed to enter the war against Japan after the defeat of Germany. He also pledged free elections in nations "liberated" by the Red Army. The breaking of this pledge would be a root cause of the Cold War. The Big Three also agreed on demanding "unconditional surrender."

In the Pacific, Allied forces were clearing or bypassing Japanese strongholds in New Guinea and preparing for an invasion of the Philippines to fulfill General MacArthur's vow: "I shall return." The landings began at Leyte in October 1944, drawing out a Japanese fleet in the climactic naval battle of the war, with the Japanese losing four carriers, three battleships, six cruisers, and 14 destroyers. The naval disaster left the Japanese garrisons on the Philippines without air support or protection of supply lines to Japan. But fierce fighting continued, demolishing Manila, which was not liberated until March 1945.

The Concluding Campaigns

One last German offensive, personally conceived by Hitler, stopped the Allied advance in December 1944 when German troops, attacking from the Belgian region of the Ardennes plateau, broke through U.S. lines. The surprise attack created a bulge in the line—hence the name Battle of the Bulge—and threatened a division of Allied forces. In the largest battle ever waged by the U.S. Army, some 600,000 soldiers fought in rain and snow along a 60-mile (97-kilometer) front. Nearly 20,000 would be killed, and another 20,000 would be captured. So many U.S. soldiers deserted under fire that General Eisenhower, believing he had to make an example, ordered the execution of a deserter. The battle ended in mid-January with 30,000 Germans dead, 30,000 captured, and the German army crumbling.

On January 16, Hitler entered an underground bunker in Berlin. Except for brief daytime trips, he would stay there for the rest of his life. By April 25 the Red Army had encircled the city. Anglo-American

The United Nations

The United Nations (UN), like the League of Nations, which had been created immediately following World War I, was born in 1945 out of another catastrophic event—an even greater war, World War II. In both cases, the intention was to create a global organization whose primary mission was to preserve the peace. Unlike the League, which failed to attract and sustain the membership of any "great powers" other than Britain and France, the UN obtained the commitment of all the major actors who had emerged victorious from the war. Indeed, the Allies, led by the United States, already had started calling themselves the "United Nations" as early as 1942. In 1944, even before

World War II was over, two conferences—one at Dumbarton Oaks in Washington, DC, and the other at Bretton Woods, NH—were held by the Allies. The purpose of those meetings was to draft a plan for the postwar international order that would include both a general-purpose organization to deal with war and peace issues (the UN) as well as a set of institutions to deal with economic matters (the World Bank and the International Monetary Fund, or IMF).

By the time the delegates from 50 countries met in San Francisco in April 1945 (*photo above*) to finalize the United Nations Charter, there was euphoria. U.S. President Harry Truman opened the conference by radio with the prediction that the participants were about to create "machinery which will make future peace not only possible, but certain." The UN came into being on Oct. 24, 1945, after the Charter, which was signed on June 26, had been ratified by the requisite number of states.

The UN founders were in one sense idealists, dreamers, and visionaries who were trying to construct a new world order based primarily on the principle of collective security, whereby a universal coalition of all member states would be mobilized against any nation committing aggression. For the first time in history, there was a blanket proscription against the first use of armed force; secondly, there was a pledge to address the economic and social problems underlying most conflicts. Yet the founders also were driven by realism and self-interest. After all, it was the victors of World War II who were the chief architects of the UN; and the "Big Five" (the United States, Britain, France, the Soviet Union, and China) gave themselves special privileges in the organization. They alone would have permanent seats on the Security Council and the power to veto Security Council actions. In addition to the Security Council, the other major organs included the General Assembly (the plenary body), the Secretariat (the administrative arm headed by a secretary-general), the World Court, the Trusteeship Council, and the Economic and Social Council.

Alas, no sooner was the ink dry on the Charter than the Cold War began, ending any hope the organization could be used as envisioned. During the next 45 years, collective security was implemented only once, if one counts the effort to punish North Korean aggression against South Korea in 1950. There also were more modest "peacekeeping" missions sent to manage conflicts in the Middle East, the Belgian Congo, and elsewhere. With the end of the Cold War in 1989, a revived UN engaged in collective security during the Persian Gulf war and more peacekeeping operations.

J. Martin Rochester

forces had halted at the Elbe River, leaving Berlin to the Soviets. While the battle for Berlin raged overhead, Hitler married his longtime mistress, Eva Braun, on April 28. That same day, Italian guerrillas executed Mussolini and his mistress. On April 30, Hitler shot himself in the right temple, and Eva took poison. Their bodies were carried out of the bunker, drenched with gasoline, and set afire. On May 7, Germany surrendered. Americans would learn about the surrender from their new president, Harry S. Truman. The vice-president had succeeded Roosevelt, who died on April 12.

The invasion of Japan was scheduled to begin in November 1945. Japanese military leaders, expecting the invasion, planned to fight to the end, hoping to kill so many Americans that the United States would sue for a negotiated peace. President Truman believed that America's secret weapon, the atomic bomb (see page 114), could end the war without an invasion. A special advisory group recommended immediate use of the successfully tested bomb. Truman agreed.

Much of Tokyo already was a blackened ruin. Flying from bases in the hard-won Mariana Islands, 279 B-29 Superfortresses had dropped 1,665 tons of incendiary bombs on the city on the night of March 9–10. Wind-whipped fires torched about 16 square miles

Germany staged its final offensive of the war in what became known as the Battle of the Bulge, December 1944–January 1945. Casualties were high on both sides, and many soldiers were captured.

(41 square kilometers), killed more than 80,000 people, and made more than a million homeless. Unable to defend Japan's skies, the military nevertheless advised Emperor Hirohito that the nation could fight on. They gave similar advice on August 6, when a B-29 dropped an atomic bomb on Hiroshima. Only when the second bomb was dropped on Nagasaki on August 9 did the emperor decide to end the war.

On August 15, Truman announced Japan's "unconditional surrender." There was a condition: The prerogatives of the emperor would be preserved. By then, the USSR, which had declared war on Japan on August 8, had taken much of Manchuria and was heading down Korea toward the 38th Parallel, the line set as the boundary between Soviet and U.S. occupation forces. For their short-lived role as a Pacific war ally, the Soviets would get the Kuril Islands and the southern end of nearby Sakhalin Island.

Although the victors created the United Nations (see page 116), the war ended with the victors no longer united. The Red Army occupied what would become East Germany; U.S., British, and French troops occupied what would become West Germany. Civil war raged in China, Indochina, and Greece as the world itself began dividing into East and West. In that sundered world, the United States and the USSR waged a new war, cold but always potentially atomic.

Thomas B. Allen

British Prime Minister Winston Churchill (left), U.S. President Harry Truman, and Soviet Premier Joseph Stalin (right) discussed the postwar world at Potsdam, Germany, in the summer of 1945.

THE SEARCH FOR A NEW STABILITY

The thought "never again" doubtless rose in legion minds as Japan surrendered on the deck of the USS *Missouri* on Sept. 2, 1945. The loss of life, destruction of humane society, and devastation of the material infrastructure of civilization brought by the Second World War seemed incalculable. Never again, most agreed, should the world's nations allow renegade dictatorships to disrupt peace. Never again, thought some, should the world populations make such sacrifices for social and economic structures that seemingly benefited only the few. Not much longer, vowed still more, would the governed masses of the world let themselves be dragged into the battles of their pale masters to serve the cause of democracy while not experiencing it themselves.

Restoring Order to a Broken World

The world was broken, and the question was how to reassemble it. Though world leaders spoke of restoring order, visions differed, as did the recipes proposed. Victorious Britain and the United States spoke of "making the world safe for democracy," yet were allied

In the decades immediately following the conclusion of World War II, major wars were fought in the divided nations of Korea, right, and Vietnam, above. With the Cold War at its height, the United States became involved militarily in both.

CAUTION
THIS IS THE M.L.R.
THE REDS DIRECT
TRAFFIC BEYOND
THIS POINT.
要注意
此地点 으로부러 前方은
共產軍 抵抗線 으로
直接通하는 通路 입니다

On board the USS "Missouri," above, in Tokyo Bay on Sept. 2, 1945, Japan formally surrendered, ending World War II. In London's Westminster Abbey on June 2, 1953, Elizabeth II, below, was crowned queen of the United Kingdom of Great Britain and Northern Ireland. Both events marked the beginnings of new eras.

with Joseph Stalin's totalitarianism in the Soviet Union. American talk of capitalist free trade and self-determination conflicted not only with Stalin's prediction of a Communist world revolution but also with British dreams of a restored empire and Commonwealth preferences.

Convinced that collective security required a better world forum than the failed League of Nations, the victorious powers created a United Nations (UN). Membership was open to all "peace-loving nations"—initially those on the winning side of the war. Soon election of additional participants became an issue on which Russians and Anglo-Americans sharply disagreed. The Communists viewed the UN as one more instrument by which the capitalist West could impose its formulas on the rest of the world. As a counter, the Muscovites employed their veto power within the UN's

Security Council. The conflict was all part of what came to be called the Cold War— "cold," because it supposedly did not involve the hot explosions of bombs and bullets between major global powers (though smaller conflicts often occurred), but a war, nevertheless, in that it involved a bitter struggle between nations with conflicting political, economic, and social systems.

Perhaps the Cold War began as early as the Russian Revolution of 1917 and the subsequent Anglo-American-Japanese intervention in the Russian civil war. According to this view, the World War II alliance against Hitler was merely an interruption dictated by necessity in the ongoing struggle between capitalism and Communism. Others point to the incompatibility of the dictatorship of Stalin with the democratic precepts of the West, the distrust engendered in

Moscow by the Westerners' failure to include the USSR in the negotiations at Munich in 1938, the apparent willingness of the West to turn Hitler against the Soviets, and the long delay in the establishment of a second front in Europe during the war. Certainly, too, national aspirations and misunderstandings of each side's motivations, fears, and attitudes played major roles.

Europe—The Focus of a New Cold War

Though the Cold War in time became global, the focal point of the struggle initially was Europe. The West—essentially the United States and a much weaker Great Britain and France—understood Stalin's desire for security for his union. No vigorous opposition was raised to his turning neighboring states such as Romania, Bulgaria, and Hungary into subservient satellites; scarcely lip service was given the notion that Estonia, Latvia, and Lithuania—Baltic states annexed by the USSR during the war—should regain their independence. But Soviet pressures on Poland, Czechoslovakia, and Germany were another matter.

Distrustful of a Germany that twice had attacked their homeland in less than a half century, the Soviet leaders favored that country's partition. They quickly achieved cession of a large chunk of East Prussia to Polish administration, while Poland was forced to cede land to the USSR. But the United States and Britain soon backed away from German dismemberment. It would mean chaos in the center of Europe and would harm the mercantile economies of Western Europe. They pressed instead for a centralized economic administration to unite the economies of the several occupation zones of Germany. The Soviets disagreed. In response, the United States, Britain, and eventually France merged their zones economically and gave the unified zone a new currency. Confrontation with the Soviets continued, resulting in a yearlong Soviet blockage of land connections from the west through East Germany to Berlin and an Allied airlift to supply Berlin. In 1949 the three Allied zones of occupation formed the Federal Republic of Germany, and the Soviet zone became the German Democratic Republic. Thus, reciprocal actions intensified Cold War tensions and ensured that the "Iron Curtain" dividing Europe, described by Sir Winston Churchill in 1946, would remain in place.

Other developments confirmed hostility between East and West. Soviet spies knew that, although the British and Americans had proposed UN jurisdiction over atomic energy, in fact, they were maneuvering to control all major sources of uranium fuel. Not wishing to be blackmailed by the West's sole possession of atomic weapons, Stalin launched a major effort to produce them in his own

After the Soviet Union had begun to blockade the land routes into the divided city of Berlin in June 1948, the Western Allies began the largest airlift in U.S. history, photos at right. Some 1.5 million tons of food, fuel, and other supplies were delivered before the Soviets lifted the blockade on May 12, 1949.

In one of the most important international actions of the second half of the 20th century, the foundation of the North Atlantic Treaty Organization (NATO) was laid on April 4, 1949, when the North Atlantic Treaty was signed in Washington, DC (*photo above*). The signatories of the treaty were the United States, Canada, Britain, France, Italy, Belgium, the Netherlands, Luxembourg, Norway, Denmark, Iceland, and Portugal.

NATO arose out of the developments of the four years since the end of World War II. Events had falsified the hope that the United States, Britain, and the Soviet Union could continue to work in harmony, as they more or less had done during the war, and that the United Nations would be competent to deal with whatever issues came up. Fissures in the alliance had appeared at the Yalta and Potsdam conferences in 1945, especially in regard to the future of Poland. The Soviet Union—which in 1940 had annexed the independent Baltic nations of Estonia, Latvia, and Lithuania—after the end of the war quickly took under its control almost the whole of Eastern Europe, installing Communist regimes and reshaping these nations' economies and social structures in conformity with Soviet ideology. As Britain's Winston Churchill said in 1946, "From Stettin in the Baltic to Trieste in the Adriatic, an iron curtain has descended across the Continent." In 1947 the United States took over financial support of endangered Greece and Turkey from Britain, and also launched the vast and generous Marshall Plan for economic aid to Europe.

The last straw was the Communist takeover in Czechoslovakia in 1948. This provided the immediate impulse for the creation of NATO. The North Atlantic Treaty was a relatively short and simple document of 14 articles. Central was Article 5, specifically based on "the right of individual or collective self-defense" recognized in Article 51 of the UN Charter. The NATO states agreed that an armed attack against one or more of them in Europe or North America would be considered an attack against them all. The essential point, the core of NATO, was the U.S. commitment to defend the nations of Western Europe against any such attack—this was an unprecedented innovation in U.S. foreign policy.

Article 2, a Canadian contribution, suggested broader aims in fostering economic cooperation and other matters, but such functions later were taken over by other European institutions. Article 9 envisaged the setting up of a council and "such subsidiary bodies as may be necessary"; but it was the alarm caused by the North Korean aggression against South Korea that transformed the alliance treaty by 1952 into a permanent international organization, with a civil and a military side, and with substantial armed forces assigned to it. The secretary-general is chairman of the North Atlantic Council, which may meet on several levels. The Supreme Allied Commander, Europe (SACEUR) is responsible in the European sector for military planning and command in war. The SACEUR invariably has been a high-ranking U.S. general. The secretary-general's post rotates among member-states other than the United States. The NATO secretariat originally was housed at the Palais de Chaillot in Paris, and military headquarters were at Fontainebleau.

Greece and Turkey joined NATO in 1952, West Germany in 1955. (Reunited Germany was a member by 1991.) It was a severe setback when France in 1966, under Charles de Gaulle, withdrew from all active military cooperation. NATO headquarters, both civil and military, were moved to Belgium. Spain joined NATO in 1982. In the early 1990s, France began increasing its role in NATO, and in late 1995 it rejoined the military committee.

The dissolution of the Soviet Union in 1991 raised difficult questions about NATO's purpose. There was a shift to peacekeeping activities, in Bosnia-Herzegovina and, later, in Kosovo. But the assurance of security made NATO membership a desirable benefit for states recently liberated from Communism. A dozen sought membership. In April 1998 the U.S. Senate approved NATO membership for Poland, Hungary, and the Czech Republic, and they became members in March 1999.

Arthur Campbell Turner

After becoming head of a new Yugoslav coalition government in 1945, Tito (Josip Broz), above, ruled Yugoslavia, a union of six constituent republics and two regions, with absolute authority and his own brand of Communism until his death in 1980.

country. Soviet explosion of a test bomb in 1949 surprised the West.

Dismayed by pressures placed on Turkey by the Soviets and by the progress of Communist rebels in Greece, in 1947, U.S. President Harry Truman had announced his intention to send military goods to countries whose freedom appeared endangered. The plan, which became known as the Truman Doctrine, was an initial step in the development of a policy of containment of Soviet and Communist expansion. A few months later, under the leadership of U.S. Secretary of State George C. Marshall, the United States announced a major economic-rehabilitation program for Europe. Though such states as Poland and Czechoslovakia expressed interest in participation, Stalin forbade it. He saw the Marshall Plan as a challenge to his own economic hegemony in Eastern Europe. In response, Stalin constructed a Council for Mutual Economic Assistance (COMECON), radically altering the trade patterns of seven of the Eastern European states and linking them to Soviet economic preferences. Yugoslavia, where Marshal Tito exercised independent leadership, was not included and was pressured by the new organization.

The Soviets also formed a Communist Information Bureau to coordinate the Com-

Winston Churchill was accompanied by U.S. President Harry Truman (shown waving his hat) as he left Westminster College in Fulton, MO, on March 5, 1946. The British leader just had warned the world that "from Stettin in the Baltic to Trieste in the Adriatic, an iron curtain has descended across the Continent."

munist parties in Europe and strengthen Soviet direction of them. Most leaders in the satellite states who put the interests of their own countries ahead of those Stalin viewed as properly the Communist—i.e., Soviet—cause were replaced by figures loyal to Moscow. In Czechoslovakia, President Eduard Benes defended democracy until Communists seized control of the nation in February 1948.

At the time, France, Britain, and the three Low Countries—Belgium, Luxembourg, and the Netherlands—were considering a defense accord. Galvanized by recognition that Russian control of Eastern Europe, with the exception of Greece and Yugoslavia, was complete, they created the Western European Union. Thanks to a delicate American suggestion, the language of the agreement was not aimed simply against the former enemy, Germany. Rather, it spoke of collective self-defense and did not name a specific enemy. That action effectively turned the pact from a precaution against Germany to a defense against the USSR.

West European leaders recognized that their promises of mutual aid did not mean much against the might of the Soviet army. What was needed was the support of the industry, technology, and troops of the United States. Despite isolationist voices, U.S. leaders were aware of the need to bolster Europe against the Soviets once the Europeans themselves had agreed to work together. Moreover, if the United States were to plan a defense against the USSR, stepping-stones into Europe were needed. Complex negotiation brought the formation of the North Atlantic Treaty Organization (NATO) on April 4, 1949, by the United States, Canada, and ten European countries (*see* page 122). Others would join later. Though American originators of the policy of containment had contemplated firm but flexible resistance to Soviet probes while developing the economic and political strengths of the West, policy implementation became focused on military responses. The growing network of allied military bases surrounding the Soviet Union did not miss Stalin's attention, and his military preparations escalated. Europe was divided, an arms race was under way, and each side in the Cold War sought allies.

The March toward Independence

There were many possibilities, for the configuration of the world body politic was changing. A process of decolonization that began as a trickle in 1946 became a torrent; between the end of World War II and 1970, about 70 new states appeared. Decolonization was not welcomed by the colonial powers. But they found themselves faced either with the expensive choice of suppressing growing nationalist movements or of working with them to guide them to an independence that might maintain, in some cases, close economic and even cultural ties with the mother country. The travails of war and reconstruction had forced Britain, France, Belgium, and the Netherlands to focus on domestic issues and had weakened their influence in their colonies. Moreover, they had encouraged colonial nationalist movements to resist German and Japanese seizure of those lands. Now these nationalist movements could not be extinguished, and their leaders aspired to total independence. The war effort had been justified in terms of democratic beliefs and the concepts of freedom. The colonial powers' right to rule thus was challenged ideologically, not only in the eyes of the subject peoples but also at home. For the Communists, who had provided leaders for resistance movements both in Europe and the colonies during the war, imperialism was an extreme example of capitalist exploitation. Nationalist leaders in the

colonies found this an attractive stance and made friends with their enemy's enemy. In time, however, countries such as Egypt found the Soviet embrace to be as dangerous to their hopes of true independence as the paternalism and economic domination of the colonial powers.

The withdrawal of Britain from India in 1947 and the birth of the states of India and Pakistan demonstrated how significantly the role of Britain in the world had changed. The rivalry between Hindu and Muslim elements that forced the creation of two states out of what had been one colony revealed also the strength of religious and cultural pas-

On Aug. 15, 1947, the British Crown Colony of India became the independent nations of India and Pakistan. Jawaharlal Nehru (at left in photo at right) became India's first prime minister; Muhammad Ali Jinnah (at right in photo at right) was appointed governor-general of Pakistan. Gamal Abdel Nasser, above, governed Egypt from the overthrow of King Farouk in 1952 until his death in September 1970.

The Birth of Israel

On Nov. 29, 1947, the United Nations General Assembly passed the partition resolution dividing the British mandate of Palestine into a Jewish state; an Arab state; and an international enclave including Jerusalem, Bethlehem, and the surrounding areas. The UN partition resolution was welcomed by Palestine's Jewish community with mass euphoria. In the early hours of November 30, crowds of Jewish youth erupted into the streets celebrating the long-awaited event, fraternizing with the British soldiers who only yesterday were the enemy. It seemed that a centuries-old dream was about to be realized; that the Zionist goal finally was achieved. Six months later, on May 14, 1948, Israel declared independence, and the Jewish state was established. The last of the British subsequently left Palestine (*photo above*).

However, Palestine's Arab community was plunged into despair. To most it seemed that the country was stolen away by the Jewish minority. The Arabs, too, massed in the streets on November 30, but in silent protest demonstrations. Many wore black armbands to mark what they called the *Nakba*, or "disaster." Soon these protests became violent, as Arab youths stoned Jewish shops, and the Jews in turn retaliated.

From the heights of Mount Scopus in Jerusalem, an observer could peer down into the city and see the crowds of Jews and Arabs approaching each other, leading to an almost inevitable violent clash. Indeed, within hours of the UN announcement, Palestine's Jewish and Arab communities were engulfed in a civil war that became part of the Arab war against Israel following its declaration of independence on May 14. This was the first Arab-Israel war—according to Israel, its War of Independence.

The partition resolution of the UN and Israel's declaration of independence precipitated a prolonged conflict, really a series of wars between Israel and its neighbors that opposed establishment of a Jewish state in what they considered an Arab land. When the partition resolution was passed, the Arabs constituted about two thirds of the population, and the Jews, one third. By the time the first Arab-Israel war ended in 1949, only one fifth of the original Arab population remained in Israel-held territory. More than 700,000 fled to the neighboring countries.

Israel has believed that the return of the refugees would create a threat to its security and undermine the Jewish character of the state. Furthermore, the Israeli government has charged that the refugees were encouraged to leave by their own leaders, although some Israeli scholars refuted this charge in the 1990s. Most property left by the refugees in 1948 was absorbed, providing land for agriculture, homes for Jewish refugees, and other property for the country's economic development.

The Arabs have insisted on the refugees' "right of return" or on payment of compensation for property left in Israel, according to resolutions passed by the UN. They maintain that the refugees were driven from their homes by Israel's armed forces. As the 1990s were drawing to an end, the fate of the refugees remained one of the most difficult issues in the peace negotiations between Israel and the Palestinians. Discussion of their future was deferred to the impending final status negotiations between the two parties.

Don Peretz

sions that would become increasingly divisive in the coming decades. Nowhere were these passions more militant than in the Near East.

Zionist hope for a Jewish homeland in Palestine had gained support from the British Balfour Declaration of 1917. Yet when the British assumed the League of Nations mandate for Palestine after World War I, they limited Jewish immigration in response to Arab protests. The Arabs had no desire to see foreigners settle on their soil and claim partition of lands Arabs had tilled so long. The issue became acute following World War II, for the Holocaust seemingly had demonstrated the need for a Jewish safe haven and national state. Britain placed the matter before the new United Nations, which in 1947 voted to partition Palestine into Jewish and Arab sectors, with Jerusalem under international control. The following year, Jewish leaders, with financial and political backing from the United States, proclaimed the state of Israel (*see* page 126). This was more than neighboring Arab states could tolerate. They attacked and were defeated—in part because of rivalries among their own leadership and partly because the Israelis were better equipped, organized, and led. Israel increased its size by nearly half and made West Jerusalem its capital. Jordan, meanwhile, annexed the West Bank of the Jordan River and took control of East Jerusalem. The stage was set for more conflicts that ensued periodically over the following years. The USSR, which initially had backed the formation of Israel, turned to aiding the Arab cause, while the United States became the chief supporter of Israel. Thus the Cold War came to include a region not only rent by nationalistic and religious rivalries but also containing the world's largest reserves of crude oil.

A Hot War

It was in Asia that the Cold War became hot. Following World War II, the peninsula of Korea had been partitioned into Soviet and American occupation zones. Negotiations for reunification failed, separate states evolved, and the United States and the USSR

removed their troops from each country. Interpreting that withdrawal as a lack of U.S. interest and confident that South Koreans would rise to back an invasion, North Korea, with Stalin's permission, sent its forces into South Korea on June 25, 1950. The South Koreans resisted, and the United States hastily marshaled an armed UN response. By October, UN forces were approaching the border of North Korea with China. Suddenly, Chinese troops appeared and drove UN forces south to the 38th parallel, the original dividing line between the two Koreas. Deadlock ensued; diplomatic negotiations resumed and stalled. In 1953 an armistice was signed and a demilitarized buffer zone created in the region of the 38th parallel. The two Koreas went their separate ways: The South developed a powerful capitalist economy but not a true democracy; the

(Continued on page 130.)

A new currency, right, was introduced in China in 1949 after the Communists took control of the mainland and established the People's Republic of China.

When World War II ended, Korea—which had been part of the Japanese Empire since 1910—became a liberated nation under joint U.S.-Soviet occupation. The dividing line between the occupation forces was the 38th parallel, which ran roughly across the middle of the peninsula. The occupation created two nations: North Korea—the Democratic People's Republic of Korea, a Soviet-installed Communist regime; and South Korea—the U.S.-backed Republic of Korea. The occupation officially ended in 1949, when U.S. and Soviet troops withdrew. But North Korea remained a Communist dictatorship and a well-armed threat to South Korea.

By then, the U.S.-Soviet Cold War had begun. U.S. interests focused on confrontations in Germany and concern over China, where a civil war had ended with the Communists victorious and allied with the Soviet Union. U.S. policy in Asia, as defined by Secretary of State Dean Acheson in January 1950, put South Korea outside the U.S. defensive perimeter in the Far East. So when North Korea invaded South Korea on June 25, 1950, the possibility of U.S. intervention was not clear.

On June 27, however, as the North Korean invaders poured down the peninsula, President Harry S. Truman ordered U.S. air and sea support of South Korean defenders, and the United Nations Security Council, which the Soviet Union was boycotting, called on member nations to give aid. Within days, North Korean troops took Seoul, the South Korean capital, and on June 30, Truman committed U.S. ground troops to Korea (*photo above*). When a reporter asked if this could be called a UN "police action," Truman agreed. The term would haunt Truman through what would be a long and bloody war.

Joining the United States in an unprecedented UN military commitment were 23 other nations, 15 of which contributed combat forces; the others provided noncombatant medical units. U.S. officials viewed the invasion as inspired by the Soviet Union, possibly to deflect Western attention from Europe. In fact, the invasion surprised the Soviets as much as the Americans. Soviet leader Joseph Stalin gave his tacit approval, sending supplies, advisers, and MiG pilots.

The North Koreans overwhelmed the South Korean army, quickly taking Seoul's port of Inchon. Ill-equipped American troops, rushed to Korea from Japan, established a beachhead at Pusan, on the southeastern tip of the peninsula. While the Pusan defenders fought to hold the beachhead until reinforcements arrived, U.S. Army Gen. Douglas MacArthur, the supreme commander of UN forces in Korea, planned a bold outflanking move: an amphibious landing at Inchon, on the west coast. The landing liberated Seoul and severed North Korean supply lines. At the same time, UN troops broke out of Pusan, and a drive began to force the North Koreans back to the 38th parallel.

MacArthur crossed the 38th parallel to capture the North Korean capital of Pyongyang in October and then, challenging Washington limits on the war, authorized a drive to the Yalu River, the North Korean–Chinese border. In a meeting with President Truman on Wake Island, MacArthur dismissed the possibility of Chinese intervention and said that UN troops could be withdrawn from Korea as early as Christmas. But as frontline UN troops neared the border, they found themselves fighting Chinese soldiers (*photo, page 129*). MacArthur's intelligence officers shrugged off the reports, unaware that 300,000 Chinese were being deployed in North Korea. The Chinese, in "human wave" attacks, inflicted huge numbers of casualties.

On November 27, in freezing cold, nearly 100,000 Chinese attacked the 1st Marine Division at the Chosin Reservoir. More than 40,000 U.S. Marines and soldiers, in an epic fighting withdrawal, reached the port of Hungnam, where they were evacuated. The Communist troops retook Pyongyang and surged southward, occupying Seoul in January 1951. The UN forces reorganized and launched an offensive in February; they took Seoul in March, drove the Chinese from South Korea, and advanced to a line just north of the 38th parallel.

The unforeseen Chinese intervention had put President Truman on a collision course with General MacArthur. In what Truman saw as a reckless crusade for a war with China, MacArthur continually ignored orders from Washington. On April 11, Truman—acting as commander in chief and backed by his military advisers—relieved MacArthur for failing to "give his wholehearted support" to U.S. policy.

Succeeding MacArthur was Lt. Gen. Matthew B. Ridgway.

Fighting would go on for two more years, both on the ground and in the air, with U.S. airmen unaware that they sometimes were fighting Soviet pilots in North Korean MiGs. The static warfare mostly involved artillery duels along the 38th parallel and fierce infantry battles. The fighting did little to change the war, but the battles—Heartbreak Ridge, Pork Chop Hill, T-Bone, Old Baldy—would reverberate in military history.

Negotiations to end the war deadlocked on two issues: prisoners and an armistice border. The Communists opposed "voluntary repatriation," a UN proposal to allow an estimated 171,000 Chinese and North Korean prisoners to decide whether they wanted to go home. The death of Soviet leader Joseph Stalin on March 5, 1953, helped to end the stalemate. Stalin may have goaded the Chinese into intervening, according to documents released after the end of the Cold War. Stalin's successor, Georgi M. Malenkov, swiftly made conciliatory gestures toward the new administration of U.S. President Dwight D. Eisenhower. Eisenhower had used "I shall go to Korea" as a campaign slogan, implying that he would end the unpopular war.

In June 1953 negotiators reached agreement on the prisoner issue and on a border that gave South Korea some territory north of the 38th parallel. But South Korean President Syngman Rhee balked, saying his troops would not honor a truce. The Communists, in turn, responded with an offensive that mauled South Korean army units. After this demonstration of North Korea's might, President Rhee relented. On July 27 at Panmunjom, just south of the 38th parallel, generals from both sides signed an armistice. The war ended; through the rest of the 20th century, however, the peninsula would be a crisis point where North Korea and South Korea still confronted each other.

Military casualties totaled an estimated 2.4 million, with 2 million more civilians killed or wounded on both sides. U.S. casualties totaled 36,916 dead and 103,284 wounded; 415,000 South Korean soldiers were killed and 429,000 wounded. The British Commonwealth—which sent troops from Britain, Canada, Australia, and New Zealand—lost 1,263 killed and 7,000 wounded. About 1,800 troops were killed from the other UN countries: Belgium, Colombia, Ethiopia, France, Greece, Luxembourg, the Netherlands, the Philippines, South Africa, Thailand, and Turkey.

Thomas B. Allen

Members of the Red Guard carried signs proclaiming the thoughts of Mao Zedong, above, as China underwent a Cultural Revolution—an attempt by Mao to remove his enemies from the Chinese Communist Party—in the latter years of the 1960s. In May 1967, Nigeria's eastern region seceded as the Republic of Biafra, below; a 30-month civil war—with Biafra suffering widespread starvation—followed.

was streamlined. Yet some of Mao's efforts proved counter-productive even as they convulsed the country. Such was the case for the "Great Leap Forward," undertaken in the late 1950s to modernize agriculture and industry through the development of production brigades in "people's communes." Even more disastrous was the Cultural Revolution (c. 1966–69), which reasserted Mao's revolutionary power but destroyed the educational and economic systems and unleashed political purges.

Asia and Africa

Elsewhere in Asia, remarkable change also came to pass. Japan, under U.S. occupation, promulgated a new constitution in 1946 that went into effect in 1947. The new constitution ended divine-right rule, established parliamentary government, extended the franchise to women, and renounced war. Local self-government, as compared to centralized national direction, was encouraged. The

(Continued from page 127.)

North remained a Communist state with limited economic development. UN troops patrolled the demilitarized zone, and U.S. troops continued to be stationed in South Korea and Japan (*see* page 128).

The role of the People's Republic of China in the Korean War underlined the significance of events in that country for the entire world. Since 1927, nationalist and Communist warlords had vied for control in China. They reluctantly cooperated against Japanese invaders but resumed their own civil war in 1945. By fall 1949, Communist troops under the leadership of Mao Zedong had defeated the nationalists under Chiang Kai-shek; the latter withdrew to Taiwan. Mao proceeded to mobilize his country, determined that it should take its place among the leaders of the globe and that no dissent should encumber his efforts to modernize. By 1960, China had become one of the top ten industrial powers in the world. In 1964 it tested an atomic bomb; three years later, it exploded a hydrogen weapon. The Chinese way of life was transformed: Industrialization was forwarded; women were given new status; and the written language

Japan's Post—World War II Economic Rise

Early in the 1900s, Japan's economic emergence still was regarded as "late development," somewhere on the time line behind Britain, the United States, and Germany. As has been pointed out by Columbia University economist James Nakamura, however, Japan's performance throughout the 20th century was unmatched. Except for a "takeoff" period (1870–1913) and during the time of the Pacific wars (1937–45), progress was more rapid for Japan than for the leading nations, including the United States.

Mobilization for, and engagement in, wars in the late 1930s and early 1940s resulted in a doubling of the output of industry, but tended to hide what the Japanese called the "dual structure." Modern industry was grafted on a semideveloped agrarian sector, and the standard of living of ordinary Japanese did not rise proportionately. Moreover, the effects of World War II destroyed half of the nation's industrial capacity. Millions of military personnel and urban civilians were killed, and an equal number were displaced from burned-out cities.

Yet the skeleton of modern industry survived; a skilled labor force reappeared. Although by century's end, many Japanese had reservations about continuing U.S.-Japan security arrangements, the majority recalled the American-led occupation as benign. Massive assistance, especially early provision of food, staved off collapse and was followed by one of the first applications of technical assistance. In the 1950s rebuilt plants were only ten years old or younger and boasted of up-to-date technology.

In this same decade, there was a remarkable appearance of free-enterprise systems throughout the world. In fact, these were mixed economies with various degrees of public control matched with private sectors. Among them, Japan's economy was unique in its record of aggregate growth.

Indeed, in the 1960s economic growth became in practice the dominant Japanese religion. Conservative leaders pledged that the nation's gross national product (GNP) would double in a decade, and citizens followed economic statistics as closely as sports scores. The actual record was nearly unbelievable: GNP (in current prices) almost doubled in five years (1955–60); more than doubled again in the next five years (1960–65); and then rose another 2.5 times in the five years following (1965–70). In this last period, the annual rate of growth (in real terms) averaged 12.1%.

By 1971, Japan had the world's third-largest GNP after those of the United States and the USSR, with income per capita at about $2,000. These results were products of conscious planning: Japan was the originator of supply-side economics. A second factor was the extraordinary capacity of the Japanese to save. Savings were plowed back into capital goods and more growth.

In the 1970s the Japanese themselves began to use advice from the Club of Rome Report, "The Limits to Growth." GNP figures were recognized as gross amounts, and per-capita income was only an average. Neither figure spoke to the basic issue of equitable distribution. As a matter of fact, the share of income accruing to labor had declined in the preceding two decades (1950–70). There was also a relatively low expenditure on social infrastructure.

Growth continued throughout the 1980s, and no one could have predicted that by the end of the century, Japan would be regarded as a carrier of the "Asian flu," an economic downturn that infected world markets.

Ardath W. Burks

Cold War and the Korean conflict stimulated the economy. The United States, eager for additional support, aided reconstruction of Japan's damaged productive capacity. Starting from scratch proved beneficial, as new technologies could be introduced. Funds devoted in earlier decades to military purposes were turned to industrial research and production. During the 1950s, Japan's economy grew at a rate of 10% per year; industrial production increased at an annual rate of 14%. Labor shortages stimulated pioneering use of advanced technology that gradually enabled Japan to win an important segment of the world's commerce for its own factories. As the American occupation ended in 1952, the close relationship between the United States and Japan—the Japanese even adopted baseball as a popular sport—could only perturb the Soviets and increase Cold War tensions (*see* page 131).

Decolonization first affected the Middle East and Asia. In some nations it was achieved peacefully. In others, as in Vietnam and Indonesia, bitter fighting took place. By the 1960s, it was Africa's turn (*see* page 134). All of that continent—save for Egypt, Liberia, and Ethiopia—was European-controlled in 1950. North Africa began the drive for independence; 1960 saw many states south of the Sahara achieve theirs. Between 1960 and 1970, 32 new African countries were born, and still more regions were pressing for independence. Many of the new states, for whatever reasons—including the performance of the colonial powers—lacked infrastructure, significant educated populations, understanding of democratic processes, and good leadership. Some harbored destructive tribal rivalries, traditions endorsing rapid population growth, and agriculture-based value systems that did not support fiscal and industrial development. Though Africa as a whole was once agriculturally self-sufficient, by 1964 it had to import food.

Resentment of colonial domination spurred the independence movement. It garnered support, often more verbal than physical, from the USSR. Americans, champions of self-determination, were caught between

On Nov. 11, 1965, Prime Minister Ian Smith's white-minority government unilaterally declared Rhodesia independent of Great Britain. The announcement caused international protest. Following seven years of guerrilla conflict in the 1970s, Rhodesia became the independent nation of Zimbabwe, with black-majority rule, in 1980.

In January 1959, Fidel Castro, above, led a revolt against Cuban dictator Fulgencio Batista. Castro subsequently formed a Communist government and became a Soviet ally. María Eva Duarte de Perón, left, the wife of Argentina's President Juan Perón, was a minister without portfolio and played a major role in Argentine affairs, including managing organized labor, in the late 1940s and early 1950s.

Latin America

South American states were already independent, though their economic and often political dependence upon the "colossus of the North," the United States, was everywhere evident. In 1948 the Organization of American States (OAS) was established under the United Nations Charter as a comprehensive regional security system. In the early 1960s, Washington began to show more concern for the development of the region. Aid was forthcoming through President John Kennedy's newly inaugurated Alliance for Progress, and industrial-growth rates moved upward. But the problems of a high birthrate, deep-rooted poverty, and great gaps between rich and poor persisted. The Soviet Union found opportunity to meddle, especially after Fidel Castro staged his successful revolution in Cuba in 1959 and elected to move close to the Communist side in the Cold War. The USSR's attempt to install missiles in Cuba, so near U.S. shores, in 1962 nearly provoked a nuclear war. Elsewhere in Latin America, left-wing regimes and politicians were sabotaged by groups

their own tradition and the need to retain the loyalty of colonialist NATO allies. Reluctant to be submerged in drawn-out guerrilla wars such as France experienced in Algeria, bereft of strong backing from across the Atlantic, and subject to criticism, the European capitals gave in to the independence movement. The transition of power to local authorities sometimes went smoothly; often it was messy indeed. Nowhere was this more true than in the Belgian Congo, which became the Republic of the Congo in 1960, when the UN had to intervene, and the possibility of a major Soviet-U.S. confrontation as a result of a government power struggle in the new nation loomed.

(Continued on page 136.)

There was something extraordinary and almost inexplicable in the fact that the decolonization of Africa—an enormous historical change affecting most of a continent nearly three times larger than Europe—occurred almost entirely in one year, 1960. Most of the areas concerned had been under French control to one degree or another, but the largest colony to become independent that year was Belgian; one large British colony and one British protectorate also gained independence in 1960.

Historical developments, of course, are never entirely tidy, and some areas of Africa were already independent by 1960, while for other areas the completion of a seemingly irresistible historical process would take a few more years or even decades. The southern littoral of the Mediterranean, from the Nile delta to the Strait of Gibraltar, was almost all independent before 1960. Egypt had been nominally independent since 1922, but British troops were stationed on its soil until 1956. In the Maghreb—Arabic for "the West"—former French protectorates Morocco and Tunisia had been free since 1956. Libya, an Italian colony before Italy's defeat in World War II, had been independent since 1951, although British troops remained until 1966. Algeria, however, was an exception; technically a part of metropolitan France, it had been involved in severe civil strife since 1954. South of Egypt, The Sudan—a former Anglo-Egyptian condominium—had been independent since 1956.

Of the 17 states admitted to United Nations (UN) membership in 1960, all except Cyprus were newly independent African countries. Prime Minister Harold Macmillan of Great Britain, addressing the South African Parliament on Feb. 3, 1960, declared, "The wind of change is blowing through the continent," and indeed it blew with hurricane force all that year. The areas for which independence arrived in 1960 were those south of the Mediterranean shore down to the northern edge of the British federation of the two Rhodesias and Nyasaland, but not including that federation or the areas in East Africa possessing white minorities. The Union of South Africa was a unique case—an independent state ruled by a white minority. Meanwhile, the elegant French solution to the colonial question—which was adopted in 1958 when the French Union was replaced by the French Community and which offered to colonies autonomy, but with continuing parliamentary and policy links to Paris—totally disintegrated in the course of 1960, with President Charles de Gaulle acquiescing gracefully.

On Jan. 1, 1960, the French-held UN trust territory of Cameroon (French Cameroons) received its independence, as did Togo (French Togoland), whose status had been the same, on April 27. The Italian-held trust territory of Somalia (Somaliland) became independent on July 1, joining the former British Somaliland Protectorate, which had become independent on June 26. On June 30 the Belgian Congo, the largest political unit in Africa, became independent and immediately relapsed into a complicated civil war. Four autonomous members of the French Community became independent in the early days of August: Dahomey, Niger, Upper Volta, and Ivory Coast. Becoming independent, but signing treaties for future cooperation with France, were the Malagasy Republic (also known as Madagascar) on June 26, and, in the middle of August, Chad, the Central African Republic (formerly Ubangi-Shari), the Republic of Congo, and Gabon. August 20 saw the emergence of Senegal and September 22 that of the Republic of Mali (Soudan). Mauritania followed on November 28. The largest remaining British colony, Nigeria, became independent on October 1.

What remained for Africa was the completion of decolonization, a process that already largely had been carried out at breakneck speed. France abandoned its 1 million white settlers in Algeria under the 1962 Evian agreement. Sierra Leone emerged from British rule in 1961, as did Uganda in 1962 and Kenya in 1963. Tanganyika (1961) joined with Zanzibar to become Tanzania (1964). In 1964, Northern Rhodesia became independent as Zambia, and Nyasaland as Malawi. Settler-ruled Southern Rhodesia proclaimed its independence in 1965 but became black-ruled Zimbabwe in

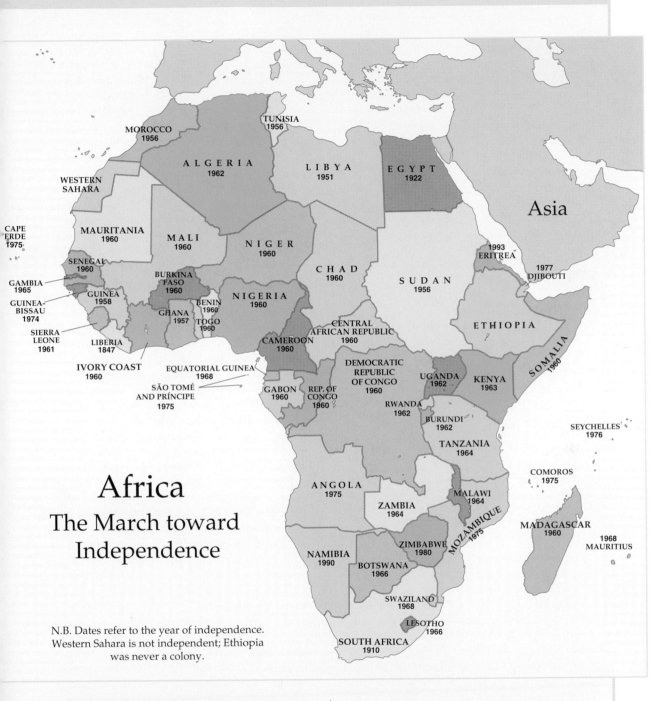

Africa
The March toward Independence

MOROCCO 1956
TUNISIA 1956
WESTERN SAHARA
ALGERIA 1962
LIBYA 1951
EGYPT 1922
Asia
CAPE VERDE 1975
MAURITANIA 1960
MALI 1960
NIGER 1960
1993 ERITREA
1977 DJIBOUTI
SENEGAL 1960
GAMBIA 1965
BURKINA FASO 1960
CHAD 1960
SUDAN 1956
GUINEA 1958
GUINEA-BISSAU 1974
GHANA 1957
BENIN 1960
NIGERIA 1960
TOGO 1960
SIERRA LEONE 1961
LIBERIA 1847
CENTRAL AFRICAN REPUBLIC 1960
ETHIOPIA
IVORY COAST 1960
CAMEROON 1960
EQUATORIAL GUINEA 1968
DEMOCRATIC REPUBLIC OF CONGO 1960
UGANDA 1962
KENYA 1963
SOMALIA 1960
SÃO TOMÉ AND PRÍNCIPE 1975
GABON 1960
REP. OF CONGO 1960
RWANDA 1962
BURUNDI 1962
SEYCHELLES 1976
TANZANIA 1964
COMOROS 1975
ANGOLA 1975
MALAWI 1964
ZAMBIA 1964
MOZAMBIQUE 1975
MADAGASCAR 1960
1968 MAURITIUS
NAMIBIA 1990
ZIMBABWE 1980
BOTSWANA 1966
SWAZILAND 1968
LESOTHO 1966
SOUTH AFRICA 1910

N.B. Dates refer to the year of independence.
Western Sahara is not independent; Ethiopia
was never a colony.

1980. Portugal hung onto its two great colonies of Angola and Mozambique until 1975. South Africa ceased to be ruled by the white 25% of its population only in 1994.

Africa was the great focus of the world's attention in 1960 and 1961. This interest progressively ebbed as independent Africa succumbed in some places to one-party systems, brutal tyrannies, frontier disputes, famines, wholesale massacres, and seemingly endless civil wars.

Arthur Campbell Turner

(Continued from page 133.)

that, according to revelations from decades later, often were linked to Washington.

Within largely Roman Catholic Latin America, members of that church took an active part on both sides of key issues. Their involvement reflected the new vitality infused in the church by Pope John XXIII. It was he who launched a call for an updating of the teachings and discipline of the church, opening it to the "winds of change." His greatest initiative was the summoning of the first ecumenical council of the Roman Catholic Church since 1870. Known as Vatican II, the council, which ran from 1962 to 1965, endorsed many specific reforms. These included use of the vernacular in parts of the Mass, revision of the calendar of saints,

Amid a storybook setting, Hollywood actress Grace Kelly married Prince Rainier III of Monaco in separate civil and religious ceremonies in Monaco in April 1956.

renunciation of former declarations assigning continuing responsibility to Jews for the death of Jesus Christ, and promotion of collegiality among bishops in the governance of the church. Even more significant was the sense of acceptance of new approaches and growth of new energies within the church. Conservative opposition to some of these changes did develop, and succeeding years would be spent redefining the extent of the reforms of Vatican II. Pope John and his successors further emphasized the relevance of the Roman Catholic Church to the modernizing world by breaking the domination of Italian clergy in the Roman curia through the appointment of many officials, including cardinals, from African and Eastern lands (*see* sidebar at right).

The Second Vatican Council

Vatican II, as the Second Vatican Council commonly is called, is, according to the count of the Roman Catholic Church, the 21st in a series of ecumenical councils that began with the Council of Nicaea in the year 325. A council—which means the bishops acting in unity with the successor of the Apostle Peter, who is the pope—is believed to be infallible, which means it is divinely protected from error in matters of faith and morals. Pope John XXIII surprised almost everyone when he called for a council in 1959, and the surprises issuing from the council (*photo, page 137*), which was held in four sessions between 1962 and 1965, and from different interpretations of the council continued throughout the 1900s.

The decades following Vatican II witnessed lively, sometimes tumultuous, controversies over how it should be understood. History shows that such controversy is not surprising in the wake of an ecumenical council, especially a council with an agenda as ambitious as that of Vatican II. Two main lines of interpretation have emerged, turning on two key words, *aggiornamento* and *ressourcement*. Briefly stated, *aggiornamento* suggests that the chief purpose of the council was to "update" the Catholic Church, bringing it into tune with the modern world. *Ressourcement*, on the other hand, means a "return to the sources" in order to more firmly ground the church's faith and life in Scripture and tradition, thus enabling it to better challenge the modern world. The usual view is that "liberals" accent *aggiornamento*, while "conservatives" accent *ressourcement*. In fact, things are much more complicated than that.

Following the council, in 1968, Pope Paul VI issued an encyclical on human sexuality (*Humanae Vitae*) that condemned artificial means of birth control and met with widespread dissent among "liberal" theologians. That dissent has played a strong role in the subsequent discussion of the council itself. For most of the period since the council, specifically since October 1978, however, John Paul II has been pope, and he has combined *aggiornamento* and *ressourcement* in ways that confound the usual liberal-conservative

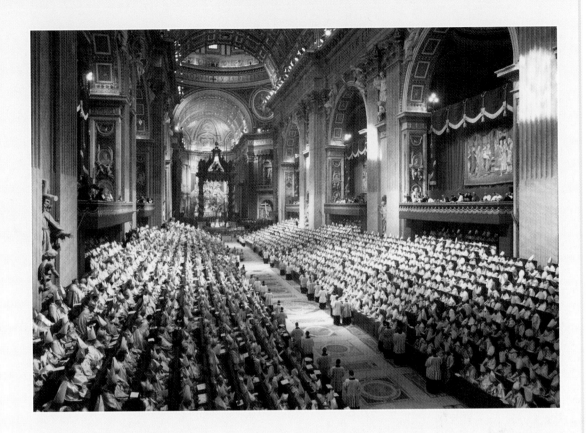

divide. John Paul is "a man of the council," having been involved in its deliberations and decisions. As archbishop of Kraków, Poland, he vigorously implemented the teachings of the council, and as pope he definitively has shaped the interpretation of the council.

John Paul understands the entire period from the beginning of the council through his own pontificate as a preparation for the third millennium, which he anticipates as a "springtime" of evangelization, Christian unity, the strengthening of democracy and human rights, and much else. This hopeful reading of the council accents its teaching about religious freedom, which condemns any effort to force a person to act against his or her conscience in religious matters; about relations with Judaism and other non-Christian world religions, which affirms many values in the world's other great religions and specifically condemns anti-Semitism; about the unity of Christians (especially reconciliation between Rome and Eastern Orthodoxy), which states that Christian reunion should be sought on the grounds that the Holy Spirit is truly at work in non-Catholic Christian communities, and that such reunion should, as much as possible, respect diverse forms of church government; and about the radical vocation of all Christians, both laity and clergy, to be "salt and light" in the modern world. John Paul has refined and strengthened this interpretation of the council by regularly convening synods of bishops from around the world to address particular problems and opportunities. These synods are an exercise of the "collegiality"—closer collaboration between bishops and the pope in exercising the church's "magisterium," or teaching authority—for which the council called.

It is argued plausibly that Vatican II was the most important religious event of the 20th century, and its significance will continue to unfold in decades to come.

Rev. Richard John Neuhaus

French military units, above, engaged in an eight-year-long war against the Viet Minh until they were defeated at the Battle of Dienbienphu in 1954. After Egypt nationalized the Suez Canal in 1956, British military forces and naval power, below, joined France in supporting Israel's attack against Egypt.

A Time of Change

Change occurred in many other places and ways. In the United States in the 1950s, the economy expanded, and a major civil-rights movement began to emerge; the subsequent decade witnessed the appearance of a counterculture and calls for increased women's rights. Developments in technology, including the jet engine, altered multiple facets of life. A space race led from a Soviet artificial satellite launched in 1957 to a U.S. Moon landing in 1969. In Western Europe the power of elite oligarchies, so strong before the war, was lessened; the franchise was expanded; and the network of social services available to persons of any level of income also was expanded. Administrative responsibilities of governments increased, as did the ranks of the civil services.

Most remarkable was the change in European attitudes toward international cooperation: A Council of Europe was formed in 1949; the European Coal and Steel Community (ECSC) appeared in 1952; and 1957 treaties created the European Economic Community (EEC) or Common Market and the European Atomic Energy Community (EURATOM). All of these organizations envisioned using economic ties to facilitate some future form of political integration for Western Europe as a whole. The industrial growth and trade expansion achieved would stimulate further economic cooperation. For example, because of concerns regarding sovereignty, the United Kingdom initially opted not to participate. Instead, it took a leadership role in the formation of the European Free Trade Association (EFTA); the latter group did not plan a common external tariff. The advantages of EEC membership became so evident, however, that Britain eventually joined in 1973. Other EFTA members did the same. The organization of the EEC also evolved, as the leadership of the Coal and Steel, Atomic Energy, and Economic communities merged into a European Commission in 1967. The Community's purview, meanwhile, expanded.

Enormous change took place from 1945 to 1970. Yet it occurred within a world desperately searching for stability. The pre–World War II world had been rejected. What emerged nonetheless had striking similarities to what had gone before. New states had been born; allies had become enemies and enemies allies; but the globe was dominated, if not precisely managed, by a contest between two armed camps. An action by one side spurred response by the other. Thus, the 1954 formation of the Western European Union and its inclusion of forces from West Germany was matched by the creation of the Warsaw Pact in 1955.

Crises reflected the determination of each side not to be bested. For example, in 1954 the French were defeated at the Battle of Dienbienphu in Indochina, and the newly independent Vietnam was divided roughly along the 17th parallel, pending elections for a united government. The Communist-led Viet Minh forces would control the north, and the French Union would be in charge in the south. Two years later, major crises developed over the Suez and Hungary. After Egypt's President Gamal Abdel Nasser nationalized the Suez Canal, Israel—with support from France and Great Britain—staged a successful military action against Egypt and captured the Gaza Strip and the Sinai Peninsula. The United Nations passed a resolution requiring the nations to withdraw from Egyptian territory, and UN Emergency Forces were sent to the area. Both the Soviet Union and the United States opposed the

Soviet troops, tanks, and planes were used to end an anti-Communist revolt in Hungary in the fall of 1956.

Israeli-French-British action. Indochina and the Middle East remained major trouble spots throughout the period. Israel was victorious in the 1967 Six-Day War, and hostilities between Communist and non-Communist (with increasing U.S. support) forces intensified in Vietnam in the 1960s.

Meanwhile, after Soviet Premier Nikita Khrushchev had delivered a speech in February 1956 denouncing Joseph Stalin, the Soviet leader who had died in 1953, the Soviet satellite nations of Poland and Hungary sought greater freedom. The USSR quelled the independence spirit in both cases. Thousands of Hungarian resisters lost their lives before Soviet tanks in the streets of Budapest. East Germany's erection of a wall separating zones in Berlin in 1961 and the Soviet crushing of reform in Czechoslovakia in 1968 also created low points in East-West relations. Those developments also revealed strong motivation not to allow events to escalate into war. The threat of mutually assured nuclear destruction was too real. Instead, talk of détente emerged, and a limited-nuclear-test-ban treaty was negotiated, even as each side attempted to influence the forces for change so they would not destroy the new stability—a stability based on nervous equilibrium between the nuclear superpower of the United States and of the Soviet Union.

Jonathan E. Helmreich

In an effort to keep East Berliners from defecting to the West, East Germany began in August 1961 to build a wall separating East Berlin from West Berlin.

CONFRONTATION AND DÉTENTE

During the 1970s and 1980s, the world changed dramatically. The period is likely to be remembered as the last half of the Cold War, an era that ended with the fall of the Berlin Wall and the breakup of the Soviet Union. It also should be remembered as a time of rapid globalization of communications and economics, and of active and widespread democratization. The world did not necessarily become a safer place following these two decades. The spread of terrorism; the development of regional conflicts in Asia, Africa, the Middle East, Latin America, and central Europe; and the dispersion of weapons of mass destruction succeeded the threat of bipolar nuclear confrontation that dominated the Cold War. At the beginning of the 1990s, the world was certainly more complex and more interdependent than two decades earlier.

From a Bipolar to a More Chaotic World

The peak of the Cold War may have been the 1962 crisis between the United States and the Soviet Union over the installations of Soviet missiles on the Caribbean island of Cuba, but confrontation between East and West, between Communist and anti-Communist forces, continued throughout much of the 1970s and 1980s. In 1971 the People's Republic of China replaced the Republic of China (Taiwan) as the official representative of China in the United Nations (UN). U.S. Secretary of State Henry Kissinger's secret visit to Beijing in 1971 and President Richard Nixon's trip to China in February 1972

signaled major steps toward a more multipolar world.

The war in Indochina, still raging in 1971, officially ended in 1975 after negotiation, U.S. withdrawal, and reunification of Vietnam under the Communist regime in Hanoi. The much-touted "domino theory"—the belief that if Vietnam fell to the Communists, other nations in the Southeast Asian region would do likewise—faded from consciousness as additional "dominoes" failed to fall. However, the U.S. experience in Viet-

In the early 1980s, Beirut, Lebanon, above, was in ruins after an invasion by Israel to destroy military bases of the Palestine Liberation Organization (PLO) and as a civil war continued. Soviet leader Leonid Brezhnev and U.S. President Richard Nixon sought détente through personal diplomacy.

nam cast a long shadow over U.S. foreign policy for the next two decades. Communist victories in Vietnam, Cambodia, and Laos also did not bring total peace to the region. Pol Pot's genocidal rule in Cambodia (1975–79) left more than 2 million dead, and "boat people" and other refugees fled from Vietnam in the late 1970s. Vietnam occupied Cambodia from 1979 to 1989.

East-West confrontation did not end with the Vietnam war. The movement of Soviet troops into Afghanistan in the closing days of 1979 began a protracted involvement that in many respects was "the Soviet Union's Vietnam." Just as the sending of U.S. troops to aid anti-Communist forces in Vietnam had serious consequences for the society and economy of the United States, the Afghani-

The Khmer Rouge, above, despotically ruled Cambodia from 1975 until 1979. Between 1 million and 2 million Cambodians were killed during that period. The future of East Pakistan was the central issue in a 1971 war, right, between India and Pakistan. India's forces overran the West Pakistanis; East Pakistan became the independent nation of Bangladesh.

stan experience had an even heavier impact on the Soviet Union. It arguably was one of the factors that led indirectly to the breakup of the Soviet empire. In Afghanistan itself, the forces set in motion by a decade of civil war and intervention continued to sustain internal oppression and instability and to breed global terrorism long afterward.

The transition from Cold War to multipolar world included the collapse of several of the strategic alliances that had been created in the decade after World War II. The Southeast Asian Treaty Organization (SEATO) and the Baghdad Pact (later known as the Central Treaty Organization), both created in the 1950s as part of the U.S.-led policy to contain perceived Communist expansion, collapsed in the 1970s. The Warsaw Pact disappeared with the end of Soviet hegemony. The only major regional security alliance to survive this period was the North Atlantic Treaty Organization (NATO), which would face challenges in the prospect of admitting new members from among the former Warsaw Pact countries in the 1990s.

The 1970s and 1980s saw the breakup of other units besides the Soviet Union. Paki-

Soviet troops completed their withdrawal from Afghanistan in mid-February 1989, following a costly campaign of nearly ten years against the Afghan "mujahidin" resistance forces, right.

stan's 1971 civil war culminated in the independence of Bangladesh. At the time, successful secession was seen as a relatively rare event. Secessionist movements previously had failed in Nigeria (Biafra) and Congo (Katanga). By the early 1990s, however, political disintegration was a much more familiar phenomenon, particularly in Yugoslavia. Threats of disintegration plagued such other nations as Sri Lanka (Tamil regions), India (Kashmir), Pakistan (Baluchistan), and the Philippines (Mindanao) during this period. Resurgent nationalisms in Canada (Que-

bec), Belgium (Flemings and Walloons), and the United Kingdom (Scots, Welsh, and the longer-term Northern Ireland problem) raised possibilities of a further redrawing of international boundaries.

Political scientist James Rosenau, in his book *Turbulence in World Politics* (1990), suggested that the world in the last half of the

There were numerous incidents of international terrorism during the 1980s. In June 1985 two Lebanese Shiite Muslim gunmen hijacked a Trans World Airlines (TWA) jetliner, above, out of Athens, Greece, and held 39 Americans captive for more than two weeks. A U.S. Navy diver was murdered during the hijacking.

20th century was becoming more chaotic. That is, the old nation-state system that had served as the organizational framework for world politics for the last few centuries was being replaced with a much more complex set of substate, suprastate, and nonstate political actors. The 1970s and 1980s not only featured disintegration of some nation-states, but also gradual integration of others into larger entities. The prime example was the European Community (now the European Union), but a variety of regional and special-interest associations also gained in prominence during this period, including the Association of Southeast Asian Nations (ASEAN) and the Organization of Petroleum Exporting Countries (OPEC) (*see* page 145).

Terrorism took many forms. Airplane hijackings became frequent and led to airport-security systems unimagined only a few years earlier. Bombings, including the use of car bombs, also became more numerous and led to increased security measures around public buildings, including embassies. The bombing of a U.S. Marine barracks in Lebanon (1983) and of a Pan American airliner over Lockerbie, Scotland (1988), were the most prominent instances, but the conflicts in both Northern Ireland and Israel provided numerous other cases. In another form of terrorism, diplomats, members of the clergy and the press, and others were held hostage by groups in various nations, especially in the Middle East. Iran's holding of 52 Americans for 444 days (November 1979–January 1981) was a prime example of such activity. The Iranians were demanding the return of their former ruler, Shah Mohammed Reza Pahlavi, a longtime U.S. ally. There were also many political assassinations during this period, including those of Britain's Lord Mountbatten of Burma (1979), Egypt's President Anwar Sadat (1981), Filipino opposition leader Benigno Aquino (1983), Swedish Prime Minister Olof Palme (1986), Indian Prime Ministers Indira Gandhi (1984) and Rajiv Gandhi—Indira's son (1991), and Pakistani President Mohammad Zia-ul Haq (1988).

Two other phenomena of the time were important: the shift away from Eurocentric world politics and the political ascendancy of religious fundamentalism. Although Europe remained a key region, the period saw other regions rise to greater prominence,

duism, and Christian fundamentalism became more politically assertive in Israel, India, and the United States, respectively.

Globalization and Privatization of Economy and Society

The world became more diverse economically during the 1970s and 1980s. In the years immediately following World War II, the United States was the dominant economic power in the world. After the mid-1960s, however, the American economic miracle faltered, in part because of President Lyndon Johnson's "guns and butter" strategy—fighting a war in Vietnam and seeking a Great Society, including a war against poverty, at home.

Other economic giants emerged. Germany and Japan, rebuilt following their defeats in World War II, enjoyed impressive growth throughout this period. Japan's economic miracle came to rival that of the United States, and a growing imbalance in U.S. trade led American businesses and workers to press for protectionist limitations on Japanese imports. Other countries in Europe and Asia, most notably the "Asian Tigers"—Korea, Taiwan, Singapore, Thailand, and Malaysia—also created economic "miracles" of their own. Several of these countries would suffer financial setbacks in the late 1990s, but during this period their economies clearly were ascendant.

The oil-producing countries, which previously had been exploited by European and U.S. companies to maintain continuing flows of cheap petroleum to Western industrial economies, discovered the merits of controlled markets. The oil crisis of 1973 had a heavy impact not only on industrial countries such as the United States and Japan, but also on Third World countries such as India and Pakistan.

Even countries that long had been considered economic lost causes—such as India, Pakistan, and Bangladesh—demonstrated growth during this period, as benefits of the

Egypt's President Anwar el-Sadat, who had negotiated a peace agreement with Israel, was buried with military honors, top, following his assassination near Cairo in October 1981. In Iran the Ayatollah Ruhollah Khomeini, above, returned from exile in February 1979 and began an Islamic revolution.

especially the Asia-Pacific rim. Religious fundamentalism perhaps was associated most closely with the 1979 revolution that witnessed the downfall of the shah and the rise to power of the Ayatollah Ruhollah Khomeini, but there were other instances of "political Islam" in Pakistan, Libya, and elsewhere. In the 1980s ultra-Orthodox Judaism, Hin-

OPEC

Until the 1970s, Americans gave little thought to the reliability of energy supplies. Oil was abundant and cheap, transforming car ownership into a key ingredient of the American dream. What oil the United States did not produce at home was readily available from big U.S. companies that had access to crude from the Middle East's vast reserves.

U.S. complacency about energy supplies ended abruptly in October 1973, however, when an obscure group of Arab-led oil producers imposed an oil embargo against the United States in retaliation for its support of Israel in the Yom Kippur War. The sudden contraction of global oil supplies that resulted caused prices to leap fourfold, to $11.65 a barrel, and forced drivers to fill their tanks only on certain days and to wait in long lines at gasoline stations.

The group, the Organization of Petroleum Exporting Countries (OPEC), had been created Sept. 16, 1960, by Saudi Arabia, Iran, Iraq, Kuwait, and Venezuela in an effort to gain greater control over their product. The embargo's success prompted six more oil producers—Qatar, the United Arab Emirates, Algeria, Indonesia, Libya, and Nigeria—to join OPEC, enabling the burgeoning cartel to tighten its hold on global oil supplies and prices. By adopting strict production quotas, members again saw their oil revenues skyrocket after the 1978–79 Iranian Revolution and the outbreak of the Iran-Iraq War in 1980, when supply disruptions pushed oil prices as high as $42 a barrel.

Led by Saudi Arabia, holder of the world's largest known oil reserves, OPEC profited handsomely from the energy crises of the late 1970s and early 1980s. But even then, the cartel had sown the seeds of its own decline. Soon after the embargo was lifted, the United States and other major oil consumers began developing alternatives to OPEC oil. By the mid-1980s they were importing large oil shipments from Mexico, Canada, and British and Norwegian fields under the North Sea, all outside OPEC's control. By 1985 the cartel's share of world supplies had declined by half, to 30%. The discipline required to set prices unraveled, as members began ignoring quotas in an effort to maintain the oil revenues on which they had come to depend.

By the late 1990s, OPEC's fortunes appeared to be all but lost. An economic crisis in Asia and unusually warm winter temperatures in Europe and North America reduced demand for oil and cut deeper into OPEC rev-

enues, as oil prices fell below $11 a barrel. No longer able to agree on production quotas, some members reversed their traditionally hostile policies toward outside interests. Even Saudi Arabia, which had expelled Western oil companies in the 1970s, invited several U.S. companies in the fall of 1998 to help develop the country's oil and gas industries.

OPEC's greatest hope for survival lay in long-term consumption trends in the United States, the world's largest consumer of oil products. Despite a quarter-century of efforts by the United States to extricate itself from the cartel's grip, its dependence on foreign oil was greater than ever, accounting for more than half the oil it consumed.

Mary H. Cooper

In May 1982 the "Queen Elizabeth II," above, transported British troops to the Falkland Islands to battle Argentina's military over the issue of jurisdiction over the South Atlantic islands, off Argentina's coast. Britain enjoyed a military victory in the conflict, but the sovereignty dispute remained. In 1990 playwright Václav Havel (poster, below) was inaugurated as Czechoslovakia's first non-Communist president since 1948.

"Green Revolution" dispelled earlier predictions of widespread famine. Although there remained obvious exceptions, such as Burma (later Myanmar) and Afghanistan, Asian and Latin American economies grew impressively during this period. Sub-Saharan Africa, however, remained stagnant, suffering multiple ills of political instability; zero or, in some cases, negative economic growth; and the rampant spread of acquired immune deficiency syndrome (AIDS).

Environmental and conservation issues were prominent throughout the 1970s. The first Earth Day was celebrated in 1970. Although environmentalism declined somewhat during the 1980s, there remained a stronger awareness of global environmental challenges than had existed earlier in the century. Many of these issues would come together in the Earth Summit in Rio de Janeiro, Brazil, in June 1992.

The 20th century was a period of rapid technological change, but no prior decades could match the speed with which technology transformed the world in the 1970s and 1980s. The microchip brought about a revolution in information technology and ushered in the personal computer. Fax machines and electronic mail also made their debut and began their transformation of global communications. A wider variety of television programs became accessible through satellite dishes, and cable news systems established worldwide networks. Television, which had brought the Vietnam war into American households more vividly than any previous conflict, gave viewers an instantaneous view of what was happening as a U.S.-led coalition tried to halt Iraqi aggression in the Persian Gulf war in 1991.

Financial markets also became global. Most stock trading before 1970 took place within a relatively small number of national markets. Two decades later,

Egypt-Israel Rapprochement

When Egypt's President Anwar Sadat rose to address his nation's parliament on Nov. 9, 1977, only he knew the surprise he was about to spring—that he was prepared to fly to Jerusalem and present Israel's Knesset (parliament) with a peace plan. Sadat's proposal shocked both Arabs and Israelis. Many Israelis refused to believe that Sadat would come; others saw the Egyptian president's proposal as part of a plot. Would he actually be on the plane from Cairo, or would a bunch of terrorists leap out and fire into the crowd of assembled notables at the airport in Tel Aviv?

When Sadat arrived in Israel, those waiting on the tarmac included former Prime Minister Golda Meir, Moshe Dayan and a group of other former generals, and the leaders of the two major parties, Labor and Likud. This summit was the first public high-level meeting between Israeli and Arab leaders since the Jewish state was established in 1948.

Following Sadat's Israeli visit and Knesset speech, November 19–21, nearly a year passed without substantial progress toward peace, as Israeli and Egyptian diplomats argued over details of an agreement. Finally, U.S. President Jimmy Carter brought Sadat, Israeli Prime Minister Menahem Begin, and their aides to Camp David in Maryland (*photo above*), where, after nearly two weeks of acrimonious arguments and threatened walkouts, the outlines for a peace settlement were accepted. More than six months later, on March 26, 1979, a final treaty was concluded in Washington, DC. President Sadat and Prime Minister Begin had been awarded the Nobel Peace Prize in 1978 for their efforts.

Since then, thousands of Israeli tourists have visited Egypt, and an Israeli academic center has been established in Cairo. There is an Egyptian embassy in Tel Aviv and an Israeli embassy in Cairo. However, Egyptian tourists rarely visit Israel.

Sadat's peacemaking moves received a mixed reception in Egypt. Although he was welcomed back to Cairo by enthusiastic crowds after his Israeli visit, many nationalists opposed the agreement and continued to boycott any contacts with Israel. In 1981, Sadat was assassinated by Islamic militants who vehemently objected to the agreement.

In addition, other Arab countries condemned Egypt for establishing relations with the Jewish state. In 1979, Egypt was expelled from the Arab League, and the league's headquarters were moved from Cairo to Tunis. Egypt also was expelled from the Islamic Conference, and boycotts were imposed in 1979 as punishment.

Relations between Egypt and Israel often have been tense since the 1979 treaty because of differences over Middle East policy involving Israel's occupation of southern Lebanon, its relations with the Palestinians and continued occupation of the West Bank, and its nuclear program, among other issues. Frequent negative references to Israel in the Cairo press, the reluctance of Egyptians to visit, and disappointingly little trade between the two countries have led many Israelis to term relations with Egypt as the "cold peace."

After Israel established ties with the Palestine Liberation Organization (PLO) in the 1990s, Cairo's relations with other Arab countries improved. Egypt was readmitted to the Arab League and the Islamic Conference, and several branches of the league moved back to Cairo. Sadat's successor, President Hosni Mubarak, was recognized again as a leader in the Arab world, and Egypt became a center of inter-Arab negotiations and diplomacy.

Don Peretz

there would be many new markets, and instantaneous communications could move money in and out of markets virtually around the world.

Other economic phenomena of this period, especially the 1980s, need to be noted: the reassertion of market capitalism, the decline of various forms of socialism, and the privatization of many forms of government. The United States, under President Ronald Reagan (1981–89), and the United Kingdom, under Prime Minister Margaret Thatcher (1979–90), provided the major ideological underpinnings and impetus toward deregulation, privatization, and other dismantling of state enterprise systems. The phenomenon, however, spread throughout the world, both through emulation and through the pressures of national and global lending agencies. The International Monetary Fund (IMF) made loans contingent upon conditions that generally sought to unleash market forces, privatize state enterprises, and reduce trade barriers.

As the Iron Curtain crumbled at the end of the 1980s, and the former Communist countries sought to secure for themselves the blessings of triumphant democracy and capitalism, the dominant ideology of the free market led to rapid but often painful change, accompanied by tremendous levels of corruption.

Regional Conflicts and Reconciliation

The 1970s and 1980s featured numerous regional conflicts. Some, such as the Arab-Israeli conflict in the Middle East and Indo-Pakistani tensions over Kashmir, dated back to the 1940s. Others, like the Iran-Iraq war (1980–88), the Soviet occupation of Afghanistan (1979–89), and the Vietnamese occupation of Cambodia (1979–89), had more immediate precipitants. In Afghanistan, Cambodia, Angola (1975–91), El Salvador (1979–92), and Nicaragua (1983–90), Soviet and/or U.S. involvement was significant. The United States also intervened with brief military actions in Grenada (1983) and Panama (1989). And in 1982, Argentina and Britain fought a brief war over the Falkland Islands (Islas Malvinas).

The decline and fall of the USSR helped to hasten the resolution of many of these conflicts. This was also a period of intensive and extensive diplomacy at many levels and in many arenas: U.S.-USSR strategic-arms-limitation talks, European security conferences, and negotiations in the Middle East, Northern Ireland, and elsewhere. East and West Germany were reunited (1990) follow-

In Nicaragua in the 1980s, civil war raged between Marxist Sandinistas and "contra" guerrillas. As supreme commander of the "contras," Col. Enrique Bermúdez (below, left) helped to train Sandinistas who switched sides.

ing the end of the Cold War. More limited dialogue and rapprochement was begun between China and Taiwan, the two Koreas, China and India, India and Pakistan, and other long-standing adversaries. The United States and China formally established diplomatic relations on Jan. 1, 1979. In the spirit of détente, the United States sold food grains to the USSR, and Soviet and American astronauts completed a joint spaceflight.

Movement toward peace in the Middle East featured both seeming breakthroughs and disappointing setbacks. The 1970s began with a civil war between Palestinians and Jordanians in Jordan in 1970, and the Yom Kippur War between Arabs and Israelis in 1973, but ended with the Camp David peace accords between Egypt and Israel in 1979 (*see* page 147). Israel took several unilateral actions in the early 1980s, including the declaration of Jerusalem as its national capital in 1980 and the destruction of an Iraqi nuclear reactor in 1981. Israel also invaded southern Lebanon in 1981 and forced the withdrawal of the Palestine Liberation Organization (PLO). Even after Israeli withdrawal in 1985, Lebanon remained a devastated society. In other Israeli-occupied territories, Gaza and the West Bank, the Palestinian *intifada* uprising against Israeli

Indira Gandhi, above, the daughter of India's leader Jawaharlal Nehru, served two terms as India's prime minister before being assassinated by Sikh bodyguards in October 1984. Following the death of Francisco Franco in November 1975, Juan Carlos, right, was sworn in as Spain's new king.

occupation that began in late 1987 led to hundreds of deaths and to thousands of Palestinians being placed in detention camps.

Democratization

In the 1970s democracy appeared to be in eclipse throughout much of the world. Many of the Asian and African nations that had become independent during the post–World War II breakup of the old colonial empires and many of the countries of Latin America had fallen under one form or another of dictatorship. South Asia had the populist authoritarianism of Z.A. Bhutto (Pakistan), Indira Gandhi (India), Sheikh Mujibur Rahman (Bangladesh), and Sirimavo Bandaranaike (Sri Lanka). In Bangladesh and Pakistan, military dictatorships followed the authoritarianism. In Southeast Asia, Ferdinand Marcos (the Philippines), General Suharto (Indonesia), and Lee Kuan Yew (Singapore) consolidated a remarkable array of authoritarian regimes in their respective countries. African dictators included Idi Amin (Uganda) and Jean Bedel Bokassa (Central African Republic), and apartheid in South Africa maintained a racial dominance

Solidarity

Originating as a Polish labor organization, Solidarity (*Solidarnosc*) became a political movement that ultimately defeated Poland's Marxist-Leninist regime. The beginnings of Solidarity reach back to the summer of 1980, when the Communist government, hard-pressed financially, ended its meat subsidies in July. The nation's cost of living rose sharply. Widespread labor stoppages brought about virtual industrial paralysis by mid-August. The leadership of the strike movement was assumed by a charismatic, intrepid, and obser-vantly Catholic electrician at the Lenin Ship-yard in Gdansk—37-year-old Lech Walesa (*at microphones in photo above*).

By the end of August, Walesa's strike committee negotiated a historic settlement with Poland's Communist rulers. It included the right of unions to be independent of government and party control and also the right to strike—both unprecedented in Soviet-style Marxist regimes. An easing of government censorship and more rights for the Roman Catholic Church also were part of the Walesa settlement.

The agreement of Aug. 31, 1980, did not end either government repression or the social and labor unrest in Poland, but it opened new vistas. Solidarity became the principal vehicle for the oppositional forces seeking freedom. In September 1981 the Solidarity movement held its first national congress in Gdansk, where Walesa was confirmed in his leadership role. The Communist regime attempted to undo the 1980 agreement by outlawing Soli-darity, jailing Walesa, and imposing martial law in late 1981. Turmoil continued.

Walesa drew valuable support from Pope John Paul II and the Catholic Church. He was released from prison at the end of 1982. In July 1983 martial law was lifted, and Walesa won the 1983 Nobel Peace Prize. Solidarity, however, remained officially illegal. It continued to struggle against the regime and gather popular support.

In early 1989 the Communist government, seeking to improve its public image, agreed to legal recognition of Solidarity both as a trade union and a political entity. In June parliamentary elections, Solidarity won 260 out of 261 of the mandates it had been allowed to contest. On August 24, after Walesa himself declined the honor, Tadeusz Mazowiecki became premier of a Solidarity-led government, breaking 45 years of Communist rule.

In December 1990, Lech Walesa won Poland's presidency by popular election. But the Solidarity movement, earlier united by opposition to the Communist dictatorship, began to splinter. It was easier for people to demand freedom than to agree on what to do with it. In November 1995, Walesa was defeated for reelection, ironically by former Communist Aleksander Kwasniewski. Although diminished, Solidarity did not disappear from Polish politics. An alliance of about 35 center-right parties calling itself Electoral Action Solidarity (*Akcja Wyborcza Solidarnosc*) received one third of the vote in the 1997 parliamentary elections.

Alexander J. Groth

of white minority over black majority. In Latin America, Chile's democratic government of Salvador Allende was overthrown in 1973, ushering in the military dictatorship of Gen. Augusto Pinochet. Military coups in Argentina (1976), Bolivia (1971 and 1979), and Peru (1976) and the development of civil wars in such spots as Nicaragua and El Salvador further added to the eclipse of democracy. Exceptions to this trend were Spain and Portugal. Both of the Iberian nations began to enjoy greater economic growth under more-democratic political systems following the deaths of their longtime dictators, Francisco Franco of Spain and Antonio Salazar of Portugal, in 1976 and 1970, respectively. They also were among the nations admitted to the European Community (Union) during this period.

The United States was implicated in the overthrow of Allende and tended to support military dictators who professed themselves anti-Communist. Popular opinion had become somewhat cynical following the failures of democracy in so many parts of the world. Perhaps, many reasoned, democracy could not be exported as easily to other parts of the world as Woodrow Wilson had thought earlier in the century. Scholarly articles and books on the subject argued that the successful development of democracy required certain social and economic prerequisites that were missing in much of the world.

The 1980s demonstrated a phenomenal turnaround in the fortunes of democracy. By the end of that decade, many countries had reestablished, or established for the first time, democratic representative political systems, and still more would do so in the 1990s. Democratization was sweeping throughout much of the world. Major changes had taken place in the Soviet Union—including *perestroika* (restructuring) and *glasnost* (openness) under Mikhail Gorbachev—and in its European dependencies, including the rise of the Solidarity trade union in Poland

As leader of the USSR (1985–91), Mikhail Gorbachev, shown above addressing the Soviet parliament, launched "perestroika" to "achieve a renewal of every aspect of Soviet life." The British flag was lowered in Rhodesia, below, and the new nation of Zimbabwe, with black-majority rule, was born on April 17, 1980.

(*see* page 150). In South Africa the release from prison of Nelson Mandela, the leader of the African National Congress (ANC), in February 1990 was an indication of the change that was about to come. In 1980 the British colony of Rhodesia became the independent nation of Zimbabwe. With almost dizzying speed, democracy was transformed from being an unexportable item to being an active export industry.

On the negative side, however, a massive, springtime 1989 pro-democracy movement in China was squelched violently by the government. China's action became a stumbling block in the development of its relations with the West, especially the United States.

In many respects, this transformation began as a function of the Cold War, with the United States reasserting American values of democracy and capitalism, and speaking out against human-rights abuses in the USSR, especially Soviet restrictions on Jewish migration to Israel. The theme quickly developed its own dynamic, however. The National Endowment for Democracy and affiliate organizations were established in the mid-1980s. By the beginning of the 1990s these affiliates were involved actively in monitoring elections, training leaders in the operation of democratic institutions, and supporting democratic development throughout the world. National and international funding agencies—such as the U.S. Agency for International Development and its counterparts in Japan, Canada, and elsewhere—also joined in this movement.

One prominent feature of democratic change in the 1980s was the rapid growth of voluntary associations and other nongovernmental organizations (NGOs). Political parties, labor unions, business associations, and other organizations were not new to most countries. In the 1980s, however, there was a

In June 1989, Chinese troops crushed student-led pro-democracy demonstrations in Beijing's Tiananmen Square, above. Hundreds were killed in the crackdown, which caused widespread condemnation in the West. In Japan in November 1990, Emperor Akihito was enthroned officially as the 125th monarch to sit on the Chrysanthemum Throne, below. He succeeded his father, Emperor Hirohito, who died on Jan. 7, 1989.

virtual explosion in the number and variety of NGOs, with emphasis on legal and political rights, women's issues, economic development, and environmental issues. This growth in what democratic theorists call "civil society" appeared to be near-universal. Political scientist Samuel P. Huntington referred to this phenomenon of the 1980s and beyond as the "third wave" of democracy, following earlier major expansions of democratic systems in the early 19th and mid-20th centuries. Whether it would be sustained into the 21st century would depend on how successful newly democratic countries were in using their governmental systems to meet the needs of their people.

Prince Charles, the heir to the British throne, and his bride, the princess of Wales—the former Lady Diana Spencer—rode through London in an open carriage following their wedding at St. Paul's Cathedral on July 29, 1981.

Demographics

Finally, it is helpful to note some of the social changes that occurred worldwide during the 1970s and 1980s amid the major global, regional, and national changes. For the most part, this was a period in which the "World War II generation" of political leaders passed from the scene. For example, France's Charles de Gaulle died in 1970. Japan's Emperor Hirohito passed away in January 1989 and was succeeded by his son, Akihito. In China, Mao Zedong and Zhou Enlai both died in 1976, ushering in new Chinese leadership. Chiang Kai-shek, the longtime leader of Nationalist China (Taiwan), died in 1975.

This period also saw the entrance of women into positions of political leadership in many countries. Before 1970 only a handful of women had held top leadership positions—in India, Sri Lanka, and Israel. As women's movements grew in the United States and other countries, women's roles changed significantly. By 1990 women had the vote in all but a few countries. And between 1970 and 1991, there were female heads of state or of government in Britain, Norway, Iceland, the Philippines, Pakistan, India, Bangladesh, Sri Lanka, Argentina, and Nicaragua. Meanwhile, economic necessity reinforced women's entry into the paid workforce, as families came to depend upon two incomes, and women headed single-parent families.

This period probably will be looked upon as the end of the industrial era, and possibly as the beginning of the information age. In 1970 most jobs in the world were in industry or agriculture. By the 1990s the service sector was the largest and fastest-growing area of employment in the United States and in many other countries.

Globally, the Green Revolution, resulting from the introduction of new varieties of seeds in the 1960s, reduced fears of worldwide famine. At the same time, the spread of AIDS in pandemic proportions and outbreaks of Ebola and other viruses led to fears of disease to rival those of plague in the Middle Ages, cholera in the 19th century, and influenza in the early 20th century.

In the 1970s there still appeared to be some movement toward overcoming disparities of wealth among and within countries. Programs of foreign and domestic assistance sought to address such disparities between rich and poor. But by the beginning of the 1990s, welfare and other forms of social assistance were being either dismantled or downgraded, and economic foreign assistance had come under similar attack. Not coincidentally, gaps between rich and poor were generally on the increase.

William L. Richter

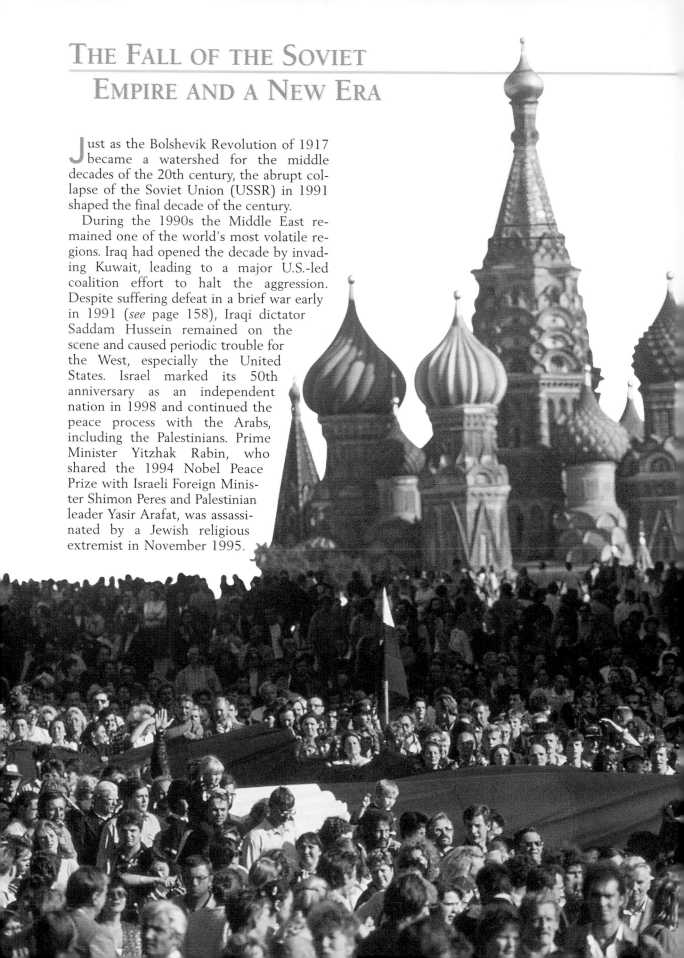

THE FALL OF THE SOVIET EMPIRE AND A NEW ERA

Just as the Bolshevik Revolution of 1917 became a watershed for the middle decades of the 20th century, the abrupt collapse of the Soviet Union (USSR) in 1991 shaped the final decade of the century.

During the 1990s the Middle East remained one of the world's most volatile regions. Iraq had opened the decade by invading Kuwait, leading to a major U.S.-led coalition effort to halt the aggression. Despite suffering defeat in a brief war early in 1991 (*see* page 158), Iraqi dictator Saddam Hussein remained on the scene and caused periodic trouble for the West, especially the United States. Israel marked its 50th anniversary as an independent nation in 1998 and continued the peace process with the Arabs, including the Palestinians. Prime Minister Yitzhak Rabin, who shared the 1994 Nobel Peace Prize with Israeli Foreign Minister Shimon Peres and Palestinian leader Yasir Arafat, was assassinated by a Jewish religious extremist in November 1995.

Jordan, which had signed a peace treaty with Israel in October 1994, ended the decade by trying to cope with the death of its longtime popular king, Hussein. Slightly more moderate leaders were chosen to lead Iran as its Islamic revolution continued following the death of Ayatollah Ruhollah Khomeini in 1989. Lebanon remained under the dominance of Syria.

With the fall of the USSR and Communism worldwide, China and Cuba were about the only nations that retained that economic system. Although China enjoyed a 10% economic-growth rate during much of the 1990s, by 1998 its money-losing government-owned businesses had become a top concern for the nation's new premier, Zhu Rongji. Meanwhile the United States tried to juggle the benefits of doing economic business with China with a concern for human rights, including the fate of dissidents, in that nation. With fanfare, the colony of Hong Kong reverted to Chinese control on June 30, 1997, following 156 years of British rule. Fidel Castro marked his 40th anniversary as leader of Cuba and played host to Pope John Paul II. A slight improvement in the Caribbean island's relations with the United States was apparent following the 1998 papal trip.

The "economic tigers" of the Asia-Pacific rim—including Indonesia, Malaysia, the Philippines, Singapore, and Thailand—suffered financial and economic meltdowns in the late 1990s. Even economic giant Japan was affected by the crisis, which, in part, was responsible for the downfall of Suharto—the leader of Indonesia for 32 years. Also, as the decade drew to a close, India and Pakistan exploded nuclear devices. Earlier, in 1991, India's former Prime Minister Rajiv Gandhi—like his mother, Indira, before him—was assassinated. Some 20 years after the union of North and South Vietnam, the Southeast Asian nation became a member of the Association of Southeast Asian Nations (ASEAN) and the Asia-Pacific Economic (APEC) forum.

On May 10, 1994, Nelson Mandela took office as South Africa's first black president. Mandela, who had spent 27 years in prison because of his anti-apartheid views, had been elected to the office in the nation's first nonracial election. The year before, Mandela and then South African President F.W. de Klerk had shared the Nobel Peace Prize in recognition of their "great political courage" in negotiating an end to apartheid. Elsewhere in Africa in the 1990s, steps were taken toward more democracy and economic growth, but outbreaks of horrific violence dominated. Two ethnic groups, the Hutu and the Tutsi, did battle in Rwanda and Burundi, and civil wars were fought in such places as Sudan, Angola, Mozambique, and Sierra Leone. Eritrea became an independent nation in 1993 and was fighting Ethiopia at decade's end. Various factions contended for power in Somalia and left the nation without a government. Zaire saw the end of the Mobuto Sese Seko regime and reverted to its former name, Democratic Republic of the Congo. Inflation was down in Latin America, and freer trade became a continental objective. Mexico's governing Institutional Revolutionary Party

The 1990s were a time of rapid world change. The decade began with the fall of the Soviet Union. Accordingly, the Russian people, page 154, gained greater freedom and a new economic system. In the Middle East, the Hashemite Kingdom of Jordan signed a peace treaty with Israel in October 1994 and ended the era by mourning the death of its longtime king, Hussein, above.

In Hong Kong in mid-1997, the British flag was lowered, and the Chinese flag was raised, above, as the colony reverted to Chinese control. On May 21, 1991, Rajiv Gandhi, right, who was India's prime minister from Oct. 31, 1984, to Dec. 1, 1989, was assassinated while campaigning to return to the post. F.W. de Klerk, below, who served as South Africa's president, shared the 1993 Nobel Peace Prize with Nelson Mandela for their "efforts in dismantling" the apartheid system.

(PRI) suffered setbacks, and a peace treaty ended a border dispute between Ecuador and Peru. With the support of U.S. President Bill Clinton and Great Britain's Prime Minister Tony Blair—two government leaders who were born after World War II—the search for peace in Northern Ireland intensified, and an agreement was reached in 1998.

Despite these at times historic developments in various parts of the world, "the story" of the 1990s was the downfall of Communism and the Soviet empire.

The Impact and Theme of a New Era

The immediate and enduring historical impact of the demise of the USSR was the end of the nearly 50-year Cold War with the West. Because the USSR was not only a militarily powerful state, but an empire as well, another momentous consequence of its end was the liberation of more than two dozen states and nations under its direct or indirect control. Even before the USSR's collapse, its outer empire in Communist East Europe had crumbled in 1989, as symbolized by the destruction of the Berlin Wall. With the fall of the Soviet Union two years later came the

breakup of the inner empire, releasing its constituent ethnic-national parts into the global mainstream of independent nation-states.

The theme of the new era that emerged from the wreckage of the Soviet empire was transition—the transition from Communist authoritarianism with its centralized economy in the direction of democratic polities and market economies. The transitional process proved to be more difficult than the post-Soviet leaders had anticipated during the euphoria that followed the end of Communism. Some of the new and new-old states fared better than others in transforming their polities and societies during the 1990s, while others remained mired in past patterns of power and control, or slipped even further back into political arbitrariness and statism. In several of the emergent nation-states, the transformation program was engulfed in internal ethnic conflict and violence, as well as international war.

Transitional success was most apparent in the erstwhile East European satellites and the former Baltic republics of the USSR—

Estonia, Latvia, and Lithuania—all of which had lived under the Soviet political-economic model only since the 1940s. Transition was most difficult for the nations of the Soviet inner empire, which by 1991 had experienced Communist authoritarianism for almost three quarters of the 20th century. By the end of the 1990s there were notable distinctions within this group of transitional states. Perhaps the most difficult transitions were in those states where the tasks of political and economic change were complicated and often interrupted by internal or external violence—in particular, in the former Soviet Union's republics of Tajikistan and Georgia, where civil wars waxed and waned through much of the decade, and in Armenia and Azerbaijan, which had been stalemated in a draining ethnic-territorial war since the late 1980s.

In Eastern Europe ethnic violence and ethnic cleansing took place on the territory of the former Yugoslavia, long an independent Communist regime but one nonetheless adversely impacted by the fall of the Berlin Wall and the collapse of the Soviet Union (*see* page 162).

Twilight of the Soviet Empire

The prevailing image of the USSR in the 1970s had been one of stability and effective control by the Communist Party leadership. The exception was the East European states, where Moscow tolerated some local variations. In the 15 union republics of the Soviet inner empire, however, the image in fact masked increasingly serious economic shortcomings as well as rising ethnic-nationalist deviations. By the time Mikhail Gorbachev assumed leadership of the Soviet Communist Party in 1985, the fault lines in the system were evident. Gorbachev responded with an ambitious and intensive program of reforms called *perestroika*, or "restructuring." This entailed several policies, including *glasnost*, an emphasis on more open information; democratization, a policy of greater public participation in policymaking; and the "new thinking," a series of foreign-policy initiatives to relax Cold War tensions. All of Gorbachev's new policies were intended to support a number of liberalizing economic measures designed to restructure the stagnating Soviet economy significantly.

(Continued on page 161.)

An agreement to end 26 years of conflict in Northern Ireland was reached on April 10, 1998. Representatives of eight political parties agreed to a revamping of the political structure of Northern Ireland. Residents supported the pact in subsequent referenda in the Republic of Ireland and in Northern Ireland.

The Persian Gulf War

After Iraq invaded and annexed Kuwait in 1990 (*photo above*), there followed almost six months of a curious period of uncertainty as to whether U.S.-led diplomatic and economic pressure would induce Iraq to leave Kuwait, and, if not, whether war would follow to bring that about. A fairly short war occurred early in 1991; but this, with its limited aims achieved for the Western coalition, was followed by an enormous and frustrating aftermath that stretched on through much of the 1990s.

Iraq's lust for acquiring Kuwait—its small, vulnerable, oil-rich neighbor—was not a novelty. The occasion had seemed ripe in 1961, when Kuwait ceased to be a British protectorate; but hastily-called-back British forces, and then a joint Arab force, had averted that threat from Abdul Karim Kassem's Iraq. The threat, however, was renewed in 1975 and in the 1980s. The plausible idea, assiduously propagated by Iraq, that Iraq had a claim to Kuwait, had little substance. Kuwait had existed as a political entity, under the same dynasty, the Al-Sabah family, since the 1750s. It first enjoyed considerable autonomy under the Ottoman Empire; then, after the 1890s and at its own request, it remained under British protection until 1961. Iraq, however, while it had a geographical basis in the Tigris-Euphrates valley, was a recent British political invention. Shortly after the end of World War I, it was patched together by combining three administrative districts (*vilayets*)—Mosul, Baghdad, and Basra—of the former Ottoman Empire. Like Jordan (at first, "Transjordan"), Iraq was awarded as a realm to a member of the Hashemite family as compensation for the family's being driven out of the Hejaz by the rising power of Ibn Saud, the founder of Saudi Arabia.

In 1990 the other Persian Gulf war, the 1980–88 war between Iraq and Iran—brought about by Saddam Hussein's invasion of Iran—had left the Iraqi dictator in tempting possession of a large, if not particularly competent, army. Hussein also had a large foreign debt and several rich and vulnerable neighbors to the south. In the first half of 1990, his conduct became more and more outrageous. In February he addressed an Arab summit in his capital in incendiary anti-Israeli and anti-Western terms. In mid-March he executed the Iraqi correspondent of a prominent British newspaper. In July his wild rhetoric was aimed more and

more at Kuwait. Hussein unjustly accused Kuwait of not assisting Iraq during the war with Iran; of territorial violations; of stealing Iraqi oil in the shared Rumaila field. But he also gave to Egypt, Jordan, and Saudi Arabia the most emphatic assurances that he would not attack Kuwait. The Iraqi leader perhaps was encouraged to do exactly that by an absence of any warnings from the outside world. Indeed, toward the end of July, the U.S. ambassador to Iraq, April Glaspie, assured Hussein that the Iraqi leader's quarrels with Kuwait were a purely local affair in which the United States had no interest.

The conquest of Kuwait by Iraq began when Iraqi tanks rolled across the border early on the morning of August 2. The conquest took only a matter of hours. The ruler of Kuwait and his family fled to refuge in Saudi Arabia.

The invasion of one sovereign state by another, and the extinction of the invaded state's sovereignty, is the supreme affront to the norms of international life. Nevertheless, neither Saddam Hussein nor anyone else could have foreseen the astounding vigor and near unanimity of the world community's reaction against his action. Responding to a massive Iraqi buildup on the Saudi frontier, U.S. Presi-

dent George Bush warned that the integrity of Saudi Arabia was a vital U.S. concern; on August 6, Saudi Arabia's King Fahd unprecedentedly agreed to permit U.S. troops to move into his country. The next day began "Operation Desert Shield," the most massive deployment of U.S. troops on foreign soil since the Vietnam war. A series of decisions by the UN Security Council in August condemned Iraq's actions and imposed economic sanctions and an air and sea blockade on the aggressor. The effect was to deprive Iraq of the fruits of conquest: Kuwaiti oil could not be marketed, and Kuwait's enormous accumulated wealth, administered from London, was beyond reach.

Various events, including the gradual release of the thousands of foreigners—in effect, hostages—resident in Iraq and Kuwait; the enforced closure of embassies in Kuwait; and, above all, a great buildup of coalition forces filled the next three months. Many weeks of intense U.S. diplomacy resulted in the Security Council's passage on November 29 of Resolution 678, authorizing member states "to use all necessary means" to make Iraq withdraw from Kuwait if it had not done so by January 15.

Abortive diplomatic contacts between the United States and Iraq continued into January 1991, but Iraq refused to withdraw from Kuwait. The date fixed by the UN ultimatum passed, and on January 17 a U.S.-led multinational military action ("Operation Desert Storm"), under the leadership of U.S. Gen. Norman Schwarzkopf, was begun to liberate Kuwait. An international coalition was committed to the effort. Thirty-five nations committed troops, warships, or planes to the allied cause; 21 had ground-combat forces in Saudi Arabia. Other states promised financial support. The United States made the largest military as well as financial commitment, with more than 500,000 personnel of its armed forces involved.

Operation Desert Storm began with massive air attacks on Iraqi forces and installations that lasted more than a month. Also, on January 17, Iraq began to fire long-range (Scud) missiles into Israel. U.S. defensive Patriot missiles were a fairly good shield, but casualties did occur. Israel did not retaliate. All the Arab states except Jordan, Libya, and Yemen at least had expressed approval of Operation Desert Storm. After the air attacks had destroyed Iraq's military command and control system and demoralized its troops, allied ground forces began their attack early on February 23. Three days later they entered Kuwait City, the capital. Before retreating from Kuwait, Iraq set on fire about half of Kuwait's oil wells (*photo above*) and caused extensive oil spills both on land and in the waters of the Persian Gulf. It would take about a year to clear up this sabotage.

Although the action against Iraq was successful for the coalition, many of Saddam Hussein's best troops and planes were withheld from combat. With all of Kuwait liberated, President Bush declared a cease-fire effective on February 27, exactly 100 hours after the ground war had begun. Although Bush's decision to stop the fighting later was criticized widely, it had two chief justifications—UN Security Council resolutions only had authorized the liberation of Kuwait, and, secondly, there was no believable replacement for Saddam Hussein's dictatorship on the horizon. The war had cost the United States less than 150 deaths.

In the course of 1991, Iraq dealt decisively with attempted rebellions in the Kurdish north and the Shiite south. This led to the imposition by the allies of no-fly zones in those two areas; but in 1996 an Iraqi foray into the north enabled Saddam Hussein to hamstring opposition there, and allied ground forces were withdrawn from that region. The armistice concluded in 1991 included provisions mandating destruction of Iraq's stock of chemical and mass-destruction weapons and of the facilities for making them; these were essential conditions for lifting the oil embargo. The UN inspectors attempting to verify compliance were frustrated year after year by Iraq's tireless strategy of delays, concealment, prohibitions, and lies. Many Iraqi weapons were destroyed, but undoubtedly many escaped detection. This led on a number of occasions to allied air strikes, but the weapons inspectors were forced out in 1998. Meanwhile, any possibility of reviving the extraordinary coalition of 1991 had unraveled. Britain alone excepted, the other former U.S. partners were more concerned with resuming economic links with Iraq than with restraining Saddam Hussein.

Arthur Campbell Turner

(Continued from page 157.)

Indeed, thanks to Gorbachev's reforms, the winds of greater freedom began to blow throughout Soviet society. Censorship was relaxed, relatively free legislative elections were held, and individuals, emerging political groups, and even entire union republics soon availed themselves of the freer atmosphere to pursue long-forbidden and -suppressed agendas.

Taking their cues from the Soviet example, the various nations of East Europe began to agitate peacefully for more autonomy from Moscow's indirect rule, and eventually even for independence. Under Gorbachev's new policy of détente with the West, the East European Communist leaders were no longer free to use force to contain the burgeoning independence movements, and by

Following the breakup of the Soviet Union in late 1991 (cartoonist comment, right), the Baltic republics of Estonia, Latvia, and Lithuania—which had been under Soviet dominance since the 1940s—became independent nations. Their presidents (above, l-r)—Estonia's Lennart Meri, Latvia's Guntis Ulmanis, and Lithuania's Algirdas Brazauskas—discussed mutual issues in Estonia in May 1997.

Christmas 1989, Poland, Czechoslovakia, Hungary, East Germany, Bulgaria, and Romania had broken free of Soviet control and shed their Communist systems.

Reciprocally, the East European freedom movements influenced the unwinding of the tightly centralized USSR, as Lithuanians, Georgians, Armenians, and Azeris began to contemplate the unthinkable—secession from the Soviet Union. The domestic reforms had worked in ways unintended by Communist reformer Gorbachev, as the logic of freedom became irresistible. The exception was the economic reforms, which succeeded in partially dismantling the centrally planned economy without, however, successfully replacing it with working market structures. By 1991 the Soviet system was in serious disarray, as the integrative mechanisms—the state economy, the Communist Party bureaucracy, and the secret police (KGB)—had weakened critically. An abortive coup attempt by the Communist old guard in the summer of 1991 merely accelerated the process of imperial decline, leading to the final collapse of the once-mighty USSR several months later, just weeks before what would have been the 75th year of the Bolshevik Revolution.

Dawn of the New Era

By Christmas 1991 the Soviet Union and its inner and outer empires were no more, and the half-century Cold War had entered history. The West was jubilant, considering itself the winner of the Cold War. Euphoria swept the newly independent countries, as elites

(Continued on page 164.)

The Breakup of Yugoslavia

The Socialist Federal Republic of Yugoslavia, which was established as the Federal People's Republic of Yugoslavia in 1945, consisted of six republics—Slovenia, Croatia, Bosnia and Herzegovina, Macedonia, Serbia, and Montenegro—and two autonomous regions: Kosovo and Vojvodina. Marshal Josip Broz Tito headed the country's Communist government from 1945 until his death in 1980. Under Tito's rule, conflicts among the country's various nationalities were kept in check.

During the 1980s the interrepublican and interethnic balance established by Tito began to unravel. The forces of ethnic nationalism swept the country, as competing republican elites sought to gain political control outside the federal Communist structure. In particular, Croatian and Slovenian aspirations for autonomy clashed directly with Serbian moves to regain dominance in Yugoslavia. Titoism had disfigured Yugoslav society by preventing the development of democratic institutions and a multinational civic society that could have held Yugoslavia together.

The disintegration of Yugoslavia stemmed from the failure to transform a Communist system into a democratic state. Failed economic reforms resulted in declining living standards, mounting social disquiet, and an erosion of political legitimacy. Republican and national leaders clashed over their political jurisdictions and control over economic resources. This weakened the principles of federalism, interrepublican equality, and central-government authority.

During the 1980s the abdication of power by the ruling League of Communists of Yugoslavia (LCY) to the republican-based Communist parties exacerbated national and republican polarization. Escalating economic problems also fueled competition for scarce federal funds; these in turn increased social and ethnic tensions throughout the federation.

The leaders of several republics, especially Slovenia and Croatia, campaigned for greater autonomy. Meanwhile, the Serbian government, under the leadership of Slobodan Milosevic (*depicted below as a doll-like figure in a prisoner's outfit*), asserted greater central control from Belgrade. Ethnic nationalism grew as each republic tried to ensure its self-determination, while shrewd politicians exploited ethnic differences in order to strengthen their powers. All six Yugoslav republics held multiparty elections during 1990. Newly formed na-

tionalist parties, which were opposed to the continuation of the Yugoslav federation, scored major victories.

As political conflicts escalated between republican elites, various Yugoslav leaders turned to nationalism to garner popular support. While Slovenia and Croatia pressed for full independence from Yugoslavia, Bosnia and Herzegovina found itself caught in the middle of the Serb-Croat dispute. The three ethnic groups (Muslims, Serbs, and Croats) were pressured to side with either Serbia or Croatia. Serb leaders were concerned that a Muslim-Croat alliance would make Serbs into second-class citizens and sever them from Yugoslavia.

Muslims and Croats grew anxious that local Serb leaders, in league with the Milosevic regime in Belgrade, would try to partition Bosnia in their quest for a "Greater Serbia."

The wars in Yugoslavia began in the summer of 1991, after Slovenia and Croatia declared independence. The Yugoslav People's Army (JNA), controlled by Serb leaders, intervened in Slovenia with the intention of removing the Slovenian government. Slovenian troops repelled the Yugoslav forces after ten days. Further negotiations failed to resolve the dispute, and Slovenia gained world recognition as an independent state by early 1992.

The government of Croatia declared the republic's independence in June 1991. However, Croatia had a sizable Serbian minority that did not want to secede from Yugoslavia and rebelled against the declaration. Armed units of ethnic Serbs were supported actively by the Yugoslav army, and by the end of 1991 they had carved out their own separate quasi-state, encompassing about one quarter of Croatian territory. The United Nations placed troops in the Serb-controlled area of Croatia but failed to return the occupied lands to Zagreb's control. During 1995 the Croatian army retook most of the territories, and Serbian residents fled to neighboring Bosnia and Serbia. The remaining regions of Eastern Slavonia were returned to Croatia in January 1998 following the UN withdrawal.

The war in Bosnia began in the spring of 1992, when the new government declared independence from Yugoslavia. Serbian nationalists, assisted by the Yugoslav army, violently occupied more than 60% of Bosnian territory; tens of thousands of Muslims and Croats were murdered or expelled from their homes. A UN Protection Force (UNPROFOR) failed to restore the country's unity or to protect its inhabitants and was withdrawn at the end of 1995. In November 1995, under international pressure, the Dayton Accords were initialed by the leaders of Bosnia, Croatia, and Serbia in an effort to end the fighting in Bosnia. A North Atlantic Treaty Organization (NATO) force was placed in Bosnia, and the country's three ethnic groups agreed to re-create a single Bosnian state consisting of two largely autonomous entities, a Muslim-Croat federation and a Serbian republic.

Macedonia was able to secede from Yugoslavia without armed conflict in November 1991 after its president, Kiro Gligorov, had been unable to negotiate a looser confederal agreement with Belgrade. Despite prolonged disputes between the majority Macedonian Slavs and the large Albanian minority, Macedonia managed to avoid violent conflicts.

In 1992, Serbia and Montenegro established the Federal Republic of Yugoslavia (FRY). The formerly autonomous regions of Kosovo and Vojvodina became part of FRY. However, the new state was beset by mounting ethnic and economic crises and growing international isolation because of Belgrade's support for Serbian secessionism in Croatia and Bosnia. The Serbian government confronted an Albanian rebellion in the province of Kosovo and a growing movement for reform in Montenegro. Both crises indicated that the breakup of Yugoslavia would continue.

By 1998 the rift between the Serbian and Montenegrin governments had widened significantly. Montenegrin President Milo Djukanovic threatened to sever all contacts with Belgrade and to hold a referendum on independence if his demands for reform were ignored. Montenegro prepared the ground for sovereignty by refusing to recognize the legitimacy of the Yugoslav federal government.

After several years of an unstable status quo, the crisis in the Serbian province of Kosovo entered a more dangerous phase in 1998. Albanian rebels mounted an uprising against Serbian rule, while President Milosevic conducted a brutal military campaign to eliminate the secessionist threat. Despite international mediation, the Serb and Albanian leaderships failed to reach an agreement on Kosovo's status. Following several massacres of ethnic Albanian civilians by Serb police and military forces early in 1999, the international community began in March to launch NATO air strikes against Serbia in an effort to force Milosevic back to the bargaining table.

Janusz Bugajski

A debate over constitutional changes in Russia led to a power struggle between President Boris Yeltsin and the parliament in the fall of 1993. Russian troops crushed the uprising by the rebellious members of parliament. Earlier in the year, Yeltsin's policies were supported by some 58% of the electorate in a referendum, poster, above. Russia was affected by a 1998 Asian economic crisis. The ruble plummeted in value, below.

(Continued from page 161.)

and public alike saw democracy and economic prosperity within easy reach. Harsh reality set in very quickly. The path of the new-old East European states, as well as the Baltic states that had regained lost independence, was eased somewhat by the fact that market societies were within collective memory, allowing for greater emphasis on moving toward political democracy. Even though transitions in those states were less complex, they were not without difficulties, as political struggles ensued over privatization, reviving party systems, sorting out winners and losers in the reemerging market, and dealing with the past, especially with those who had collaborated with the former Soviet rulers. The transitional journey of the remaining 12 new states of the former USSR was considerably more complicated. Because of the Communist system's long dominance, few within living memory had experienced a market system. In addition, the roots of the authoritarian system had gone much deeper than in Eastern Europe or the Baltics. Perhaps no single country had as complicated and difficult a transitional road from past to future as did newly sovereign Russia. For the Russians, the transition was not only political and economic, but also involved the problem of redefining the state from the empire or demi-empire it had been for 1,000 years into a modern republic, and the psychological adjustment of involuntarily downscaling from superpower status to an ordinary great power, and a weak one at that.

Toward a Russian Democracy

For Russia, New Year's Day 1992 ushered in not only a new year, but the post-Soviet era. The political system of the new Russia was a jerry-built assemblage of institutions forged

in the twilight of the USSR. The constitution originally had been written in the Soviet period, in 1978, but by the dawn of the new era it had been amended heavily to accommodate various reforms. These included a working two-tier legislature that had been progressive in the Gorbachev period, but now was a rather cumbersome legislative mechanism dominated by former Communist Party and Soviet bureaucratic officials jealous of its powers and resistant to radical economic change. Then there was the presidency, a strong, single-seat executive established in 1991. The first direct, popular election of a president in Russia was held in June of that year and was won by Boris Yeltsin, a former Soviet Communist leader, in a field of six candidates. A new constitutional court, the first institution of its kind in Russia's long history, also was established in 1991, and was endowed with the power of judicial review. Finally, as part of Russia's received political system, the state, while nominally called a federation, was in fact a unitary, centralized colossus controlling 89 constituent units; some of these were called republics, but most were classified as regions.

The initial post-Soviet polity did not function well, and all agreed that a new Russian constitution was needed. However, by early 1993, serious differences had surfaced between President Yeltsin and his parliamentary opposition over whether Russia should be a presidential or a parliamentary republic. By summer, constitutional reform was stalemated, as were the profound legislative-executive differences over the pace and scope of market reforms. Yeltsin promoted a fast transition to a market economy, including the decontrol of Soviet-era prices and the privatization of state property. As these policies produced hyperinflation, the reduction of industrial subsidies, and widespread impoverishment, parliament opted to slow the reforms and keep the social safety nets intact. Another major problem was the uncontrolled leakage of power from the central government to the republics and regions. In effect, as provincial leaders witnessed the infighting in Moscow, they took advantage of

the political disarray to pursue local agendas often at variance with national policy.

Russia's multiple tensions exploded in the fall of 1993. In August parliament had moved to strip the president of his executive powers. Yeltsin counterattacked, suspending parliament and calling for new legislative elections. The standoff erupted in violence. By October the president had prevailed, the parliamentary rebels had been arrested and the provinces reined in, and a pro-presidential draft constitution was being rushed to completion. By early 1994, Russia's new constitution had been ratified, new legislators had been elected, and a system of strong executive power was in place.

While the new constitution of 1993 resolved the legislative-executive power struggle, the economy continued its downward spiral. The selling off of state property had favored corrupt insiders. Great concentrations of legal and illegal wealth had emerged, and a huge gap opened between the new "haves" and the majority "have-nots." The state's inability to collect sufficient taxes led to serious shortfalls in the public funding of judicial reform, education, and health care. Strikes over unpaid wages became frequent and included teachers and doctors along with miners. Finally, in 1998 a major economic crash and currency devaluation left the Russian economy in dire straits.

As 1994 ended, Russian forces, above, invaded the breakaway republic of Chechnya in an effort to enforce central authority. The struggle continued until a 1996 cease-fire and a 1997 peace agreement.

(Continued on page 168.)

Steps toward a United Europe

The 20th-century movement to unite Europe—which culminated in the formation of the 15-member European Union (EU), with a population of 374 million and a gross domestic product (GDP) higher than that of the United States—began with attempts at political and military rather than economic integration. In 1948, Britain, France, Belgium, the Netherlands, and Luxembourg formed an ineffective military alliance known as the Western European Union. A brief attempt in 1950–54 to form a European Army under a common political authority failed ignominiously. The Council of Europe, the first multinational European political body, formed in 1949, soon turned into an impotent debating society. Only when French planning director Jean Monnet persuaded his nation's foreign minister, Robert Schuman, to propose in 1950 the union of Europe's coal and steel industries in a supranational European Coal and Steel Community (ECSC) did Europe's economic unification begin.

The ECSC, which was formed by Belgium, France, Italy, Luxembourg, the Netherlands, and West Germany in 1952, was the model for the future European Economic Community (EEC)—later the EU. It had a four-part constitutional structure—an executive, a parliament, a court of justice, and, most importantly, a ministerial body representing the national governments. It began the integration of the European economy by introducing freedom of movement of goods, labor, and capital within the coal and steel industries of the community. And it was a financial success. When the foreign ministers of the ECSC met in Messina, Italy, in June 1955, the Dutch and Belgian foreign ministers proposed that the Community build on the success of its sectorial integration by creating a common market, in which all sectors of the economy would be integrated in a more ambitious community, with common institutions and coordinated supranational policies. After two years of hard negotiation, the treaty creating the EEC or Common Market was signed in Rome on March 25, 1957. The new Community began work on Jan. 1, 1958.

The executive appointed to implement the Treaty of Rome was a nine-member European Commission based in Brussels. A Council of Ministers represented the national governments. The Court of Justice of the ECSC in Luxembourg was to act on disputes in the EEC also, while the ECSC assembly, later called the European Parliament, was to supervise the Community's functioning. The first task of the EEC was to dismantle barriers to free trade, like tariffs and quotas, among its six members; it achieved this goal in ten years. A Common Agricultural Policy (CAP) was formulated, with great difficulty, through which the farmers of the EEC were to be protected by a complicated system of import levies, price supports, and subsidies for agricultural improvement. The cost was enormous, soon taking one half of the Community budget. But the overall success of the Community was immediate. Between 1958 and 1968, trade among members quadrupled, product per worker rose 4.9%, and the GDP increased 4.7% annually. These results encouraged Britain, whose first application for membership had been vetoed by French President Charles de Gaulle in 1963, to reapply, and it joined, with Ireland and Denmark, in 1973.

Almost immediately, however, Europe went into a long recession as a result of the rise in oil prices following the Arab-Israeli war of 1973, and the EEC's leaders took several steps to maintain momentum. To replace fixed exchange rates, which they and the United States had been applying since the Bretton Woods conference of 1944, they agreed to keep their currencies within a narrow range of each other, in a system called "the snake in the tunnel." The Community's leaders were to

The euro, photos, page 166, became the official currency of 11 European nations on Jan. 1, 1999. The prices above compare the costs of popular items in French francs and euros.

meet regularly each year to hammer out Community policy in an important new institution called the European Council, whose twice-yearly meetings came to be called the European summit. In 1979 the European Parliament was enlarged and elected by universal suffrage, and a new European Monetary System (EMS) was begun. A European Currency Unit (ecu) based on a basket of national currencies could be used in financial transactions both within the Community and internationally, and fluctuations in the value of national currencies would be held down by a new Exchange Rate Mechanism (ERM).

Early in the 1980s, François Mitterrand, the Socialist president of France, and Helmut Kohl, the Christian Democratic chancellor of West Germany, determined to make new efforts to advance both the political and economic unification of the Community, which they felt was stalled. First, new members were admitted—Greece in 1981 and Spain and Portugal in 1986—as a reward for their restoration of democratic government. Second, the Single European Act, approved by the Council in 1986, revised the Treaty of Rome for the first time. The act streamlined voting procedure in the Council, slightly increased the powers of the European Parliament, and required the abolition by 1993 of all remaining barriers within the Community, not only in industry and agriculture but in private services, insurance, and banking. Achievement of these goals helped lead Europe into renewed prosperity.

Meanwhile, the European Commission, presided over in 1985–95 by Jacques Delors, was refining plans for the Community to move into monetary union and to fuller political and defense collaboration. Delors' proposals were embodied in a far-reaching new treaty approved at a summit in Maastricht, the Netherlands, on Dec. 1, 1991. It came into force on Nov. 1, 1993, when the Community changed its name to the European Union (EU). The Maastricht Treaty rather vaguely required the European Council to establish common foreign-policy objectives and to frame "a common defense policy, which might in time lead to a common defense." Monetary union was to be achieved in stages. In 1994 a European Monetary Institute (EMI) was established in Frankfurt as the nucleus for a future European Central Bank (ECB). In 1995 the future common currency was named the euro. In May 1998 the Council—now swollen to 15 members with the accession of Austria, Finland, and Sweden to the EU in 1995—declared that 11 would-be members of the monetary union had met the criteria for participation: a budget deficit of less than 3% of GDP and public debt of less than 60% of GDP. Greece had not; Britain, Denmark, and Sweden had opted out. In July 1998 the EMI became the European Central Bank. On Jan. 1, 1999, the euro became the official currency of the so-called euro-11, although the national currencies would continue in use until replaced between January and June 2002 by euro notes and coins.

Monetary union was expected to launch the EU on a new boom. Costs of international business would be reduced. Price stability and transparency would increase competition and encourage capital flows. The euro would challenge the dollar as the principal instrument of world trade. The proof of the EU's astounding success was that, in 1999, 13 countries were pressing to be admitted to membership.

F. Roy Willis

The foreign ministers of the Czech Republic, Hungary, and Poland joined U.S. Secretary of State Madeleine Albright on March 12, 1999, as the three former Soviet-bloc nations became members of the North Atlantic Treaty Organization (NATO).

(Continued from page 165.)

Economic difficulties, in turn, made the transition from empire to federal republic more difficult. Regional separatism surged again, as provincial leaders found it necessary to fend for their constituents without help from Moscow. Beginning in the mid-1990s, the Yeltsin administration countered these centrifugal pressures by negotiating dozens of bilateral power-sharing and revenue-sharing treaties between the central and subnational governments. While the treaty process quieted the restiveness, it also institutionalized wide disparities between provinces depending upon their leverage in the bargaining process with the center.

From Superpower to Great Power

Although Russia remained a major nuclear power, it lost a crucial aspect of its erstwhile superpower status—the ability to project conventional power abroad. A casualty of the country's economic crisis was the Russian military. While still large in size, the armed forces were a shadow of themselves. This was evident when Moscow took military action to subdue its secessionist Chechen Republic in late 1994. What was expected to be a very short campaign turned out to be a nearly two-year debacle for Moscow. The highly motivated but outnumbered and lightly armed Chechens outlasted a poorly led, inadequately supplied, and demoralized Russian army of 40,000 with strong air support.

Abroad, the condition of Russian power was, if anything, worse. Loudly protesting Western policy toward Iraq, Serbia, and Libya, Russia was unable to back words with even the threat of action. Russia's attempt to project its influence over the former Soviet republics, other than the Baltics, also fell short. The Commonwealth of Independent States, an organization of former Soviet republics formed in 1991, through which the foreign ministry sought to build a system of common defense and economic and customs arrangements, was foundering by the end of the decade. The ultimate test of Russia's new postimperial status—the country's yearning to be admitted to the concert of Western industrial democracies—also met with setbacks. Largely due to Russia's economic turmoil and international financial dependency, the G-7 (the Group of Seven major industrialized states) did not enlarge itself to the G-8 to include Russia until 1998. In addition, the possibility of joining the European Union looked, at best, very long term. Finally, adding insult to injury, the West expanded the North Atlantic Treaty Organization (NATO) into East Central Europe over Russia's very strong objections.

Russia and the New Era in Perspective

In spite of its enormous problems, Russia took risks and achieved far more in its quest for a post-Soviet identity than did its neighbors, such as Ukraine, Belarus, and Kazakhstan. In order to continue its arduous transition, however, Russia faced a formidable agenda as the 20th century was ending. Nonetheless, the Russians had broken with their authoritarian past, had dared to change radically, and, in spite of uneven progress and periodic setbacks, had advanced in their multidimensional transition toward a democratic, postimperial, and economically better future. Such a future would involve facing a more united Europe (*see* page 166).

Robert Sharlet

UNITED STATES SCENE

Celebrations at the U.S. Capitol in honor of the bicentennial of the U.S. Constitution, 1987

A New Century, a World War, and the 1920s

Technically, Americans knew the 20th century would not commence for a full year. Nevertheless, as Jan. 1, 1900, dawned, people across the land felt, as the *New York Tribune* put it, "that something momentous had happened to the calendar." Setting aside the quibbling over the literal interpretation of the calendar, the nation that only barely had come into existence at the birth of the 19th century could scarcely wait for the official start of the 20th. "We step upon the threshold of 1900...facing a still brighter dawn of civilization," exulted *The New York Times*.

The optimism was easy to understand, considering the country's past achievements. A puny infant wedged into a corner of North America with fewer than 6 million citizens at the beginning of the previous century, the United States now sprawled across the continent from coast to coast, with a population of more than 75 million. Drawing on its vast natural resources and the restless energy and ingenuity of its populace, this still burgeoning republic had lost no time in fulfilling what many considered to be its Manifest Destiny on the mainland. Then, just as the old century concluded, the United States had established itself as a force to be reckoned with among the powers of the globe by waging and winning a war beyond its own shores against a tottering onetime giant of the Old World, the Kingdom of Spain, adding new possessions— Puerto Rico in the Caribbean and the Philippines in the Pacific—to what fast was becoming an American empire.

TR's Stamp on the Presidency

No one was better suited to the national mood than the politician who would assume the presidency as the new century was beginning—Theodore Roosevelt (known as TR). Viewed with suspicion because of his maverick bent by party bosses like Mark Hanna, who had steered William McKinley to the White House in 1896, Roosevelt had gained the presidency only by accident, in fulfillment of the whim of Tom Platt, Republican boss of New York state. After Roosevelt—helped by his exploits as organizer and leader of the Rough Riders in the Spanish-American War—had managed to get himself elected governor of the Empire State, Platt had become fed up with Roosevelt's freewheeling reformism and con-

In the early years of the 20th century, an increasing number of immigrants, top—some 8.8 million in the period 1900–10 alone—were admitted to the United States, and Theodore Roosevelt, page 171, was the nation's dominant personality. TR, who as vice-president took over as president following the assassination of William McKinley in September 1901, was elected to a full term in 1904. Meanwhile, in 1916, Jeannette Rankin, above, a social worker and suffragette from Montana, became the first woman to be elected to the U.S. House.

sequently arranged for the hero of the charge up San Juan Hill to become McKinley's running mate in 1900. In doing so, Platt disregarded the misgivings of Hanna, who presciently warned that Roosevelt's elevation to the vice-presidency would mean "that there's only one life between that madman and the White House."

Sure enough, McKinley was assassinated by a deranged anarchist in the first year of his second term, and Roosevelt took over the presidency. His personality and his rhetoric won him support among a middle class made anxious by the growing power of industrial capitalism on one hand and the increased militancy of the trade-union and Populist movements on the other. His flair for showmanship bolstered his appeal. A cross between St. Vitus and Saint Paul was the way visiting British statesman John Morley described him.

Reflecting the idealistic strain in the national character, Roosevelt presented himself as a progressive reformer determined to tame the excesses of big business, and he promised the country a "square deal." To live up to that rubric, he gained enactment of measures giving the government expanded authority to regulate the railroads and the meatpackers, and filed an antitrust action against the Northern Securities Company, a mammoth railroad combine. But TR was reluctant to challenge directly the Republican Party hierarchy and its allies in the business community. Though he was called a trustbuster, he sought merely to regulate the big corporations, not wreck them. "We draw the line against misconduct, not against wealth," he told Congress in 1902.

Roosevelt found an additional outlet for his energies by extending U.S.

influence abroad, making the phrase "speak softly and carry a big stick" the motto for his foreign policy. The most enduring demonstration of this doctrine was the creation of the Panama Canal, to allow the swift deployment between the Atlantic Ocean and the Pacific Ocean of the great fleet he envisaged for the United

Prohibition

At midnight on Jan. 16, 1920, when the 18th Amendment to the Constitution, known as Prohibition, went into effect, it became illegal to manufacture, sell, export, or import intoxicating liquors in the United States. Congress had passed the prohibition amendment in December 1917; state ratification was completed in January 1919. The Volstead Act, named for its chief supporter, Republican Rep. Andrew J. Volstead of Minnesota, was enacted in 1919 to enforce Prohibition. Anti-alcohol groups—such as the Woman's Christian Temperance Union (WCTU), formed in 1874, and the Anti-Saloon League, formed in 1895—had

led the antiliquor fight. When the 18th Amendment took effect in 1920, 33 states already had legislation on the books banning the sale and consumption of alcohol.

Several factors were behind the antialcohol movement. One was a reaction to the alcoholism and lawlessness that grew rapidly in the West following the Civil War and Gold Rush days. There also was a widespread negative reaction to the rapid growth of cities and the drinking establishments that proliferated there, many of which condoned gambling and prostitution. Another factor was anti-immigrant sentiment espoused by evangelical Protestant groups concerned about the drinking habits of recent European émigrés.

The 18th Amendment ushered in the era of Prohibition, a time period that coincided with the decade known as the Roaring 20s and the "jazz age." This was an era during which, for many Americans, social mores were loosened, wild parties were in vogue, women known as "flappers" sported short haircuts and short dresses, and many chose to disobey the new law prohibiting them from drinking alcohol. In short, Prohibition and the Roaring 20s did not mix very well. Many Americans obeyed the new liquor law, and alcohol consumption declined greatly during Prohibition. However, many Americans also broke the new law. "Evasion of the law began almost immediately," historian Frederick Lewis Allen wrote, "and strenuous and sincere opposition to it—especially in the large cities of the North and East—quickly gathered force. The results were the bootlegger, the speakeasy, and a spirit of deliberate revolt that in many communities made drinking the 'thing to do.'"

Organized crime controlled the distribution and sale of illegal alcohol during Prohibition. Notorious bootleggers such as Al Capone and George "Bugs" Moran held sway over multimillion-dollar illegal-alcohol empires. That state of affairs led to a series of gang wars and murders, including the infamous St. Valentine's Day Massacre in Chicago in 1929. On a less malignant scale, Prohibition also brought about significant changes in American attitudes about alcohol. These included the increased popularity of distilled spirits such as whiskey, gin, and vodka; the use of the hip flask; the birth of the cocktail party; and "the general transformation of drinking from a masculine prerogative to one shared by both sexes together," as Allen put it.

With growing public criticism of organized crime's hold on the liquor industry and a parallel feeling that Prohibition was overly restrictive, in February 1933, Congress adopted a resolution repealing the 18th Amendment. The resolution became the 21st Amendment to the Constitution. Prohibition formally ended on Dec. 5, 1933, when Utah became the 36th state to ratify the 21st Amendment.

Marc Leepson

States. When the government of Colombia, which then ruled Panama, balked at the idea, Roosevelt encouraged Panamanian nationalists to revolt and declare their independence. Later, when he asked Attorney General Philander Knox to provide a legal rationale for his conduct, Knox replied wryly, "If I were you I would not have any taint of legality about it."

Elected by a landslide in his own right in 1904, Roosevelt undercut his potential for leadership by declaring at the outset that he would not seek another term, a pledge he later privately complained he would give all he possessed to renounce. And his frustration grew after he left the White House, when his own handpicked heir, William Howard Taft,

failed to measure up to Roosevelt's expectations. Out of patience with Taft, Roosevelt did run for president again, in 1912. But the third-party insurgency he led had the effect of assuring Taft's defeat and the victory of Democratic standard-bearer Woodrow Wilson, who had won national renown as a reform governor of New Jersey.

The Wilsonian Era

Just as Roosevelt infused the presidency with the energy and dynamism that marked the 20th century, President Wilson sought to instill in the office a moral vision that he felt the new age badly needed. Wilson's devotion to morality made possible his greatest achievements but also created in him a rigidity that ultimately spoiled the brightest dreams of his presidency. Wilson started off splendidly, signing into law tariff reduction on a scale not undertaken in half a century, currency reform reordering the structure of the nation's financial system, as well as antitrust legislation breathing new life into federal efforts to regulate business.

In the final year of his first term and during his second term, though, Wilson faced a different and more formidable challenge, as his plans for domestic reform were over-

Germany's torpedoing of the British liner "Lusitania," which killed more than 100 Americans, in May 1915 was a major factor that led to the U.S. entry into World War I. At war's end, victory parades for the returning U.S. troops occurred in many cities, including New York, right, and towns throughout the country. Sen. Henry Cabot Lodge, chairman of the foreign-relations committee, successfully led the opposition to the Treaty of Versailles that would have ended the war and established the League of Nations. A cartoonist of the day illustrated a view of Lodge's action, above.

With their hair bobbed, wearing short skirts, and enjoying the emerging automobile market, the flappers became the symbol of the "Roaring 20s"—an era in which Americans recklessly pursued wealth and pleasure.

shadowed by the Great War raging in Europe. At first, President Wilson tried desperately to resist U.S. involvement in the face of demands from the war hawks led by Roosevelt that the national interest required a forceful response to German aggression. "There is such a thing as a man being too proud to fight," he declared three days after the torpedoing of the British liner the *Lusitania*, which killed more than 100 Americans and outraged the public. Finally, when Wilson no longer could help himself in the face of German resumption of unrestricted sub-

marine warfare and was forced to lead Americans into battle, he adumbrated his own moral vision of the conflict. He called for a war that would end all wars and make the world safe for democracy—a pledge to be guaranteed by Wilson's plan for a League of Nations.

But that dream was soon in jeopardy. After the million-man American Expeditionary Force led by Gen. John J. (Black Jack) Pershing had helped the Allies win victory in 1918, Wilson encountered opposition from Republican Senate leaders—notably Henry Cabot Lodge of Massachusetts, the chairman of the foreign-relations committee—to ratification of the treaty that would have established the league that Wilson had proposed. Republican supporters of the league urged Wilson to compromise, but Wilson—remaining true to his principles and his unyielding nature—refused to give any ground at all, and the league failed to win the required Senate ratification. While campaigning for the league, Wilson suffered a stroke that made him an invalid during the final months of his presidency. So far as the United States was concerned, the league's doom was sealed

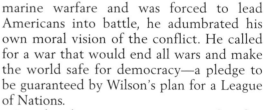

Warren Harding, the 29th U.S. president, died suddenly in San Francisco, CA. His funeral, left, was held at the nation's Capitol on Aug. 8, 1923.

in the 1920 election. In that presidential campaign, the Democratic nominee, Ohio Gov. James W. Cox, and his vice-presidential running mate—a young assistant secretary of the navy and distant cousin of Theodore Roosevelt, named Franklin Roosevelt—who backed the league, were crushed by the Republican ticket of Ohio Sen. Warren G. Harding, who promised a return to "normalcy," and Massachusetts Gov. Calvin Coolidge.

The Roaring 20s

As the League of Nations passed into history, Americans turned their backs on the idealism of Roosevelt and Wilson and embarked instead on an unprecedented decade-long binge that became known as the "Roaring 20s." It was an era that became celebrated for the reckless pursuit of pleasure and wealth, symbolized by such new cultural artifacts as the irrepressible flappers, with their bobbed hair and short skirts, and the ubiquitous speakeasies, with their obliging bootleggers and abundant supplies of bathtub gin. Prohibition (*see* page 172)—the so-called noble experiment,

★ FOR PRESIDENT ★
ALFRED E. SMITH
HONEST · ABLE · FEARLESS

which backfired on a massive scale—the emergence of the automobile, and the popularity of motion pictures combined to create a revolution in manners and morals, shattering the Puritan code that had restrained Americans since the nation's birth. The scandals of the Harding administration and the death of Harding himself in 1923, from never-fully-explained causes, were shrugged off by the uninhibited jazz-age culture. Lending a semblance of legitimacy to the country's mood was the economic boom that followed a brief postwar recession, sparked and symbolized by the Great Bull Market on Wall Street.

"The business of America is business," declared Coolidge when he succeeded Harding, and with unemployment falling and stocks soaring, no one cared to gainsay him.

In the 1928 race for the White House, Secretary of Commerce Herbert Hoover (above right) *easily defeated New York Gov. Alfred E. Smith—the first Roman Catholic to run for president. Hoover succeeded fellow Republican Calvin Coolidge* (above left), *who had chosen not to seek reelection.*

Coolidge had been in Vermont, visiting his father, when he received the news of Harding's death. His father, a notary public, administered the presidential oath of office.

As the good times rolled, Coolidge easily won election in his own right in 1924 over a divided Democratic Party. In 1928 the Republicans' nominee, Herbert Hoover—Harding's and Coolidge's widely respected secretary of commerce—easily defeated New York Gov. Al Smith to become the third successive Republican president. Smith, the first Catholic in history to seek the presidency, was hurt in the election campaign by uneasiness about his religious faith. Hoover's victory by more than 350 electoral votes seemed to represent a ratification of the wisdom of the free-enterprise system that had brought the nation the greatest prosperity in its history.

As it turned out, though, Hoover had been in the White House for less than a year when that rosy perception began to be transformed by a chain of upheavals that would bring the once proud national economy to the brink of collapse.

Robert Shogan

In what would become one of the most cel-ebrated and trenchant headlines of the cen-tury, *Variety* jeered, "Wall Street lays an egg." But even the harsh argot of show business was not sufficient to capture the extent of the disaster that overtook the stock market in October 1929. Day after day, once-gilt-edged securities tumbled in value, while the bulls who had ruled Wall Street for most of the decade panicked and ran. "The present week has witnessed the greatest stock-mar-ket catastrophe of all the ages," the *Commer-cial & Financial Chronicle*, a publication not given to overstatement, reported in its Nov. 2, 1929, edition. One statistical measure of the scope of the autumn havoc: The total loss in value of all securities amounted to $30 billion, an amount nearly as much as the entire cost of U.S. participation in World War I and greater than the national debt.

The Great Depression

This financial collapse by itself did not bring about the Great Depression. But the practi-cal and symbolic fallout from the market's crash generated anxiety and pessimism that before long pervaded the entire economy, worsening the impact of other tangible prob-lems. The seeming prosperity of the Roaring 20s had obscured other weaknesses such as the overexpansion of business concerns and overproduction of goods and commodities. Throughout the decade an average of more than 20,000 businesses, including about 600 banks, had been failing annually. Among the troubled industries were mining, textiles, and, particularly, farming, which had never really recovered from the slump immediate-ly after World War I.

To make matters worse, European coun-tries were in weakened condition, in part because of U.S. policies. Washington insisted on prompt repayment of war debts, draining cash from economies abroad still struggling to overcome the impact of the Great War. Moreover, the high import duties of the United States—capped by the now notorious Smoot-Hawley Tariff, which President Her-bert Hoover proudly signed into law in 1930 with six gold pens—made it difficult for other countries to market their products to

From the prairies to the plains, farmers burned bridges and turned over trucks to stop the flow of goods to market. In an Iowa town, an angry mob surged into a courtroom in the midst of foreclosure proceedings, dragged the judge from the bench, threw him in the dirt, tore off his clothes, and stopped just short of lynching him.

"No one has starved," Hoover claimed. But in Harlan county, KY, miners' families lived on dandelions and blackberries, and in Pittsburgh, steelworkers recalled to the mills by a brief flurry of orders collapsed from hunger at their machines. And in New York City in 1932, as Hoover was in what would be his last year in the White House, 29 persons actually did starve to death.

FDR and the New Deal

No wonder then that in the presidential elections of that year, Americans turned their backs on 12 years of Republican regimes and sent Democrat Franklin D. Roosevelt (FDR) to the White House. The new chief executive just had concluded four years as governor of New York, where his efforts to promote social reform, along with his famous name, helped gain him national attention. Yet his performance as governor was uneven, providing ammunition to detractors, notable among them the columnist Walter Lippmann, who had dismissed FDR as "a pleasant man, who, without any important qualifications for the office, would like very much to be president."

American customers. The United States, wrote historian Robert McElvaine, wanted "to be the world's banker, food producer, and manufacturer but to buy as little as possible from the world in return. This attempt to eat the world and have it too was the epitome of a self-defeating policy." The economic malaise deepened and spread, sending shock waves rippling through the nation's political and social structure. As Thurman Arnold, one of the early figures in Franklin Roosevelt's New Deal, later summed up the national condition: "The world was standing on its head." Commerce and industry ground to a halt, bankruptcy was rife, and farmers saw land they had tilled all their lives vanish under the sheriff's hammer.

In the depths of the Great Depression, 13 million jobless walked the streets (*photo, pages 176–77*). Some sold apples, and some sought a way out. When the government of the Soviet Union announced openings for 6,000 skilled workers, 100,000 Americans applied. Despair hardened into violence. After months without paychecks, miners in West Virginia looted the company stores.

Partly through the dynamism of his personality, Franklin D. Roosevelt, above, sought to lead Americans out of the doldrums of the Depression. Shortly after taking office, President Roosevelt oversaw enactment of emergency banking legislation to aid private banks, right.

Social Security

The federal government's Social Security System went into effect on Aug. 14, 1935, in the middle of the Great Depression. On that day, President Franklin D. Roosevelt, surrounded by members of Congress and his administration, signed into law a landmark piece of legislation that set up the nation's first permanent old-age pension system (*photo below, right*).

The Social Security System was funded initially by a 2% payroll tax—half paid by employers and half by employees—on the first $3,000 worth of workers' wages. Self-employed individuals would pay their own Social Security taxes when they filed federal income-tax returns. Benefits were payable at age 65. On Jan. 31, 1940, a retired law clerk in Vermont received the first Social Security check, for $22.54.

By the end of the century, the Social Security System had grown enormously. During the 1999 fiscal year, for example, the federal government paid out $427 billion to some 49 million Social Security beneficiaries. The system, at century's end, was the primary source of retirement income for some 80% of Americans. For nearly one fourth of retired Americans, Social Security checks made up 90% of their total income.

Social Security was broadened significantly in its first 25 years. Dependents and survivors of deceased workers were guaranteed benefits in 1939. Agricultural workers, the self-employed, members of the armed forces, and the disabled over age 50 were added to the system in the 1950s. Social Security taxes and benefits were increased for all recipients in the 1960s and 1970s.

Beginning in the early 1980s, serious questions were raised about the Social Security System's future. The problem was the upcoming retirements of the 76-million-strong baby-boom generation, those born between 1946 and 1964. Because of the huge number of people scheduled to receive retirement benefits, the Social Security System's retirement fund was projected to be bankrupt by the third decade of the 21st century. It was not until the late 1990s that Congress and the Bill Clinton administration put forward substantive solutions to try to fix Social Security. Several proposals called for allowing individuals to invest some or all of their Social Security retirement funds in stocks and nongovernment bonds. Since 1935, these funds were invested solely in long-term U.S. Treasury securities held in a government account. They earned about 6% annually in 1999.

Others argued against putting Social Security in the stock market. They called instead for gradually increasing payroll taxes, raising the

cap on taxable Social Security earnings (from the 1999 limit of $72,600), cutting cost-of-living adjustments, reducing Social Security benefits for nonworking spouses, and raising the retirement age (from 65 to 67 or even to age 70). All sides in the debate agreed with Sen. Daniel Moynihan (D-NY), who said in March 1998: "Social Security's problems become more difficult the longer we delay. If we continue to treat this program as the untouchable 'third rail' of American politics, we could find one day in the not very distant future that the system has vanished."

Marc Leepson

tions by restoring public confidence in the system. "The only thing we have to fear is fear itself—nameless, unreasoning, and unjustified terror," he declared in the most memorable passage from his 1933 inaugural address. And he made sure Americans knew that he was ready to act aggressively, vowing to ask Congress for powers as great as "if we were in fact invaded by a foreign foe."

Roosevelt at first moved cautiously, to avoid adding to the sense of public alarm. Instead of nationalizing the banks, as some on the left had wanted him to do, the new president gained enactment of an emergency banking bill to aid private banks. And he cut nearly half a billion dollars in government spending by trimming payments to veterans and shrinking the paychecks of federal workers. To offset the deflationary impact of these moves, he took the

Roosevelt's campaign for the presidency against Hoover in 1932, successful as it was, nevertheless tended to bear out the misgivings about his lack of gravitas. Roosevelt said little about his specific plans for dealing with the national crisis, beyond offering the vague promise in his convention acceptance speech of "a new deal for the American people." Roosevelt's victory owed more to public disgust with the GOP and to his own captivating personality than it did to his platform. "No one who voted for him did it because he presented himself as learned or competent in all the matters he talked about," Rex Tugwell, a charter member of FDR's Brains Trust, later pointed out. "They voted for the big easy smiling man who had no fear of failing at anything, who seemed capable even of saving sinners from themselves."

Once in office, though, Roosevelt, reacting to the national crisis, at times displayed a boldness that surprised his detractors. With the country's economy in ruins, its social and civic institutions undermined, its populace demoralized, and its government seemingly helpless, he launched a program of reforms unprecedented in their scope. But he was careful to lay the groundwork for his innova-

The National Recovery Administration (NRA) and the Works Progress Administration (WPA) were two of the "alphabet agencies" established during Roosevelt's New Deal to fight the Depression. The NRA was designed to encourage labor and business to establish codes of fair competition; it failed, however, and was declared unconstitutional by the Supreme Court in May 1935. The WPA disbursed some $11 billion in work relief from 1935 to 1942.

nation off the gold standard, thus easing the plight of debtors and exporters.

But the outlines of the New Deal's activist approach to dealing with the crisis soon began to emerge during the celebrated first 100 days of the special session of Congress that had been convened immediately after FDR's inauguration. During this period, as Roosevelt scholar Arthur M. Schlesinger recorded, Roosevelt sent 15 messages to Congress and guided 15 major laws to enactment. One immediate consequence was the birth of an array of "alphabet agencies" that for the first time in the nation's history extended the reach of government into the lives of ordinary citizens. First on the New Deal agenda were relief programs for those hardest hit by the hard times. Most of them were directed by Harry Hopkins, the former social worker who would become Roosevelt's closest adviser. Hopkins began by disbursing nearly half a billion dollars in grants to states and local agencies as head of the Federal Emergency Relief Administration (FERA). And within the next two years he would spend three times that amount in direct grants and work relief through the Civil Works Administration (CWA).

On other fronts, under FDR's prodding, Congress created the Civilian Conservation Corps (CCC), which ultimately hired more than 2.5 million young men to conserve the nation's fields and waters; the Home Owners Local Corporation (HOLC), which provided cheap credit for home purchases; and the Public Works Administration (PWA), which funded billions of dollars' worth of public projects. To curb the excesses of stock-market speculators, which had helped bring about the crash of 1929, the Securities and Exchange Commission (SEC) was established with power to regulate the securities industry. The Federal Deposit Insurance Corporation (FDIC) was set up to backstop banks by federally insuring bank accounts. Inspired by Roosevelt's zeal for developing

As secretary of labor under President Roosevelt, Frances Perkins had to deal with the many labor-management disputes that resulted from the plethora of New Deal legislation. A member of the administrations of New York Governors Alfred Smith and Franklin Roosevelt and a central figure in the labor-reform movement of the 1920s and early 1930s, she was the first woman to serve in a presidential cabinet.

An area of 150,000 square miles (390,000 square kilometers) in southwestern Kansas, southeastern Colorado, northeastern New Mexico, and the panhandles of Oklahoma and Texas became known as the "dust bowl" after it was devastated by drought in the 1930s. Counties in the dust bowl lost 60% of their population due to migration. The 1932 kidnapping and murder of the infant son of Charles Lindbergh, who in 1927 had completed the first nonstop transatlantic flight, were front-page news, below, and caused much public concern.

natural resources and his suspicion of private utilities, the Tennessee Valley Authority (TVA) came into being, to build dams, control floods, and generate cheap electric power throughout the Southeast—literally lighting up the world of millions of Americans in that region.

Some legislative experiments of the New Deal—for example, the National Recovery Administration (NRA), which was designed to encourage labor and business to set up codes of fair competition within each industry—flopped. Under the NRA's Blue Eagle emblem, workers were supposed to be guaranteed the right to bargain collectively and to receive a minimum wage, while companies were expected to agree on pricing and production policies. But critics said the NRA codes favored big companies, and the agency was floundering even before the Supreme Court declared it unconstitu-

tional in May 1935. Somewhat more successful, though also controversial, was the Agricultural Adjustment Administration (AAA), which sought to raise farm prices by paying subsidies to growers who agreed to abide by production quotas.

Through it all, President Roosevelt displayed the flexibility that became his hallmark, though the trait frustrated many of his admirers. "His mind does not follow easily a consecutive chain of thought," his secretary of war during World War II, Henry Stimson, once complained in his diary, adding that keeping track of the president's ideas was "very much like chasing a vagrant beam of sunshine around a vacant room." Reinforcing such critiques was Roosevelt's own description early in his presidency of his approach to economic policy. "It is a little bit like a football team that has a general plan of game against the other side," he said. Each succeeding play could be called, he explained, only after it was clear how the preceding play had turned out.

Bolstered by the 1934 elections, which added to the Democratic majorities on Capitol Hill, Roosevelt pushed another wave of landmark bills through Congress, gaining approval for the Works Progress Administration (WPA), which disbursed some $11 billion in work relief from 1935 to 1942; the National Labor Relations Board (NLRB), which assured labor's right to unionize; and, probably most important of all, Social Security (*see page 179*), which provided for federal payment of old-age pensions.

All these efforts earned President Roosevelt the enduring loyalty of millions of Americans and helped forge a powerful new coalition for the Democratic Party built around low-income whites in the South and city dwellers, minorities, and union members in the North. These factors contributed to his 46-state landslide reelection victory in 1936 over the Republican nominee, Kansas Gov. Alfred Landon. The victory emboldened him to hasten the pace of economic reform to deal with the problems of "one third of a nation ill housed, ill clad, ill nourished," as he remarked in his 1937 inaugural. Determined to confront the Supreme Court, which continually had thrown judicial roadblocks in the path of his legislative programs, Roosevelt made the most serious blunder of his presidency by proposing legislation that would empower him to add a maximum of six new justices to the court if justices reaching the age of 70 did not retire. What Roosevelt called "court reform" critics called "court packing," and Congress rejected his plan.

Other second-term headaches followed. The economy slumped, and the Republicans made dramatic gains in the 1938 midterm elections. Late in 1938, historian Walter Millis wrote that the New Deal had been "reduced to a movement with no program, with no effective political organization, with no vast popular party strength behind it, and with no candidate." Given the time-honored custom limiting American presidents to two terms, Roosevelt seemed nothing more than a lame-duck politician who had lost his grip, facing the dead end of his career. But then in 1939 the outbreak of war in Europe altered the American political landscape as it confronted the nation with a crisis that was as profound as the Great Depression had been.

World War II

American attitudes toward the mounting threat of aggression in Europe had been shaped by the nation's disillusioning experience in World War I and its aftermath, and by the country's traditional isolationism. Moreover, Roosevelt did little in the first few years of his presidency to counter these forces. He was too preoccupied with his reform program at home to focus his energies on the potential problems arising from the growing strength of Adolf Hitler's Nazi regime in Germany and Hitler's alliance first with Italian dictator Benito Mussolini and later with the warlords of Japan.

John Dillinger, the notorious bank robber who twice escaped from jail and was declared "Public Enemy Number 1," was shot by federal agents outside a Chicago theater on July 22, 1934. Wendell Willkie, right, staged a vigorous campaign against President Roosevelt's economic policies in 1940 but lost the November election by nearly 5 million votes.

Besides, in pushing his New Deal program through Congress, Roosevelt often made common cause with legislators from both parties from the West who were progressive on domestic issues but strongly opposed to U.S. involvement abroad. Thus Roosevelt went along with Congress in banning Americans from making loans to nations that had defaulted on war debts and in prohibiting the United States from shipping arms to any nations, including former allies Britain and France, in the event of war. And when war erupted, Roosevelt reaffirmed American neutrality and promised the country that he would do all he could to avoid the conflict abroad.

But Hitler's early successes, particularly his dramatic conquest of France in the spring of 1940, made that difficult task even harder. The United States embarked on a vast rearmament program, funneling some aid through the Lend-Lease program to Britain, which fought alone for awhile, and then to the Soviet Union after Hitler invaded that country in June 1941. In 1940, Roosevelt ran for and won an unprecedented third term, defeating Republican standard-bearer Wendell Willkie, after promising Americans that he would not send their sons to fight in foreign wars.

But even after the election, a great debate between isolationists and interventionists raged in the country until the Japanese

With encouragement from "Rosie the Riveter," poster above, millions of American women left their homes and joined the workforce for the first time during the World War II years. Gen. Dwight Eisenhower directed the invasion of Normandy for the Allies in 1944 and was supreme commander of the North Atlantic Treaty Organization (NATO) in the early 1950s, photo above. On Oct. 20, 1944, Gen. Douglas MacArthur kept a promise made more than two years earlier and landed with his troops at Leyte to direct the invasion of the Philippines.

Following the sudden death of President Roosevelt on April 12, 1945, Vice-President Harry S. Truman, a former U.S. senator from Missouri, was sworn in as the 33d president by Chief Justice Harlan F. Stone. Truman's wife and daughter as well as key congressmen witnessed the moment at the White House.

ended the argument by attacking the U.S. fleet at Pearl Harbor. That military disaster proved a boon in the long run because it unified the country behind Roosevelt's leadership. At the outset, President Roosevelt—together with British Prime Minister Winston Churchill and Soviet Premier Joseph Stalin—decided to make the defeat of Hitler, who had declared war on the United States right after Pearl Harbor, the first priority of the Allies. They then would finish off the Japanese; that strategy led to victory.

As the United States made itself into the arsenal of democracy, the boom triggered by the needs of war production finally ended the Great Depression and wrought vast social changes. More than 16 million men and women were called to the colors, mostly through a system of conscription that had begun before Pearl Harbor. Millions of women abandoned or modified their traditional roles as homemakers and entered the workforce for the first time—a development memorialized by the wartime hit song "Rosie the Riveter." And millions of blacks left the South for jobs in the teeming urban centers of the North and Midwest, gaining political muscle that presaged significant changes in racial relations in the postwar world.

In 1944, with the war still raging, Roosevelt ran successfully for a fourth term, defeating New York Gov. Thomas E. Dewey by more than 3.5 million votes and carrying 36 states. For the sake of party unity, Roosevelt had abandoned his incumbent vice-president, Henry A. Wallace, a controversial figure to many Democrats, and chose as his running mate Sen. Harry S. Truman of Missouri. Truman had made himself a national figure by leading a congressional investigation of inefficiency and corruption in defense production. President Roosevelt, however, was tired and ill and died of a cerebral hemorrhage in Warm Springs, GA, on April 12, 1945, less than three months after taking the presidential oath for a fourth time. Suddenly the man from Independence was thrust into the world spotlight with the responsibility of concluding the war effort. When the new chief executive asked the just-widowed Eleanor Roosevelt if he could do anything for her, she replied: "Is there anything *we* can do for *you?* For you are the one in trouble, now."

Robert Shogan

TRUMAN, THE COLD WAR, AND IKE

It was late on a wintry afternoon in 1947 when Undersecretary of State Dean Acheson got the bad news from the British. Two official documents informed him that His Majesty's government, its economy crippled, no longer could continue aid to Greece and Turkey, leaving both countries vulnerable to Communist conquest. "They were shockers," Acheson wrote later of the British messages. He quickly passed the word to the White House, where President Harry Truman had to deal with the crisis.

Truman's Fair Deal

The nation Truman led, after succeeding to the presidency on Franklin D. Roosevelt's death in April 1945, had been officially at peace for a year and a half. Most Americans still were striving to get their lives back to normal. That was the theme of the motion picture *The Best Years of Our Lives*, starring Frederic March, which won the Oscar for best picture in 1947. In a more practical vein, relief at the end of wartime shortages was soured by dissatisfaction with rising prices. "People talked endlessly of how much more they had enjoyed on much less before the war," reported *Time*.

In the face of this introverted mood, President Truman had to consider whether to ask the war-weary citizenry for a new commitment about which all that was certain was that it would involve high risk and great costs. Politically the new president was on shaky ground. Only a few months before, in the November 1946 midterm elections, his Democratic Party had taken a severe beating, which left the Republicans in control of Congress.

Truman, though, did not shrink from challenges. Only a few months after taking office he had given the order to drop the atom bomb on Japan, thus speeding the end of World War II, a decision over which he later famously claimed he never lost any sleep. And soon after Acheson sounded the alarm, the president proclaimed the Truman Doctrine, pledging U.S. support for Greece and Turkey and other nations threatened by Communism—and changing the course of history. "It was the opening shot in the Cold War," said Truman biographer Alonzo Hamby. And in June 1947 the promise of military support was followed up with the

Harry S. Truman, Franklin D. Roosevelt's successor in the White House, did not hesitate to put his own stamp on the presidency. Fast-paced walks were a Truman trademark, right. Dwight and Mamie Eisenhower, page 187, who had moved more than 25 times during his military career, took up residence at the White House in January 1953.

unveiling of the Marshall Plan (*see* page 189), which formalized U.S. backing for the economic regeneration of the nations most imperiled by the Red Army or subversion.

Although the Republican Congress gave the battle against Communism abroad its blessing, efforts to deal with domestic issues were marked by partisanship. Postwar labor unrest drove up prices, fired public resentment, and inspired the Republican-con-

trolled Congress to pass the Taft-Hartley Act. The act was aimed at cutting back some of the power labor had gained during the New Deal era. Truman vetoed the bill, but his veto was overridden on June 23, 1947.

Still, Franklin Roosevelt's successor pressed his efforts not only to extend the New Deal reforms but to move into new areas, such as civil rights. He established the President's Committee on Civil Rights,

A cross-country campaign tour in a 17-car special train helped Harry Truman win a full presidential term in November 1948. After President Truman relieved Gen. Douglas MacArthur, below, as military commander in the Far East in April 1951, the general received a hero's reception and addressed Congress upon returning to the United States. Truman and MacArthur had disagreed about policy regarding the Korean War.

whose landmark 1948 report paved the way for future legislation in the field. The chief executive also ordered the integration of the armed forces. Though Truman entered the 1948 election campaign as a hopeless underdog, the president accused the Republicans of trying to undo FDR's activist legacy and won a stunning upset victory over New York Gov. Thomas E. Dewey, the Republican nominee. The Democratic Party regained control of the House and Senate. Two third-party candidates—South Carolina's J. Strom Thurmond of the States' Rights Party and former Vice-President Henry A. Wallace of the Progressive Party—each captured more than 1 million votes. Thurmond took 39 electoral votes.

The victorious Truman proposed a legislative program, with his own cognomen, "The Fair Deal," embracing most notably a plan for national health insurance. Although a housing act that included a provision for public housing was enacted in 1949, Truman's domestic agenda stalled as the battle against Communism came to dominate his presidency. At home, Sen. Joseph McCarthy (R-WI) began to make himself a national figure by accusing Truman of harboring Communists in the State Department. Abroad, the North Korean invasion of South Korea in June 1950 led to U.S. intervention on a massive scale in support of the South Koreans and to a costly and divisive war.

The limited nature of the conflict, which the United States officially referred to as a "police action," made it inevitably an unpopular war badly damaging Truman's

Marshall Plan

On June 5, 1947, U.S. Secretary of State George Marshall, speaking at the Harvard University commencement, startled the world by offering Europe—West and East alike—economic aid on an unparalleled scale for the reconstruction of the European economies that were proving incapable of recovering from the devastation of World War II.

As Secretary Marshall noted, "the visible destruction was less serious than the dislocation of the entire fabric of the European economy," and only the United States was capable of providing the assistance needed to avoid "economic, social, and political deterioration of a very grave character." The Soviet Union, however—deeply suspicious that the United States was using aid to establish superiority in the Cold War confrontation and, in particular, to interfere in Soviet planning—refused the aid and compelled its various East European satellites to do the same.

Sixteen West European countries enthusiastically established a common organization for coordination of their planning and distribution of the aid, called the Commission of European Economic Cooperation and later the Organization for European Economic Cooperation (OEEC). Between 1948 and 1952 they shared American aid of $13 billion ($88 billion in current dollars). Britain received the largest share, $3.2 billion; Iceland the smallest, $29 million. The aid was mostly in the form of foodstuffs and raw materials but also in advanced machinery and technical aid. Recipients paid for the aid in their national currencies; these payments were deposited in "counterpart funds" used largely for rebuilding infrastructure, such as roads and harbors. Because Western Europe already had a trained workforce and a strong industrial and agricultural base, aid quickly brought positive results. The recipients' gross national product jumped 15% to 25%, while industrial production rose 35%. Industries targeted for investment, such as steel and chemicals, showed great increases in productivity. Inflation was checked, confidence in the currencies was restored, and unemployment was reduced greatly. Trade among OEEC countries increased 70%.

Political results were also noteworthy. The U.S. government and people became accustomed to accepting the responsibility of sharing American wealth, and the Marshall Plan became the standard by which all future aid programs were tested. Large numbers of Americans became acquainted with their counterparts in European political and economic life, thus laying the foundation for a wider Atlantic community. Europeans realized that acceptance of U.S. aid did not require political subservience, but that their own economic recovery was bringing them to an equal partnership within the Western alliance. Within the OEEC, as Marshall had hoped, Europeans had become accustomed to working together in coordinating national policies for the common good.

But there were shortcomings. Tariffs barely were reduced. Capital and labor did not circulate freely across frontiers. Little was done to avoid duplication of capital investment or harmful competition. New European organizations were needed. It was the disappointed administrators of the OEEC—for example, Paul-Henri Spaak of Belgium and Jean Monnet of France—that led Europe from the OEEC directly into true economic integration by creating the European Coal and Steel Community in 1952 and the European Economic Community in 1958. By so doing, they prepared the way for today's European Union.

F. Roy Willis

After defeating Adlai Stevenson, the Democratic governor of Illinois, for the presidency in November 1952, Dwight D. Eisenhower kept a campaign promise and visited the battlefields of Korea, left. Stevenson (below, caught in what would become a famous photo) had tried to focus his presidential campaign on "talking sense" to the American people, but was overwhelmed by the "I Like Ike" momentum.

own personal standing. Yet Truman refused either to pull out or to run the risk of expanding the war, even when World War II hero Gen. Douglas MacArthur publicly argued otherwise. For this insubordination, Truman fired MacArthur, surely one of the most unpopular actions ever taken by a U.S. chief executive. MacArthur returned to the United States to a big reception and spoke before a joint session of Congress. As it turned out, Truman's steadfastness and determination as a leader would win him higher marks from future historians than from the contemporary electorate. His standing in the opinion polls sank, and he decided not to seek another term in the White House in 1952. On March 29 the president told a Jefferson-Jackson Day dinner in Washington that he had served his "country long—and I think, efficiently and honestly," and that he would "not accept a renomination."

"I Like Ike"

For their part, the Republicans nominated the World War II hero Dwight D. Eisenhower over "Mr. Republican," conservative Sen. Robert Taft of Ohio. Eisenhower had assumed the presidency of Columbia University after the war and then had returned to military service to command the allied forces of the North Atlantic Treaty Organization (NATO), the alliance forged to block a Soviet attack on the West. Eisenhower selected a young California senator named Richard Nixon as his running mate. Following the nominating convention, it was

reported that the senator had benefited personally from a "slush fund" established by millionaires. Nixon turned to the relatively new medium of television to deliver a nationwide speech to defend himself. He detailed modest personal items belonging to him and his family, including Checkers, a spaniel given to his children by an admirer. He vowed that he would not return the dog. The address, which became known as the "Checkers speech," was a success with the public, and Nixon's place on the ticket was cemented.

On the campaign trail, Eisenhower, flashing his famous grin, rallied broad support behind the appealing if enigmatic slogan "I Like Ike." He swept to an easy victory over Democratic standard-bearer Adlai Stevenson, the governor of Illinois, and Republicans gained control of Congress. Eisenhower soon set about keeping his campaign promise to

McCarthyism

Historically "McCarthyism" meant the airing of weakly grounded, irresponsible charges of pro-Communist loyalties or sympathies. The term derives from the activities of Sen. Joseph R. McCarthy (R-WI), *photo below*, who, on Feb. 9, 1950, charged that the U.S. State Department swarmed with Communists or their sympathizers.

As was typical with McCarthy, there was dispute over precisely what he charged and how many disloyal employees he cited—the figures 205, 57, and 81 all cropped up. A Senate subcommittee took up his claims. As one accusation was discredited, he moved, ducking and weaving, to another. The subcommittee split on party lines, with the Democratic majority calling McCarthy's claims "a fraud and a hoax." However, this verdict came less than a month after war broke out in Korea. Anxiety over the North Korean (and later Chinese) Communist belligerency made the senator's charges plausible to a number of Americans. Additionally, the electoral defeats of several of McCarthy's foes, for which he received credit, prompted many fearful colleagues to avoid antagonizing him, enabling him to run roughshod.

As the Korean War dragged on, the sour political environment nourished McCarthy's style of politics. He never organized a following or a sustained political program, but his scattergun attacks continued to command headlines. That he assailed the White House, even after the Republicans under President Dwight D. Eisenhower captured it in 1952, helped rouse growing disquiet over his excesses. After his undignified brawl with the Department of the Army was aired in televised hearings during the spring of 1954, his political stock fell sharply. In December his colleagues censured him. He was condemned for contempt of the Senate Elections Subcommittee and for breaching Senate decorum, how-

ever, not for excessive anti-Communism. McCarthy promptly disappeared from national political influence. He died in 1957.

McCarthy's skills at self-promotion were such that both allies and enemies mistook McCarthy for the broader phenomenon he epitomized. He was not the inventor, the exclusive practitioner, or the most effectual enforcer of anti-Communism. Other lawmakers explored Communism long before he did. Only in 1953–54 did he chair a committee that did so. Rep. Martin Dies (D-TX) had probed into un-American activities from 1938 until 1945. Thanks to aggressive pursuit by Rep. Richard M. Nixon (R-CA), in 1948 the House Un-American Activities Committee helped expose the involvement of former New Deal bureaucrat Alger Hiss in Communist intrigues. Earlier, in 1947, President Harry S. Truman had established a loyalty program to remove and exclude Communists from government posts. This and similar efforts were built on precedents from the late 1930s and the war years under President Franklin D. Roosevelt. The first "Red Scare" in 1919–20 had witnessed the infamous Palmer Raids against Communists and other radicals. Thus, McCarthy trod a well-worn path.

When the senator's critics used the term "McCarthyism," they unwittingly obscured this broader set of phenomena that both predated and outlived McCarthy, who was merely the rashest of the anti-Communist demagogues. Today the word has lost some of its original context, coined as it was at the height of the Cold War, when fears of the Soviet danger and charges of Communist infiltration were at a peak. The term now enjoys common use to rebuke those in public life accused of trumpeting ill-founded charges and smears or exhibiting excessive prosecutorial zeal or moralism.

Richard M. Fried

end the fighting in Korea. He visited the battlefield in December 1952, and a Korean armistice was signed on July 27, 1953.

McCarthyism and Civil Rights

Other problems proved harder to solve. One came from within Eisenhower's own party, in the person of Wisconsin's Senator McCarthy. By the time Eisenhower entered the political arena, McCarthy was viewed as a threat not only by Democrats but also by many Republicans who regarded his high-handed tactics in pursuit of Communists as endangering civil liberties. The senator's charge that the army was "cuddling Communists" led to the McCarthy-Army hearings, which dominated the press for two months in 1954. Although Eisenhower personally disapproved of McCarthy's methods, the president—in part because of his strong inclination to avoid controversy—was reluctant to criticize the senator publicly. Ultimately, McCarthy's reckless conduct led to his censure by the U.S. Senate in December 1954, bringing an end to the obsessive fear of Communism that had come to be known as McCarthyism (*see* page 191).

At about the same time as the controversy over McCarthy reached its height and then faded from prominence, another and far more complex issue, the problem of race relations, which had been dubbed "the American dilemma," arose to confront and frustrate Eisenhower. The relationship between the white majority of Americans and the Negro minority had vexed the nation since its birth, but it was forced to a critical point during Eisenhower's presidency in May 1954. On May 17 the Supreme Court, now led by Eisenhower's own appointee, Chief Justice Earl Warren, unanimously ruled in *Brown v. Board of Education* that segregation of public schools was unconstitutional (*see* page 193). In addition, the civil-rights movement was born the following year when Rosa Parks, a 42-year-old African-American seamstress, refused to give her seat on a Montgomery, AL, bus to a white man. A yearlong protest of the bus system by African-Americans resulted.

On Sept. 30, 1953, President Eisenhower named California Gov. Earl Warren, above, chief justice of the U.S. Supreme Court. In 1955, Rosa Parks, below left, a 42-year-old African-American seamstress, refused to give her seat on a Montgomery, AL, bus to a white man, sparking the U.S. civil-rights movement. In 1957, President Eisenhower sent federal troops to Little Rock, AR, to ensure the integration of Central High School.

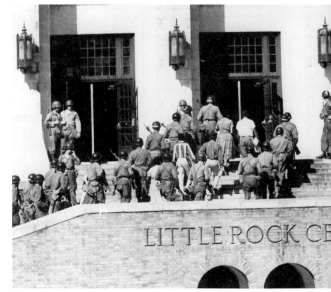

Brown v. Board of Education of Topeka, KS

In the landmark 1954 decision *Brown v. Board of Education of Topeka, KS*, the Supreme Court of the United States reversed the "separate but equal" doctrine that had provided the constitutional cover for legalized segregation since the *Plessy v. Ferguson* decision of 1896. Although the *Brown* decision applied specifically only to public education, it had far-reaching implications. It involved the federal government directly in civil rights and provided a constitutional impetus for social change.

The *Brown* case followed a series of lawsuits brought during the 1940s by the Legal Defense Fund of the National Association for the Advancement of Colored People (NAACP) to end racial segregation in higher education. NAACP lawyers argued that because education was integral to legal equality and economic opportunity, racial discrimination in schooling violated the equal-protection clause of the 14th Amendment. After victories in the court that opened all-white law and graduate schools to blacks, the NAACP turned to grade-school education. Led by Thurgood Marshall, the NAACP initiated suits in Kansas, South Carolina, Virginia, Delaware, and Washington, DC. The five cases were consolidated as *Brown* and reached the Supreme Court in December 1952. A divided court put off making a decision. When Earl Warren was named chief justice in 1953, he negotiated a unanimous decision from the justices, thereby giving the controversial ruling the authority necessary to make possible its acceptance. The court was convinced by historical arguments that segregation was not an immutable folkway and by sociological arguments that segregation damaged black children's sense of self-worth. It concluded that "in the field of public education the doctrine of 'separate but equal' has no place" and that separate educational facilities were inherently unequal.

The *Brown* decision did not lead to school desegregation immediately. In 1955 the court handed down a second *Brown* decision that ordered compliance "with all deliberate speed." The decision left actual implementation to federal district courts and local school districts, in an effort to preempt opposition to school desegregation by involving those most immediately affected in establishing its timetable. Border states and large urban areas moved rapidly toward desegregation, though not integration, of schools, but across much of the South, "massive resistance" became the strategy encouraged by politicians who stood at schoolhouse doors to block blacks' entrance to all-white schools. A series of violent incidents, especially at Central High School in Little Rock, AR, in 1957, periodically forced federal intervention to protect black students, but full implementation of *Brown* did not come until the court ordered a prompt end to any further delays in 1968.

Despite the mixed results on school desegregation, the effects of *Brown* were profound. The decision spoke to more than public education when it struck down the "separate but equal" doctrine that had sustained Jim Crow for more than half a century. Southern whites understood this and launched a wide-scale war against "federal invasion" of their "sacred rights," as blacks invoked *Brown* to press for equal rights and access to public facilities of all kinds.

Randall M. Miller

The Democratic Party, under two Texans—Senate Majority Leader Lyndon Johnson (above, left) and House Speaker Sam Rayburn—controlled Congress for six of Eisenhower's eight years as president.

The upheaval that confronted President Eisenhower in the wake of that court decision and the birth of the protest movement had been building steadily for more than a decade, in part because of the changes in the nation's moral and political environment wrought by World War II. Another factor was the Cold War, which pitted the United States against the Soviet Union in intense competition for the support of the emerging nations of the world, made up almost entirely of people of color.

Eisenhower, once again displaying his dislike for controversy, tried to steer clear of the bitter arguments that erupted following the high court's desegregation ruling. But in 1957, Arkansas Gov. Orval Faubus' repeated defiance of a federal court ruling ordering the desegregation of Central High School, in Little Rock, left Eisenhower with little choice except to send in federal troops and to federalize the National Guard in order to enforce the court order. The action outraged many defenders of segregation in the South. But the president's handling of the confrontation with Faubus also drew criticism from civil-rights advocates. They argued that if Eisenhower had used his moral authority to support the court's ruling, Faubus would have been obliged to retreat, thus avoiding much of the racial polarization triggered by the use of federal troops.

Vice-President Richard Nixon (bottom, center) and Soviet Premier Nikita Khrushchev discussed the merits of free enterprise in a "kitchen debate" in Moscow in 1959. John Foster Dulles (top, right), a former international lawyer and State Department adviser, served as Eisenhower's secretary of state from 1953 until illness forced him to resign in 1959.

Eisenhower's own appeal remained strong throughout his presidency, as evidenced by his overwhelming reelection—again against Adlai Stevenson—in 1956. In September 1955 the president had suffered a heart attack, but he recovered in time for the campaign. Yet despite his own popularity, the president had difficulty transferring that rapport with the electorate to his party. Republicans lost control of Congress in 1954 and remained in the minority on Capitol Hill during Eisenhower's tenure. Under the president's watch, however, the Department of Health, Education, and Welfare (HEW) was established; a massive federal highway-building program was launched; and the National Aeronautics and Space Administration (NASA) came into existence.

Foreign Affairs

While president, Eisenhower used his stature as a military leader to attempt to slow down the arms race. In December 1953 he pro-

In August 1960 a Soviet military tribunal in Moscow found Francis Gary Powers, the pilot of a U.S. U-2 spy plane that had been shot down over the USSR the previous May, guilty of espionage. The incident further dampened U.S.-Soviet relations. President Eisenhower, who supported Richard Nixon in the 1960 presidential race, conferred with the Democratic president-elect, John F. Kennedy (below, right), following the balloting.

posed an Atoms for Peace plan under which nations would pool their atomic information and materials for mutual advantage. In January 1957 the president outlined the Eisenhower Doctrine, which pledged U.S. military aid to fight Communist aggression to any Middle East nation requesting it. As president, Eisenhower relied heavily on his secretaries of state—John Foster Dulles (1953–59) and Christian A. Herter (1959–61).

In attempting to hold down defense spending so as to reduce the burden on the federal budget, Eisenhower found himself under attack from Democrats. The president's political opponents were desperate to find a weakness in his political armor and sought to depict the hero of Normandy as reckless on the nation's security. Stung by these attacks, Eisenhower offered a rare glimpse of his feelings at a press conference when he said: "This is a charge that I think is despicable; I have never made it against anyone in the world."

And in his farewell address to the nation, in perhaps his most widely praised and best remembered utterance, he warned Americans against granting too much influence to "the military-industrial complex." But in the same speech, Eisenhower was forced to confess to "a definite sense of disappointment" that he had not been more successful in slowing down the arms race. One reason was the downing of a U.S. spy plane in May

1960, which torpedoed a planned summit conference with Soviet leader Nikita Khrushchev, who had visited the United States in 1959, as well as with the leaders of Britain and France. To add to Eisenhower's distress, he was caught red-handed trying to mislead the country and the world. After the Soviet Union announced it had shot down the U-2 plane, Eisenhower authorized a statement falsely claiming that the plane was on a meteorological mission, a cover story that was shattered when Khrushchev revealed that the pilot of the plane, Francis Gary Powers, had been captured alive.

As he left the presidency, Eisenhower was given credit for avoiding war. But his young successor, John Kennedy, with the threat of nuclear catastrophe unabated, would be challenged severely to keep the peace.

Robert Shogan

THE NEW FRONTIER, GREAT SOCIETY, CIVIL RIGHTS, AND VIETNAM

As the Eisenhower presidency and the decade of the 1950s drew to a close, most Americans had every outward reason for contentment. Although the Cold War persisted, the end of the Korean War in Eisenhower's first term meant that no American troops stood in harm's way. At home, the greatly enlarged middle class was absorbed with tapping into the new opportunities for affluence created by the post–World War II boom. Under the circumstances, few political leaders saw evidence of a groundswell for change.

A New Era—The 1960 Campaign

They saw, in fact, just the opposite. "The country wants to be comfortable, it doesn't want to be stirred up," Senate Majority Leader Lyndon Johnson of Texas, the highest-ranking elected Democrat in the land—who was preparing to seek the presidency in 1960—told historian Arthur Schlesinger. But at least one Democrat who shared Johnson's ambitions for the White House, John F. Kennedy—the junior senator from Massachusetts—disagreed. Kennedy saw the apparent public complacency as merely a veneer, masking a restlessness that had been produced by the economic, social, and political ferment that had marked the postwar era.

Between 1940 and 1960, America's population increased by 47 million, from 132 million to 179 million. Nearly all of this growth was registered in the metropolitan areas, which showed a jump to 113 million from 70 million. During the same 20-year period,

the gross national product increased fivefold, from $100 billion to more than $500 billion. Also striking were the gains in family income from 1950 to 1960. At the beginning of the 1950s, 10% of American families earned under $2,500 measured in 1978 dollars; by 1960 only 5% were below that level. And while in 1950 fewer than 50% of American families had incomes in excess of $10,000, again measured in 1978 buying power, by 1960 that figure had climbed to nearly 68%. Educational levels were improving, too. In 1940 only 35% of the population had completed four years of high school or more. By 1960 that figure had jumped to 41%, and college graduates in the population had increased from 4.6% to 7.7%.

The most important consequence of this dynamic from Kennedy's perspective was the erosion of traditional partisan allegiances and the undermining of the authority of the once-supreme party bosses. As the party leaders confronted changing constituencies with increasingly complex interests, they found it harder to define and dominate political debate. Voters were more independent. Increasing income and leisure had fostered the emergence of an influential class of intellectuals—in the media, the foundations, and academia—who generated and manipulated political information and who found a growing audience for their output.

And then there was television. The magic box had become a pervasive and intrusive force, at once enlightening and confusing, informing, and distracting. Between 1950 and 1960 the number of American families owning television sets had increased tenfold, to more than 45 million, or nearly 90% of the population. The medium's capacity for instant projection of ideas and personalities into living rooms everywhere created a voice that drowned out the traditional political chain of command.

As he planned his run for the presidency, Kennedy sought to take advantage of these circumstances, not with some radical ideological message but rather through the force of his personality. His youthful vigor—at 43

On Jan. 20, 1961, 43-year-old John F. Kennedy was sworn in as the 35th president of the United States by Chief Justice Earl Warren, page 196, top left. In 1964, Lyndon B. Johnson (top right, at left), who had taken over the presidency following Kennedy's assassination in November 1963, was elected to a full term in the White House. Both he and his vice-presidential running mate, Hubert Humphrey (top right, at right), had challenged Kennedy for the Democratic presidential nomination in 1960. With the civil-rights movement growing in the mid-1960s, the United Klan of America held an open-air cross burning near Edinburg, MS. During the same period, the United States was becoming more involved in a war in a distant spot called Vietnam.

he would become the youngest elected president in history—and his record as a World War II hero cast him as a macho role model for males, while his handsome features and sophisticated manners captured the hearts of their wives, and his elegant rhetoric stirred the intelligentsia. Kennedy needed all these gifts to overcome opposition to his nomination within his own party from those who feared his Roman Catholic faith would doom his candidacy, as it had wrecked the chances of Al Smith, the first Catholic to be nominated for president, in 1928. As it turned out, though Kennedy did lose some support because of anti-Catholic feeling, his

broader horizons—overseas and in outer space. In his inaugural address, Kennedy pledged his country "to pay any price, bear any burden, meet any hardship, support any friend, oppose any foe to assure the survival and success of liberty." And early in his presidency he set as a national goal the sending of an American to the Moon before the young decade was ended—an objective that would be reached in July 1969, after he had been killed.

Foreign affairs brought the first major setback for the Kennedy presidency, and one of the worst blows to American prestige in the postwar era. An April 1961 attempt, spon-

Vice-President Johnson joined President Kennedy, Mrs. Kennedy, President and Mrs. Truman, and others in enjoying the inaugural parade, above, left. Glamour and style characterized the Kennedy White House. In April 1962 the Kennedys honored Nobel Prize winners, including Pearl Buck and Robert Frost, at a White House dinner.

determination to challenge bigotry endowed his candidacy with a moral fervor and helped him to gain his party's nomination. Another asset for Kennedy was his choice of Lyndon Johnson to be his running mate. Johnson helped the ticket carry his native state of Texas, and this was critical in Kennedy's narrow victory over the Republican nominee, Vice-President Richard Nixon.

The New Frontier

Kennedy's slender margin restricted his freedom of action on domestic issues, as he himself privately conceded by quoting Thomas Jefferson's remark that "great innovations should not be forced on slender majorities." Seeking action, he turned his attention to

sored by the Central Intelligence Agency, to overthrow Cuban ruler Fidel Castro by landing an insurrectionary force at the Bay of Pigs failed. Planning for the invasion had begun under the Eisenhower administration, but, as Kennedy later admitted, he blundered in allowing the enterprise to go forward. However, continuing tensions between the United States and Cuba ultimately would lead to one of Kennedy's greatest triumphs—facing down Soviet Premier Nikita Khrushchev in the Cuban missile crisis in October 1962 (*see* page 199). Moreover, President Kennedy skillfully built on that military success to achieve a significant diplomatic triumph—a nuclear-test-ban treaty with the Soviet Union, which was

The Cuban Missile Crisis

In 1962 the Cold War between the United States and the Soviet Union raged full blast. Potential flash points for an explosion were spread across the globe, from Indochina to the Congo, but no spot was more dangerous than Cuba—the largest island in the Caribbean Sea, known for its beautiful beaches.

The rise to power in Havana of Fidel Castro, an avowed Marxist-Leninist, had created a potentially grave threat to U.S. security. In early 1961 the United States had sought to end that threat by sponsoring an invasion of Cuba by anti-Castro forces at the Bay of Pigs. This venture failed miserably, giving the new U.S. president, John F. Kennedy, a black eye. But Kennedy learned from that fiasco. His basic mistake, he concluded, was to take the advice of so-called military and intelligence experts without seriously challenging them. Next time, he promised himself, he would trust his own judgment.

The next time came soon enough. In October 1962, U.S. spy planes detected evidence of Soviet missile emplacements in Cuba (*photo, right*), 90 miles (145 kilometers) from the U.S. mainland. It was a stunning discovery. Soviet leader Nikita Khrushchev's démarche, if he got away with it, as Kennedy later said, would "materially...and politically change the balance of power" between the two great adversary states.

The president decided he must act, but to avoid a nuclear holocaust he acted with caution. When some advisers urged an air strike or an invasion, Kennedy insisted instead on imposing a blockade on Cuba to cut off further missile shipments. While the world held its breath, a Soviet ship steamed up to the U.S. naval cordon and then turned back. "We were eyeball to eyeball and the other fellow just blinked!" Secretary of State Dean Rusk exulted.

As the crisis neared its climax, Attorney General Robert Kennedy later reported, there was "almost unanimous agreement that we had to attack." But his brother, the president, held off. "It isn't the first step that concerns me," he explained, "but both sides escalating to the fourth and fifth step—and we don't want to go to the sixth because there is no one around to do so."

When Premier Khrushchev countered the U.S. demand that the Soviets withdraw their missiles from Cuba by insisting that the United States remove its own missiles from Turkey, President Kennedy observed: "...Most people would regard this as not an unreasonable proposal." Seizing upon Khrushchev's suggestion, Kennedy sent his brother Robert to tell Soviet Ambassador Anatoly Dobrynin that,

even before the onset of the missile crisis, he himself had decided to remove the missiles from Turkey, and that if the confrontation over Cuba ended peacefully, they soon would be taken out. The president also wrote Khrushchev, assuring him that the United States would not invade Cuba if the missiles were withdrawn.

The next day, Premier Khrushchev agreed to remove the missiles from Cuba. In victory, President Kennedy was magnanimous, welcoming the Soviet leader's "statesmanlike decision" and ordering members of his administration not to gloat or claim a victory. Kennedy had a larger objective in mind—a lessening of world tensions, which he helped achieve with the nuclear-test-ban treaty negotiated by the United States and the USSR the next year.

Robert Shogan

negotiated in the summer of 1963 and ratified by the U.S. Senate in September of that year. The accord, which forbade atmospheric testing of nuclear weapons and ultimately was signed by most nations, represented the first check on the arms race since the beginning of the Cold War.

Elsewhere, though, the deep-rooted antagonisms between the United States and the Soviet Union proved harder to reduce. In Europe the greatest danger loomed over the shaky status of the United States and its Western allies that occupied West Berlin. To demonstrate his determination to make the United States uncomfortable in Berlin, Khrushchev in 1961 erected the Berlin Wall, dividing the eastern and western sectors of the city. President Kennedy responded by

The 1963 March on Washington

The 1963 March on Washington was part of the emerging strategy of mass demonstrations and "direct action" used by civil-rights leaders to mobilize broad elements of the public in civil-rights causes and to focus media attention on particular injustices. In 1963 they hoped the March on Washington also would pressure the John F. Kennedy administration to follow up on the president's June 1963 address on America's moral obligation to secure civil rights for all citizens and to make good on its promise to see enactment of a federal civil-rights bill. The Aug. 28, 1963, March on Washington (*photo, right*) was directed by A. Philip Randolph, a longtime civil-rights advocate and labor leader who had organized the March on Washington Movement in 1941 that forced the Franklin D. Roosevelt administration to end segregation in the defense industry.

Randolph enlisted the National Association for the Advancement of Colored People (NAACP), the Southern Christian Leadership Conference (SCLC), the Student Nonviolent Coordinating Committee (SNCC), and the Congress of Racial Equality (CORE), in various degrees of enthusiasm, for a rally at the nation's capital for jobs and freedom. At first, President Kennedy balked at the idea of the march, fearing that violence would embarrass his administration, but he acceded to it after assurances from Martin Luther King, Jr., and others that the march would be ecumenical and peaceful. Bayard Rustin assumed principal responsibility for planning.

On August 28 more than 200,000 people of different races and religions arrived in the capital, carrying banners calling for "jobs and free-

dom" and singing "freedom songs." They gathered between the Washington Monument and the Lincoln Memorial, where they sang with popular singers and listened to long speeches on a hot, humid day. The locked arms of blacks and whites swaying and singing together "We Shall Overcome" bespoke, for a moment, the "beloved community" promised by the civil-rights movement, just as young

calling National Guard and reserve units to active duty and by telling a wildly cheering crowd during a visit to the beleaguered city: "*Ich bin ein Berliner!*"

And in Asia, in one of the most fateful decisions of his presidency, Kennedy, trying to meet the threat of Communist success in Indochina, quietly expanded the nation's involvement in Vietnam by dispatching U.S.

people playing in the Reflecting Pool on the mall symbolized a new baptism of reform spirit. The high point came with King's "I Have a Dream" address, which closed the rally and stamped its moral authority on the public mind. In his speech, King told of his dream "that one day this nation will rise up and live out the true meaning of its creed," and that "all of God's children, black men and white men, Jews and Gentiles, Protestants and Catholics, will be able to join hands and sing in the words of that old Negro spiritual, 'Free at last! Free at last! Thank God almighty, we are free at last.'"

The media portrayed the march as a success, as did President Kennedy and many of the march's leaders. The millions of Americans who watched the rally and heard the speeches on television also shared in the march's spirit of community and promise. And King's peroration would echo thereafter as the mantra of the civil-rights movement. Behind the scenes, though, the more militant civil-rights leaders, especially from the SNCC, criticized the march as too much show and too little "direct action." The failure of Congress to pass a civil-rights bill in 1963 seemed to justify the criticism. Indeed, it would take Kennedy's assassination the following November and the political genius of President Lyndon Johnson to get the Civil Rights Act of 1964 through a reluctant Congress. But the March on Washington had galvanized national support in the attack on segregation and had enshrined King as the shining figure of the civil-rights movement and the experience of the march as its shining moment.

Randall M. Miller

troops. The troops ostensibly were supposed to act only in an advisory role to the forces of South Vietnam.

At home, in the arena of civil rights, Kennedy initially had decided not to seek new legislation, calculating that the influence of conservative southerners in the Congress would prevent enactment of antisegregation measures. But the energy and determination of the burgeoning civil-rights movement forced his hand. Throughout the South, sit-ins, "freedom rides," bus boycotts, mass marches, and other protests—many led by the eloquent Martin Luther King, Jr.—and the brutal response of local police using clubs, fire hoses, and dogs captured the nation's sympathy. Those actions also gained support from the Justice Department, headed by the president's brother, Robert Kennedy, and led President Kennedy himself to propose a broad new package of civil-rights measures. "The heart of the question is whether...we are going to treat our fellow Americans as we want to be treated," Kennedy told the nation in a dramatic televised address in June 1963. A massive, peaceful March on Washington in August 1963 also had an impact on the movement (*see* page 200).

But for all the president's forceful rhetoric and the impassioned protest of civil-rights activists, his program seemed to be going nowhere on Capitol Hill when an assassin's bullets claimed his life in Dallas on Nov. 22, 1963 (*see* page 202). It remained for his successor in the Oval Office, Lyndon Johnson, himself a man of the South, to overcome that region's historic resistance to the struggle against segregation. The shocking tragedy of the assassination that elevated Johnson to an office many doubted he could have won on his own would haunt his presidency. But the immediate impact of Kennedy's slaying was to unify the nation in a way not seen since Pearl Harbor, a mood Johnson was quick to exploit.

The Great Society

A master strategist who had learned the inner workings of Washington at the feet of Franklin Roosevelt, Lyndon Johnson shrewdly laid claim to Kennedy's legacy in his first postassassination address. Reminding the nation of the goals Kennedy had set forth, most of which remained to be reached, he

Dallas movie theater for the murder of J.D. Tippett, a Dallas police officer. Tippett was questioning Oswald about the Kennedy murder when he was shot and killed. Oswald, a 24-year-old former U.S. Marine who had spent time in the Soviet Union, denied that he had killed the president. On November 24, Jack Ruby, a nightclub owner in Dallas, shot and killed Oswald as he was being transported to another jail by Dallas police (*photo, page 203*). The act was seen live by millions on television. Ruby claimed that he shot Oswald to avenge the president's death. Jack Ruby was convicted of Oswald's murder on March 14, 1964; he died of cancer on Jan. 3, 1967.

The JFK assassination—and the television coverage that began 15 minutes after the shots were fired and ended with Kennedy's funeral three days later—shook the nation. It was "the greatest simultaneous experience in the history of this or any other people," historian William Manchester wrote. The sight of young John F. Kennedy, Jr., saluting his father's coffin was a particularly poignant moment (*photo, left*).

The events in Dallas also gave rise to many theories about Oswald's guilt and the role of others in the Kennedy assassination and Oswald murder. To counter well-publicized conspiracy rumors, President Lyndon B. Johnson, Kennedy's successor, appointed a seven-member commission headed by Supreme Court Justice Earl Warren to look into the matter. The panel's conclusions,

At 12:30 CST on the afternoon of Nov. 22, 1963, President John F. Kennedy was riding in an open limousine through downtown Dallas with his wife, Jackie, and Texas Gov. John Connally and his wife, Nellie. It was the second day of a political visit to Texas during which Kennedy was working to stop infighting within the Democratic Party in Texas and to rally that state's Democrats to support his 1964 reelection.

As the presidential motorcade passed the Texas School Book Depository building, several gunshots were fired. Connally was wounded. President Kennedy was hit in the head and the neck. He died a half hour later in Dallas' Parkland Hospital emergency room.

Later that afternoon, Lee Harvey Oswald, a Book Depository employee, was arrested in a

recalled that Kennedy had said at the start of his presidency, "Let us begin." Now the new president declared: "Let us continue."

President Johnson's first objective was the enactment of President Kennedy's civil-rights program, which he accomplished in midsummer of 1964. Then, setting out on his own, he proclaimed his vision of a Great Society—"a place where the meaning of man's life matches the marvels of man's labor"—and, as the first installment on that promise, launched nothing less than a "War on Poverty."

But these proposals turned out to be only appetizers for the far-reaching menu he would press upon Congress. To clear the way for that effort, Johnson in 1964 won a landslide victory over the GOP's hapless candidate, Arizona Sen. Barry Goldwater, whom Democrats succeeded in depicting, with the help of Goldwater's own ill-considered utterances, to be a right-wing extremist. On election day, not only did Lyndon Johnson himself win the presidency in his own right by more than 15 million votes, but the Democrats gained the biggest advantage they had enjoyed in Congress since the heyday of Johnson's early hero, Franklin Roosevelt.

Johnson's agenda was tailored to match his party's majorities. The president seemed to offer something for nearly every national interest of consequence. Medicare for the elderly and federal aid to education for young middle-class families were the major

known as the Warren Report, were released in September 1964. The 888-page report, based on the testimony of 552 witnesses, concluded that Oswald acted alone, that he fired the three shots that killed Kennedy and wounded Connally, and that Oswald killed Tippett. The Warren Report did not put an end to the conspiracy theories, which included claims that the assassination was carried out by agents of Cuba or the Soviet Union and that Kennedy was killed on orders of American organized-crime leaders.

A U.S. House of Representatives select committee began an extensive review of the assassination in 1976. The committee's report, released in 1979, said there was a "high probability" that a second gunman had fired on the presidential motorcade and that it was "likely" that a conspiracy was involved in the murder. By 1999, however, historians generally were in agreement that Lee Harvey Oswald acted alone in assassinating President Kennedy.

Marc Leepson

After African-Americans launched a protest drive in Birmingham, AL, in 1963, officials used police dogs and fire hoses to disperse marches. Such tactics intensified sentiment in favor of civil rights.

1964 DEMOCRATIC NATIONAL CONVENTION

The Democrats chose their 1964 presidential ticket—Lyndon Johnson and Hubert Humphrey, above—at their national convention in Atlantic City, NJ, in August. One month earlier, the GOP had met in San Francisco and nominated "Mr. Conservative," Barry Goldwater, right, as their standard-bearer.

components of his Great Society blueprint; they headed a laundry list of other programs in areas ranging from the arts and Appalachia to water pollution and weather forecasting. An added and momentous starter was voting rights. Not content with enactment of the landmark 1964 law striking down segregation in public accommodations, the civil-rights revolution had stormed another barricade of racism—voting rights. This drive led to a new cycle of demonstrations and violent attempts by local authorities to suppress them. President Johnson adopted the proposal of civil-rights activists to appoint federal voting registrars to ensure the access of blacks to the ballot box and made the stirring battle cry of the civil-rights movement his own. "We shall overcome," he declared in a stirring speech to Congress in March 1965; the legislature then sent the voting-rights bill to the White House for Johnson's signature on Aug. 6, 1965.

Yet all of these achievements on the domestic front could not solve the terrible dilemma abroad that posed the gravest threat to Johnson's plans for the Great Society, and this was the war in Vietnam. The 15,000 or so military advisers whom Kenne-dy had shipped to Indochina clearly had proved inadequate to stem the Vietcong revolt against the government of South Vietnam. That left Johnson with the agonizing choice of escalating the war or pulling out. Whichever decision he made, he knew would damage his presidency. "I knew from the start," Johnson would say later, "that if I left the woman I really loved—the Great Society—in order to get involved with that bitch of a war on the other side of the world, then I would lose everything at home. All my programs." But Johnson was equally convinced that the Great Society would be doomed because its progenitor would lose credibility if he appeared to abandon the anti-Communist cause in Indochina.

Vietnam and Its Consequences

President Johnson's thinking about Vietnam was influenced by the pre–World War II debate in the United States over intervention versus isolationism. "Like most men and women of my generation, I felt strongly that World War II might have been avoided if the United States in the

President Johnson honored President Truman (below, right) by signing the Medicare bill into law at the Truman Library in Independence, MO, on July 30, 1965. Truman had been an early supporter of a national health-insurance measure.

1930s had not given such an uncertain signal of its likely response to aggression in Europe and Asia," the president later wrote. This judgment inclined him toward relying on a military solution to Vietnam.

Mindful, though, that his political allies had branded Republican Goldwater a warmonger in the 1964 campaign, Johnson was reluctant to make a public commitment to rely solely on the use of force in Vietnam. Consequently the U.S. strategy there was shaped largely by unplanned events and cloaked in ambiguity, leading opponents of the war to accuse Johnson of deception and bad faith.

The first such event was an apparent attack by the North Vietnamese on U.S. destroyers in the Tonkin Gulf in the summer of 1964. Johnson used the murky circumstances of the Tonkin Gulf incident to pressure Congress into adopting a resolution giving approval in advance for "all necessary measures to repel any armed attack against the forces of the United States and to prevent further aggression." Critics later charged that this resolution amounted to "a blank check" for Johnson to operate at will in Southeast Asia.

The belief that if South Vietnam fell to the Communists, other nations of Southeast Asia would suffer the same fate was behind the Johnson administration's escalating effort to help South Vietnam. By November 1965, some Americans were protesting that the war effort was hindering the enactment of the president's Great Society program at home.

Then in early 1965 a Vietcong attack on the U.S. barracks in Pleiku, South Vietnam, that killed nine Americans led Johnson to launch a sustained campaign of "tit-for-tat" bombing raids against North Vietnam. But the war continued to go badly for the United States and its South Vietnam ally, and the

In January 1968, U.S. Marines, right, fought to hold their position in Hue, South Vietnam, as the Communists launched a major offensive during the Tet holiday. Two months later, President Johnson partially halted the bombing in Vietnam and declared that he would not seek reelection in November, and Sen. Eugene J. McCarthy, below, was an antiwar presidential candidate.

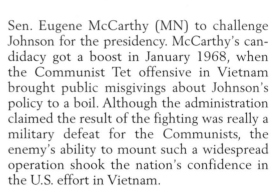

United States began sending more ground troops to Vietnam, first to defend U.S. installations, then to launch attacks with South Vietnamese army units. Without a formal declaration or presidential acknowledgment, the United States had gone to war.

As the U.S. troop strength climbed toward 500,000 and casualties mounted, protests against the war intensified. Unimpressed by the claims of the Johnson administration that there was "light at the end of the tunnel," opponents of the war, following the trail blazed by the civil-rights movement, took to the streets in the nation's capital and many of its cities. As the 1968 election campaign approached, leaders of the antiwar movement persuaded Democratic

Sen. Eugene McCarthy (MN) to challenge Johnson for the presidency. McCarthy's candidacy got a boost in January 1968, when the Communist Tet offensive in Vietnam brought public misgivings about Johnson's policy to a boil. Although the administration claimed the result of the fighting was really a military defeat for the Communists, the enemy's ability to mount such a widespread operation shook the nation's confidence in the U.S. effort in Vietnam.

In the nation's first 1968 presidential primary, in New Hampshire in March, McCarthy, the peace movement's candidate, won enough votes to claim a moral victory over Johnson. In short order, Robert Kennedy, who had won election to the U.S. Senate from New York in 1964, announced his own candidacy for the nomination. Johnson, with his dream of a Great Society in ruins,

After the Republican Party again turned to Richard Nixon as its presidential candidate in 1968, the former vice-president selected Spiro Agnew (left), the 50-year-old governor of Maryland, as his running mate. The Nixon-Agnew ticket won a squeaker over Hubert Humphrey and Edmund Muskie in November.

206

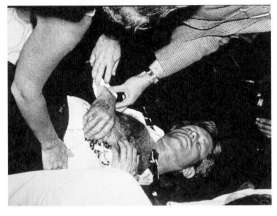

On April 4, 1968, civil-rights leader Martin Luther King, Jr., was shot fatally in Memphis, TN. Following King's funeral in Atlanta, right, his widow, above, took her husband's place at a sanitation workers' march in Memphis. On June 5, Sen. Robert F. Kennedy, below, was assassinated after winning California's Democratic presidential primary.

dropped out of the presidential race to devote himself to the quest for peace. That action cleared the way for Vice-President Hubert Humphrey to run.

Though the Democratic Party's established leaders had been weakened by the changes of the postwar era, they had sufficient influence to help Humphrey gain the nomination. But his triumph was tarnished by the tragedy and violence that marked the conclusion of the bitter battle for the Democratic nomination. The assassination of Robert Kennedy in June, following his victory in the California primary, had traumatized the nation and robbed the Democrats of the leader best able to exploit the reputation of John Kennedy and to hold together the fractious elements of the old New Deal coalition. At the time of Robert Kennedy's death, the nation had not recovered from the assas-

sination of civil-rights leader Martin Luther King, Jr., two months earlier. And the rioting in Chicago during the Democratic National Convention, along with the chaos within the convention hall, provided Americans, via television, with the image of a party unable to control even its own deliberations, let alone lead the way out of the Vietnam quagmire.

The only real winner at the Democratic convention was former Vice-President Richard Nixon, the Republican nominee. In the general election, a three-way contest involving Alabama's Democratic Gov. George Wallace, who exploited the white backlash against the civil-rights movement, Nixon won the White House by a margin almost as narrow as was his 1960 defeat by John Kennedy.

Robert Shogan

Richard Nixon, Watergate, and the Aftermath

As Richard Nixon took office as the 37th president, the war in Indochina presented a giant stumbling block, overshadowing all other concerns and threatening to prevent any accomplishments—foreign or domestic. Nixon wanted to end the war, but he wanted to do so, as he later emphasized, "in a manner that would save the South Vietnamese people from military defeat and subjection to the domination of the North Vietnamese Communist regime." Just as important, he wanted the war to end in a way that would maintain U.S. credibility as a world power, so he could carry out his double-barreled grand strategy—establishing diplomatic relations with Communist China and détente with the Soviet Union.

Though mindful of the potential power of the peace movement that had forced Lyndon Johnson to give up the presidency by not seeking reelection in 1968, Nixon worried that any steps he took toward peace might

make it harder to bargain with the North Vietnamese, who would view such concessions as signs of weakness. As president, Nixon intended to wind down the war in Indochina, following a policy he called "Vietnamization." But he was determined to move at his own pace, not in response to the antiwar movement. His basic approach to solving the dilemma of Vietnam was to make the Vietnam settlement part of a "global transaction," allowing the United States to take advantage of the split between China and the USSR, which Nixon realized could be of enormous benefit to the United States.

Richard Nixon and the Silent Majority

Once he took office, Nixon's initial bargaining objective in Vietnam was to get the North Vietnamese to withdraw from South Vietnam as a condition for ending U.S. involvement. Nixon's grand strategy combined diplomatic finesse with military might, and while it focused on Vietnam, it also scanned broader horizons in the Communist world. Nixon looked to Moscow, where he sought détente, and at the same time looked to Beijing, where he laid the groundwork for a dramatic new relationship.

Underlying Nixon's global blueprint was his political strategy at home, which was dependent on holding the support of middle-class Americans, who were frustrated by the Vietnam war but also concerned about protecting the nation's security. The president achieved this rapport in part by pitting himself against the antiwar protest movement, whose raucous style and aggressive tactics a good many Americans found unsettling. Nixon unveiled this strategy in November 1969 in one of the most successful speeches of his presidency, when he chided the protesters for "the bitter hatred" that infused their opposition to the war, pledged to withdraw all U.S. troops from Vietnam, and directly appealed to what he described as "the great silent majority of my fellow Americans" to back his policies. Recalling that he had promised during his campaign for the White House to end the war in a way that also could win the peace, Nixon added: "The more support I can have from the American people, the sooner that pledge can be redeemed."

By morning the White House had received the biggest response ever to a presidential speech—more than 50,000 wires and 30,000 letters, nearly all of them favorable—and Nixon's standing in the polls soared. Nixon himself later wrote that, as a result of the

After Richard Nixon became the first president to resign from office, on Aug. 9, 1974, he and Mrs. Nixon (at right in photo, page 208) were escorted to a waiting helicopter on the White House lawn by his successor, Gerald Ford, and Mrs. Ford. In the 1972 presidential race, Nixon had overwhelmed his Democratic challenger, Sen. George McGovern (SD) (top photo, right). U.S. Rep. Shirley Chisholm of New York (top photo, center) was among those who challenged McGovern for their party's nomination. The "Jesus People," photo above, an unorganized movement of young people committed to Christian fundamentalism, came to the fore in the early 1970s.

The Woodstock Generation

The nation's first mammoth outdoor rock festival took place Aug. 15–17, 1969, near the town of Woodstock, NY. Billed as "Three Days of Peace and Love," the Woodstock Music and Art Fair featured many popular rock acts of the day, including the Who, the Doors, Jimi Hendrix, and Bob Dylan. The event drew a crowd estimated at up to 500,000 young people, many of whom sported the trappings of the counterculture: long hair, bell-bottom blue jeans, open drug use, and liberated sexual attitudes. The singer Janis Joplin called the crowd "a new minority group." In fact, those who attended the Woodstock concert were part of a majority: the 76-million-strong baby-boom generation, the largest in U.S. history. Baby boomers were born in the 18 years following World War II (1946–64).

Also known as the Woodstock generation, the Dr. Spock generation, the television generation, the rock 'n' roll generation, the '60s generation, the Vietnam generation, and the Yuppie generation, the baby-boom generation and its needs shaped important segments of American society beginning in the early 1950s, when baby boomers first entered the nation's schools in record numbers. This huge influx of students caused severe overcrowding and teacher and classroom shortages in elementary schools in the mid-1950s and in secondary schools in the 1960s. The nation's high-school population doubled between 1950 and 1975.

The boomers began crowding the nation's colleges in the 1960s. When they reached adolescence, the oldest segment of the generation put an indelible stamp on the decade of the 1960s, during which a "youthquake" reverberated throughout the American social landscape, influencing everything from hairstyles to lifestyles. Many Woodstock-generation members spent their young adult years in the 1960s and early 1970s disdaining the social, religious, moral, and political values of their parents' generation. Some forsook the corporate-job market in order to work for social change, joining the civil-rights, public-interest-law, environmental, feminist, anti–Vietnam war, and other antiestablishment movements.

As the members of the Woodstock generation entered the workforce in the early and mid-1970s, they bore the brunt of the economic difficulties of that time. Conversely, as the older members approached middle age and the younger ones entered the labor force, many former counterculture adherents enthusiastically embraced mainstream society, taking advantage of the economic boom of the 1980s and 1990s. In addition, many baby boomers who had put off childbearing during their 20s began to raise families in the early 1980s, and the Woodstock generation produced a baby boomlet of its own by mid-decade.

In January 1993, 46-year-old Bill Clinton assumed the presidency, becoming the first baby boomer to hold the nation's highest political office. The election symbolized the Woodstock generation's ascendancy to the upper reaches of political and economic power in the United States.

Marc Leepson

speech, "I had the public support I needed to continue a policy of waging war in Vietnam and negotiating for peace in Paris until we could bring the war to an honorable and successful conclusion." In the 1972 election, Nixon—while standing firm on his Vietnam policy—won a landslide victory over the Democratic nominee, George McGovern, a 50-year-old U.S. senator from South Dakota who had built his candidacy around opposition to that policy. Ultimately Nixon did achieve his aims—withdrawal from Vietnam, détente with the Soviets, and the beginning of a relationship with the Chinese.

But prolonging the war caused much bitterness and resentment. And although Nixon gained the backing of the silent majority, a vocal and determined minority of Americans actively opposed his policies. Their opposition was intensified in May 1970 by Nixon's decision to "clean out major enemy sanctuaries" in Cambodia. Protests erupted on campuses around the country, notably at Kent State University in Kent, OH, where four students were killed by National Guardsmen called out to suppress the protests. In October 1970, nearly a year after his silent-majority address, Nixon appeared ready to make peace in Indochina. He proposed allowing North Vietnamese forces to remain in Vietnam, an idea he previously had rejected, while U.S. troops made a staged withdrawal. But the North Vietnamese rejected Nixon's proposition, demanding that any agreement must include the ouster of Nguyen Van Thieu's South Vietnamese government. Thieu was doomed anyway, as later events demonstrated, but Nixon was unwilling to accept direct responsibility for his downfall. A truce was not signed until January 1973, under terms that allowed Thieu to stay in power.

Meanwhile, Nixon moved dramatically to offset public discontent about the slow pace of his peace negotiations. Abruptly contravening the unyielding opposition to anti-

National Guardsmen breaking up a demonstration by more than 1,000 students at Kent State University in Kent, OH, on May 4, 1970, shot and killed four students and injured at least eight others. The shootings caused considerable anguish, not only on the Kent State campus, below, but also nationwide.

EQUALITY OF RIGHTS UNDER THE LAW SHALL NOT BE DENIED OR ABRIDGED BY THE UNITED STATES OR BY ANY STATE ON ACCOUNT OF SEX

American women entered the 20th century with few rights and little influence outside the home. But their role in American society expanded rapidly. Within a few decades, women had won the right to vote and had enlarged their presence in the workforce beyond the traditional "feminine" jobs of teaching, nursing, and clerical work. When men were sent to fight in World Wars I and II, women became family breadwinners, working in traditionally male-dominated settings.

But after the soldiers resumed their jobs following World War II, progress in women's rights abruptly ceased. During the conservative 1950s, women returned to their roles of wives, mothers, and housekeepers.

The women's-liberation movement was born in the 1960s as a reaction to what its leaders saw as systematic repression of women's rights. In her landmark book of 1963, *The Feminine Mystique*, Betty Friedan sounded the call for equal rights for women. Activists organized and lobbied Congress for change. In 1963 lawmakers passed the Equal Pay Act; in 1964 they outlawed sex discrimination with the Civil Rights Act.

Introduction of the birth-control pill in the 1960s gave women new freedom from unwanted pregnancies. As technological advances reduced the number of jobs requiring muscular strength and made the workplace more hospitable to women, female employment grew, surpassing 50% by the late 1970s.

The National Organization for Women (NOW), formed in 1966, advocated legalized abortion nationwide, a goal that was reached with the 1973 U.S. Supreme Court ruling in *Roe v. Wade*. It was during the 1970s that the women's-liberation movement reached its peak. In 1972 alone, Gloria Steinem founded *Ms.* magazine as a forum for feminist ideas; Title IX ensured that women had equal opportunity to participate in programs (most notably sports) offered by educational institutions that received federal funds; and Congress passed the Equal Rights Amendment (ERA) to the U.S. Constitution.

But antifeminist sentiment also was strong and only grew with the emergence of more radical feminist groups in the 1970s. This resentment exploded in the 1980s, when conservative ideas enjoyed a resurgence with the support of President Ronald Reagan. Antifeminist, antiabortion groups demanded that *Roe v. Wade* be overturned. They also accused the feminist movement of forcing women to abandon their traditional stronghold, the family, only to be exploited in the male-dominated workplace.

Although abortion rights survived the antifeminist backlash, the ERA failed to be ratified. Nevertheless, the women's-liberation movement left a lasting mark on American society. Although a resilient "glass ceiling" kept women from gaining a significant presence in corporate boardrooms, by the end of the 20th century, nearly half of all managerial and professional positions were held by women.

Mary H. Cooper

Communism that had marked his political career, he traveled to the People's Republic of China in February 1972 to begin the process of establishing normal relations with that country. As the presidential election approached, he thus was able to present himself to the country as a peacemaker. On the domestic front, he already had moved boldly to bolster the faltering economy by installing sweeping controls over wages and prices in 1971. In 1970 the U.S. Post Office was converted into an independent U.S. Postal Service, and in 1972 legislation establishing revenue sharing, under which needed funds for state and local governments were allotted through direct federal payments, was enacted.

As Nixon dealt with another domestic challenge—race relations—his tactics often produced controversy and division. In winning his party's nomination and the general election in 1968, Nixon had made plain, as part of his overall appeal to middle-class voters, that as president he would be an ally of white southerners, sympathetic to their anxieties about the threat of racial integration. The votes of southern whites helped to elect Nixon president; he carried five southern states. Once in office, he sought to solidify southern support. He challenged the Supreme Court's strong stance against segregation by ordering the Justice Department to resist its orders. When that approach failed, Nixon sought to change the court. He twice

The U.S. Senate confirmed, by wide margins, the nominations of two Nixon appointees to the U.S. Supreme Court—William H. Rehnquist (left) and Lewis F. Powell, Jr. (right)—in December 1971.

tried to fill a court vacancy with conservative southern judges, but each nomination was rejected by the Senate, in part because of the nominee's views on civil rights.

For all of Nixon's machinations, school desegregation in the South went forward anyway, with the full authority of the high court behind it. Meanwhile, Nixon's southern supporters helped him win his overwhelming reelection victory in 1972, a triumph that he was confident would "give the Republican Party the new majority momentum that would give it a new lease on life."

Nixon's Second Term and Resignation

President Nixon also was convinced that his own landslide victory at last had given him a mandate to tame Congress and the balky bureaucracy, too. "There are no sacred cows," he told members of his White House staff on the day after the election. "We will tear up the pea patch." Shortly after the election, he stepped up the bombing of North Vietnam and then announced broad new impoundments of funds appropriated by Congress. At the same time, he began selecting his most trusted White House aides for posting in the cabinet agencies during his second term, hoping to strengthen his control over the executive branch as he girded for confrontation with Congress.

In accordance with a Vietnam cease-fire agreement signed in 1973, North Vietnam began releasing American prisoners of war. Lt. Col. Robert L. Stirm, left, received a warm welcome home from his family.

Just as the Cold War defined U.S. foreign policy for much of the second half of the 20th century, it had a powerful impact on domestic politics, particularly after the struggle against Communism turned hot and bloody in the jungles of Vietnam. Ultimately the Vietnam war set the stage for the Watergate scandal, which forced Richard Nixon to become the first American president to resign the office in disgrace.

Earlier the Vietnam protest movement had crippled Lyndon Johnson's presidency, leaving him no choice but to abandon his plans to run for reelection in 1968. Nixon, after succeeding Johnson in the White House, was determined not to let the protest movement get the best of him. But his battle against those who resisted his Vietnam policies warped his presidency in ways he could not foresee or control.

As biographer Joan Hoff-Wilson wrote, Nixon's conduct of the ending of the war "established secrecy, wiretapping, and capricious personal diplomacy as standard operation procedures in the conduct of foreign policy that ultimately carried over into domestic affairs." In his own self-revealing analysis, Nixon wrote that in his struggle against the peace movement, "I was sometimes drawn into the very frame of mind I so despised in the leaders of that movement"—their willingness to justify any means in order to achieve their goal of ending the war.

The excesses that came to be known as Watergate were foreshadowed in 1971 by the Pentagon Papers case, when Nixon vainly sought to prevent newspaper publication of a classified Defense Department study of the Vietnam war, claiming it threatened national security. Seeking to gather evidence to discredit Daniel Ellsberg, the former National Security staffer who had released the papers in 1971, a covert White House unit called "the plumbers" had burglarized his psychiatrist's

files. Later, John Ehrlichman, Nixon's chief domestic adviser, defended the break-in, telling the Senate Watergate investigating committee (*photo below*) that it was "part of a very intensive national security investigation," whose authorization was "well within the president's inherent constitutional powers."

Not all the misdeeds lumped together under the Watergate rubric were connected directly to Vietnam. The scandal began to emerge in June 1972 with the arrest of five burglars who were attempting to break into Democratic Party headquarters in Washington's Watergate complex. The culprits

had ties to the Committee for the Re-election of the President (known by the acronym CREEP), which it turned out was involved in a systematic campaign of perpetrating "dirty tricks" designed to embarrass and confuse the Democratic opposition.

But the basic rationale for these heavy-handed campaign tactics, including the burglary of Ellsberg's psychiatrist's office, later was described by former Nixon speechwriter William Safire as "an attitude of us against them," an outlook rooted in the tensions arising from the president's battle against the war protesters.

Nixon steadfastly denied any role in the burglary or in the cover-up of the crime. But his doom was sealed in the summer of 1973, when it was revealed that he secretly had taped all his Oval Office conversations (*photo, page 214*). The turning point in the case came in October 1973, when Nixon ordered the firing of special prosecutor Archibald Cox for insisting that Nixon turn over tapes that Cox wanted as evidence. In turn, Elliott Richardson and William Ruckelshaus resigned as attorney general and deputy attorney general, respectively. Both had refused to dismiss Cox. That action, which came to be known as "the Saturday night massacre," brought a storm of pub-

lic indignation down on Nixon's head and set the stage for the House of Representatives to launch an impeachment inquiry.

Nixon fought on. But in July 1974 the House Judiciary Committee voted three articles of impeachment against the president— for obstructing justice, abuse of power, and impeding the impeachment process. Additional taped disclosures of his role in trying to cover up the Watergate burglary led most members of his own party to desert his cause, and on Aug. 9, 1974, Nixon resigned the presidency (*photo above*).

Robert Shogan

But Nixon's hopes for his party and for his own second term as president were undermined by the scandal of Watergate. The mysterious burglary of Democratic Party headquarters in June 1972, which at first had been dismissed as a trivial "caper," took on increasing and ominous significance as sordid revelations of the behavior of the president's closest advisers began to emerge, first in a trickle, then in a flood (*see page 214*).

In the midst of his own difficulties, President Nixon was confronted by a scandal involving his vice-president, Spiro Agnew, who was forced to resign in October 1973 by revelations of payoffs he had received during his tenure as governor of Maryland. He pleaded nolo contendere to one count of income-tax evasion. In the first use of the 25th Amendment to the Constitution, Nixon selected House Republican leader Gerald Ford of Michigan as his vice-president. Though the choice of Ford was popular, it did little to lessen the outcry against Nixon because of the Watergate scandal, fed by new disclosures of wrongdoing. His incumbency, which had been of great benefit to Nixon during his 1972 reelection campaign, when he was able to make his breakthrough visit to Communist China and establish economic controls to ward off inflation, now became an added burden for the beleaguered chief executive. When oil and gas supplies dwindled during the Arab oil embargo in 1973, the public's resentment of the shortages added to the anger against Nixon. The president sought to draw public attention away from the Watergate scandal and other domestic problems by touring the Middle East in June 1974 and by signing arms-control accords with Soviet Party Chairman Leonid Brezhnev in Moscow the following month. But the mounting drive for impeachment forced him to resign in August.

The Gerald Ford Administration

The major challenge facing Nixon's successor, Gerald Ford, was to restore the credibility of government in the wake of the Watergate scandal. He was handicapped in that effort by the fact that he was the first president to take office without having run in a national election. Ford, nevertheless, initially won public approval with his first speech, in which he announced, "Our long national

nightmare is over," and by his natural and open manner. His choice of former New York Gov. Nelson Rockefeller as his vice-president also was applauded widely.

A month after taking office, though, Ford stunned the nation by issuing a "full, complete, and absolute" pardon to Nixon for any Watergate crimes he might have committed. Though some historians later concluded that Ford had acted in what he believed was the national interest, the abruptness of his decision and his failure to adequately explain his reasoning caused damage from which his presidency never recovered.

Ford had other problems, notably the vicissitudes of the economy. He grappled, with little success, first with inflation and then with a severe recession. In the 1974 congressional elections, the public's concern over the ailing economy and resentment of the Nixon pardon took a heavy toll on Republican congressional ranks, leaving Ford facing huge Democratic majorities. His response was to adopt what came to be called a veto strategy. "During his brief tenure," a Brookings Institution study concluded, "President Ford undoubtedly vetoed more bills raising important substantive issues than any previous president." There were setbacks overseas, too. In April 1975 the South Vietnamese government collapsed, marking the

final defeat for the long U.S. struggle against Communism in Indochina.

As the nation was celebrating its bicentennial, Ford won his party's presidential nomination in Kansas City, MO, in August 1976 only after a bitter struggle against conservative forces led by former California Gov. Ronald Reagan. That competition left him and his vice-presidential candidate, Sen.

Jimmy Carter, Mrs. Carter, and other family members walked to the White House after the former Georgia governor was inaugurated as the 39th president.

Robert Dole of Kansas, in a weakened condition for the general-election campaign against the Democratic challenger, former Georgia Gov. Jimmy Carter, and his running mate, Sen. Walter Mondale of Minnesota; Carter and Mondale won a narrow victory in November.

Jimmy Carter—A Political Outsider

Carter's status as a little-known political outsider, and his stress on his born-again Christian background, helped him gain nomination and election amid the disillusionment that colored the post-Watergate political environment. But once he was in power, Carter's inexperience in national affairs hindered his efforts to deal with the nation's problems, and his moralizing struck some Americans as sanctimonious. He proposed sweeping measures to reform the welfare system and the tax code, and to remedy what he called the energy crisis. But he failed to generate public support behind his ideas, and his accomplishments fell far short of his objectives. Two cabinet posts, the departments of energy and education, were established during the Carter presidency, however.

Carter won high marks from foreign-policy experts for gaining Senate approval of the Panama Canal treaties, which provided for turning over the canal to Panama by the year 2000, and for hosting the Camp David negotiations between Israel and Egypt that were hailed as paving the way toward a lasting peace in the Middle East. It was also during the Carter administration that China and the United States established full diplomatic relations.

But Carter's activism in foreign affairs could not ease his problems at home. When the USSR invaded Afghanistan, Carter called for a boycott of the 1980 Summer Olympics in Moscow. The overthrow of the shah of Iran caused a severe shortage of gasoline in the United States, while consumer prices and interest rates soared out of control. Carter's efforts to rally the country behind him by declaring that the nation was suffering from "a crisis of confidence" and by firing a number of his top advisers only added to public anxiety and distress.

In the midst of Carter's domestic difficulties, Iranian extremists seized control of the U.S. embassy in Tehran and held more than 50 Americans hostage. Carter rededicated his

In Panama City on June 16, 1978, President Carter and Panama's Brig. Gen. Omar Torrijos (top right) exchanged the instruments of ratification of the new Panama Canal treaties. Under the agreement, jurisdiction over the canal would pass from the United States to Panama. "No-frills" groceries that sold at cheaper prices than major brand names were introduced in the 1970s as a means for the American public to combat ever-increasing inflation.

presidency to freeing the hostages, but diplomatic efforts were of no avail, and an attempted military rescue ended in disaster. Although Carter defeated Sen. Edward M. Kennedy (MA) for the Democratic presidential nomination in August 1980, the public's frustration over the hostages and resentment of the economic turmoil helped bring about Carter's defeat and the election of Republican Ronald Reagan to the presidency in November.

Robert Shogan

Ronald Reagan brought to the presidency strong convictions and the skill to communicate his beliefs to the public. These assets allowed him to set in motion a series of changes that his admirers hailed as the Reagan Revolution and that even his critics conceded redefined the U.S. political agenda. Reagan's policies had two major imperatives: at home, to check the power of the federal government; and abroad, to meet the threat from Communist regimes. The struggle against "the evil empire," as Reagan called the USSR, offered an additional advantage, because if the government's resources were expended on national security, they would not be used on domestic programs.

The Reagan Revolution

More than any other modern president since Franklin Roosevelt, Reagan presented himself as holding a firm ideological position. But the distinctive quality of his political philosophy was that it was drawn largely from the circumstances of his own life. Reagan spoke in his own natural idiom—that of a sports announcer, which had been his first full-time work, and of a movie actor, the trade that had occupied much of his adult life—with a compelling simplicity.

His first task after succeeding Jimmy Carter in the White House was to remedy what he called "the worst economic mess since the Great Depression." Reagan prescribed a giant cut in income-tax rates and drastic budget reductions, which mainly reduced benefits to low-income Americans and others dependent on such federal programs as food stamps, Medicare, public-service jobs, unemployment compensation, urban mass transit, and student loans. Meanwhile, Reagan also carried out a huge increase in defense spending that jibed with his ideological imperative to curb the threat of Communist aggression. "Defense is not a budget issue. You spend what you need," Reagan told his budget director, David Stockman.

Democrats in Congress, meanwhile, were demoralized by the Carter presidency and depleted in numbers—in his 1980 victory, Reagan also had helped Republicans gain control of the U.S. Senate. They put up little resistance to the Reagan program. The president dominated the political landscape, not only because of his ideas but also because of his personality. Gaining the release of the Tehran hostages at the start of his presidency gave his popularity an early boost, and the courage and grace he showed after he was felled by a would-be assassin's bullet in his first months in office made him a national hero.

The rationale for Reagan's tax cuts was supply-side economics, the theory that a reduction in tax rates would stimulate the economy to generate more than enough revenue to cover the cuts. Budget director Stockman questioned the theory and urged reductions in such federal entitlement programs as Social Security to keep deficits from getting out of hand. But Reagan was unwilling to take the political risk such action would involve. As it turned out, Stockman was right. The federal-budget deficit would soar to record levels by the time Reagan left office.

Reagan's leadership was tested during his second year in the White House by a severe recession, which cost his party dearly, especially in the House, in the 1982 midterm election. But apart from agreeing to a $100 billion tax increase, which he described merely as loophole closing, Reagan stuck to his supply-side theories. And when prosperity returned full blast in 1983, "Reaganomics" got the credit, boosting Reagan's popularity to new highs and helping him win a 49-state landslide reelection in 1984 against Democrat Walter Mondale, who had been Carter's vice-president. Mondale made campaign history by naming a woman, U.S. Rep. Geraldine Ferraro of New York, as his running mate. For his part, Reagan also had helped advance the feminist cause during his first months as president by naming Sandra Day O'Connor to the U.S. Supreme Court; she was the first woman so honored.

The worst blemish of Reagan's presidency was the Iran-contra scandal, which reflected

Fifty-two U.S hostages who had been held in Iran since November 1979 were released, above, just as Ronald Reagan took office; the new U.S. president warned that terrorism henceforth would be met with "swift and effective retribution." Reagan won reelection by a landslide in 1984 over Democratic challengers Walter Mondale and Geraldine Ferraro, right.

The Bush Administration

In winning the presidency over the Democratic candidate, Massachusetts Gov. Michael Dukakis, in 1988, George Bush, Reagan's vice-president, benefited from the continued economic boom that was part of Reagan's legacy. Bush sought to distance himself from Reagan's conservatism by promising "a kinder, gentler presidency." But his domestic initiatives were modest, and he had difficulty gaining their enactment by the Democratic-controlled Congress. (The Democrats had retaken control of the Senate in 1986.) In 1991, Bush nominated Clarence Thomas, a 43-year-old African-American judge, to succeed Thurgood Marshall on the U.S. Supreme Court. Thomas was confirmed only after Senate hearings that focused on charges of sexual harassment brought against him by Anita Hill, a former colleague.

As Bush himself implicitly conceded, he was more interested in foreign than domestic

his administration's frustration in coping with the Communist regime in Nicaragua and with Mideast terrorism. Overzealous aides sold arms to supposedly moderate Iranian officials in hopes of gaining the release of U.S. hostages, and sent the money paid for the weapons to *contras*—guerrillas opposing the leftist Nicaraguan government. Though Reagan claimed to be unaware of most of these machinations, their disclosure seriously damaged his reputation. In other foreign-affairs developments, the U.S. embassy in Lebanon was destroyed in 1983 as U.S. forces participated in a multinational force in Lebanon; 241 U.S. servicemen were killed in the terrorist attack. Reagan repaired some of the damage to his prestige caused by the Lebanon tragedy by sending U.S. troops to the Caribbean island of Grenada in an "effort to restore order and democracy."

Reagan got much higher marks for his handling of relations with the Soviet Union. Though early in his presidency he was accused of warmongering because of his arms buildup and advocacy of the "star-wars" missile-defense program, his success during his second term in reaching a missile-reduction agreement with Moscow was hailed as presaging the end of the Cold War.

President Reagan's second term saw triumphs and embarrassments. He and Soviet leader Mikhail Gorbachev exchanged visits, above, right, and concluded an arms treaty in 1987. Meanwhile, the administration was embroiled in the Iran-contra affair. Marine Lt. Col. Oliver North, above, testified about the secret arms sales. Reagan's vice-president, George Bush, right, won the 1988 presidential election.

Bill Clinton and the Perils of the Presidency

When the Watergate scandal forced Richard Nixon to leave the White House in disgrace in August 1974, many Americans hoped that episode would be just an aberration in the history of the presidency. Instead, the nightmare of Watergate ushered in a long period of travail and trauma for the nation's highest office, culminating with the impeachment of President Bill Clinton on the threshold of the new millennium.

Three of Nixon's five successors—Gerald Ford, Jimmy Carter, and George Bush—saw their tenures end in defeat at the voting booth when they lost the confidence of the electorate. The other two post-Nixon presidents, Ronald Reagan and Clinton, each won reelection, but each also suffered through shattering scandals that tarnished his legacy and, in Clinton's case, threatened to oust him from office.

Partisan rivalries and a divided government contributed to these difficulties. The readiness of the Republican-controlled Congress to move against scandal-ridden Democrat Clinton was foreshadowed by the aggressiveness of Democratic congressional majorities in probing Watergate under Republican Nixon and the Iran-contra affair under Republican Reagan.

Character weaknesses gave ammunition to presidential foes. Nixon's insecurity, bordering on paranoia, created a siege mentality in his White House. Reagan's neglect of his responsibilities allowed his aides to wreak havoc with the law. And Clinton's lack of self-discipline could be blamed for much of his trouble.

The environment that led to Clinton's impeachment was established during his 1992 campaign for the presidency, when charges of sexual dalliance and draft evasion focused attention on his character and behavior. Early in his presidency, the detritus from an investment he and First Lady Hillary Rodham Clinton had made many years before in a controversial Arkansas real-estate venture called Whitewater led to the appointment of an independent counsel, Kenneth Starr. Meanwhile, sexual-harassment charges brought against Clinton by a former Arkansas state employee, Paula Jones, added to his embarrassment and to the legal pressures he faced.

In early 1998, as Clinton was beginning his sixth year in the White House, his difficulties came to a head. Whitewater counsel Starr turned up allegations that the president had tried to conceal an illicit relationship with a young White House intern, Monica Lewinsky, in order to avoid undermining his defense against Paula Jones' harassment suit. A huge uproar ensued, lasting for more than a year. After vehemently denying the charges for seven months, the president confessed that he had misled the nation. In December 1998 the House of Representatives, acting on evidence provided by Starr, voted largely along partisan lines to impeach the president on charges of perjury and obstruction of justice. Clinton was the first elected U.S. president ever to be impeached. The only other impeached chief executive, Andrew Johnson, had succeeded to office from the vice-presidency after Lincoln's assassination.

The robust economy helped save Clinton in the Senate, where neither charge gained a majority, much less the two-thirds vote required for conviction. While polls showed that most Americans disapproved of Clinton's personal behavior, they feared that ousting him might disturb the nation's prosperity. Others argued that, while Clinton had dishonored his office, he had not abused his power. Afterward, Clinton said he hoped his acquittal would lead to "a period of reconciliation and renewal." But history suggested that the bitterness aroused by his struggle for survival would linger to plague his successors.

Robert Shogan

The presidency of Bill Clinton started on a hopeful note, as his wife, Hillary Rodham Clinton, above, campaigned for health-care reform. The reform attempt was unsuccessful, and Clinton's tenure was plagued by ever-more-serious problems, as independent prosecutor Kenneth Starr, right, brought allegations against him that led to a vote of impeachment.

affairs. In his first year in office, Bush had authorized U.S. federal troops to oust Panama's dictator, Manuel Noriega. It also was in the diplomatic arena that Bush registered the major achievement of his presidency, marshaling the international coalition that launched "Operation Desert Storm" in 1991 and forced Iraqi ruler Saddam Hussein to abandon his conquest of Kuwait. That victory turned out to be the high-water mark of the Bush presidency. Soon afterward, the economy slid into recession, and Bush's popularity plummeted. Unable to cope with the slump, Bush and his vice-president, Dan Quayle, were defeated in the 1992 election by the Democratic ticket of Arkansas Gov. Bill Clinton and Tennessee Sen. Albert Gore. Maverick billionaire Ross Perot, who ran as an independent, captured 19% of the vote. It was the largest percentage for any third-party candidate since Theodore Roosevelt ran on the Bull Moose ticket in 1912.

The Clinton Presidency

Clinton, whose campaign for the presidential nomination had been plagued by charges of womanizing and draft evasion, entered office with the support of only a minority of the electorate and had difficulty from the start. Seeking to redeem his campaign promise to overhaul the nation's health-care system, he put his wife, Hillary Rodham Clinton, in charge of the reform effort, but his proposal failed to win congressional support. The president did gain congressional approval for the North American Free Trade Agreement (NAFTA) with Canada and Mexico. Capitalizing on Clinton's weaknesses, however, Republicans gained control of both houses of Congress for the first time in 40 years in the 1994 midterm elections. A ten-point plan, the Contract with America, which was reminiscent of President Reagan's economic program, was the basis of the GOP platform. Once in power, however, Republicans, led by House Speaker Newt Gingrich of Georgia, overplayed their hand, forcing a shutdown of the federal government in a budget dispute with Clinton. As voters rejected GOP efforts to carry out the conservative programs pledged in the Contract with America, Clinton gained popularity by contrast.

Helped by a booming economy, Clinton easily won reelection over Republican standard-bearer Bob Dole in 1996. But Clinton's foes continued to pursue reports of scandal, and in 1998 an independent counsel, Kenneth Starr, turned up evidence that the president had carried on a sexual liaison with a young White House intern and then had tried to cover it up. Starr's allegations led to Clinton's impeachment on charges of perjury and obstruction of justice. The Senate acquitted him of both charges in February 1999 (*see* page 221).

Meanwhile, a federal-budget surplus was realized in 1998, and Clinton had signed a major welfare-reform bill in 1996. On the diplomatic level, Clinton focused on developments resulting from the breakup of the former Yugoslavia, Israeli-Palestinian issues, and efforts to help bring peace to Northern Ireland.

Robert Shogan

BUSINESS AND INDUSTRY

The New York Stock Exchange

An Overview

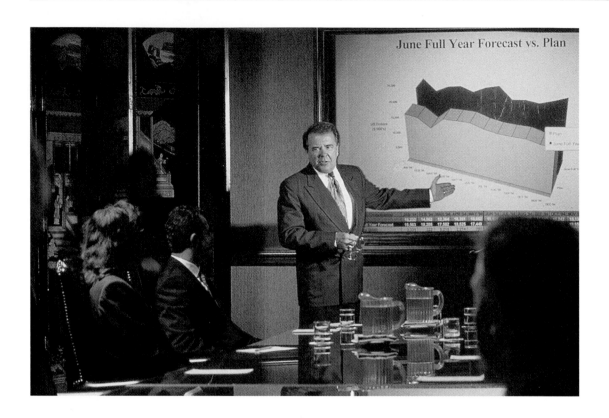

The 20th century began with an explosion of industrial activity fueled by the technological advances of the Industrial Revolution. With the steam engine, precision machine tools, and an urban workforce already in place, manufacturers were poised to embark upon a flurry of industrial activity that was to alter radically the way people live and work the world over. Most of the century's industrial innovations came from the United States, where a democratic political system and deference to free-market economic principles unleashed a surge of inventions, industrial output, and consumption that was unprecedented in human history.

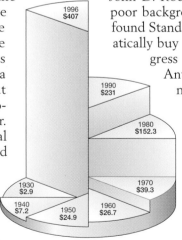

U.S. Corporate Profits After Taxes
(in billions)

The Tycoons and the Assembly Line

That the United States offered favorable conditions for business development already was apparent at the turn of the century,

when some of the country's most memorable tycoons already were amassing their fortunes. John D. Rockefeller had emerged from a poor background in upstate New York to found Standard Oil Company and systematically buy out his rivals. Even after Congress passed the 1890 Sherman Antitrust Act to discourage such monopolistic practices, Rockefeller built Standard Oil into the world's first major multinational corporation. Rockefeller and his contemporaries—steel magnate Andrew Carnegie and financiers J. Pierpont Morgan and Andrew Mellon—set the stage for the American business expansion that would follow.

The Industrial Revolution had begun in Britain, but by the turn of the century the American Midwest had emerged as a world center of manufacturing. It was in Detroit, MI, that the modern industrial age was born in 1913 with the invention of a radical new production technique, the assembly line. The brainchild of Clarence W. Avery, a manager at Henry Ford's Model T factory in the Detroit suburb of Highland Park, the assembly line revolutionized the way workers made products. Rather than putting together a product from start to finish, assembly-line workers concentrated on just one phase of the production process, as a carefully paced mechanical belt moved parts around the factory floor from one assembly station to the next.

The assembly line greatly quickened the pace of production and helped give rise to the Roaring 20s, a decade of rapid industrial development and economic growth. By 1923, Ford was turning out 1.8 million Model Ts a year, nearly a tenfold increase over the number produced in 1913. As other manufacturers adopted the assembly line, unit costs plummeted, bringing cars and many other complex manufactured goods within reach of working Americans for the first time. The Model T's sticker price, for example, fell from more than $900 to less than $300 over the decade.

New Management Techniques

The assembly line was just one aspect of a revolution in manufacturing practices to come out of Detroit. At General Motors, Ford's main automotive rival, Alfred Sloan developed corporate-management techniques that improved productivity, in part by speeding up the pace of assembly. Resentful of the faster pace and monotony of assembly-line work, workers left factories in droves, while those who remained joined labor unions to protect their interests. As a result, manufacturers were forced to raise wages and offer pensions and other benefits that were to become the hallmark of U.S. union-negotiated labor contracts. In coming decades, the system of mass production based on fast-paced assembly and organized labor that took hold in Detroit quickly spread throughout the industrial world.

Modern advertising and marketing practices also took root in the 1920s to promote sales of the myriad new consumer products turned out by U.S. industry. Americans responded eagerly, buying cars, appliances, and other new products as fast as manufacturers could produce them. As consumption

American industrialist and philanthropist John D. Rockefeller (1839–1937) (at left in photo at left) established the Standard Oil Company. Its first service station, above, opened in Columbus, OH, in 1912. Rockefeller's son—John D. Rockefeller, Jr. (1874–1960) (at right in photo at left) primarily devoted himself to philanthropy.

The Great Stock-Market Crash of 1929

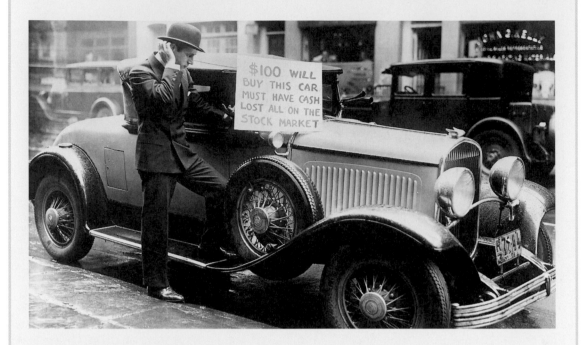

$100 WILL BUY THIS CAR MUST HAVE CASH LOST ALL ON THE STOCK MARKET

Of all the financial calamities in modern history, the most notorious struck Wall Street in October 1929, when the great bull market of the Roaring '20s collapsed in a thunderous crash. The initial panic was concentrated in a single week, from Wednesday, October 23, through Tuesday, October 29. But its aftereffects would be felt for many years to come, in the lives of countless individuals who lost fortunes and in the history of a country that was about to enter the Great Depression.

On successive days, the Dow Jones industrial average suffered two of its biggest percentage losses ever—13.5% on October 28 and another 11.7% on October 29. The average finished October with a net loss for the month of 20.4%. In his book *Only Yesterday*, Frederick Lewis Allen told of the shares of White Sewing Machine Company, which had fallen from a high of $48 to $11.12 by Monday, October 28. The next day, "Black Tuesday," a buy order was executed for $1 a share.

At least one prominent trader killed himself in the aftermath of the debacle. Although historians have noted that the suicide rate in New York actually did not increase during this period, the image has been burned into the nation's consciousness of a time in which many lives were ruined. "Wall Street Lays an Egg," *Variety* declared in one of the most famous newspaper headlines ever published.

The causes of the crash, and its role in setting the stage for the Depression to come, have been debated ever since. One theme on which almost all commentators agree is that the world was witnessing the bursting of a speculative bubble—that years of excessive enthusiasm in the stock market had made a letdown inevitable, perhaps even necessary.

For all the trouble and loss it inflicted, the crash also provided the impetus for quite a number of positive events in the years that followed. Using lessons learned from the crash, Congress enacted a series of laws in the 1930s and 1940s that created the U.S. financial regulatory structure that still remains in use—including the Securities and Exchange Commission (SEC) and the Federal Deposit Insurance Corporation (FDIC)—as well as the modern mutual-fund industry and other important engines of prosperity. The crash also contributed to a greatly increased understanding of the way markets, and economies, work.

Chet Currier

expanded, so too did the innovative practice of buying on credit.

Wealthier Americans also used credit to buy stocks, sometimes paying as little as 10% of a stock investment in cash. As long as businesses flourished in the infant consumer market, fortunes were made on the strength of borrowed money. But the speculative bubble finally burst on Tuesday, Oct. 29, 1929, when the bottom fell out of the stock market, wiping out nearly $30 billion in investments (*see* page 226).

The Great Depression, World War, and the 1950s

Although "Black Tuesday" affected only a small minority of Americans directly, fallout from the stock-market crash was widespread and set the tone of the decade to follow. By the early 1930s, almost 30,000 businesses had gone under, throwing millions of Americans out of work. At the Great Depression's depth, almost one quarter of the entire U.S. workforce was unemployed.

The Great Depression marked the end of the boundless faith in unfettered capitalism that had fueled the century's early industrial development and the beginning of a system of government regulations to mitigate the free market's adverse impacts. Under President Franklin D. Roosevelt's New Deal, stock-market regulations were adopted to prevent excessive speculation; bank deposits were insured; and workers gained pension rights, workplace-safety standards, and other protections.

The outbreak of World War II spurred demand for planes, tanks, and other industrial goods, and helped pull the U.S. economy out of the Depression. After the war, returning soldiers went to work, started families,

and moved to the suburbs (*see* page 230), launching the next great consumer-driven business expansion. The appearance of television as a mass medium in the 1950s greatly strengthened the influence of advertising over Americans' buying habits. Consumer spending accelerated further at the end of the decade, when Bank of America and American Express introduced the first plastic credit cards.

This was the heyday of big corporations, which lured talented workers with the promise of lifetime employment and generous benefits. The corporate culture, personified by the complacent, gray-suited "organization man," made companies like International Business Machines (IBM), General Electric (GE), and Procter & Gamble household names among the rapidly growing middle class. At the same time, banking, insurance, and other service industries were displacing traditional manufacturing companies as the U.S. economy's driving force. By 1956, white-collar office workers for the first time outnumbered blue-collar production workers in the United States.

After World War II the American veteran, above, bought a "gray flannel suit," joined a corporation, and moved his growing family to the suburbs. George Meany, right, helped negotiate the merger of the American Federation of Labor (AFL) and the Congress of Industrial Organizations (CIO) in 1955. He then served as the first president of the merged union, the AFL-CIO, until November 1979.

Automation

As the 20th century ended, the term "automation" was heard much less often than in the 1950s and 1960s. During those decades, the popular notion of automation was exemplified by the introduction of robots into factories. A story that may be apocryphal—but is nonetheless indicative of the popular conception of automation—made the rounds among industrial-relations specialists: An automobile executive showing United Auto Workers President Walter Reuther through a plant using the latest state-of-the-art production asked, "Walter, how are you going to collect dues from these robots?" Reuther replied, "How are you going to sell them cars?"

This dialogue, whether true or not, reflected a widespread concern that automation greatly would reduce the need for manpower, leading

to unemployment and loss of purchasing power, and thereby creating major economic problems in the United States. This concern led President Lyndon Johnson to establish the National Commission on Technology, Automation, and Economic Progress in 1964. The commission's charge was to identify and assess the effects of technological change on production and employment, and to recommend specific steps that should be taken to promote the positive effects and to prevent and alleviate the adverse impact of change on displaced workers. It made a number of rec-

ommendations, but it did not anticipate the extent to which simplified robots would be employed as standard production machines or the fact that computers would become indispensable tools in businesses, offices, schools, and daily activities.

Automation has come to be used as shorthand for the much more meaningful term "technological change," which includes new methods of production and new designs of products and services. Examples include automation of a machine tool, reorganization of an assembly line, substitution of plastics for metals, bookkeeping by electronic computer, and many others. While technological change was recognized as generally beneficial, it also reawakened fears that it would lead to widespread unemployment.

In ensuing decades, computerization proceeded at a rapid pace in nonmanufacturing industries. The U.S. Department of Labor has projected that, by the year 2006, employment in computer and data-processing services will reach 2.5 million. The fastest-growing demand is expected for database administrators, computer-support specialists and scientists, engineers, and systems analysts.

As computers take over more and more tasks formerly performed by humans, scientists warn that they have significant limitations. For example, no computer can be programmed to deal with contingencies that cannot be anticipated. As computers become more and more embedded as the underlying performers of a wide variety of social and organizational tasks, they also become more invisible. Gene I. Rochlin, a physics professor at the University of California at Berkeley and the author of *Trapped in the Net: The Unanticipated Consequences of Computerization*, warns: "It is all too easy to forget that [computers] are also idiots, having no information other than what has been supplied them, and capable of doing no more than has been programmed into them....Over time, they will be increasingly out of sight, but they must never be out of mind. Otherwise, it is humans, and not the computers, who will become invisible idiots."

Jack Stieber

Fast-food restaurants, left, grew rapidly and contributed to the boom in franchising in the 20th century. In fact, the "Golden Arches" of McDonald's became one of the world's most recognized symbols. The American public experienced gasoline shortages, especially in the 1970s and 1980s, and considered changes in gas prices, below, as their personal barometer of the cost of living.

A New Corporate Culture

By the 1960s it was becoming apparent that the rise of big business had failed to benefit all of society. The gap between middle-class workers and poor Americans grew, setting the stage for the social unrest and the civil-rights movement that marked the decade. The growing clout of corporations also helped change the flavor of communities across the country. Big discount-chain stores such as Kmart and Sears appeared in suburban shopping centers, driving smaller, downtown stores out of business and gutting urban centers.

Another aspect of the prevailing corporate culture was a boom in franchising. Interspersed among the suburban mega-stores were fast-food restaurants and motels, such as Howard Johnson, Burger King, and Marriott. The biggest franchise operation of them all was McDonald's—based on a small burgers, fries, and shakes operation in San Bernardino, CA. After opening his own McDonald's fast-food restaurant in Des Plaines, IL, in 1955, entrepreneur Ray Kroc developed the franchise into the biggest restaurant company in the world; by century's end it had some 7,500 locations in the United States and more than 100 other countries.

Decades of intensive industrial development came at a high cost to the environment. In the 1970s urban smog, dying rivers, and waning populations of birds poisoned by pesticides gave rise to the environmental movement. Over the decade, Congress passed landmark legislation to curb air and water pollution, forcing businesses to invest in new technologies to help protect the environment. Concern over the country's environmental health mounted with a series of energy crises that exposed the growing U.S. reliance on oil, a dwindling and highly pol-

The Postwar Housing Shortage

In August 1945 the guns stopped firing, and the bombs stopped falling. World War II was over. In the following months, soldiers, sailors, and airmen began returning home to resume their lives. Many rejoined wives and children, and many others soon married and began their families. The housing stock, especially in the industrial cities of the Midwest and the East, was woefully inadequate for their needs. Little housing had been built during the Depression or the war. The result was severe overcrowding, with many families doubling up with parents and other relatives or staying in inadequate housing that lacked amenities like indoor plumbing or central heat.

In order to build single-family housing (the American dream) on a large scale, developers looked beyond city borders that often had been sealed several decades before. Annexation laws made suburban incorporation easy, and the housing needs of the veterans created a market for the explosion of new communities beyond central-city borders. The new housing developments varied in cost and design. Those geared to workers frequently shared the same layout, perhaps best epitomized by the mass-produced Levittowns (*photo*). Low production costs made such new communities attractive to returning GIs.

Available land and eager developers were not alone in stimulating this rush to suburbia. The mortgage-loan guarantees offered by the

federal government contributed significantly to the housing boom and to central-city decline. In the 1930s the Home Owners Loan Corporation (HOLC) set federal standards for property appraisal that came to govern the granting of Federal Housing Administration (FHA) and Veterans Administration (VA) mortgage-loan guarantees. The HOLC institutionalized redlining—discriminatory practices that would ensure race and class segregation in new subdivisions. Redlining meant that homes in older areas of cities were ineligible for the loan guarantees, as were homes in areas where African-Americans lived. Loans to African-American families in cities and suburbs also did not occur. Most FHA and VA mort-

---

luting energy source. An embargo on oil exports to the United States imposed by Arab producers in 1973 also triggered sudden increases in gasoline prices and sustained inflation that would last for more than a decade.

New Industrial Techniques

The 1970s witnessed a second major innovation in industrial practices, this time arising in Japan, where manufacturers adopted "just-in-time" inventory practices to reduce excess storage requirements and costs. Japanese workers were organized into teams and given more responsibility for product quality

than were traditional assembly-line workers. As American consumers chose low-cost, high-quality autos and electronic products from Japan over their domestic counterparts, U.S. manufacturers were forced to adopt the new industrial techniques or die.

In their effort to trim costs—an effort that intensified during the 1980s—American companies "downsized" their payrolls by eliminating middle-management jobs, "outsourced" many production and office jobs to nonunion southern states and low-wage Third World countries, and merged with competitors to broaden their markets. A major victim of these trends was the mid-

gages were granted to new housing outside core-city limits. Federal guidelines thus enabled suburban growth at the expense of neighborhoods in central cities. Discriminatory practices were quite common then throughout the lending and real-estate industries. The HOLC criteria extended the imprimatur of the federal government and served to sanction the standard private practices.

Many cities—such as Philadelphia, Detroit, Pittsburgh, and St. Louis—achieved their peak populations in 1950. By 1960 the flight to new housing at the periphery began to take its toll. The central cities grew poorer, smaller, and more heavily minority.

The Levittowns and the many other postwar housing projects built away from the city centers spurred additional construction, including freeways, strip malls, and large, enclosed shopping malls. All of this development added to downtown and central-city decline. Available land, low building costs, and amenable state-incorporation laws led to America's unique suburbanization. The federal use of restrictive lending practices made possible the waves of settlement by white home buyers. Yet, were it not for the lack of housing construction in the prewar and war years and the huge number of GIs needing housing after the war, the urban fabric might not have taken quite the form it did.

Lana Stein

western industrial heartland, which was transformed during the 1980s into the "Rust Belt," plagued by rising poverty and unemployment.

By the mid-1980s the service sector largely had displaced manufacturing as the main engine of the U.S. economy. Unlike the male-dominated union jobs of heavy industry, many of the new service jobs were provided by nonunion businesses and paid relatively low wages. But there was a vast pool of underemployed job-seekers who were ready to accept these conditions. Shedding their traditional role as homemakers, American women entered the job market in droves to

supplement family incomes that had been eroded by corporate downsizing and years of inflation.

The 1980s also witnessed a stock-market boom unparalleled since the Roaring 20s. Financial-service companies such as banks and brokerage houses flourished, as institutions and individuals alike invested heavily in stocks. Corporations merged and engaged in hostile takeovers, causing stock values to gyrate and transforming Michael Milken and other "yuppie" investment bankers, brokers, and corporate raiders into instant millionaires. As it had after the earlier boom, the stock market eventually crashed. On "Black Monday," Oct. 19, 1987, stock values dropped by almost 25%. But this time, thanks to regulations put in place after the earlier crash, the stock market rallied quickly.

The Information Age

The third great industrial innovation of the century was the development of computer

In the tight job market prevalent during the early 1990s, some Americans were forced to resort to innovative approaches in their search for employment, below. By March 1999, however, the U.S. employment rate was at 4.2%—a 29-year low.

The Conglomerate

Beginning in the 1960s, Harold Geneen built ITT, a listless owner of telephone companies, into an amalgam of large corporations in fire insurance, hotels, auto parts, credit, book publishing, street lighting, pumps, and oil and gas production. Buying, managing, and selling, ITT actually owned hundreds of companies over three decades, making it one of the largest and most successful conglomerates ever.

As Geneen explained in *The Synergy Myth*, his biographical account of the creation of the $6 billion-a-year ITT Corporation, "an operating conglomerate is a centrally managed company that gets deep into each of its operations." A conglomerate, he said, is not just a pudding stone of companies without relation to each other. "Its job is to own *and* operate companies," he said. Unlike a holding company, which invests in a company but rarely gets involved directly in managing it, a conglomerate does both. "It allows the individual groups a high degree of autonomy, but always subject to review and discipline from the top." Its task, "creating harmony from diversity, defines the mission of building a conglomerate," Geneen wrote.

Geneen was not alone in creating these large entities, nor was he by any means the first. Operating from the small town of Wakefield, RI, Royal Little spun Textron in the 1950s out of a small synthetic-yarn business, following his theory of "unrelated diversification" wherever opportunity promised. Over a period of three decades,

Textron was involved in woolens, hardware, helicopters, cement, cable television, outboard motors, fiberglass, pharmaceuticals, golf courses, bookselling, resorts, cattle ranching, and bowling alleys.

Among the postwar conglomerators, General Tire & Rubber Company was among the more stable and successful, diversifying from tires into rocket engines, entertainment, chemicals, plastics, and space. Gulf & Western Industries (*photo, left*), Litton Industries, and Ling-Temco-Vought became multibillion-dollar operations, created by visionary entrepreneurs using creative financing techniques advanced by equally inventive bankers.

New as they seemed to be, conglomerates had a long history. Such well-known companies as General Motors and duPont had been in seemingly unrelated enterprises for a long time, but they had developed their various interests gradually, ever mindful of antitrust laws. The new conglomerators expanded swiftly, with size and diversification as goals, and into such varied industries that they avoided accusations of monopoly. But their efforts were sometimes haphazard, and the rage to conglomerate reached its peak by the 1970s, undone mainly by its financial pyramiding and the less expansive economic times. "Conglomerate mania" left a legacy, however, and some of the much larger mergers of the 1990s benefited from its legal, regulatory, financial, and marketing lessons.

John Cunniff

More and more women joined the workforce in the century's latter years. Although women still largely were excluded from the top levels of corporate management, nearly half of all managerial and professional positions were held by women at century's end.

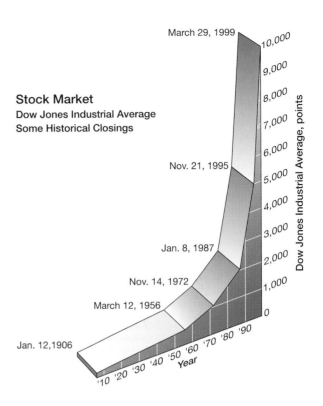

Stock Market
Dow Jones Industrial Average
Some Historical Closings

March 29, 1999 — 10,000

Nov. 21, 1995

Jan. 8, 1987

Nov. 14, 1972

March 12, 1956

Jan. 12, 1906

Dow Jones Industrial Average, points

Year

technology. In 1951 two engineers, John W. Mauchly and J. Presper Eckert, Jr., created UNIVAC, the first large mainframe computer that was available commercially to business and government agencies. But it was the Apple Computer Company, a business literally started in a California garage, that launched the information age by introducing the first easy-to-use personal computer (PC), the Apple II, in 1977. Four years later, IBM, the leading business-computer manufacturer at the time, rolled out its own PC. Apple countered in 1984 with the first Macintosh. As these models were joined by innumerable PC "clones," prices for personal computers plummeted, making them accessible to individuals as well as businesses.

The biggest high-technology fortunes were made by young entrepreneurs—such as Microsoft's Bill Gates—who founded start-up companies to produce word-processing programs and other computer software. Hired by IBM to create the operating system for its personal computer, Gates went on to dominate the software market with Microsoft's DOS and Windows systems and become the world's richest individual. New software products came on the market when the Internet—originally set up to facilitate communications among government agencies and university research labs—became more easily accessible to the public in the early 1990s with the creation of the World Wide Web and the introduction of Internet browsers and electronic-mail software.

As the world leader in computer and telecommunications technology, the United States thrived in the ongoing information age. Its fortunes mounted after the Soviet Union and its satellites collapsed at the beginning of the 1990s, and the free-market principles that had fueled business and industrial development in the United States and other Western countries became the guiding force of economic policies throughout the world. American businesses flourished in the expanding global market for goods and services, producing a period of sustained economic growth, low unemployment, and negligible inflation. Once again, U.S. stock values soared to record levels.

The U.S. economy was so strong in the 1990s that, as of the end of the first quarter of 1999, it had escaped harm from a financial crisis that swept through much of East Asia in 1997, spread to Russia in 1998, and threatened to infect Latin America. As the 20th century wound down, the United States remained the world's dominant player in the realm of business and industry.

Mary H. Cooper

ADVERTISING

It has been said that advertising has existed ever since about 160 B.C., when street hawkers in Carthage promoted local wine merchants and were compensated according to how much wine was sold. But it was not until the 20th century that the advertising industry—and the modern advertising agency—truly came into their own and began playing a key role in the culture, lifestyle, and economy of the United States.

Simply put, the story of the ad business in the 20th century can be divided into two parts—before television and after television. Conveniently, that division came virtually in the middle of the century, or the late 1940s, to be exact, when television sets began to be mass-produced and gradually became afford-able enough that a large percentage of American families could buy one. Before television, advertising was restricted to print and radio. Print included newspapers, maga-zines, outdoor boards, and, to some degree, direct mail or "junk mail," as many nonadver-tising practitioners call it.

At the end of the 19th century, advertising "agents" were essentially independent brokers of newspaper space. They served as middle-men between advertisers and the media, sell-ing newspaper space at full retail rates to merchants after purchasing the space at dis-counted rates directly from the newspapers. In those days, the agents provided no help in preparing the ads themselves—that chore was left in the hands of the advertiser. But by the beginning of the 20th century, the adver-tising agency as we know it today had emerged in New York, Chicago, and Philadel-phia, as the "agents" began increasing the kinds of services they provided to clients. Such services included creating the advertise-ments, buying media space, and negotiating for the best possible location for the ads within the newspapers.

In the years before World War I, some of the more enterprising agencies were develop-

Whether on radio in the 1930s and 1940s or on television in the 1950s and 1960s, bellhop Johnny Roventini, right, was a trademark with his "Call for Philip Morris." Cigarette advertising was banned from U.S. television and radio beginning in 1971.

ing a reputation as hucksters and wheeler-dealers that made false claims for the products they advertised, especially highly questionable potions and lotions. But as the industry grew and the marketplace matured, agencies became committed to more-honest forms of advertising. The industry reshaped itself, and by the 1920s it emerged as a respectable, often high-powered, and lucrative business. In 1926, speaking at the tenth annual meeting of the American Association of Advertising Agencies, President Calvin Coolidge said: "It [advertising] is the most potent influence in adapting and changing the habits and modes of life, affecting what we eat, what we wear, and the work and play of a whole nation."

Another significant factor in the development of the advertising industry was the concept of the brand. By the 1920s, as products proliferated and consumers matured, the idea of a product's "status" surfaced, as manufacturers discovered that consumers were developing loyalties to certain products. To reinforce that loyalty, marketers turned to advertising; the result was a boon for ad agencies. It was the birth of modern marketing as it existed at the end of the 20th century. Brands were at the heart of marketing, powered by the advertising that built, supported, and maintained them. This strategy was adopted by the biggest advertisers of the day and remained the guiding marketing philosophy of the biggest advertisers in the world—companies like Procter & Gamble and General Motors.

The ad industry also played a key role when the nation found itself embroiled in World War II. Only two months after the Japanese bombed Pearl Harbor, the War Advertising Council was formed to help the federal government persuade Americans of the importance of the war effort and the need for sacrifice. The Council immediately began to create ad campaigns to sell war bonds, support blood drives, recruit factory workers and nurses, and promote conservation of resources, and to develop slogans like "loose lips sink ships." The War Ad Council represented the birth of public-service advertising; the organization later became known as the Ad Council, which was responsible for developing most of the public-service advertising seen in the 1990s. This advertising included hard-hitting and effective ads addressing such issues as drunk driving, drug abuse,

The White Rock goddess, above, first was introduced in 1893 and, although "modernized" over the years, became one of the century's oldest and most recognized advertising symbols. Doyle Dane Bernbach's "Think Small" campaign for Volkswagen, right, helped put the German car on U.S. roads in large numbers during the 1960s.

Think small.

Dealer Name

child abuse, air pollution, and conservation. Some of the most famous Ad Council efforts included ads featuring Smokey Bear ("Only you can prevent forest fires") and the campaign for the United Negro College Fund ("A mind is a terrible thing to waste").

More than any other factor, the introduction of television in the late 1940s changed the face of advertising forever and was probably the single biggest development of the 20th century for the ad industry. It allowed marketers to reach more people than ever before in history, and to do it faster and more comprehensively. Advertisers not only could show their products, but could demonstrate them as well. The results were astonishing. Sales figures for products advertised on television skyrocketed, and commercials became more and more sophisticated, as ad agencies and their clients began to realize the incredible power of the new medium. In fact, it was ad agencies that were responsible for television programming in the early 1950s. It was the advertising agencies—not the networks or high-priced, star-spangled production companies—that actually produced television shows for their clients. This was especially true of daytime programming; "soap operas" are so-called because it was soap companies that originally sponsored them. Advertising's role in the birth of television also spawned many new industries—such as market research, opinion research, and audience measurement.

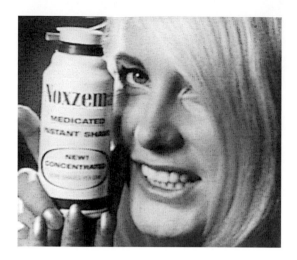

By the middle of the century, advertising truly became an engine that powered the economy. The more product a company sold, the more people the company could employ to make the product, create the package for the product, print the labels on the package, drive the trucks that delivered the product, stock the product on store shelves, and so on. All those people earned salaries, paid taxes, and pumped money back into the overall economy. To put the entire century into perspective, consider the following: In 1900 an estimated $450 million was spent on advertising in the United States. By 1999 that figure had increased to an astonishing $212 billion.

As television matured, so did advertising. In the mid-1960s an event occurred in the industry that reshaped it forever. This was known as the "creative revolution," and after it, advertising never looked the same. Up until the mid-1960s, most advertising, both print and broadcast, generally was straightforward. It was filled with information about the product and often employed a hard-sell approach through constant repetition of the brand's name and attributes. But a group of highly creative ad executives in New York, led by Bill Bernbach of the Doyle Dane Bernbach ad agency, decided to try something different. They broke all the rules that had existed up until that time and created

In 1995, Noxzema's 1960s ad "Take it off, take it all off" and Wendy's 1980s ad "Where's the beef?," featuring actress Clara Peller, were judged by the trade publication "Advertising Age" as two of the "50 best" commercials of television's first 50 years.

advertising that spoke more directly to consumers' interests. These new ads not only informed people about products, but did it in a way that was more entertaining than ever before. Perhaps the best example of this new trend was Doyle Dane Bernbach's campaign for the Volkswagen Beetle. The Beetle ads employed a self-deprecating, yet tasteful and elegant style that consumers loved and responded to. Other clients that reaped the benefits of this trend included Alka-Seltzer, Polaroid, American Tourister Luggage, Levy's Rye Bread, and Cracker Jack. Bernbach's influence was huge. Many young copywriters and art directors cited him as one of the reasons they chose advertising as their profession.

Another equally influential 20th-century advertising figure was Marion Harper. What Harper brought to the business side of the ad industry was as important and long-lasting as what Bernbach contributed to the creative side. In 1961, Harper, an executive with the McCann-Erickson ad agency, began buying other ad agencies and marketing-service companies and created the first holding company for ad agencies. The creation of this organization, christened the Interpublic Group of Companies, marked the first time a single parent company owned separate ad agencies that operated, conflict-free, under the same corporate umbrella. It was an idea that stuck, and in many ways it paved the way for the round of mergers and acquisitions among ad agencies that began in the mid-1980s and continued into the 1990s.

Harper's work in the 1960s paved the way for advertising luminaries like Charles and Maurice Saatchi, a pair of Iranian-born, London-bred brothers who created an advertising empire in the 1980s through a round of acquisitions that rocked the industry at the time. The Saatchis' chief financial architect, Martin Sorrell, later left the brothers and started his own holding company, WPP Group, after acquiring two venerable mainstays of Madison Avenue: Ogilvy & Mather and J. Walter Thompson. Not to be outdone

On January 24th, Apple Computer will introduce Macintosh. And you'll see why 1984 won't be like "1984."

A Chiat/Day campaign that was inspired by George Orwell's novel "1984" and introduced the Apple Macintosh computer during pro football's 1984 Super Bowl game, top, was shown only once but became a legend in the ad world. Companies long have turned to celebrities to market their products, and popular comedian Bill Cosby, above, was a longtime spokesperson for Jell-O. Speedy Alka-Seltzer sought to calm everyone's stomach during the 1950s.

by their British counterparts, American admen entered the fray with the formation of another holding company, Omnicom Group, which was created through the merger of three leading U.S. agencies—Doyle Dane Bernbach, Needham Harper Worldwide, and BBDO International.

After their formation in the 1980s, all of those companies continued to grow through acquisitions, leaving the landscape of the American advertising agency changed forever. Gone were the midsized independent ad agencies, most of which were swallowed up by the conglomerates. The industry had become polarized: There were huge, multinational holding companies on one end, and small, creatively driven boutique ad shops on the other.

John Wolfe

Agriculture

Never has agriculture changed so dramatically as in the 20th century. In 1900 nearly half of the U.S. population lived on farms. Draft animals, along with backbreaking human labor, provided power for farmwork. Farms were family operations where everyone from young children to senior adults worked. Most U.S. and Canadian farms were highly diversified. Enterprises included dairy cows for the family's milk, butter, cream, and cheese needs and for cash income. Vegetable gardens, an orchard, and such livestock as hogs, sheep, and chickens were essential. Families were partially self-sufficient, with much of their fuel, food, and clothing produced at home. Horses provided transportation, with the farm family taking only an occasional train trip. Farmers performed carpentry, blacksmithing, and butchering; made their own clothes; and took care of other essential activities. Neighbors shared work, and the social structure centered around relatives, neighbors, country schools, and local churches.

As the century ended, less than 3% of the U.S. population lived on farms. Scientists were mapping the tens of thousands of genes in each of several major crops. Agriculture utilized genetically modified crops and other biotechnology research, space-age geographic position systems, instant electronic market information, computerized record keeping

238

and marketing, and other developments unimaginable in 1900.

The seeds of change already were sown by 1900, with improvements in horse-drawn equipment, the gasoline engine, and electricity. The years 1910–19 saw rapid spread of traction engines (later called tractors) across the U.S. countryside and a decline in the draft-animal population. As the century progressed, farm families adopted innovations used by their city cousins, including electric lights, indoor plumbing, telephones, radios, automobiles, television, and computers. Universities in each state linked farmers with the latest research and scientific developments. With mechanization and rising worker productivity, the size of farms increased, while the number of farms declined. The 1930s Depression interrupted these trends when unemployment in the cities brought family members back to the farm. In the 1930s plant breeders developed hybrid-seed corn, the first of many scientific innovations in crop production. Dramatically improved varieties spread rapidly across the countryside, increasing agricultural productivity. Rural electrification led to milking machines and other equipment to reduce hand labor.

The post–World War II years brought numerous scientific developments, including manufactured fertilizer, chemical weed and insect control, genetic improvements in crops and livestock, better knowledge of crop and animal nutritional needs, and improved farm machinery. By the late 20th century, sophisticated farm equipment had computers monitoring internal processes and warning when trouble occurred. The differences between the living standards of farmers and their urban counterparts narrowed considerably. Other changes included less interaction with and reliance of farm families on neighbors, and an increased focus on urban-based social activities. The children of farmers went to city schools, in contrast to the one-room schools of the first half of the century. In areas far from industrial centers, the smaller farm population led to declining populations of rural towns, increased average age of rural residents, and declining availability of community services. Areas near indus-

Technological innovations wrought great changes in the U.S. agriculture industry during the 20th century. Farmers moved from using old-fashioned plows and threshers, page 238, to more sophisticated machinery—and even computers, above. The resulting rise in efficiency and worker productivity led to an increase in the acreage of farms, even as their number declined, page 238, graph.

trial centers saw rural populations increase as city residents moved to small part-time or hobby farms.

Agriculture in most developed nations followed that of the United States. Agricultural sciences helped farmers provide abundant food and natural-fiber supplies for a several-fold increase in global population. Even so, major challenges remain for the 21st century, as world population and food needs continue to expand, and farms in some developing countries remain largely untouched by modern technology.

Robert Wisner

THE AUTOMOBILE INDUSTRY

1908 Franklin Touring Car

As the 20th century dawned, the automobile industry was fast emerging from its raw beginnings and taking the shape of an international volume-production industry. Whether "horseless carriages" and their transportation offspring actually "defined" the century is questionable, but no single mechanical creation ever did more to change the lifestyle of its users.

The Early Days

By 1900, approximately 50 entrepreneurs already were exploring ways to build and sell gasoline-powered automobiles. Many individuals had built test vehicles of their own, primarily in Europe, but the first to build more than a single car were brothers Charles E. and J. Frank Duryea of Springfield, MA, in 1896. That same year, with 13 Duryeas built, Charles Brady King drove his four-cylinder automobile through downtown Detroit, followed on a motorized "Quadricycle" by an Edison Illuminating Company engineer named Henry Ford.

With promoters and mechanics furiously developing automaking ventures, the roots of what would be General Motors a decade later were planted in Lansing, MI, with the formation of Olds Motor Company by an engine builder named Ransom E. Olds. Ford had registered the Detroit Automobile Company in 1899, but he was preceded as the nation's first mass-producer of motor cars by Olds, whose curved-dash one-cylinder runabout Oldsmobile reached an output of 425 in 1901 and 2,500 the next year.

One year later, in 1903, Ford Motor Company was organized to produce Model A cars, fully five years before the phenomenally successful—and cheaper—Model T replaced it. Also in 1908, General Motors Corporation was born. The launch pace of the auto industry in the first decade of the new century was like a whirlwind, as investors, mechanics, and salesmen all clamored to board the bandwagon. The first national automobile show drew 48,000 persons, paying 50 cents apiece, to New York City's Madison Square Garden in November

240

1911 Oldsmobile Limited Touring Sedan

1900. No fewer than 51 exhibitors showed their wares, and few mourned the end of the bicycle as a transportation necessity.

The fledgling auto industry, demonstrating the exploratory genius of its technical creators, emerged with a variety of power plants and body styles. Of course, gasoline was offered as a fuel source, as were electricity and steam. Cars powered by electricity or steam were easier to operate than the early gas-powered vehicles. High carriage designs competed with a low-wheeled "French" body, which was more stable. Until Henry Ford turned the Model T into a highly "affordable" product for the working class, in the second decade of the century, most of the first cars were out of reach for any buyers but the wealthiest.

The first automakers found quite a challenge in raising money to organize and then staying solvent. No one in the early days was more successful at cobbling a company together than William Crapo Durant, a carriage salesman who in 1904 drove David Buick's Model-B near Flint, MI, and set about organizing an automaking company to rival those of other carriage manufacturers such as Ford and the Studebaker brothers in South Bend, IN. Durant bought out Buick in 1904, eventually absorbed Oldsmobile, and created General Motors in 1908, with Buick

1935 Model CZ "Airstream 8" Chrysler

as the nation's largest-selling car. Cadillac was purchased by GM a year later.

Despite financial and policy disputes that plagued the first automakers, Ford and Durant found other ways to generate cash. Sales of franchises to farsighted bicycle and carriage dealers or outside investors generated cash for exclusive territories and built the distribution system still prevalent today. The United States overtook France in auto production in 1905 and never relinquished its supremacy.

A Time of Growth

Though the first automakers were spread far and wide, the fact that expansionist pioneers such as Durant and Ford were located in the Detroit area undoubtedly established the

1920 Ford Model T Touring Car

Motor City as the center of the U.S. auto industry. Major suppliers—led by GM axle builder Charles Stewart Mott, of Utica, NY—located new plants in southeastern Michigan to become more accessible to their primary customers. A dozen auto-manufacturing plants were clustered in southeastern Michigan or northwestern Ohio alone, including such famous names as Dodge, Essex, Hudson, Hupmobile, Oakland (later to become Pontiac), Packard, and Willys. GM was headquartered in New York City until 1922, when it relocated to a new building in midtown Detroit.

As automobile sales boomed in the World War I decade, with GM adding Chevrolet as a challenger of Ford in the entry-level market, Durant undertook a series of financial manipulations that led to his unseating in

1920. The Du Pont family of Delaware, owning a controlling stock interest, installed as chief executive officer a stolid management expert, GM Vice-President Alfred P. Sloan, Jr., who reorganized the corporation into a paradigm for all industry during his 33-year reign as president and chairman. Under Sloan's leadership, focusing on strong vehicle divisions functioning as profit centers, GM overtook Ford to become the world's highest-grossing corporation in dollar revenues by the 1930s—a position it retained throughout the century. GM's brands dominated their segments from the 1920s until the 1990s, building GM's share of the U.S. market to a high of 50.7% in 1962 and inspiring calls in the 1950s for a "breakup" under the nation's antitrust laws.

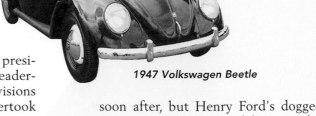

1947 Volkswagen Beetle

1955 Studebaker Regal Commander Station Wagon

GM's rise against a torpid Ford Motor Company, clinging to the aging Model T through the 1920s, was not without challenge from other new and existing competitors. The most successful of the post–World War I "upstarts" was Chrysler Corporation, founded in 1925 by former GM manufacturing executive Walter P. Chrysler. Chrysler in 1928 acquired the Dodge car and truck line and introduced the entry-level Plymouth car, giving the fast-growing new company strengths that carried it through the Depression, which drove out of business such venerable names as Jordan, Graham-Paige, Cord, Auburn, Essex, and Hupmobile.

GM, Ford, and Chrysler—the "Big Three" automakers, as they came to be called—were targeted in the mid-1930s by the newly organized United Automobile Workers (UAW) union. A bitterly fought sit-down strike in 1936–37 at GM's plant in Flint, MI, ended with recognition of the UAW. Chrysler Corporation acceded to the union

soon after, but Henry Ford's dogged resistance to "outside" control kept Ford a nonunion shop until 1941.

World War II brought about a total stoppage of new-vehicle production while the auto plants produced tanks, airplanes, and other military vehicles, including the Willys-built Jeep. The latter evolved into the highly popular sports-utility segment. Victory against Japan in 1945 set the stage for a post–World War II boom in new-car sales to a deprived American public. The Big Three and five independents emerged from the war eager to supply the demand, except that the elderly Henry Ford's neglect of company matters forced a "palace" revolt and replacement of the founder as top executive by his 28-year-old grandson, Henry Ford II. A group of 14 Army Air Force "whiz-kid" officers was brought in to streamline the company and barely save it from bankruptcy. Only one automaker ever has emerged from bankruptcy in the industry's 100-year history—Studebaker, during the Depression. A future company executive in the "whiz-kid" group included Robert S. McNamara, who later would serve as secretary of defense.

The early post–World War II years lured three newcomers to the industry, with the most prominent being Henry J. Kaiser, a West Coast shipbuilder. Kaiser-Frazer Corporation built both a small car called the Henry J, which was sold by Sears Roebuck as the Allstate, and full-size sedans. The venture failed following the recession of 1954, as had

1964 Ford Mustang

1970 Toyota Corolla 2-Door Station Wagon

other postwar ventures of Preston Tucker and Powel Crosley. The 1954 downturn also prompted independent automakers to merge. Hudson and Nash combined to form American Motors; George W. Romney, the future governor of Michigan, served as a chairman of American Motors. Studebaker and Packard also joined forces.

The Century's Later Decades

The 1960s brought fuel-emissions and safety standards to the auto industry. Safety regulations flowed in large measure from crusader Ralph Nader's attacks on the rollover propensities of Chevrolet Corvair cars. GM Chairman James M. Roche publicly apologized for hiring detectives to harass Nader. Early in the decade, Chrysler Corporation met supplier payola charges hurled by a gadfly shareholder by ousting its newly appointed president, William C. Newberg.

Imported-car sales took off, with the rear-engine Volkswagen Beetle notching a record 600,000 sales a year in the United States, portending the Japanese-car "invasion" that started in the 1970s. Americans' preferences for midsize and full-size cars and trucks left a big economy-car gap that importers exploited in the 1970s and 1980s. Toyota, Nissan, and Honda introduced successful small-sized cars and pickup trucks. The Big Three responded with cars, such as the Ford Pinto and Chevrolet Vega, that suffered from

serious quality problems. Import sales kept mounting, helped by the Arab oil embargo in 1973–74 and the Iran hostage crisis of 1979–80. Volkswagen opened an assembly plant for its Golf/Rabbit subcompact car, successor to the Beetle, in 1978, foretelling a wave of Japanese "transplant" plants in the United States and Canada beginning in 1982.

The seesaw business pattern at Chrysler Corporation continued in 1978, after Henry Ford II fired Ford's longtime President Lee A. Iacocca, who had achieved an icon status in the 1960s when he unveiled the sporty Ford Mustang car. Chrysler hired Iacocca as its president and then made him chairman and CEO, giving the flamboyant executive the opportunity to resurrect the floundering and nearly insolvent company. Another Chrysler shake-up in 1992, resulting in

1986 Ford Taurus

Iacocca's involuntary departure, set the stage for the climactic merger with Daimler-Benz AG in 1998.

Ironically, 1992 also brought about a drastic top-level realignment at GM. Lackluster products and continuing decline in GM's market share prompted the GM board to depose Chairman Robert C. Stempel, after a mere two-year reign, and replace him with an executive vice-president, John F. (Jack) Smith, Jr. GM's Saturn initiative of the late 1980s, establishing an autonomous compact manufacturer with its own plant, combined with industry-record-sales years in the United States of 16.1 million and 15.8 million new vehicles in 1986 and 1988, respectively, had not kept GM out of the red in the early 1990s. Ford, Chrysler, and the imports kept steadily chipping away at GM's market penetration, culminating in 1998 in a total overhaul of the system that Alfred P. Sloan crafted. Meanwhile, at Ford, William Clay Ford, Jr., became chairman at age 41.

Maynard M. Gordon

1998 Dodge Durango

BANKING

For the American banking industry, 1999 began as had many other years of the 20th century—in the midst of legislative controversy. In 1999 the House Banking Committee was considering removing the barriers enacted during the Depression era that separate banks, brokerage firms, and insurance companies. Similar legislation had failed in Congress for 20 years.

One issue in the 1999 debate was increasing concentration in the financial industry. Is it good for consumers? The number of United States banks and banking organizations fell by almost 30% between 1988 and 1997. At the end of 1997 there were 7,233 commercial banks and bank holding companies, plus 1,665 thrifts—mostly savings and loan institutions—for a total of 8,898. The share of total domestic banking assets held by the ten largest banking organizations rose from one fifth to one third. The share of assets held by the top 50 organizations rose from one half to two thirds. Several mergers, such as the deal between Citicorp and Travelers Group announced in April 1998, were giant ones. Together, Citicorp and Travelers provided banking, insurance, and brokerage services to more than 100 million customers in some 100 countries. Another notable merger deal was the planned acquisition of Bankers Trust in New York by Deutsche Bank, the largest German commercial bank.

At the start of the century, the trend was in the opposite direction: Small banks were flourishing. The trend toward small banks was encouraged by state laws and by rules of the comptroller of the currency limiting banks to a single office. There were 13,000 banks and only 119 bank branches in the entire nation in 1900. The number of banks multiplied to 27,000 by 1913. Most were state-chartered, small, and located in country towns, providing credit to the numerous farmers of the day. In the bigger cities national banks were growing, providing credit to expanding business empires that thrived as railroads stretched across the nation.

A financial panic in 1907 prompted Congress to appoint a National Monetary Commission. Its recommendations led to passage of the Federal Reserve Act of 1913. Under

During much of the century, customers visited their local bank, above, to make deposits and withdrawals. By the 1990s, however, people could take advantage of the widely present automatic-teller machines (ATMs), page 245, for such transactions.

President Woodrow Wilson, the Federal Reserve (the Fed) became the nation's first true central bank. It facilitated national check-clearing and fund-transfer arrangements. It helped finance World War I by, in effect, printing money. National banks had to be members of the new Fed. State-chartered banks, at least the larger ones, joined the system for the various advantages it offered. By 1921 there were 31,000 banks in the United States, more than at any other time. But failures among these so-called "unit" banks were common. Some states liberalized their branching laws between 1929 and 1939. And some banks formed holding companies to operate multiple banks within states or even across state lines. In 1927, Congress passed the McFadden Act, allowing national banks to branch within the cities of their main offices.

By the mid-1920s, many commercial banks had become financial department stores—something they sought to attain again toward the end of the century. In the big cities some banks underwrote stock and bond issues and even traded in securities, usually through subsidiaries. A high bank-failure rate in the 1920s and the Great Depression of the 1930s revealed a downside to branching restrictions. Some 3,000 banks closed their doors in 1933. Unit banks, often those in rural areas, were hit by local economic troubles, such as bad years for farmers. Banks trading in securities actually failed at a lower rate in the 1930s than unit banks.

Disturbed by the banking failures of the Depression, Congress passed the Banking Act of 1933 (later called the Glass-Steagall Act). It separated commercial and investment banking and created federal insurance of deposits by establishing the Federal Deposit Insurance Corp. (FDIC). It prohibited interest payments on demand deposits (normal checking accounts) and limited interest on savings accounts. It also permitted national banks to branch to the extent that state banks were permitted to branch. Interstate banking was not allowed. Deposit insurance was the financial safety that allowed branching restrictions to continue with only marginal changes until the 1980s. Usually 75 to 150 mergers per year took place during that period.

Further, bank charters were hard to obtain. Regulators feared over-banking, blaming the banking troubles of the Depression on this factor. During World War II, banks purchased $100 billion in government bonds—nearly half of those bonds sold—thereby helping to finance the war and expanding the money supply. Price and wage controls held down inflation. After the war, consumer credit flourished, with bank credit cards first appearing in the 1950s. A hike in oil prices in 1973–74 brought huge flows of money from the Middle East. These deposits were reinvested in developing countries, such as Brazil and Argentina. In 1982 a drop

in oil prices prompted Mexico to default on its debts, setting off a developing loan crisis that lasted through that decade. More than $100 billion was at stake, some of it written off eventually by the banks.

As inflation increased during the 1970s, interest rates rose. Banks were prohibited from paying interest on demand deposits, and interest rates on savings accounts were limited. So consumers fled to money-market mutual funds. The funds' holdings grew from $4 billion in 1977 to $220 billion in 1982. Seeing the unfairness of its own laws, Congress passed legislation deregulating interest rates on savings and time deposits beginning in 1981. This gave banks a renewed opportunity to compete. Thrifts also got into trouble when a huge gap opened between the interest they received from mortgages, their prime assets, and the interest they had to pay on deposits, their liabilities. During the 1980s, some 1,200 savings-and-loan institutions were forced to close, costing taxpayers perhaps $200 billion.

After 1981, merger activity exploded. Restrictions on branching faded. During the 1980s, 20 states liberalized in-state branching laws. By 1990, 36 states authorized statewide branching, and only two prohibited it. In the early 1980s, states began allowing bank holding companies from other states to buy banks within their borders. By 1990 all but four states allowed at least some cross-border purchases.

Finally, the Riegle-Neal Interstate Banking Act of 1994 eliminated interstate banking restrictions. It set the stage for booming merger activity. Through actions by regulators, legislators, and the courts, the Glass-Steagall prohibitions on mixing commercial banking with investment banking and insurance were weakened.

David R. Francis

COMMUNICATIONS

At the dawn of the 20th century, the communication industry was in its infancy. By the close of the 20th century, the communication industry had matured greatly and had become a substantial portion of the U.S. gross domestic product (GDP).

Today's home is bombarded by a tremendous variety of communication media, delivered to the home in a wide variety of ways—from radio waves to physical delivery. The home is so full of communication media—many of which are taken for granted—that one wonders whether there is room for anything else. This remarkable profusion of communication media—along with the industries to develop and distribute them—occurred during the 20th century. The telecommunication, cinema and television, publishing, and audio segments of the communication industry had total revenues of $500 billion in 1995, or about 7% of the gross domestic product. Half of the revenues

of the communication industry were coming from the telecommunication segment, mostly telephone communication over fixed wires and mobile radio.

In the entertainment segments of the communication industry, most revenues are in the sale of content—the business of software—as opposed to the sale of such hardware as television sets and radios. In the telecommunication segment, most revenues are in the sale of the service to interconnect people, as opposed to the sale of telephones and other telecommunication equipment. It can be misleading to apply general conclusions from one segment to another.

The telecommunication industry has had impact far beyond just communication and

During the early years of the century, the arrival of the mail was a much-anticipated event. By century's end, such companies as Federal Express guaranteed one-day delivery of mail seven days a week.

stimulates many other segments of the economy. Considerable commerce, such as the ordering of airline tickets and the transfer of financial funds, is conducted over telecommunication networks. The various goods that are ordered over the telephone—and increasingly through the Internet—are shipped by physical delivery. In 1995 the total revenues of the United States Postal Service, United Parcel Service, and Federal Express were $78 billion, or almost as much as the entire cinema and television segment of the communication industry. Much of today's electronic mail (E-mail) is sent over the Internet, using personal computers as a communication terminal. In this way, the communication and computer industries have converged. The sale of personal-computer hardware and software in the United States generated $78 billion in 1995. Although the basic concepts for the programmable computer can be traced back to Charles Babbage in the early 19th century, the digital computer did not achieve its tremendous potential until the second half of the 20th century with the invention of the transistor and integrated-circuit chips.

Over-the-air television broadcasting began in the United States on a full commercial scale in 1945, and 49% of households had a TV set by 1953—a phenomenal market penetration in less than a decade. TV antennas appeared on the roofs of most homes, but most antennas had disappeared by the end of the 20th century due to the great penetration of cable television. Cable television began as a community antenna—thus the term CATV—in 1958 as a means to obtain television reception in areas distant from large cities, but then spread to large cities and their suburbs as a way to obtain a better picture and more programs. In 1970 only 9% of TV households in the United States had cable, but by the late 1990s, 65% of TV households obtained their television from cable. In fact, as the 20th century ended, only about 30% of Americans were receiving their television programming directly over the air.

Network television has been experiencing a steady decline in viewership, and over-the-air broadcast television seems to be dying. The salvation of broadcast television may be digital broadcasting, which can offer high-definition images and many programs in the space of one channel. But most people watch television because of the quality of the program content—not because of the technical quality of the picture. The failure of the first field-sequential standard for broadcast color television demonstrates the essential importance

Communication Industry Revenue 1995

- USPS + UPS + FedEx $78 billion
- Publishing $82 billion
- Audio $33 billion
- Personal Computers $78 billion
- Cinema and Television $133 billion
- Telecommunication $269 billion

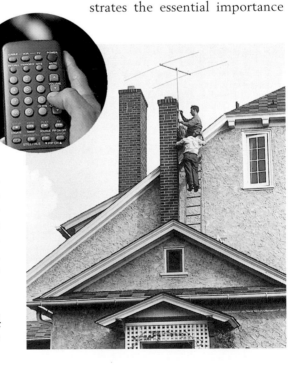

Until the arrival of cable television in the 1960s–70s, antennas were fixtures on the roofs of homes that had television sets. The remote-control unit, inset, became an added convenience for the TV viewer.

of backward compatibility in the entertainment segment of the communication industry. The color standard of the National Television Standard Code (NTSC) that replaced it in the United States was backward compatible with the black-and-white sets already in widespread use. Incompatible digital television well might face a similar ill fate, even though the policy of the U.S. government in the late 1990s promoted digital television.

Communications policy and government intervention have shaped the structure and nature of the communications industry in the United States considerably. When it seemed that AT&T would dominate the new radio-broadcasting industry, the government coerced AT&T to sell its radio network to the newly formed Radio Corporation of America (RCA) in 1926. Under threat of government censorship, the motion-picture industry voluntarily created a code for rating movies in terms of sensitive content. The government broke apart vertical integration in the motion-picture industry. But toward the end of the 20th century, media companies began acquiring each other in a frenzy of merger activity. The telecommunication segment likewise seemed afflicted with merger

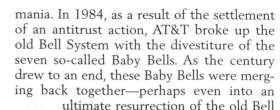

mania. In 1984, as a result of the settlement of an antitrust action, AT&T broke up the old Bell System with the divestiture of the seven so-called Baby Bells. As the century drew to an end, these Baby Bells were merging back together—perhaps even into an ultimate resurrection of the old Bell System. Industry structure seemed cyclical—going from monopolies and vertical integration to competition, and then back to the ways of the past.

Market forces—particularly competition—also have played a central role in shaping the communications industry. Competition in the provision of telephone service first came to telephone instruments and then to long-distance service. Yet all the mergers occurring in the telecommunication industry at the close of the 20th century seemed to be eliminating opportunities for increased competition.

The tremendous success of television and consumer electronics after World War II created great expectations for communications technology for the second half of the 20th century. A video dimension was added to the telephone to create the Picturephone in the early 1970s. The television set was attached to the telephone line to facilitate access to computerized databases in the early 1980s.

But consumers did not respond overwhelmingly to these advances. Most consumers did not want to be seen while speaking on the telephone, nor

The telephone underwent a transformation in the 20th century. From the early, somewhat cumbersome model, above, the telephone has advanced to the handheld version of the 1990s, near left. With the former, a user had to contact an operator to make a call and shared the telephone line with others; the latter permits the making and receiving of calls from any location that offers the necessary service. In addition, very compact pagers, far left, now keep doctors, sales representatives, repairmen, and, in fact, almost anyone in constant contact with their offices and customers.

did they want to interact with their television sets. The communication industry learned the hard way that technology could not be forced on consumers.

Communication systems and products must be easy to use and satisfy the real needs of consumers. The success of the Internet and its World Wide Web is due to the ease of use of browsers and search engines, with their point-and-click features. The Internet shows the success of decentralization. Rather than one gigantic database of information, the Internet and World Wide Web are a conglomeration of many dispersed, decentralized databases; all are accessed seamlessly. E-mail—one of the prime uses of the Internet—is an extension of the use of text as a means of interpersonal telecommunication and thus should be viewed as a natural progression of the telegraph of the 19th century. It is much easier to use, however, and far more widespread.

People seem to want to keep in contact everywhere at all times through telecommunication over a wide variety of media, such as the telephone, E-mail, wireless, facsimile (fax), and even telephones in airplanes. Facsimile—invented in the 1840s—languished until universal standards, developed in the 1980s, finally stimulated its growth and widespread application.

One thinks of the 20th century as the century of great advances in the communications industry. Yet many of the basic concepts and principles for the communications technology and communication industries of the 20th century were developed in the 19th century. Radio waves were discovered by Heinrich Hertz in 1887 and had been observed as an "etheric force" by Thomas Alva Edison in 1875. Automated switching of telephone lines was invented in 1889 by Almon B. Strowger. The diode and triode vacuum tubes that were so essential to modern electronics were invented in 1904 by John Ambrose Fleming and in 1906 by Lee de Forest, respectively.

The major accomplishments of the 20th century were the large-scale commercializa-

The Western Union telegram, the main means of rapid, written communication for much of the 1900s, was superseded by the fax machine at left, and E-mail.

tion of the revolutionary innovations of the 19th century and also the mathematical optimization and continued evolutionary improvements of these innovations. The major invention of the 20th century in communication technology was the transistor, invented in 1948 at Bell Labs by John Bardeen, William Shockley, and Walter H. Brattain. The transistor has been improved greatly with the large-scale integrated circuits that are the foundations of the computer and electronics industries.

The basic concept of capturing sound in a recorded form was truly a revolutionary invention by Edison in 1877. Edison's tinfoil-cylinder phonograph then was improved, first with the disc phonograph of Emile Berliner in 1887 and then with the long-playing vinyl disc of Peter Goldmark in 1948. Along the way, the waxed-cardboard cylinder improved Edison's tinfoil cylinder in 1885, and the stereo disc improved the LP disc in 1958. The digital compact disc appeared in 1982 and brought near-perfect sound quality, along with an absence of wear and tear. But Edison's initial invention of the phonograph remained the only truly revolutionary event in the long history of recorded sound. Much progress in communication has been evolutionary—even though the term "revolution" has been overused greatly.

A. Michael Noll

At the outset of the 20th century, large corporations were beginning to dominate various parts of the U.S. economy. The retail industry was part of this trend, with three large organization types developing and prospering. These were the large mail-order establishments, which concentrated their significant selling operations in rural communities; the large department stores, which dominated the urban sales market; and the large chain-store operations, which had central management and focused on a specific area of retail—i.e., food or soft goods.

Initially, these large retail institutions integrated all of the elements of the economic process by controlling manufacturing, distribution, and the sale of merchandise at the retail level. However, by 1910 a transformation was occurring in which retailers began to specialize by focusing exclusively on the selling of goods to consumers. The manufac-

turing and distribution of products were left to others to develop and perfect.

Evolution of the Department Store

By the early 1920s the success of large mail-order houses, department stores, and chain stores was evident. Their niche was to offer a multitude of goods in one location. Their competition, often the small-town store-keeper, was able to match neither the prices nor the variety of goods these businesses offered to the customer. Further, these organizations were developing a strong service component as well. They promoted the service image with their liberal return policies, their fixed-price policies, and their superior marketing techniques, which included advertising and offering frequent sales and coupon giveaways. Loyalty to the local shopkeeper was beginning to wane, and many shopkeepers either went bankrupt, joined buying cooperatives in an attempt to compete, or

Main Street Kansas

Mall of America

converted their operations to the department-store concept.

In the 1930s large department stores controlled the retail markets in many metropolitan communities. Stores like Siegel-Cooper of New York; Marshall Field's of Chicago; Carson, Pirie, Scott of Chicago; Filene's of Boston; Famous-Barr of St. Louis; John Wanamaker's of Philadelphia; Lazarus in Cincinnati; and Macy's of New York were becoming institutionalized in the cities in which they operated. The opponents of large

In the early 20th century, most people in the United States shopped at individually owned and operated businesses that focused on selling a single type of product, such as food, clothing, or hardware. Their storefronts lined the streets of small to midsize American towns, page 250. But department stores and chain outlets began to encroach upon local shopkeepers, particularly after the advent in the mid-1950s of the enclosed shopping mall, which allowed consumers to shop in a variety of stores under one roof. In 1992 the 78-acre (32-hectare) Mall of America, above, in Bloomington, MN, became the largest U.S. shopping complex.

retail stores, who earlier had attempted to undermine large-retail expansion through special tax requirements and other anticompetitive measures, were no longer viable opposition to these powerful entrepreneurs. Because of the tremendous success of the retailers, investment bankers were willing to offer vast capital outlays to them. Many retailers began expanding into other large cities. Because they were so well funded, many were able to survive the Depression, which extended through much of the 1930s.

Mail-order sales were weakening during this period, in part because the rural share of the national income was declining. Mail-order titans Sears, Roebuck and Company and Montgomery Ward recognized that retail stores located in cities were the wave of the future, and both companies devised plans to enter the department-store milieu. Gen. Robert Wood, who left a leadership role in Montgomery Ward for a similar role with Sears, limited expansion efforts to a few large stores on the outskirts of cities with

The hallmark of the traditional small business in America, such as the 1950s-era grocery above, was attentive personal service, with the shopkeeper frequently knowing customers by name and catering to their individual needs. In contrast, the modern superstore of the 1990s, right, emphasized the wide variety of goods it offered—everything from groceries to gardening equipment to furniture to computer supplies—as well as bargain prices.

populations in excess of 100,000. Conversely, Montgomery Ward developed a plethora of modest-size stores in small towns. Wood's decision turned out to be the better one, enabling Sears to cope better with the upcoming Depression. In fact, Montgomery Ward nearly went bankrupt during this period and never was able to compete effectively with Sears again.

During this era, the chain-store concept prospered predominantly in food stores like Kroger's and A&P. However, chain-store retailers including J.C. Penney, Kresge's, and W.T. Grant's became successful with the implementation of the "junior department store" concept. Chain-store retailers did not offer a wide range of items as did department stores. They confined their product lines to one area, e.g., soft goods.

In the 1930s the completion of the railroad and telegraph networks allowed retailers to realize economies of scale with distribution systems going from coast to coast. The urban population was increasing, and reliable and efficient passenger bus and rail systems were carrying both urban and rural consumers into the cities for their shopping treks. Further, the increasing use of automo-

biles and the expansion of highway systems throughout the 1940s and 1950s brought customers from small cities into the larger ones. The department-store niche charged low prices and had low profit margins, but achieved increased total profits because of high volume. This strategy also allowed for the proliferation of national brands, resulting in brand loyalty among consumers. Merchants, recognizing and promoting this trend, seized on the opportunity to shape and mold the market. Prior to this time the commodity, not the brand name, dictated the terms of business.

A Changing Marketplace

Although most department stores prospered throughout the 1960s, a new organizational

The Credit Card

For most of the 20th century, customers were able to say: "I'll charge it, please," or "Put it on my card!" In fact, credit cards were introduced to select customers by the retail industry in the 1910s, by the gasoline industry in the 1920s, and by the airline industry in the 1930s. However, it was not until the late 1940s that unrestricted, or universal-type, credit cards were offered.

For the first half of the 20th century, credit-card use was reserved for the wealthy and was restricted to a specific company or industry. However, the post–World War II period brought the largest economic boom in the history of the United States. For the first time in the country's history, most Americans had discretionary income. Enter Alfred Bloomingdale, Frank McNamara, and Ralph Schneider. In 1949 they developed the idea of an unrestricted, or universal-use, card. Their company, Diners Club, promoted the card as a convenience for the mobile, affluent consumer. Thus, the "travel-and-entertainment" (T&E) credit-card industry was born.

By the mid–1950s, American Express and Carte Blanche had entered the T&E credit-card field. Bank of America and Chase Manhattan Bank initiated substantive credit-card operations geared toward the mass market. Shortly thereafter, more than 100 banks throughout the United States were offering bankcards. Typically, banks did not charge an annual fee to their customers. They made their profits through the fees that they charged merchants and through fees charged to customers who did not pay off their accounts each month.

Many banks had difficulty making their operations profitable. Chase Manhattan closed its credit-card operations in the early 1960s, and other smaller banks followed. They were unable to compete with the T&E-card industry because bankcards were not accepted nationwide. In the mid-1960s, however, Bank of America overcame that obstacle by licensing BankAmericard (later to be called Visa) to other banks nationwide. This concept met with immediate success. Other large banks joined together and formed a second nationwide bankcard network, the Interbank Card Association (later to be called MasterCard).

The growth of the credit-card industry, especially the sector devoted to the bankcard, has skyrocketed since the 1960s. For many consumers, the credit card has become a cash substitute, used not only for major purchases but also for routine expenses such as groceries. In fact, some suggest that credit-card companies have become too successful and have promoted unwise spending habits for many Americans, putting millions in financial jeopardy. For example, at the beginning of the 1990s the average U.S. household had a credit-card debt of approximately $1,600. By the middle of the decade, the average credit-card debt had risen to $3,400. Concomitantly, both credit-card delinquencies and personal bankruptcies, often caused by credit-card debt, were at the highest levels in U.S. history.

A growing trend in the 1990s was the debit card. These cards resemble credit cards and can be used in most establishments just like credit cards. In a transaction using one of these cards, the holder's bank account is debited electronically for the amount of the purchase. These cards are favored for their convenience, and usually also function as ATM cards. Another similar recent innovation is the phone card, which allows its holder to use a certain amount of prepaid telephone time.

Mel J. Zelenak

competitor, the discount store, and an old competitor, the specialty shop, showed enormous sales strength. The retail market again was transformed, and discount stores and specialty shops secured substantial market share away from department stores.

Through most of the 1960s, the department-store sector of the retail industry did not perceive competition from the discount companies as a serious threat. Indeed, department-store sales revenues doubled during the decade. Discounters, however, increased sales revenues by nearly 1,000%. By the time major retailers reacted, they were unable to reverse the trend. Additionally, they miscalculated the popularity of Sunday store openings, further exacerbating their woes. In the early 1960s, more than half the U.S. states had "blue-law" statutes. Blue laws regulated the types of products (mostly necessities) that could be sold on Sundays. For the most part, these laws were not enforced, because they were considered antiquated and because it was too difficult for authorities to determine which goods were "necessities." The department-store retailers and their trade association, the National Retail Merchants Association, strongly resisted Sunday openings. They felt the additional day would do little to increase sales revenues and substantially would increase their overhead. However, discount stores disagreed, and most of them opened for business. It was quickly determined that Sunday was a popular sales day—nearly 30% of the weekly sales of discount stores occurred on Sundays.

A further problem for the department stores was the growth and renewed popularity of specialty stores. These shops, which were part of the retail market for the entire century, were able to compete with department stores because they offered unique and better-quality merchandise, had more knowledgeable sales employees, and featured prices comparable to those in department stores. Many department stores attempted to compete by creating in-store boutiques and specialty lines of their products. They began to promote high-fashion merchandise,

emphasized prestige-building activities, and expanded customer service.

Eventually, department stores attempted to win back their market share by opening on Sundays, reducing prices on some items, increasing the number of special-event sales, and stressing service. However, they were showing their age; they suffered from employee and customer apathy, and their labor-intensive nature made it difficult for them to cut costs. They quickly lost their niches in the marketplace. Several retailers attempted to diversify into other nonretail related areas, but most of those efforts were counterproductive, because they took the focus away from their retail efforts. The efforts appeared to be too little and too late.

Rise of the Discount Store

By the early 1980s, various analysts were predicting that, within the next decade, Kmart would overtake Sears as the Number 1 retailer in the nation. Kmart's niche was to develop stores in middle-size cities, those with at least 20,000 residents. Its stores were large and offered a wide array of merchandise at low prices. However, some experts felt that Kmart's long-term forecast was at risk, because the company was notorious for being poorly stocked, providing poor service, and having dismal store layouts. Enter Wal-Mart, a regional discount organization whose national headquarters was in a small Arkansas town, Bentonville. By the late 1980s, Wal-Mart and its low-profile leader, Sam Walton, were being noticed by Wall Street but were not yet being taken seriously by competitors. After all, even as late as 1990, Sears was three times larger than Wal-Mart, and Kmart was twice its size. Additionally, Wal-Mart's base since its inception in the early 1960s was in

The Wal-Mart discount chain, started in 1962 by entrepreneur Sam Walton, above, launched an aggressive expansion campaign in the late 1980s, competing directly with other discount outlets, such as Kmart. Its efforts proved phenomenally successful. A decade later, Wal-Mart had become the largest retailer in the world, with more than 2,400 stores nationwide and $137.6 billion in sales.

Buying products from home always has appealed to the American consumer. Mail-order catalogs, above, and the Internet, right, were among the most popular shopping trends of the late 1990s.

substantial portions of their retail operations. Other prominent rivals, including Macy's and Federated Department Stores, announced plans to merge. The 1990s also exhibited substantial gains in specialty stores like the Gap, the previously noted success of Wal-Mart, and the infusion of personal computers into millions of American homes.

Looking to the Future

The 20th century began with the biggest change in retail in history—the development of the department store. The century ended with what many experts predict will be the biggest change in retail since the advent of the department store—Internet shopping, known as electronic commerce or e-commerce. At the beginning of the millennium, it is in its infancy and is a minuscule part of a $2.6 trillion retail economy. Nonetheless, Internet shopping is gaining consumer acceptance, with Internet sales estimated at more than $6 billion for 1998. Most analysts

small midwestern towns. However, by the late 1980s, Wal-Mart expanded its operations and competed directly with Kmart and other retail giants. Wal-Mart had an abundance of capital to proceed, as Sam Walton was considered the richest man in America. The plan to open stores nationwide was very successful, and, by the mid-1990s, Wal-Mart became the largest retailer in the world.

Major Changes in the 1990s

The 1990s were a decade of major changes and innovations in retail. Early in the decade, there was the phenomenal success of television home shopping, with QVC (Quality, Value, Convenience) and HSN (Home Shopping Network) becoming the premier forces in home shopping. The 1990s was also the decade of retail shake-ups. Numerous long-established retailers including Macy's, Caldor, Bradlees, Jamesway, and Montgomery Ward all filed for bankruptcy protection. Significant financial problems led numerous other established retailers, including Kmart and Dayton Hudson, to sell off

predict that consumer purchases will approach $20 billion by the millennium. Business-to-business trades over the Internet will reach $175 billion by 2000, according to the GartnerGroup, and more than $1 trillion by 2003, according to Michael Putnam, an analyst with the Forrester Research consulting company.

Retailers continue to expand their offerings on the World Wide Web. Virtually every major retailer either already is selling on-line or is poised to do so. With the increased interest in the Web among shoppers, and the greater commitment among business and government entities to support electronic commerce, it is evident that this new form of shopping is the wave of the future.

Mel J. Zelenak

THE STEEL INDUSTRY

The U.S. steel industry began the 20th century with a notable event. In 1901, Andrew Carnegie sold his steel mills to J.P. Morgan, the famed banker, for $480 million. One Carnegie complex was the Edgar Thomson works in Braddock, PA, the first large-scale steel plant in the United States.

The sale made Carnegie, who came to America from Scotland with his family as a lad of 12, the "richest man in the world," Morgan said. Carnegie subsequently became famous as a philanthropist, bestowing many gifts to libraries. Morgan combined the steel company that Carnegie had been building since 1873 into the newly formed United States Steel Corp., now the USX Corp. That combination gave U.S. Steel about 65% of the nation's steelmaking capacity. In 1906, Gary, IN—with its swamps, sand dunes,

abundant water, and good rail-transportation potential—became a key steel town for U.S. Steel. It was named after Judge Elbert Gary, chairman of U.S. Steel. Two years earlier, Charles M. Schwab, who had resigned as the first president of U.S. Steel, formed Bethlehem Steel. Headquartered in Pittsburgh, it became a keen rival of U.S. Steel.

This was a time when steel rapidly was becoming a key industry in the United States. Annual production was 1.4 million short tons in 1880. It was 11.2 million tons in 1900, 28 million tons in 1910, 111.6 million by 1953, and 100 million at the end of the century. In the last half of the 1800s, much steel was used for rails. But as the new century moved forward, steel was in rising demand for automobiles and countless other products. Steel beams were the key material that made pos-

The rapid growth of U.S. industries such as automaking and construction in the early 1900s increased the demand for steel, generating an increase in iron and steel mills in such locales as Homestead, PA, below.

sible the skyscrapers sprouting rapidly in America's cities.

Because of its importance, the steel industry frequently was big news. In 1919, 350,000 steelworkers were on strike for three months. Twenty people, 18 of them workers, died in the turmoil. Judge Gary refused union demands for recognition and an eight-hour day. The strike failed to accomplish those goals but strengthened the union in the long run. In 1923, U.S. Steel and other major steel firms gave in to pressure from Washington and abolished the 12-hour day in favor of eight hours. By 1937, Big Steel had signed pacts with the Congress of Industrial Organizations, which later merged with the American Federation of Labor to become the AFL-CIO, to represent steelworkers for bargaining purposes. The union won a 40-hour week. A 1949 strike of more than 500,000 steelworkers resulted in company-funded pensions. A move by President Harry Truman in 1952 to nationalize the mills, shut down by a strike, was ruled unconstitutional by the Supreme Court.

Steel beams, which are laid out to cool after being forged, top, *are the key element that facilitates the construction of high-rise skyscrapers,* bottom, *which have changed the look of cities worldwide.*

In 1962 a price hike by the steel industry challenged President John F. Kennedy's efforts to restrain inflation. After the president strongly questioned the necessity for the price hike and threatened a governmental investigation of the industry, the increase was rescinded. With economic recovery in Western Europe and Japan in the 1950s and 1960s, steel imports began flowing into the United States and became troubling for the U.S. industry for the remainder of the century. U.S. Steel shut down ten factories in 1979. LTV, the parent company of the nation's second-largest steel firm, filed for bankruptcy in 1986. By then, the ranks of steelworkers had thinned from 450,000 in 1979 to 200,000, as steel companies became more efficient and lost market share to imports from many nations. The United States negotiated so-called Voluntary Restraint Agreements that held back the flood of steel imports from 1982 to 1992. Critics accused the industry of being slow in modernizing to meet the competition.

By the end of the century, the U.S. steel industry was as modern as any in the world in terms of man-hours needed to produce a ton of steel. Labor productivity doubled in the decade prior to 1998. Mini-mills, using scrap metal, were thriving. But the industry and its 170,000 workers were at the barricades again, seeking help from Congress and the president to block imports of what they termed "dumped" steel from Russia and other economically depressed nations.

David R. Francis

An elegant dining car was a key feature of Pennsylvania Railroad's "Broadway Limited." The "Limited" began its New York City–to–Chicago run in 1902 and competed with the Pullman Company's "Twentieth Century."

At the close of the 20th century, when one can fly from London to Paris in an hour or from New York to London in five hours or less, it is surprising to recall how vastly different travel was in the United States at the beginning of the century. Although leisure travel is a distinctly modern phenomenon, it predated railroads, automobiles, and travel agents by several decades—while thoughts of air transportation were merely flights of fancy.

Today the travel and tourism industry accounts for the largest portion of money spent in international commerce, and annual tourism expenditures in the United States exceed $500 billion. According to a 1998 report from the World Travel & Tourism Council, tourism is also the world's third-largest retail industry, with a global workforce of 233 million people.

Train Travel

Perhaps no other event made such a sudden, dramatic difference in the speed and comfort of travel in the United States as the arrival of the transcontinental railroad. By the turn of the century, five railroads spanned the continent, linking the East's burgeoning population centers with the West's major scenic attractions.

Train travel not only increased the number of people on the move; it forced companies associated with rail travel to standardize times and scheduling. Shipping lines benefited from improved rail connections to seaports, which led to an increase in the number of passengers who had money and time to travel to Europe and beyond.

Middle-class Americans also began to travel, taking shorter, more frequent journeys in their own country. Railroads responded with summer-excursion fares designed to lure vacationers westward. Travel agencies organized low-cost tours, promoting attractions with detailed guidebooks, and new hotels and resorts opened to cater to travelers on budgets. Tent camps and cottages were built in parks and other scenic areas for people who preferred casual camping to the formality of the resorts built by the railroads.

Auto Travel

U.S. roads were much poorer than those in Western Europe—where Thomas Cook & Son offered the first auto tour from England to Switzerland in 1900—with the result that travel by car took longer to catch on in the United States as a practical alternative to railroad travel. The first recorded transcontinental journey by automobile took place in 1903; it started as a bet and ended as a publicity stunt for the Winton Motor Carriage Company, an early American automobile manufacturer. It took 63 days and 6,000 miles (9,656 kilometers) to get from San Francisco to New York—and this without roads in many places.

Thanks primarily to the automobile industry, the first transcontinental highway was built in 1915 along a route that resembled today's Interstate 80, and the first guidebook was published to encourage Americans to take to the road. Early motorists consulted "Blue Books" of each state, which provided detailed road descriptions, mileage between major towns, and basic information about each town. Directions, however, relied on landmarks—a "green house at a turnoff," for example—creating a problem if the house was repainted another color.

Thanks in part to Henry Ford's 1908 introduction of the Model T, which dramatically reduced the cost of automobiles, auto registrations in the United States skyrocketed from a mere 8,000 in 1900 to 500,000 in 1910, and to 8 million—about one car for every 13 Americans—by 1920. Americans now buy more than 10 million new cars and trucks annually.

To accommodate motorists looking for roadside lodging in the United States, ubiquitous motor inns sprang up along major highways. The country's first motor hotel, the aptly named Motel Inn, opened in 1925 in San Luis Obispo, CA, halfway between Los Angeles and San Francisco.

Air Travel

World War I left Americans with no choice other than to "See America First." San Francisco's 1915 Panama-Pacific International Exposition drew 19 million people. One of the most popular exhibits was the Ford Motor Company assembly line, which

As more and more people began to travel by car in the 1920s and 1930s, a new type of lodging—the motel or "hotel for motorists"—was born. The supersonic transport was a revolutionary development in the history of aviation. Passenger service was inaugurated on the Anglo-French Concorde, above, in 1976.

turned out a car every ten minutes. Another was a detailed replica of the Panama Canal, which opened in 1914. But perhaps the most popular attraction was the daily appearance of the latest in transportation technology—a tiny, single-engine airplane.

Though Orville Wright doubted planes would compete with trains or cars, or fly at speeds much faster than 45 miles (72 kilometers) per hour, others predicted that travel would see an unimaginable change. Commercial aviation floundered until Charles A. Lindbergh's 1927 flight from New York to Paris. Suddenly the airplane had come of age. In 1929, Transcontinental Air Transport—the forerunner of TWA—offered a unique 48-hour transcontinental service that required passengers to split the trip between Ford Tri-Motors and Pullman-car trains. The planes

With cruising increasing in popularity in the late 1990s, the Princess Line introduced the world's largest cruise ship, the "Grand Princess," above.

flew only in daylight, leaving the passengers to board trains for nighttime passage over the mountains.

The age of international jet travel was inaugurated on Oct. 26, 1958, when Pan American World Airways flew a Boeing 707 from New York to Paris with 123 passengers aboard. Jets cut long-distance travel time in half.

Travelers now jet to countries around the world. More than 200 airlines serve Europe—the most popular tourist destination—from all over the globe. Almost every country has its own international airline as well as domestic commuter lines.

That upsurge of tourism also triggered a need for more lodging. Today's air travelers

choose from some 10 million hotel and motel rooms worldwide.

Cruising

Hundreds of years before the airplane, ships provided transportation between continents. The time, expense, and effort required for early ocean voyages encouraged travelers to stay at their destination as long as possible and cover as much ground as they could. In the early part of the 20th century, competition developed among shipping companies, leading to fare reductions, increases in speed, and the design and construction of such early floating palaces as Cunard Line's *Mauretania*, *Lusitania*, and *Aquitania*, as well as the White Star Line's ill-fated and much-dramatized *Titanic*.

As late as the 1950s, travel by ship was the most popular way to cross the Atlantic. But jet planes, which saved both time and money, eventually doomed such passenger transportation. Many shipping lines scrapped their vessels before the novel concept of selling ships as destinations rather than transportation was developed. Today the cruise industry is one of the fastest-growing segments of travel. More than 20 cruise lines operate around the world, and 13 new ships were to enter service in 1999 to serve an estimated 9 million passengers.

Looking Ahead

A study entitled "Changes in Leisure Time: The Impact on Tourism" concluded that 21st-century travelers will be targeting products that offer maximum thrills in minimum time. The World Tourism Organization predicts that the next millennium's hot new trends will include undersea travel and journeys to "the ends of the earth." Millions of passengers already have booked voyages in commercial submarines, and thousands have signed up for commercial spaceflights, following the dreams of such 20th-century astronauts as John Glenn, Buzz Aldrin, and Neil Armstrong.

Barbara J. Braasch

SCIENCE AND TECHNOLOGY

A laboratory technician stores frozen virus samples for research purposes.

OVERVIEW

When the most spectacular century in the history of science began, most people thought Earth was just 50 million years old. Nobody dreamed that the continents drifted across Earth's surface on huge plates of rock. Earth seemed to be the only planet in a universe with just one galaxy, the Milky Way.

So far as chemists knew, everything in the universe was made from the 92 naturally occurring elements on the periodic table of the elements. Synthetic elements like plutonium, the nuclear-weapons material, were pure science fiction. Nobody ever had made a synthetic element or expected the periodic table to reach 112 elements.

Physicists thought that the atoms in elements were "indivisible." A whole realm of subatomic particles that make up atoms—including neutrons, protons, quarks, and antiquarks—were undiscovered. Many physicists felt their science was at a dead end. Everything worth discovering about the structure of matter and the laws of motion had been discovered. Were they wrong! The nature of light, relativity, quantum mechanics, radioactivity, and the principles that led to nuclear weapons would revolutionize the entire field.

People knew little about their own roots as a species. Only a few ancient fossils had been unearthed to document humanity's origins. Nobody thought humans had been on Earth for 2.5 million years.

The age of technology, invention, and science in service of humanity was just dawning. Few people even had seen an automobile, electric light, telephone, phonograph, radio, or product made from plastics or synthetic fibers. And the Wright brothers, the pioneers of aviation, owned a bicycle shop in Dayton, OH.

An Older, More Dynamic Earth

As the 20th century progressed, scientists developed a better understanding of Earth. In 1907, U.S. chemist Bertram Borden Boltwood concluded that Earth was 2.2 billion years old. Many scientists thought Earth was 20 million–50 million years old, based on the time needed for it to cool from a molten mass at its formation to present temperatures. Boltwood discovered a better "clock"—uranium's breakdown, or "decay," into lead. By measuring the proportion of uranium and lead, he could calculate a rock's age with greater precision. Scientists later showed that Earth actually was formed about 4.5 billion years ago.

In 1912, German geophysicist and meteorologist Alfred Wegener challenged the idea that Earth's surface rests on a solid, unchanging mass of bedrock. Wegener developed the theory of continental drift. All the continents originally were one supercontinent, "Pangaea," which broke apart into the existing continents. They drifted apart, floating on molten rock deep beneath the surface. Wegener concluded that the continents still were drifting away from one another. Scientists ignored the theory for more than 50 years, because no one could explain how continents might move. In 1962, U.S. geologist Harry Hess provided the answer. Hess discovered seafloor spreading, the process in which molten rock rises up from cracks in the seafloor. It cools, forms new seafloor, and forces the existing seafloor apart. Geologists later realized that Earth's crust consists of huge plates of rock that spread, carrying the continents, as molten rock oozes up at their edges.

A Bigger, Expanding Universe

Twentieth-century astronomers made breathtaking advances in understanding the universe. They developed ways of measuring immense distances between stars; discovered new objects like black holes, pulsars, and neutron stars; built powerful terrestrial and space-based telescopes; learned how stars are born, mature, and die; discovered that comets are "dirty snowballs" of ice and dust; drew the first accurate portraits of other planets in the solar system; and even reported the existence of planets orbiting other stars.

Konrad Lorenz (1903–89), page 262, an Austrian-born pioneer in ethology—the study of animal behavior—researched and described "imprinting," a process that occurs at a genetically predetermined time in which an animal identifies with another individual, usually of its own species. The goslings in the photo had imprinted with Lorenz. U.S. astronomer Edwin P. Hubble (1889–1953), above, demonstrated the existence of galaxies outside our own and established that the universe is expanding.

The Transistor

Transistors are semiconductor devices that amplify and switch electronic signals. They are the principal components of microchips, which often contain millions of these minuscule devices imprinted upon their surfaces. Deeply embedded in everything electronic, they are the "nerve cells" of the Information Age.

John Bardeen and Walter Brattain, working at Bell Laboratories as part of a team of physicists led by William Shockley, invented the point-contact transistor in 1947. A few years later, in 1951, Shockley developed a much better version called the junction transistor. The three men (*photo, right*) shared the 1956 Nobel Prize for physics in recognition of their work.

Major wartime advances in silicon and germanium technology had generated new opportunities for useful products that were used to develop the first practical semiconductor amplifiers. Bell Labs executives recognized that these advances might lead to solid-state alternatives to the bulky, balky vacuum tubes and electromechanical switches in use throughout the telephone system. By doping slivers of high-purity silicon and germanium with small amounts of impurities, Bell scientists found clever ways to induce and manipulate electrical currents inside these semiconductors, achieving the desired amplifying and switching actions.

Commercial transistors began to roll off production lines during the 1950s, soon finding ready applications in lightweight devices such as hearing aids and portable radios. Texas Instruments produced the first transistor radio in late 1954; the Regency TR1, which sold for $49.95, used four germanium transistors to amplify radio signals. Transistors also began to replace vacuum tubes in the new digital computers being manufactured by IBM, Control Data, and other companies. The combination of their small size, very low power consumption (resulting in low heat generation), and extremely long life made transistors by far the superior choice for use as electronic switches in computer circuitry.

As the 1950s ended, Texas Instruments and Fairchild Semiconductor Corporation developed integrated circuits, in which several transistors and other electrical components were etched into the surface of a single silicon chip. Now known as microchips, these circuits have experienced an exponential growth in complexity—from about 100 components per chip in the mid-1960s to almost 1 billion by the end of the 20th century. In 1970, Intel introduced the microprocessor, which sported an entire central processing unit (CPU) built into a microchip.

More than any other single factor, the explosive growth in information technology made possible by the transistor led to the vast changes that swept through modern life at the end of the millennium. The computing power that once required rooms full of bulky, fragile electronic equipment could be included easily in units that can sit on a desktop, be carried in a briefcase, or even rest in the palm of the hand. Words, numbers, and images flashed around the globe instantaneously via transistor-powered satellites, fiber-optic networks, cellular phones, and telefax machines.

The information age would be inconceivable without the transistor, which put immense power into the hands of ordinary people everywhere. Cheap, portable, and reliable equipment based on the transistor can be found in almost every village and hamlet in the world. This tiny invention made the world a far smaller and more intimate place than ever before.

Michael Riordan

Few discoveries, however, could match two early breakthroughs made by U.S. astronomer Edwin P. Hubble. He originated the modern idea of the universe and discovered that everything in the universe is expanding, with objects moving away from each other. Hubble began work in 1919 at the Mount Wilson Observatory in California, whose 100-inch (254-centimeter) telescope then was the world's most powerful. Astronomers in that period thought that Earth's home galaxy, a disk-shaped mass of stars called the Milky Way, was the universe. It seemed possible, since U.S. astronomer Harlow Shapley just had calculated the Milky Way's size—an astounding 300,000 light-years in diameter. A light-year is about 6 trillion miles (9.6 trillion kilometers).

In 1924, Hubble discovered that the universe is bigger by far than had been believed. The discovery came while Hubble was viewing the Andromeda nebula, one of many glowing clouds of gas that most astronomers regarded as unimportant features of the Milky Way located relatively close to Earth. One star in Andromeda turned out to be a Cepheid variable, a particular kind that astronomers can use to gauge distances. Hubble calculated that Andromeda was about 800,000 light-years away, well beyond the universe's boundary as set by Shapley. Andromeda eventually was recognized as the galaxy closest to the Milky Way. Thanks to Hubble, the Milky Way was found to be just one of billions of galaxies in the universe.

Hubble made another revolutionary discovery a few years later. Astronomers earlier had noted that light from nebulae looked redder than expected. It actually was shifted toward red wavelengths in the electromagnetic spectrum. The red shift probably occurred, they concluded, because nebulae were moving away from Earth. A similar shift occurs in sound waves, with the pitch of a police car's siren changing as it moves past an observer. Hubble discovered that nebulae farthest away from Earth were moving the fastest. The discovery supported the "Big Bang" theory for the universe's origin, which was proposed in 1927 by Belgian astrophysicist Georges Lemaître. The Big Bang explained Hubble's findings and became the leading theory of how stars, planets, and other celestial objects came into existence. Hubble calculated that the Big Bang began about 2 billion years ago. Astronomers later pushed back the universe's origins to about 15 billion years ago.

Matter, Energy, and Einstein

Two scientific theories about the behavior of matter—the quantum theory of energy and the theory of relativity—discovered early in the century had enormous impact on the world.

In 1900, German physicist Max Planck developed one of the strangest and most useful scientific theories of the 20th century—the quantum theory of energy. Planck realized that matter does not absorb and release energy in a continuous stream, as previously thought. Rather, energy comes in tiny packets, which later were named "quanta." The quantum theory made strange predictions about the invisible world of the atom and subatomic particles. It stated, for instance, that light is both a particle and a wave, and that subatomic particles can jump from one point to another without moving through the space in between. Quantum theory created a field called quantum electronics that led to development of the laser in 1960 and semiconductor chips for computers.

The theory of relativity was developed by Albert Einstein, perhaps the greatest scientific genius of the century. In 1905, Einstein, an obscure clerk in the Swiss patent office in Bern, published the first of two theories that shook the foundations of physics. In his special theory of relativity, Einstein proposed

In 1927, Belgian priest and astrophysicist Georges Lemaître (1894–1966), above, proposed the "Big Bang" theory regarding the origin of the universe.

(Continued on page 268.)

DNA: The Molecule of the Century

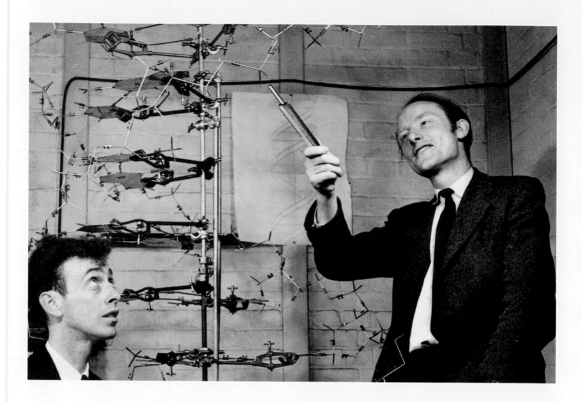

It is most unusual to be able to designate a single chemical compound as having had an outstanding impact on humanity in a particular century. However, this is exactly what occurred in the case of DNA (*deoxyribonucleic acid*), the molecule that forms the genetic material of all cellular organisms. The discovery of the chemical nature and three-dimensional structure of DNA led to an understanding of how all other components of cells are formed, and of how the hereditary material is duplicated prior to the division of any cell. This information helped establish the field of genetic engineering, which has made possible great strides in increasing world food production and combating diseases.

A DNA molecule consists of two linked series of units called nucleotides. Each nucleotide is composed of three subunits: a phosphate group that is linked to a sugar molecule that, in turn, is attached to one of four nitrogen-containing bases. The phosphate group of each nucleotide also is bonded chemically to the sugar compound of the adja-

cent nucleotide, thus forming a polynucleotide chain. The four bases found in DNA are adenine (A), guanine (G), thymine (T), and cytosine (C). It is the sequence of bases in the DNA, which makes up each gene, that determines the sequence of amino acids in each protein of an individual.

In 1953, James Watson and Francis Crick (*photo above*) proposed their model of the three-dimensional structure of DNA. They hypothesized that a molecule of DNA consists of two joined parallel polynucleotide chains that are coiled in the form of a double helix (like the steps of a winding staircase). The backbone or outside margin of each chain consists of the sugar-phosphate sequence. The bases project inward from this backbone, into the helix. The bases of one chain are attached to the bases of the other chain by weak chemical bonds called hydrogen bonds. The pairing between bases of the two chains is quite specific. Every A-containing nucleotide of one chain is located opposite a T-containing nucleotide in the other chain. Correspondingly, G-containing nucleotides are located opposite C-containing nucleotides. This specificity of matching bases is called complementarity.

The field of genetic engineering became a driving force for the improvement of human health and survival with the discovery of various ways to transfer genes from one organism to another. It began in 1964, when Werner Arber isolated so-called restriction enzymes from bacteria. These enzymes cut the DNA of any organism in a staggered fashion such that there are two to four unpaired nucleotides projecting from each polynucleotide chain. These overhanging nucleotides are called "sticky ends," because they can form hydrogen bonds with complementary sticky ends of other similarly cut sections of DNA. The added segment of DNA can come from a member of the same or a foreign species and can contain one or more genes. Any transferred gene continues to function just as it did in the organism from which it came. If an organism carries a foreign gene, it is referred to as transgenic.

The above technique has been used to advantage in the production of such medicines as insulin for diabetics, growth hormone for physically retarded individuals, and interferon for fighting viral infections. In these cases, a normal human gene for each of the needed proteins was transferred to the DNA of an individual bacterial strain, which then produced the particular chemical compound cheaply, abundantly, and in pure human form.

Another technique for gene transfer involves the introduction of a gene, obtained through the use of a restriction enzyme, directly into the fertilized egg of a farm animal. If it is a human gene and is incorporated into one of the animal's chromosomes, the animal will produce the human protein in its tissues. In addition, the animal can be bred to produce a herd carrying the human gene. As a result of using this procedure, scientists now have available the proteins alpha-1-antitrypsin, which helps fight emphysema and is produced in the milk of transgenic sheep; tissue plasminogen activator, which dissolves internal life-threatening blood clots and comes from the milk of transgenic goats; and lactoferrin, which has

bacteria-fighting capabilities and comes from the milk of transgenic cows.

Food production constantly is being hampered by crop-eating insects. There is, however, a bacterial species, *Bacillus thuringiensis*, that, for reasons unknown, is capable of producing insecticidal toxins. Genetic engineers have been able to transfer the toxin-producing genes from the bacteria to crop plants—including tobacco, cotton, tomatoes, potatoes, corn, and wheat. The transgenic plants produce the toxins in their tissues, thereby killing any insects that feed on them. The toxins have been shown to be safe for humans and wildlife.

A most imaginative use of DNA in medicine has been as a therapeutic drug against infectious organisms. In this approach, a very short and chemically modified polynucleotide chain is synthesized artificially that is complementary to and will bind permanently with a specific section of the microorganism's DNA. Under these conditions, the organism's hereditary material cannot be duplicated, and the organism cannot multiply. This procedure, known as antisense therapy, severely reduces the damage that can be caused by the infection. The U.S. Food and Drug Administration (FDA) has approved the use of DNA as a therapeutic agent against the cytomegalovirus, which causes an eye infection that can lead to blindness. This type of infection occurs in about 20% of advanced-AIDS patients.

The ultimate medical use of DNA is gene therapy, which has as its goal the delivery of normal genes to cure a wide range of untreatable inherited or acquired diseases. What has delayed the progress of gene therapy is the need to find efficient mechanisms (vectors) for getting the therapeutic genes into the specific tissues affected by the various diseases. The most commonly used vectors have been viruses, in which the disease-causing genes have been replaced with beneficial human genes. Although people with cystic fibrosis, hypercholesterolemia, and melanoma have had the severity of their diseases reduced by gene-therapy procedures, none had been cured completely by century's end.

Louis Levine

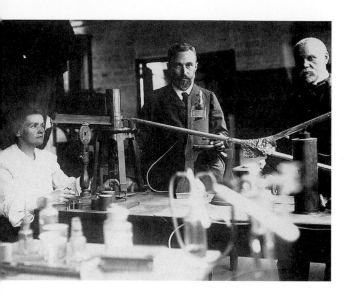

(Continued from page 265.)

that the speed of light—186,000 miles (299,792 kilometers) per second—is constant and represents the universe's speed limit. Nothing, he said, can travel faster. When objects approach the speed of light, weird things happen, and the ordinary laws of physics no longer apply. An object's mass, for instance, becomes infinitely great. Time slows down, so that a twin on a long space mission at light speed would return younger than his Earth-bound sibling. Einstein formulated a famous equation, $E = mc^2$. The amount of energy (E) released from matter equals its mass (m), or "weight," times the speed of light (c) squared. Since light travels at 186,000 miles (299,792 kilometers) per second, this meant that a minute amount of matter could release immense amounts of energy. The formula raised the possibility of nuclear weapons and nuclear-power reactors. In 1916, Einstein published the general theory of relativity, which expanded his earlier theory.

A New Portrait of the Atom

Marie and Pierre Curie helped to explain a strange property of certain atoms that had been discovered in the 1890s in uranium. French physicist Antoine-Henri Becquerel found that uranium atoms spontaneously disintegrated, or "decayed," releasing energy that later was named alpha, beta, and gamma rays. Marie Curie showed that certain other elements, including radium, which she isolated in a pure form, also had this unusual behavior, which she named "radioactivity." In

1910 she published a detailed explanation of radioactive substances. As director of the Pasteur Institute and a radioactivity laboratory in Paris, Marie Curie helped to pioneer medical uses of radium and other radioactive materials. In 1903 the Curies and Becquerel shared the Nobel Prize in physics. In 1911, Marie Curie was awarded the Nobel Prize in chemistry for her isolation of radium. She was the only person in the 20th century to win the Nobel in both sciences.

Danish physicist Niels Bohr used the quantum theory in 1912 to develop a more accurate model of the structure of atoms. British physicist Ernest Rutherford had taken the first step in 1909. He showed that the central nucleus of an atom contains most of its mass and has a positive electric charge. The negative charge is in the electrons, which orbit the nucleus. Bohr perfected Rutherford's model, proposing that electrons orbit in "shells," each of which holds only a

Polish-born French chemist Marie Curie (1867–1934), top left, shared the 1903 Nobel Prize in physics with her husband, Pierre Curie (1859–1906), for their work in radioactivity. She also was presented with the 1911 Nobel Prize in chemistry for isolating radium. Danish physicist Niels Bohr (1885–1962), above, was responsible for discovering the modern theory of atomic and molecular structure.

specific number of electrons. Bohr concluded that electrons jump from one shell to another as an atom absorbs or releases heat or light energy. The jump occurs in a quantum way, with the electron never existing in an in-between form. Bohr's work led to the development of quantum mechanics, which deals with the behavior of objects in the atomic and subatomic worlds.

Atoms lost their status as indivisible in 1919, when Rutherford discovered the proton, a positively charged particle inside the nucleus of the atom. British physicist James Chadwick discovered another subatomic particle, the neutron, in 1932. The neutron gave scientists a tool for smashing atoms and seeing what happens when they disintegrate. Since neutrons have no electric charge, they are not deflected by the electrons surrounding the nucleus of an atom. Instead, they collide with the nucleus. Two years after Chadwick's discovery, Italian physicist Enrico Fermi bombarded uranium with neutrons. The uranium atoms split, in a process later named nuclear fission. As they split, they released their own neutrons, which could strike other uranium atoms, making them split. The process continued in a nuclear chain reaction. Scientists realized that fission would release enormous amounts of energy, according to Einstein's famous equation, $E = mc^2$. If a chain reaction went slowly in a controlled way, it produced heat. That became the basis of nuclear-power reactors. An uncontrolled chain reaction would produce an explosion. In 1942 the U.S. government started the Manhattan Project, the secret effort to make a bomb based on nuclear fission. Success came by 1945, and scientists tested the first atomic bomb in the New Mexico desert. In August 1945 two bombs were dropped on Japan in an effort to speed the end of World War II.

Better understanding of the atom led to the discovery of new chemical elements. Early in the century, scientists knew that 92 natural elements existed—from Number 1, hydrogen, to Number 92, uranium. Rutherford's research showed that bombarding an atom of one element with protons could change it into a different element. In 1930, U.S. physicist Ernest Orlando Lawrence, at the University of California, Berkeley, built the first cyclotron, or atom smasher, a machine that allowed scientists to bombard

Italian-born American physicist Enrico Fermi (1901–54), above, was instrumental in the development of the atomic age. The 100th element, fermium, is named for the 1938 Nobel Prize winner in physics.

many different kinds of atoms. Cyclotrons also became the basic tool in an international effort to produce new chemical elements. For example, plutonium, which proved to be a better nuclear-weapons material than uranium, was discovered in 1940. Research in the United States, Germany, and the former Soviet Union expanded the periodic table to 112 elements by the century's end.

Ancient Origins

The study of humanity's origins became a full-fledged science in the 20th century. Scientists unearthed treasure troves of fossilized human bones and other artifacts, and developed new instruments and techniques to analyze them. For the first time, humans could look backward through 2.5 million years of their own evolution and glimpse how the species came to be.

Many new insights emerged from research done by the Leakey family, which made a spectacular series of discoveries in the Olduvai Gorge in northern Tanzania in East Africa starting in the late 1930s. The husband-and-wife team of Louis and Mary Leakey helped

(Continued on page 273.)

The modern environmental movement has its roots in the activities of pioneering conservationists like John Muir, who founded the Sierra Club and wrote treatises in the later years of the 19th century and early years of the 20th century lamenting the loss of wilderness. Muir found an audience in President Theodore Roosevelt, an avid outdoorsman and onetime rancher, who advocated a progressive policy built around preserving public lands for the American people, not wealthy resource interests. During his tenure as president, Roosevelt withdrew tens of millions of acres of forests, parks, and wildlife refuges from development, often antagonizing western timber, mining, and real-estate interests.

A different focus on land stewardship evolved in the wake of the dust-bowl catastrophe of the mid-1930s. Mechanized farming had plowed up vast grasslands in the wheat belt of the West and Southwest, leaving dryland farming the predominant economy. The combination of drought and winds left the land vulnerable to massive soil degradation: One 1934 windstorm was estimated to have removed 350 million tons of soil from Montana and Wyoming. In the wake of the disaster, new government policies were developed that instituted soil-conservation practices.

The population at large did not begin to grasp the serious threats human activities posed to the environment until several decades later. In 1962, Rachel Carson (*photo, page 271*), the editor for publications at the U.S. Fish and Wildlife Service, published *Silent Spring*, a seminal book that was serialized in several popular magazines. It detailed the dangers common pesticides posed to wildlife. Among the chemicals singled out was DDT, a chlorinated hydrocarbon widely used after World War II to reduce the incidence of malaria. Carson, who repeatedly was disparaged by the chemical industry and other critics, demonstrated how some pesticides can cause long-term damage because they are not biodegradable and can remain in the soil and water for years. One species that particularly suffered was the bald eagle, whose population declined to 417 known nesting pairs in the lower 48 states by 1963. Many countries, including the United States, eventually banned DDT and similar substances and replaced them with less-harmful agents. The population of bald eagles rebounded to the point where they no longer are listed as endangered.

By the late 1960s, environmentalism was spreading through campus activism, though efforts often were fragmented and derided as alarmist. After a 1969 oil spill fouled beaches at Santa Barbara, CA, Sen. Gaylord Nelson (D-WI) urged the various groups to come together on April 22, 1970, for the first "Earth Day," a series of demonstrations and teach-ins designed to pressure lawmakers to enact tougher environmental laws. The event crystallized the "green movement," popularized such practices as recycling, and built public pressure that helped win passage of federal laws, including the Environmental Quality Policy Act, the Clean Air Act, and the Clean Water Act. Air pollution in such cities as Los Angeles (*photo, page 270*) and water pollution in such rivers as the Cuyahoga in Cleveland, OH (*photo, right*), were among the targets of the legislation.

The 1970s and 1980s saw a series of high-profile incidents focus more public attention on toxic threats to the environment. The 1978 chemical-dumping

emergency at a residential area adjacent to Love Canal near Niagara Falls, NY; the near meltdown at Pennsylvania's Three Mile Island nuclear plant in 1979; a 1984 gas leak at a pesticide plant in Bhopal, India, that killed more than 2,000 people; and the 1989 *Exxon Valdez* oil spill in Prince William Sound, AK (*photo, page 272*), collectively intensified the debate on environmental protection and gave environmentalists more clout with public-policy makers.

Environmentalists also became more politically savvy in fighting industry efforts to evade compliance. This was evident in the case of the 1970 Clean Air Act, which was designed to set emissions standards for 200 toxic chemicals but resulted in only six being regulated in ten years. Environmentalists changed their strategy, lobbying for disclosure of industrial-emissions data instead of more regulations. A 1986 federal reporting requirement gave Americans a snapshot of what pollutants were being released in their communities and led to 1990 amendments to the original act. By 1996 emissions of the chemicals covered in the law had fallen 45%.

Environmental groups also used scientific findings to help with court cases over ecological laws. During the 1980s, studies by the National Audubon Society and others hypothesized that the northern spotted owl was in danger of extinction due to destruction of its habitat by logging in old-growth forests of the Pacific Northwest. As a result of legal action, in 1991 a court ordered the suspension of most such logging, over timber-industry objections that thousands of jobs would be lost. In 1994 the Bill Clinton administration filed court documents to make the suspension permanent

unless further challenges were successful. Some scientists, however, maintained that the owl was not endangered and that the environmentalists' claims were overstated.

Such victories transformed leading environmental groups by the mid-1990s into established political lobbies. Organizations such as the League of Conservation Voters were publishing scorecards evaluating local and national lawmakers on key environmental votes. The Sierra Club was boasting 550,000 members and a $40 million annual budget. It spent about $7 million on election-related activi-

ties—including television advertisements endorsing candidates—during the 1996 campaign cycle. Some Sierra Club members criticized the group's leaders for abandoning Muir's conservation ethic and dabbling in such debates as the fight over immigration controls. But the group's size and might also earned it access to members of Congress and, particularly, the Clinton administration.

Environmentalists, meanwhile, continued to press for protection of marine mammals, controls on heavy-metals discharges, and limits on agricultural runoff. One major unresolved issue of the 1990s was how to dispose of more than 80,000 tons of nuclear waste from commercial power plants and weapons facilities of the Cold War era. Although some of the waste was being buried in salt caverns deep beneath Earth's surface, environmentalists, scientists, and government officials disagreed on the safest way to store large quantities of this hazardous material.

The environmental movement also branched into broader societal issues. In the 1990s, groups pressed the concept of "environmental racism," contending that minority-group members may face higher-than-normal exposure to pollution as a result of public-policy decisions. Studies by Robert Bullard, a professor of sociology and director of the Environmental Justice Center at Clark Atlanta University, indicate that African-Americans are far more likely than white Americans to be exposed to harmful lead; that Hispanics may be at greater risk of living in areas where soot pollution is a problem; and that incinerators and hazardous-waste facilities are more likely to be sited in poor black neighborhoods.

Adriel Bettelheim

(Continued from page 269.)

start the science of paleoanthropology, the study of human origins. Their son, Richard, joined in the research and made other important findings. Leakey research challenged the conventional belief that humans originated in Asia, and put man's roots firmly in Africa. The Leakeys showed that humans evolved earlier than previously had been thought, and found evidence that several different types of early humans existed in Africa. Scientists previously thought that humans had a single ancestor. During 1976–77, Mary Leakey discovered a trail of fossilized footprints, preserved in volcanic ash, where humanlike creatures had walked 3.5 million years ago. The prints, which were found in Tanzania at the bottom of a watering hole, suggested that man's ancestors walked upright much earlier than had been believed.

An important advance in the analysis of ancient artifacts came in 1947, when U.S. chemist Willard Libby developed radiocarbon dating. It gave scientists an accurate way to determine the age of ancient wood, cloth, and other plant-based artifacts as old as 40,000 years. Libby realized that plants absorb and store carbon-14, a naturally radioactive material in the atmosphere. Storage stops when the plant dies, and the carbon-14 then begins to decay at a constant rate. By measuring the amount of remaining carbon-14, Libby's technique can determine when the organic sample died.

The first scientific answers to the age-old question of the chemical origins of life on Earth came during the 20th century. In 1953, U.S. chemist Stanley Miller reproduced, in a sealed laboratory chamber, conditions believed to have existed on Earth millions of years ago. The chamber contained water, hydrogen, methane, and ammonia. Electric sparks arced through the chamber to simulate lightning. Residue containing amino acids, the building blocks of living things, formed inside the chamber. Miller's work lent support to the theory of chemical evolution, which suggested that life originated from organic chemicals that reacted with each other.

Researchers also expanded their knowledge of the extent of life's realm on Earth. For half a century, scientists had thought that life occurred in a thin layer near the surface, and within a narrow range of temperature,

Mary and Louis Leakey, above, together with their son, Richard, advanced the study of human origins— paleoanthropology. The Leakeys did much of their work in East Africa, including northern Tanzania.

pressure, and other conditions. In the mid-1960s, Thomas Brock of the University of Wisconsin at Madison discovered microbes thriving at 210°F (99°C) in a boiling hot spring in Yellowstone National Park. Scientists in the 1970s and 1980s discovered other "extremophiles," organisms that thrive in extreme environmental conditions, including the cold, dark, "dead zones" of the ocean depths.

Life's possible domain expanded even further in 1996, when the National Aeronautics and Space Administration (NASA) announced evidence that microscopic life may have existed on Mars more than 3 billion years ago. This find was based on the detection of what some scientists said were fossilized remains of microbes in an ancient Martian meteorite that landed on Earth 13,000 years ago; they were discovered in 1984.

Science Serving Mankind

The 20th century was the century of synthetics. Chemists developed a wide variety of materials stronger, lighter, and more durable than those found in nature. The list includes cellophane, polyvinyl chloride (PVC), polyurethane foam, polyethylene, synthetic rubber, polyester, polystyrene, Plexiglas, Formica, and Kevlar. Synthetics be-

(Continued on page 276.)

The 20th century was marked by public concern over the long-term effects of a number of human activities. This concern resulted in discussions that aimed to bring attention to and generate political pressure for a reversal of several dangerous trends, including the

ongoing destruction of the world's forests, the threatened extinction of various plant and animal species, and the continued pollution of the environment. As the century concluded, and people looked forward to the benefits that would accrue from the anticipated scientific achievements of the 21st century, they were faced with yet another debate—this one on the issue of cloning.

Cloning is the term applied to any natural or artificial process that produces two or more individuals having identical genes. The debate over cloning had its origin in a 1997 announcement by Ian Wilmut and his colleagues at the Roslin Institute in Edinburgh, Scotland. The scientists explained that, in 1996, a sheep (which they named Dolly) was born that had its origin in the fusion of an adult mammary-gland cell with an egg cell from which the chromosomes had been removed. This meant that the chromosomes of the artificially "reconstructed" egg cell came from the nucleus of the mammary-gland cell. Therefore, Dolly and the sheep that provided the nucleus had identical sets of chromosomes, hence identical sets of genes. As a result, Dolly and the adult sheep that served as the donor of Dolly's chromosomes are members of a clone. They are, in effect, the equivalent of a set of identical-twin sheep, despite the fact that the adult sheep was 6 years old when Dolly was born.

What troubled people about the cloning of Dolly was not that a sheep could be cloned, but rather the realization that, if it could be done with sheep, it theoretically also should be possible with humans. This, in the view of many, would constitute an unnatural method of human procreation. However, the fact must be considered that human clones have been produced normally and naturally since the birth of the first set of identical twins. Identical human twins occur once in every 300 births. There are about 88 million births each year worldwide; therefore, there are approximately 293,000 human twin clones formed naturally each year. In addition, the births of sets of identical triplets—and, extremely rarely, higher multiples—further confirm the normal and natural occurrence of human clones. It was the concept of the purposeful manipulation of human cells to create clones that presented a moral dilemma for many.

The production of Dolly stimulated further work in this field. In 1997 researchers R. Yanagimachi and T. Wakayama, at the University of Hawaii, Honolulu, were able to clone mice (*photo above*), using as nuclei donors adult cumulus cells (specialized cells of the ovary that surround an egg as it matures). The scientists also were able, in turn, to use cumulus cells from the cloned mice to clone a second and subsequently a third generation of mice. The cloned mice—as also was true of Dolly—were able to produce offspring as the result of normal mating and gestation. The success of cloning involving sheep and mice may indicate that adult cells from any tissue of the body can be used for cloning. There is also the implication that all species of mammals may be capable of being cloned.

As was to be expected, the successful cloning of mice served to stimulate further the debate on cloning. Some people urged that research on all aspects of cloning of human material be outlawed. They are understandably troubled by the low rate of success in sheep (1 per 277) and mice (average of 2 to 3 per 100), and what is expected would be a comparable experience for human beings. There are also questions about the biological and legal relationship of the cloned individual to the person who provided the donor cell. And, finally, there is the fear that, in unscrupulous hands, cloning could be used to produce armies of brutal murderers and mindless slaves.

Those in opposition to a ban on cloning research view cloning as a potentially beneficial process. They are quick to acknowledge that cloning failures would result in great disappointment for the participants, but they expect that research would lead to appreciably higher levels of success. As for biological and legal questions, the cloning of either a wife or husband (in couples who were unable to produce children) would be, in effect, the production of a delayed identical twin of that person. The care and raising of a child by an older sibling who assumes a parental role is not unknown. Finally, with respect to the fear of the possible consequences of cloning in unscrupulous hands, it was pointed out that human history shows it was not necessary to clone humans in order to have armies that commit atrocities, or to be able to subject people to abject slavery.

In agreement with those opposing experiments involving human cloning, U.S. President Bill Clinton banned all federal funding of research in this area. He also asked the National Bioethics Advisory Commission to examine the legal and ethical issues involved in such experiments. A similar committee formed of members from various European countries and Japan was organized independently to examine the same issues. Both committees agreed that there should be a ban on the cloning of a total human being. However, beyond this very important point of agreement, there were differences in the specific recommendations made by the two groups.

The U.S. committee specifically urged that medical research involving the cloning of human DNA and human cell lines be continued. The European-Japanese committee also considered the question of animal cloning. It was recommended that all animal cloning, both of the total animal and of its cell lines, be continued. This recommendation was in support of the fact that, except for environmentally caused variations, all members of a clone have precisely the same characteristics. Therefore, if a particularly desirable animal is produced as a result of genetic engineering or a breeding program, cloning becomes the most efficient way of obtaining large numbers of organisms with the same traits. With respect to cloning of human cells, the committee urged that research be continued on the cloning of human organs for replacement purposes.

At the dawning of the 21st century, it would be up to individual countries, as influenced by the public debate on this issue, to pass laws that not only specify the types of cloning experiments that will be prohibited, but also regulate the types of cloning experiments that will be permitted.

Louis Levine

The Birth of Dolly

1. Embryologist Ian Wilmut removed a cell from the udder of a 6-year-old Finn Dorset ewe. He placed the cell in a nutrient-deprived culture, causing the active genes to switch off, and ensuring that the cell's DNA would keep working after the transplant.

Udder cell

Nucleus

Finn Dorset ewe (nucleus donor)

2. An unfertilized egg cell was removed from a second sheep—a Scottish blackface ewe. The egg's nucleus and DNA were extracted with a needle, but the cellular equipment necessary to produce embryos was left intact.

Egg cell

Cell fusion

3. The egg and udder cells were placed next to each other and given a jolt of electricity, causing them to fuse. A second jolt prompted cell division, forming an embryo.

Fused cell

Finn Dorset lamb (clone)

Dividing cell

Embryo

4. After six days, the embryo was implanted in the womb of a third (Scottish blackface) ewe. Five months later, in July 1996, a Finn Dorset lamb named Dolly was born.

(Continued from page 273.)
came mainstays in fabrics, packaging materials, shopping and trash bags, bottles, electronics equipment, automobile parts, and even artificial turf, which replaced natural grass in sports stadiums.

Belgian chemist Leo Hendrik Baekeland started it all in 1907 with his invention of the first completely synthetic plastic, Bakelite, by reacting phenol and formaldehyde in a special processing unit. Bakelite, which was introduced in 1909, quickly replaced natural materials used for electrical insulation, buttons, knobs, tool handles, and many other products. Synthetics like Bakelite seemed so promising that, in 1928, the DuPont chemical company opened the first research laboratory to discover new materials. DuPont chose Wallace Hume Carothers, a Harvard University chemistry professor, as its director. Carothers developed a synthetic rubber named neoprene that went on the market in 1932. In 1938, DuPont began selling another product of Carothers' research. It was a synthetic fabric that Carothers called "66 polyamide" but that DuPont renamed nylon. The "artificial silk" was a smash success with consumers, especially in women's stockings.

The discovery of the synthetic fiber nylon, above, by Wallace Hume Carothers in the 1930s revolutionized many things—not the least, women's stockings. U.S. agronomist Norman Borlaug, right, was awarded the 1970 Nobel Peace Prize for his "great contribution" in spurring the world's food production.

In a single day after its introduction, women bought 4 million pairs.

People in the 20th century were the first in history with the ability to travel and communicate quickly over great distances. One milestone in the transportation revolution occurred in 1903, when Wilbur and Orville Wright flew the first self-powered airplane, *Flyer 1*, over the sand dunes at Kitty Hawk, NC. *Flyer 1* traveled 120 feet (4 meters). To open the age of flight, the Wrights conducted basic aeronautical research to find a wing shape that would produce enough "lift" to defy gravity. They also had to design and build the first effective airplane propellers and a light, powerful gasoline engine.

Another transportation milestone was the mass production of automobiles from standardized parts. The first automobiles were built by hand and were very expensive. Only a few wealthy individuals even could dream of owning one. In 1913, Henry Ford built a moving assembly line in his Ford Motor Company plant in Detroit. Workers assembled cars from identical parts that would fit any vehicle of the same model. More people could afford to buy the Model T cars that rolled off Ford's production lines. Ford sold more than 15 million Model T cars by 1927, when production stopped.

Advances in communications made the world seem smaller and opened the era of wireless transmission of messages. In 1901,

The building of a 31-mile (50-kilometer)-long tunnel system across the English Channel from England to France in the late 1980s and early 1990s was one of the civil-engineering marvels of the 20th century. Trains could travel through the Channel Tunnel, above, at a speed of 90 miles (145 kilometers) per hour.

Italian inventor Guglielmo Marconi transmitted the first radio signals across the Atlantic Ocean. Radio continued as mainly a one-to-one means of communication—between ships at sea and individuals, for instance—until 1920, when station KDKA in Pittsburgh, PA, began the first regular commercial broadcasts. Television added images to voices and music in the 1930s; it first was demonstrated at the 1939 New York World's Fair. Color television came along on a large scale in the mid-1960s, and ultrasharp high-definition TV in the late 1990s.

Wonders of the 20th-Century World

The 20th century was a golden age of engineering, when humans built skyscrapers, bridges, dams, and other structures that were bigger, higher, longer, and stronger than ever before in history. One of the greatest civil-engineering marvels was the Channel Tunnel, or "Chunnel," which went into full operation in 1995 after seven years of construction. The 31-mile (50-kilometer)-long tunnel system under the English Channel linked England and France, fulfilling a dream that dated to the early 1800s. Drive-on/drive-off shuttle trains carrying cars and trucks travel in two tunnels that are 25 feet

(8 meters) wide and run on each side of a smaller service tunnel.

Other technological advances of the 20th century made people happier and more comfortable in many different ways. Willis Carrier, a U.S. engineer, invented air-conditioning in 1902. Carrier developed a mathematical formula, published in 1911, that still is used in the design of air-conditioning systems.

As the world population grew at a faster rate than food production, scientists in the 1960s predicted that great famines would sweep Asia before the end of the 20th century. U.S. agronomist Norman Borlaug led the Green Revolution, an effort to develop high-yield varieties of basic food crops that produced more grain when grown with fertilizers, pesticides, and irrigation. Borlaug developed "miracle wheat," which tripled grain production in Mexico and increased yields by 60% in Asia. "Miracle rice" and other improved varieties soon followed, preventing global famine. In the 1990s agricultural scientists recognized the need for a new Green Revolution based on plants that would produce sustained high yields without expensive fertilizers, pesticides, and scarce irrigation water.

Michael Woods

MEDICINE AND HEALTH

Medicine at the turn of the 20th century was a crude and imprecise science. Doctors understood that many of the worst diseases were caused by microorganisms invisible to the naked eye, but lacked the drugs to do anything except alleviate symptoms. X rays had found useful application only recently, and the options for pain relief were limited largely to aspirin, morphine, and heroin. Surgery was risky and prone to complications: When President William McKinley was shot by an assassin in 1901, doctors groped bare-handed in his abdomen in a futile search for the bullet. With no antibiotics, the prognosis was grim; eight days later, the president died of gangrene.

Early Developments

As the century progressed, medical science made enormous strides in perfecting surgical techniques, diagnosing ailments, curing infectious diseases, and understanding the molecular underpinnings of the body's functions. Appalling childhood-mortality rates have been eliminated, and life expectancies have lengthened. In 1900 the average person in the United States could expect to live 47 years, and the leading causes of death were pneumonia and tuberculosis. By the century's end, the average life expectancy in the United States was 76 years, and most common bacterial infections had been eliminated or rendered controllable in developed nations.

The era of modern drug development began in the first years of the century, when German biochemist Paul Ehrlich found that synthetic dyes being manufactured by the German chemical industry could bind to, and destroy, certain microbes. In 1909 he synthesized arsphenamine, a drug that could kill *Treponema pallidum*, the organism that caused syphilis, a venereal disease that for centuries was a cause of disability and death. Arsphenamine, known by the trade name salvarsan, was a vast improvement over the

Medical technology underwent major advances in the 20th century. The CAT (computerized axial tomography) scan, right, was introduced in the early 1970s.

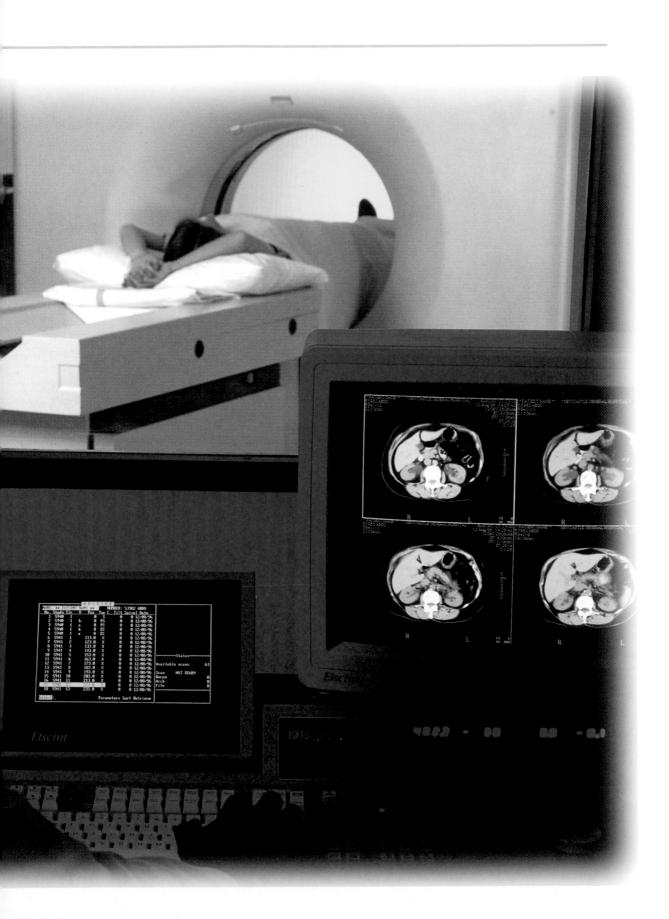

old remedy—the poisonous metal mercury—but still was toxic, and many painful injections were required before it cured the disease.

Ehrlich's work showing that molecules could bind to each other if their shapes were complementary inspired further research. Twenty-five years later, Gerhard Domagk, a scientist at the German drug and chemical company I.G. Farben, found that a synthetic compound called sulfonamide could treat streptococcal disease. This marked the beginning of sulfa drugs—and the end of a number of bacterial infections. Sulfa drugs were particularly effective in preventing blood poisoning, then a common complication in women following childbirth. The sulfa drugs actually did not kill bacteria but disrupted their molecular mechanisms, preventing them from multiplying in the host. That allowed the host's immune system to destroy them.

The early synthetic antibiotics began to make a dent in some of the world's deadliest infections. But Louis Pasteur's 19th-century experiments had indicated that natural biological agents also could kill harmful bacteria. In 1928, Scottish bacteriologist Alexander Fleming accidentally discovered how when he carelessly left staphylococcus germ cultures sitting in a petri dish near an open window. When he returned days later, he found mold had contaminated the colony—but had killed the germs. Fleming named the mold juice penicillin and began applying it to other infectious microbes. He grew disappointed, however, when he could not make it cure a skin infection.

The discovery remained largely unnoticed until a decade later, when Oxford University pathologist Howard Florey decided to test penicillin in mice by infecting them with enough streptococcus bacteria to cause a fatal infection. The mice survived, indicating that the drug had enormous potential. But it was difficult to extract enough of the active ingredient in the mold juice to produce a full treatment. Doctors first tried recovering penicillin from patients' urine. As World War II consumed the resources of European industry, it was left to American drug companies to perfect the technology to make the drug in large quantities. By 1944 the Allies had enough penicillin to treat troops with it during the Normandy invasion. A chemical cousin, streptomycin, was isolated by Russian-born microbiologist Selman Waksman, who was working in the United States in 1944, and proved to be the first antibiotic effective against tuberculosis.

These new drugs (see page 282) improved the quality of life in many households and added to a pharmaceutical arsenal that, until the 1930s, was relatively limited. Drugs and early vaccines existed for a handful of specific illnesses, such as smallpox and diphtheria. A Canadian research team, led by Frederick Banting in the early 1920s, isolated insulin from the pancreas, providing a way to control diabetes—then a major cause of death.

Polio's Reign of Fear

Perhaps the most dramatic episode in 20th-century drug development was the race to find a vaccine for polio—a crippling, often-fatal disease. Polio is transmitted by a virus that first colonizes the intestines, then attacks the central nervous system, killing cells in the spine or brain stem that control muscles. The disease mostly struck children. It hit the United States in a series of epidemics beginning in 1916. Public awareness intensified with the election of President Franklin D. Roosevelt, who had contracted the disease in 1921 and became a

Rows of tents served as a makeshift hospital in Lawrence, MA, during the 1918–19 influenza epidemic that killed nearly a million people worldwide. Australian nurse Elizabeth ("Sister") Kenny (1886–1952), below, became famous for her method of treating victims of polio, a disease that traumatized parents until the development of a vaccine in the 1950s.

passionate advocate for a cure, though the news media tacitly agreed to downplay Roosevelt's leg braces and use of a wheelchair. The post–World War II baby boom brought an alarming rise in polio incidence; by 1952 the number of new cases annually had risen to 59,000. Public pools and parks were closed, and parents ordered their children not to drink from public water fountains. The March of Dimes launched a nationwide campaign to raise money for a cure.

Relief came only after researchers learned how to isolate and grow the virus in tissue cultures. They also discovered that three distinct strains of polio existed, meaning a person would have to be immunized against all three to be protected completely. In 1953, Jonas Salk produced a vaccine consisting of weakened, or "killed," virus that proved 80% to 90% effective in trials. Public-health officials rushed the vaccine into mass production. Four years later, Albert Sabin produced another vaccine, based on live virus, that pro-

(Continued on page 284.)

German bacteriologist and immunologist Paul Ehrlich (1854–1915), page 280, top, was a pioneer in the development of 20th-century drugs. Canadian physician Sir Frederick Banting (1891–1941), page 280, bottom, led the researchers who isolated the hormone insulin in the early 1920s.

The Wonder Drugs

At the beginning of the 20th century, infectious diseases were the leading cause of death in the United States. In 1900 more than 30% of deaths were caused by tuberculosis, pneumonia, or diarrhea. The average life span was 47 years. Infant mortality was high, and young children, 1 to 5 years of age, had a greater than one-in-ten chance of dying, often from an infectious disease. The death of more than one young child in the same family was all too common. For many infections, all the physician could do was to treat the symptoms, while the family hoped that the fever would break before the patient succumbed.

Despite this grim picture, there was cause for optimism. The 19th century had been a time of marked improvement in the quality of life in the industrialized world. Hygiene and sanitation had improved, nutrition and housing were better, and food and water were safer. Science and technology also provided new opportunities for intervention in infectious diseases. The research of Louis Pasteur, Robert Koch, and others had shown that infections were caused by living microorganisms, not some miasma that rose from swamps.

By the turn of the century, scientists had learned a great deal more about these organisms and their interactions with the human body. Pasteur had shown that it was possible to prevent infections by using vaccines. Now, Paul Ehrlich theorized that it should be possible to kill the bacteria that caused the infection without harming the infected person. Ehrlich, who had been trained as a pathologist, had noticed that, when viewed under the microscope, human tissues and bacteria absorbed different stains. Thus, he believed that it should be possible to identify a toxic substance—his "magic bullet"—that would be absorbed selectively by the bacteria. With Erhlich's discovery in 1909 of arsphenamine, an arsenical compound that could cure syphilis, the world had its first wonder drug. Although patients receiving arsphenamine (known by the trade name salvarsan) had serious side effects, this magic bullet was the first antimicrobial agent, a substance with selective toxicity for microorganisms.

British bacteriologist Sir Alexander Fleming (1881–1955) discovered the antibacterial agent lysozyme as well as the "wonder drug" penicillin.

The discovery of salvarsan stimulated further research for safer drugs to treat additional infections. In 1935 prontosil, a second antimicrobial agent related to the sulfonamides, was discovered, and in 1941 a new era started with the production of a new type of antimicrobial drug, an antibiotic called penicillin. Antibiotics have been defined as substances produced by microorganisms that are antagonistic to other microorganisms at low concentrations. Both salvarsan and prontosil were chemicals that were synthesized by researchers. Penicillin, on the other hand, was produced by a living organism—a mold. Since researchers assumed that penicillin was produced by the mold as a weapon to fight bacteria, it seemed logical to search for additional new antibiotics in places where there were many competing microorganisms, such as soil and sewage. Over the next 20 years, several new antibiotics were discovered in such settings. At the same time, chemists began modifying the structures of new and old antibiotics to reduce their side effects, to modify how they were absorbed or metabolized by the body, and to increase the types of bacteria killed.

Following the introduction of antibiotics, the mortality from certain infections—such as pneumonia, meningitis, and typhoid fever—fell dramatically. Complications of infections that often led to chronic disability were reduced. The incidence of certain diseases declined, as antibiotics prevented infected persons from transmitting the illnesses to others. Antibiotics and vaccines were contributing to the continued decline in many infectious diseases, a decline that had begun with better nutrition and improved hygiene and sanitation. For the first time, however, antibiotics allowed physicians to modify clearly the outcome of infection. The effectiveness of the "wonder drugs" was perhaps the major factor influencing the emphasis on curative medicine that would characterize much of the health care of the 20th century. Faith in medical technology grew, and many predicted the eventual elimination of most infectious diseases.

Yet the war with the microbes was not over. There had been early signs of chinks in the armor of the antibiotics. Soon after the introduction of penicillin, strains of *Staphylococcus aureus* became resistant to the drug and caused outbreaks of serious infections in hospitals. As other organisms became resistant to additional antibiotics, the pharmaceutical industry searched for new drugs. Researchers began to understand the ways in which bacteria became resistant to antibiotics: The bacteria could produce enzymes to break down the antibiotic; they could pump the antibiotic outside the cell wall, where it no longer would be effective; they could change the structure of the antibiotic's target, preventing binding; and they could overproduce the target, making the amount of antibiotic in the cell inadequate. In addition, bacteria could exchange resistance genes among themselves. The use of an antibiotic provided the pressure for selecting resistant bacteria by killing the antibiotic-sensitive bacteria and giving any resistant strain an evolutionary advantage. Thus, the more an antibiotic was used, the more likely it became that that bacteria would become resistant.

Antibiotics were being used and misused extensively. In humans, the wonder drugs were used not just for serious or life-threatening bacterial infections, but to prevent infections or when an infection was only suspected or even unlikely. Persons with a fever or a cold (a viral infection not responsive to antibiotics) often were treated—just to be safe. In 1992 more than 110 million courses of antibiotics were prescribed in physicians' offices, and about 20% to 50% of these prescriptions were unnecessary. In animals, antibiotics also were being used to treat infections, but in addition, they were being given, often in feed, to prevent infections and to promote growth. It was estimated in the 1980s that 16 million pounds of antibiotics were given to animals annually. More and more bacteria were becoming resistant to commonly used antibiotics—not just bacteria that are transmitted from person to person, but also organisms such as *Salmonella* and *Campylobacter* that are transmitted through the food chain from animals to humans. But despite the emergence of resistance, there always seemed to be a new antibiotic ready to be used.

In the late 1980s, however, things began to change dramatically. New infectious diseases were emerging, and diseases once thought conquered were resurgent. This development led to increased antibiotic use and increasing resistance, but new antibiotics were no longer on the shelves. Pharmaceutical companies, believing that there were enough antibiotics, had stopped developing new ones. Within a few years, certain strains of bacteria that were resistant to all available antibiotics had emerged, causing untreatable infections. The pharmaceutical industry restarted research to modify existing drugs or to design new antimicrobial agents using newer molecular techniques, but new drugs were still years away.

The potential for untreatable bacterial infections was particularly high at the end of the 20th century. While the next wonder drugs were in development, efforts were under way to use available antibiotics more wisely and to prevent bacterial diseases by using existing and new vaccines and by practicing better hygiene and infection control.

Mitchell Cohen, M.D.

(Continued from page 281.)

voked a more powerful, lasting immune response. The Sabin vaccine also was easier to administer. Instead of being injected, it was swallowed on a cube of sugar. Through oral administration of the vaccine, the live polio was attenuated in the acidic environment of the stomach, so it did not actually give patients the disease. Polio's reign of fear thus ended by the 1960s.

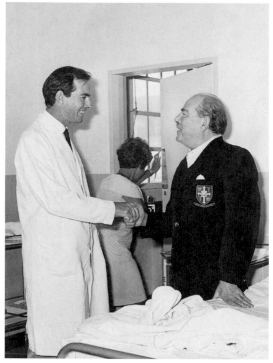

Research on the cause and treatment of heart disease intensified during the 1960s. Dr. Christiaan Barnard (above left) made headlines by performing the world's first heart-transplant operation in 1967.

Disease-Causing Conditions

Despite great advances against microbial threats, medicine still had to overcome poor hygiene and a lack of understanding about how diseases spread. Response to those challenges laid the foundation for the branch of medicine known as epidemiology, which seeks to prevent disease-causing conditions.

Scientists were mystified for years about what made the influenza pandemic that killed nearly a million people worldwide from 1918 to 1919 so deadly—especially for youthful victims, whose overall vigor helps them defeat normal flu strains. Years of research determined that the most deadly strains of the ever-mutating influenza virus may be passed from birds to pigs and then to humans. Then, human-to-human transmission can be worsened by the crowding of modern living. That aspect was exacerbated by massive troop movements during the closing months of World War I, when the pandemic hit. By the late 20th century, vaccination against the likeliest flu strains to arise was common.

Other epidemiological breakthroughs came from the U.S. Public Health Service, founded in 1902. In the early years of the century, the agency's vaunted "microbe hunters" made headway against some of the world's most exotic and fatal diseases, such as yellow fever. The health service also ushered in an era of public-health awareness by demonstrating the relationships among poor living conditions, meager diets, and bad health. One notable example was the discovery of the cause of pellagra, a mysterious disease that killed tens of thousands of people in the rural South.

Doctors believed the disease was caused by bacteria, possibly delivered to humans through insect bites. Public-health physician Joseph Goldenberger, however, noticed that the sufferers' diets tended to be restricted to cornbread, cornmeal mush, syrup, and pork. He theorized that the disease was really a nutritional deficiency. Subsequent research showed that the disease could be prevented by administering niacin, a B vitamin found in whole grains, poultry, and other foods.

Similar epidemiological studies in Washington, DC, and other cities of typhoid fever—fostered by contaminated water supplies—contributed to the establishment of the modern sanitation movement. In the second half of the century, research shifted to chronic diseases, particularly cancer, heart disease, neurological diseases, and arthritis. Much of this work is coordinated by the National Institutes of Health, a sprawling U.S. government research facility in Bethesda, MD, that grew out of the health service's hygiene lab.

Surgical Advances

World War II was responsible for some of the century's greatest surgical advances. Military doctors, facing massive battlefield injuries, perfected antibiotics, anesthesia, and blood transfusions to perform increasingly elaborate operations. Orthopedists began using pins and wires to fix bone fractures, and per-

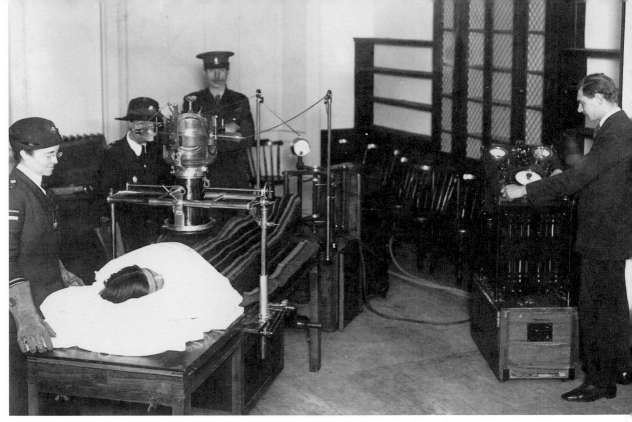

Wilhelm Conrad Roentgen discovered X rays in 1895. The first mobile X-ray machine, above, was in use some 25 years later. Both breast cancer and prostate cancer were receiving intense publicity as the 1990s ended. A mammogram, below left, a special type of X ray with very low levels of radiation, remained the most prevalent technique for detecting breast cancer. The colored computed tomography scan of an axial section through the human pelvis, below right, reveals an enlarged prostate with cancer (green area).

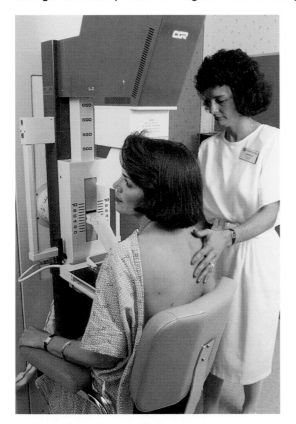

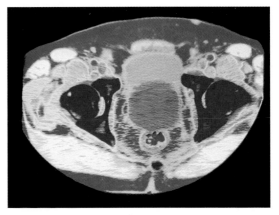

formed the first hip replacements. U.S. Army surgeon Dwight Harken developed techniques to remove shell fragments from the heart. This led to early open-heart surgery, in which doctors cooled patients' body temperatures to reduce the need for oxygenated blood, allowing them to stop the heart for up to ten minutes at a time. The development of the heart and lung machine in 1953 made the process less cumbersome and further increased success rates.

Rarely has a consumer product undergone such a radical shift in public attitudes as has tobacco in the United States. During both world wars, the U.S. government issued free cigarettes to soldiers at the front. Advertisements claimed that smoking actually benefited health by calming jittery nerves and even soothing scratchy throats. Cigarettes became an essential prop in Hollywood movies. The good publicity paid off. By 1963, Americans age 10 and older were smoking an average of 12 cigarettes a day.

But attitudes quickly changed after 1964, when the first surgeon general's report was released to the public, implicating smoking in the growing incidence of lung cancer. Numerous later studies showed smoking to be a principal cause of other cancers, emphysema, and heart disease.

Federal, state, and local governments launched an all-out war on smoking, imposing taxes on tobacco products and regulating their sale. Beginning in 1966, tobacco companies were required to include on all cigarette packs and advertisements a warning of smoking's health hazards. In 1971, Congress banned all television and radio advertising for cigarettes.

In the early 1970s, governments began taking a more direct approach against smoking by restricting it in public places. The first federal rules came in 1973, when the Civil Aeronautics Board required commercial airlines to offer nonsmoking sections. By 1990 smoking was banned on all domestic flights of six hours or less, as well as on intercity buses. The first smoking bans in federal-government offices went into effect in 1987 and later were extended to nearly all federal facilities. State and local governments have been even more restrictive. In 1973, Arizona became the first state to bar smoking in public buildings, and nearly all other states have adopted similar restrictions.

As a result of these efforts, as well as antismoking advertising by the American Cancer Society and other groups, per-capita cigarette consumption had dropped to seven cigarettes a day by 1992. The percentage of adult smokers also had fallen, from 40% in the mid-1960s to less than 30%.

Some organs were beyond repair and simply needed to be replaced. That was not possible until the 1960s, when scientists found a way around the body's tendency to reject foreign tissue. The technique involved new drugs that could suppress a patient's immune response and prevent disease-fighting cells from attacking the donated organ. Some early kidney transplants were performed in the United States in the 1950s. In 1967, South African surgeon Christiaan Barnard performed the first heart-transplant surgery, taking an organ from a 23-year-old woman who had been killed in an automobile crash and implanting it in a middle-aged man, who died 18 days later. Despite early difficulties keeping patients alive, doctors eventually perfected techniques to quickly spot signs of rejection and immediately administer immunosuppressive drugs. (*See* page 288.)

Surgery was aided by new and improved diagnostic tools. After the advent of X rays, first used to photograph bones and to shrink cancerous tumors, medicine became dependent on radioactive isotopes to trace biological pathways and view the components of the body in new, nonsurgical ways. In 1971, English electrical engineer Godfrey Hounsfield perfected a machine that took X rays of sections of the body and used a computer to put the patterns together. This CAT scan (for *computerized axial tomography*) allowed doctors to identify the precise location and size of previously undetectable tumors and cysts. A second imaging technique, called *magnetic resonance imaging* (MRI), arrived in the mid-1980s. This device uses a giant magnet to subject the patient's body to a powerful magnetic field, allowing technicians to identify small differences in the atoms of soft tissue. This gives doctors a

The tobacco industry, however, did not give up without a fight. For years, cigarette manufacturers rejected the scientific evidence linking smoking with disease, calling it speculation. To make up for declining sales of cigarettes in the United States, they beefed up exports, especially to developing countries where the cigarette habit had yet to take hold. At home, they lured nonsmokers by targeting teenagers with advertising figures, such as Joe Camel, which was introduced in 1988. This strategy appeared to work, as daily smoking among teenagers rose 73% in ten years.

In the 1990s antismoking activists took their fight to the courts. In 1998 they won an important legal victory when the four major tobacco companies—Philip Morris, R.J. Reynolds Tobacco Company, Brown & Williamson Tobacco Corporation, and Lorillard Inc.—were required to pay 46 states a total of $206 billion over 25 years to help pay for treating disease caused by smoking. The companies also were required to help discourage teenagers from taking up the cigarette habit by eliminating advertising targeted at younger consumers.

Mary H. Cooper

powerful and accurate diagnostic tool to spot subtleties such as changes in the white matter of the brain that are signs of multiple sclerosis.

Some diagnostic tools actually are used to hone surgical techniques. Laparoscopic surgery features a laser-guided probe that is used to explore areas such as the stomach and intestines. In some cases, the laser is used to seal and heal stomach ulcers and other wounds. In the 1990s light-activated dyes called photofrines began to be injected into tumors. Once activated, they could destroy cancer cells while leaving most healthy cells intact.

The Central Nervous System and the Brain

Wartime medicine also contributed to a new understanding of the central nervous system and the mysteries of the brain. The brutal trench warfare of World War I spurred investigations into a mental condition suffered by many veterans, known as traumatic shock. Scientists discovered that cells release substances—including histamines—as a result of injury. Some such releases cause allergic disorders. Further studies revealed that messages between nerve cells are transmitted by chemicals. The actions of these "neurotransmitters" can be inhibited by drugs, such as benzedrine (amphetamine); the antidepressant Prozac; and tranquilizers, such as chlorpromazine.

This led to the first widespread use of psychotropic drugs to treat mental illness. For centuries, sufferers of schizophrenia and other serious disorders were warehoused in asylums and often held up to social ridicule. The United States saw a dramatic increase in new cases of schizophrenia during the first five decades of the century, prompting intense debate between psychoanalysts, who

The 20th century witnessed probably the most prolific expansion of knowledge in the field of medicine in history. With the evolution in understanding human anatomy and the physiology of how organs work, the perennial dream of replacing terminally diseased organs with healthy ones became a reality.

Organ transplantation is defined as the replacement of a vital organ, such as the heart or kidney, or tissues, such as skin, that are diseased and have been rendered nonfunctional. Replacement of the tissue or organ with material from the same individual is called autotransplantation; when the material comes from another human being, it is called allotransplantation; and when it comes from a different species, it is called xenograft transplantation.

Three problems complicated the development of organ transplantation. The first was achieving the surgical ability to remove a diseased organ and replace it with a healthy one. The second was understanding the immune system so that these newly replaced organs would not be rejected by the body. And the third was obtaining enough organs to meet the overwhelming need.

In the early 20th century, surgeon Alexis Carrel first developed the capability of anastomosing (connecting) blood vessels, thus allowing organs to be removed and new organs to be sutured to the blood supply to enable the flow of life-sustaining nutrients into them. Once this technique was established, the next hurdle to be overcome was preventing rejection—that is, the fact that the immune system is programmed to attack and kill any genetically foreign objects, such as newly grafted organs, within the human body.

Through the 1920s, 1930s, and 1940s, an understanding of the immune system slowly evolved. Lymphatic vessels, lymph nodes, bone marrow, the spleen, and the thymus came to be known as vital parts of the immune system. It then was discovered how the immune system recognizes and kills foreign substances within the body—by attacks by humoral antibodies and by activation of certain immune cells that destroy the foreign tis-

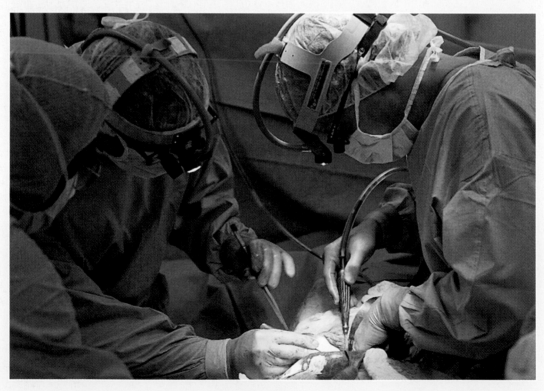

sues. Over the next 20 years, immunologists painstakingly dissected the immune system in order to understand exactly how these immune cells worked. In time, the immune system was understood well enough that pharmaceutical industries, together with academic institutions, were able to develop immunosuppressive drugs to prevent organ rejection. These medicines dramatically increased the success of organ transplantation—not just for kidneys, but for other vital organs such as the heart, lungs, and liver.

To solve the third problem—finding human organs for transplantation—a national system needed to be devised to encourage organ donation throughout the United States and to assure equitable allocation of these organs. In 1984, Congress passed the National Transplant Act, which directed the development of a national organ-procurement network called United Network of Organ Sharing (UNOS). This nonprofit organization, accountable to the federal government, was to be comprised of grassroots organizations from every city, state, and region of the country.

UNOS' organizational structure allowed for representation not only of physicians and scientists, but also of patient-advocacy groups and religious organizations. UNOS, through its various subcommittees, developed various methods of equitable allocation. It also was charged with educating the public so that the great benefits that accrued to terminally ill patients and, in the end, to all Americans would be understood. Through UNOS, the United States developed an efficient and active organ-retrieval network that became the model for the rest of the world.

Nonetheless, as the 20th century closed, there still was room for improvement, as the need for organs continued to outnumber organs donated. Further research and solutions, including the use of xenografts and the possibility of cloning human organs so that more organs would be made available from those retrieved, were in development. Living related transplantation also had become a popular and humanitarian gesture for Americans.

Robert Mendez, M.D.

believed the condition was the product of faulty child-rearing, and biologists and psychiatrists, who thought it might stem from a genetically derived chemical imbalance in the brain. In 1954 the U.S. Food and Drug Administration (FDA) approved chlorpromazine for the treatment of schizophrenia. In its first decade, the drug was given to an estimated 50 million people around the world. It produced mixed blessings: Tens of thousands of mental patients whose psychoses were controlled were deinstitutionalized, but many failed to continue taking the drug when they were out on the streets. The suc-

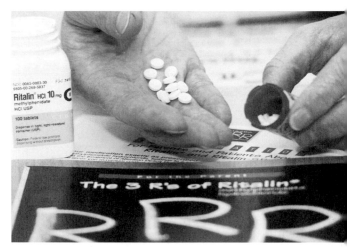

Ritalin became the drug of choice for treating attention deficit disorder (ADD), a condition affecting school-age children that was identified in the 1970s.

cess also spawned next-generation drugs such as Valium. The drug was hailed for its ability to diminish stress and anxiety but also proved dangerously addictive.

The Genetic Code

Arguably the century's most significant development in medicine and biology was the unveiling of the genetic code, which established that DNA molecules carry hereditary characteristics in living things. U.S. biochemist Oswald Avery first outlined the composition of DNA, or deoxyribonucleic acid, in the 1940s. But it was the U.S.-English team of biologist James Watson and biophysicist Francis Crick that identified the molecule's double-helix structure in 1953 and explained how biological traits—including hereditary diseases—could be passed from generation to generation. This opened the new field of genetics and, by the 1980s,

AIDS

Few diseases in the 20th century spawned public fear and frustrated scientists as much as AIDS (acquired immune deficiency syndrome). The immunodeficiency first was identified in 1981, although it is believed to have existed in sub-Saharan Africa since the 1950s. As recently as the mid-1990s, a diagnosis of AIDS was tantamount to a death sentence; by century's end the disease had claimed an estimated 14 million lives. However, in the late 1990s multiple-drug "cocktails" transformed the disease

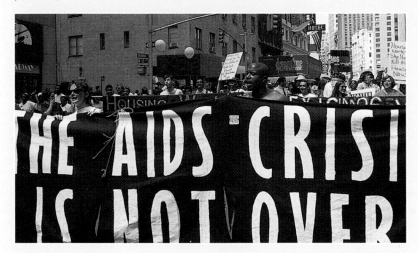

into a manageable chronic condition for many people. The new treatments were allowing some infected people to live longer but do not actually cure the disease. The treatments had unpleasant side effects; they also could cost upward of $15,000 per year.

AIDS is caused by the human immunodeficiency virus (HIV), an insidious killer that attacks the T-cells, or lymphocytes, that the human body uses to fight infections. As HIV steadily reduces the body's resistance to disease, patients often fall victim to "opportunistic infections," such as pneumonia, meningitis, or tuberculosis. Death can occur from any of these causes, as well as from dementia and wasting syndrome, which are believed to be caused by the virus itself. The virus is transmitted through infected blood, through semen that enters the body during sexual intercourse, or via the injection of contaminated blood or needles into blood vessels. The disease struck the homosexual community and intravenous-drug users particularly hard, though the majority of the new cases in the late 1990s were being transmitted through heterosexual sex.

Finding drugs to fight the disease proved frustrating. The first antiviral AIDS drug, AZT, helped some patients but is toxic and only works for about two years, after which the virus becomes resistant. Other drugs can interfere with reverse transcriptase, a key enzyme in the virus' molecular machinery, but do not provide a cure. In 1995 researchers gained new hope with a new class of drugs called protease inhibitors. The drugs interrupt another important enzyme in HIV, protease, and can suppress replication of the virus effectively. The drugs must be administered in large doses, often in tandem with AZT-like drugs, to reduce the presence of the virus over long periods of time.

By century's end, AIDS patients often were taking batteries of three- and four-drug "cocktails" to reduce the chance of the virus mutating and becoming drug-resistant. This cut the AIDS mortality rate to the point where the disease fell out of the top ten causes of death in the United States for the first time since 1990. Yet the news was not all positive. The drugs were not available in poor nations, particularly in Africa, where 80% of the world's AIDS deaths occurred. Health officials also noted that the drugs had not slowed the global epidemic; about 16,000 more people were estimated to be infected each day, and more than 33 million adults and children were believed to be living with the disease.

Adriel Bettelheim

NEXT...!

DR. KEVORKIAN
FINAL OPINION

BROOKINS
Richmond Times-Dispatch

Bioethics—medical ethics—came to the forefront in the 1990s, as new issues involving health care, human enhancement, and human experimentation arose. Retired Michigan pathologist Jack Kevorkian was a leading proponent of physician-assisted suicide, cartoon above. With medical costs escalating and some medical procedures facing new questioning, alternative forms of medicine—including the ancient Chinese technique of acupuncture, right—became more popular. Contact lenses offered those with imperfect vision an alternative to wearing glasses. The soft-lens version, below, was introduced in 1965.

gave scientists the ability to read the genetic code in DNA, isolate genes, and clone them.

By century's end, doctors routinely screened unborn babies for genetic diseases and a growing number of congenital disorders, and could diagnose the problems before birth. Scientists in the growing field of gene therapy could pinpoint and isolate a defective gene, grow a "healthy" version, and potentially insert it in the faulty gene's place. Scientists also were involved in the Human Genome Project, a $3 billion, 15-year effort to map all of the human body's approximately 80,000 genes and identify previously unrecognized genes that govern diseases like cancer.

The advances have given scientists a starting point for potential cures for cancer, AIDS (*see* page 290), cystic fibrosis, and a host of other afflictions. But they also have encouraged researchers to search for genetic links to commonplace behaviors, such as violence, risk-taking, and sexuality. This has led to difficult ethical questions about whether society is excessively "biologizing" behavior and discounting underlying economic and social conditions. Some fear the trend is rekindling the "eugenics" movement that in the early 20th century singled out some groups as biologically inferior and unworthy of reproduction.

The study of the genetics of disease has spawned a booming biotechnology industry that annually churns out dozens of new drugs aimed at particular diseases. Knowledge of the genetic makeup of some cancer cells, for instance, has allowed the development of a series of antibodies that can speed therapeutic agents to afflicted parts of the body. The agents help the body recognize distinctive proteins on tumor cells—called antigens—and signal the host's immune system to attack them as invaders. These "immunotherapies" work in ways similar to vaccines but do not actually prevent cancer. They remain critical, because cancer cells mutate and mask their identities, making it nearly impossible for the body to spot and kill them.

Adriel Bettelheim

SPACE EXPLORATION

"Everything in space obeys the laws of physics. If you know these laws, and obey them, space will treat you kindly. And don't tell me man doesn't belong out there. Man belongs wherever he wants to go—and he'll do plenty well when he gets there."

Wernher von Braun
February 1958

Thousands of artificial satellites now circle the Earth. All but one planet within the known confines of our solar system have fallen under the passing sensors of a spacecraft. Wheel markings from a robotic rover slink between rocks on faraway Mars. And the boot imprints from a dozen astronauts dot the Moon's cratered and dusty terrain. These are but a few space-exploration milestones realized in the 20th century. They were made possible by the bold imaginings of space pioneers, a majority of whom never witnessed their visions turn into reality.

Such was the case with Russian schoolteacher and mathematician Konstantin E. Tsiolkovski, considered the founder of astronautical theory. Tsiolkovski's thoughts on liquid-fueled rocketry were published in 1903, providing him a springboard for some 30 years of speculative writing on multistage rocketry, the placement of artificial satellites into orbit, the building of space stations, and the prospect of interplanetary travel. But the actual building of rocket hardware fell to an American, Robert H. Goddard. A physics professor and avowed tinkerer, Goddard began his rocket research in 1909, leading up to a 1914 patent for a multistage-rocket design and to his writing a seminal paper, published by the Smithsonian in 1919, titled "A Method of Reaching Extreme Altitudes." Goddard turned paperwork into working hardware, launching the world's first liquid-propelled rocket on March 16, 1926. His Aunt Effie Ward's cabbage patch in Auburn, MA, served as a convenient launch locale. The history-making liftoff saw Goddard's rocket fly all of 2.5 seconds, arc to an altitude of a little more than 40 feet (12 meters), then plow into the ground.

Goddard, transplanting his rocket research to the remote desert area near Roswell, NM, developed and tested numbers of liquid-propellant rockets from 1930 into the early 1940s. Dozens of rocket tests were carried out, with vehicles reaching altitudes of more than 8,250 feet (2,514 meters). Goddard himself saw more in his experiments than gyrostabilization hardware, exhaust vanes, and fuel pumps; he, too, was an "imagineer," envisioning eventual exploration of the Moon and beyond. "There can be no thought of finishing," Goddard would write, "for 'aiming at the stars,' both literally and figuratively, is a problem to occupy generations, so that no matter how much progress one makes, there is always the thrill of just beginning."

Inspired in part by Goddard's early work, Hermann Oberth—by birth a Transylvanian but by nationality a German—also helped push forward the rhetoric of spaceflight into reality. By publishing *The Rocket into Planetary Space* in 1923, Oberth detailed virtually every principle that governs spaceflight today. A later work by Oberth, *The Way to Space Travel*, was published in 1929 and expanded upon his ideas. His thoughts stirred the creative juices of space-exploration enthusiasts worldwide. Among that number was a young German, Wernher von Braun, who later would spearhead the U.S. space efforts.

It was the emergence of World War II that placed rocket development on a trajectory, not to the stars, but on a pathway for use as a weapon of destruction. The first true ballistic missile—called the V-2 (Vengeance Weapon

The 20th century marked exciting advancement for space exploration—from the early rocket research of Robert H. Goddard and his colleagues, above, to the launch of "Zarya," the first piece of the International Space Station, page 292, in November 1998.

The launching of Vanguard III, above, on Sept. 18, 1959, completed the first satellite program conducted by the United States. Three satellites were placed successfully in orbit during the program.

2)—was brought into being by German rocket teams led by von Braun. The rocket's development and use against Great Britain and the European continent was backed by German dictator Adolf Hitler. As World War II was winding down, advancing armies of both the United States and the Soviet Union collected not only V-2 components and key documents, but the elite of the German rocket team as well. Many of the German rocket team, including von Braun, surrendered to U.S. forces. The V-2 rocket—made possible by the vision of Tsiolkovski, Goddard, Oberth, and, later, von Braun—paved the way for rockets capable of lofting the first artificial satellites into orbit, thus setting humankind on a quest to explore the neighboring planets and the universe at large.

Beeps Heard Round the World

It weighed just 184 pounds (83 kilograms). Its electronic innards were stuffed within a metallic sphere measuring a modest 23 inches (58 centimeters). On Oct. 4, 1957, radio receivers around the Earth heard the "beep, beep, beep" that signaled the dawn of the space age. As the first artificial Earth satellite, the Soviet Union's Sputnik 1 (meaning "traveler") was hurled skyward atop a modified intercontinental ballistic missile (ICBM) from the Baikonur cosmodrome. Sputnik 1 not only served as a propaganda coup for the

Soviets, but doubled as a political slap in the face to U.S. world leadership. Indeed, the event bolstered Soviet claims of scientific and technological superiority over the West, and especially the United States, a view that was adopted widely by nations around the globe.

Perhaps more striking was Russia's Sputnik 2. Shot into space a few weeks later, Sputnik 2 not only was six times heavier than its predecessor, but it also carried the first living animal into orbit—the dog Laika, who became the first passenger to circle Earth. It became obvious that the Soviet Union's space agenda also listed the eventual launching of humans into orbit. The one-two punch of Soviet missile and satellite prowess transformed space into a stage for governmental one-upmanship. Space became a Cold War battleground to exhibit technical skill, economic strength, and political clout.

The U.S. entry to kick-start a national space program, spawned by U.S. participation in the International Geophysical Year, proved a disastrous undertaking. The navy's Project Vanguard booster, crafted to hurl spaceward an 8-pound (3.6-kilogram) grapefruit-sized satellite, fell back on its Cape Canaveral, FL, launchpad on Dec. 6, 1957, following two seconds of flight. One news-

On April 12, 1961, Maj. Yuri Gagarin of the Soviet Union became the first person to orbit the Earth. His "Vostok I" spacecraft circled the Earth for 108 minutes at a maximum altitude of 203 miles (327 kilometers).

paper headline summed up the embarrassing setback: "American Sputnik Goes Kaputnik!"

A crisis atmosphere permeated the U.S. Congress. President Dwight D. Eisenhower ordered a U.S. Army team to move quickly and place an American satellite into orbit. Team leader Wernher von Braun orchestrated the response, successfully using a Jupiter C rocket to place the first U.S. satellite into space on Jan. 31, 1958. Explorer 1 weighed a mere 31 pounds (14 kilograms), yet it relayed back the first scientific evidence that Earth was enveloped in bands of high-energy charged particles. These layers later were named the Van Allen belts after James Van Allen, the scientist who designed the Explorer 1 instrument that first detected the radiation fields.

The U.S. response to Soviet Sputniks also manifested itself in the establishment of the National Aeronautics and Space Administration (NASA). On Oct. 1, 1958, NASA, the U.S. civilian space agency, began its task of scripting the country's future in space exploration. Both superpowers—the Soviet Union and the United States—now were engaged in a "space race" of technical and scientific proficiency, as well as political stature in the eyes of the world. The early years of the so-called space race were dominated by a string of headline-stealing Soviet firsts, such as the first probes sent toward the Moon, one of which relayed images back to Earth of the Moon's far side. The U.S. program struggled to gain momentum, with modest success. Establishing a family of boosters proved daunting, as American rocket specialists experienced a number of launch failures, all within the glare of the public spotlight.

Comdr. Alan B. Shepard, Jr., was the first American astronaut to fly into space. His May 5, 1961, suborbital flight in a Mercury capsule from Cape Canaveral, FL, lasted a mere 15 minutes.

On June 16, 1963, Lt. Valentina V. Tereshkova became the first woman to travel in space. She and fellow Soviet astronaut Lt. Col. Valery Bykovsky, who had preceded her into space, completed twin orbital flights.

A strange shadow fell across stark terrain on July 20, 1969. In a place called the Sea of Tranquility, serenity was broken. Just a few feet above the grayish landscape, an oddly shaped craft hovered almost motionless. Slowly, a set of outstretched landing legs greeted streaks of powdery soil and rock stirred by the vehicle's rocket motor. The material jetted across a vista that is billions of years old.

"Houston, Tranquility Base here. The *Eagle* has landed" were the first words spoken from another world. Nearly 240,000 miles (386,232 kilometers) away, back on Earth, hundreds of millions of people issued a collective sigh of relief as astronauts Neil Armstrong and Edwin (Buzz) Aldrin piloted *Apollo 11*'s lunar module to a touchdown.

Sitting on the Moon, Armstrong and Aldrin peered through lunar-module windows at the never-before-visited territory that awaited. Circling in lunar orbit, fellow *Apollo 11* astronaut Michael Collins sat alone in the command module, *Columbia*. Collins was poised to greet the two moonwalkers on their return from the lunar surface for the trip back to Earth. Six and one-half hours after touchdown, the *Eagle*'s square hatch opened, with Armstrong slowly easing his way down a nine-rung ladder. A small black-and-white camera attached to the landing craft had been activated, showing the astronaut ready to step onto the Moon's surface.

On July 20, 1969, at 10:56 P.M. EDT, Neil Armstrong lifted his left boot off the lunar module's footpad. Planting it firmly on the Moon, he radioed back to Earth: "That's one small step for [a] man, one giant leap for mankind." Dressed in his bulky, but life-protecting space suit, Armstrong quickly gathered a scoop of lunar soil. In the event of an emergency and a need to depart the landing site quickly, at least a small sample of the lunar surface could be returned to Earth.

"The surface is fine and powdery," Armstrong radioed back. "I can kick it up loosely with my toe. It does adhere in fine layers like powdered charcoal to the sole and sides of my boots. I go in only a small fraction of an inch, maybe an eighth of an inch....There seems to be no difficulty in moving around, as we suspected. It's even perhaps easier than the simulations." Each of Armstrong's footfalls, thanks to the Moon's vacuum, sent surface material spraying outward for a distance before coming to rest.

Joining Armstrong on the Moon, astronaut Aldrin (*photo, above left*) described the scene he saw through his helmet visor: "Magnificent desolation," he said. The two astronauts spent two hours and 31 minutes exploring their immediate vicinity. They adopted a two-footed mode of travel, rather like a kangaroo hop, due to the Moon's weak gravity—one sixth that on Earth. Before stepping off the lunar landscape, the astronauts planted the American flag (*photo, page 297*); took a congratulatory long-distance call from then U.S. President Richard Nixon; set up an array of experiments, including a seismic-instrument package to detect future "moonquakes"; and collected 48.5 pounds (22 kilograms) of lunar rock and regolith, the Moon's top-surface material.

Their adventuring at an end, Armstrong and Aldrin blasted off from the Moon in the *Eagle*'s

ascent module, subsequently linking up with command module *Columbia* and colleague Michael Collins. Splashing down in the Pacific Ocean on July 24, 1969, the crew of *Apollo 11* made possible an epic milestone in the human exploration of space. A plaque on the *Apollo 11* lunar-module descent stage at Tranquility Base summarized the story:

Here Men from the Planet Earth
First Set Foot upon the Moon
July 1969 A.D.
We Came in Peace for All Mankind.

In retrospect, Project Apollo can be viewed as the 20th-century equivalent of pyramid building. The effort was a monument to technological competence, steadfastness, and a willingness for humankind to reach beyond its grasp. The larger dimension of that pyramid was a workforce that transformed President John F. Kennedy's hopes for a "great new enterprise" into actuality. A team of highly skilled government, industry, and university talent comprised more than 20,000 companies and some 400,000 people throughout the United States.

Leonard David

Under NASA's aegis, Explorer- and Pioneer-series spacecraft were tasked to chart the space environment, relaying scientific data as to radiation, micrometeoroid, and solar-flare hazards. Data gleaned from these satellites helped discern the magnitude and severity of radiation belts that were found to girdle the Earth.

Starting in the 1960s, civilian space activities prompted a host of successes, pointing out the utility of satellites to benefit day-to-day life on Earth. For instance, telecommunications satellites could carry the nation's business, be it for mail delivery, banking, printing, or teleconferencing. Navigation satellites proved ideal for merchant shipping and fishing concerns. Weather satellites were brought into service and began saving thousands of lives through advance warning of impending hurricanes.

Significant strides during NASA's early years were made in the satellite-applications arena. For example, a 100-foot (30-meter) inflatable satellite, dubbed Echo, was orbited in 1960 to reflect radio signals from one point on Earth to another. These experiments and other investigations were forerunners of what has become an explosive growth in satellite telecommunications services. The U.S. Telstar, Early Bird, Relay, and Syncom satellites made possible the commercial satellite operations that are enjoyed routinely today. These satellites demonstrated the unique attributes of having spacecraft handle telephone, television, and data transmissions around the globe. In similar avenues, NASA's work in the 1960s with meteorological satellites, specifically Project Tiros (Television and InfraRed Observation Satellite), proved the utility of watching the world's weather from space. Likewise, the NASA Landsat satellites, the first of the series lofted in 1972, illustrated how spaceborne sensors could assist in assessing and managing the Earth's precious resources, in searching for pockets of oil and minerals, in measuring the growth of crops, in imaging sources of pollution, and in documenting urban expansion.

Virtually every country in the world uses satellites for communications and obtaining weather data. Since 1970 a number of other countries have become members of the "spacefaring" club—that is, they have the ability to launch satellites. These countries

The March 1969 "Apollo 9" mission, above, helped prepare for the "Apollo 11" lunar landing later in the year. The Earth-orbital "Apollo 9" mission included a rendezvous of the lunar module with the command and service modules of the Apollo craft.

include China, India, Israel, and Japan, along with the European Space Agency (ESA)—a consortium of nations.

Going the Lunar Distance

Nothing defines the risk and challenge offered by space exploration more than human space travel. In April 1959, NASA introduced to the nation and the world seven test pilots—M. Scott Carpenter, Leroy G. Cooper, John Glenn, Virgil Grissom, Walter Schirra, Alan B. Shepard, and Donald Slayton—as the Mercury astronaut corps. The single-seat Mercury capsule opened the door to U.S.-piloted space exploration. But even in this domain, the Soviet Union took an early lead role. Strapped inside a Vostok spaceship on April 12, 1961, Soviet cosmonaut Yuri Gagarin became the first human to orbit the Earth. In contrast, the United States lobbed Mercury astronaut Alan Shepard the following month on a suborbital flight lasting a mere 15 minutes.

Once again, U.S. leadership was called into question. Providing focus to NASA's human space program, President John F. Kennedy placed the nation on a bold quest. On May 25, 1961, Kennedy requested Congress to support Project Apollo. "I believe that this nation should commit itself to achieving the goal, before this decade is out, of landing a man on the Moon and returning him safely to Earth. No single space project in this period will be more impressive to mankind or more important for the long-range exploration of space, and none will be so difficult or expensive to accomplish." This visionary call to action was embraced by the country. The Moon had became an undeclared finish line for the space race.

From 1962 into mid-1963, solo-seat Mercury capsules took astronauts on globe-circling missions. Similarly, Soviet cosmonauts—including the first woman in space, Valentina Tereshkova—chalked up increasing amounts of time in Earth orbit. Flying in reconfigured Vostok capsules, named Voskhod, the first multiple-person crews were orbited by the Soviet Union in 1964 and 1965. From one of these Voskhod flights, the first walk in space was achieved by a cosmonaut. Two-seater U.S. Gemini spacecraft flew in 1965 through 1966, allow-

The 118-foot (36-meter)-long, 85-ton "Skylab," below, the first American space station, went into space on May 14, 1973. During an eight-month period, three three-man crews traveled to the orbiting "Skylab" and conducted various studies and tests.

The 13-ton (11,600-kilogram), $1.55 billion Hubble Space Telescope, above, was lofted into orbit by the space shuttle "Discovery" on April 24, 1990, and has transmitted color images of the planet Saturn, below. Earlier probes by the U.S. Voyager 1 and 2 had revealed that Saturn has more than 100 rings.

ing astronauts to hone the skills of rendezvous and docking, techniques crucial to fulfilling the objectives of Project Apollo.

For NASA to stretch beyond Earth orbit and reach for the Moon, rockets far larger and more powerful were required. In a project led by the renowned Wernher von Braun, the mammoth Saturn V launcher was constructed to hurl Americans over cislunar space to land on Earth's neighboring Moon. Throughout the 1960s, U.S. robotic lunar explorers—Ranger, Lunar Orbiter, and Surveyor—provided invaluable scientific data to support astronaut landings. Thanks to the efforts of hundreds of thou-

sands of government workers, aerospace contractors, and suppliers, NASA's $25 billion Project Apollo led to the first human footprints on the aeon-aged lunar surface on July 20, 1969 (see page 296). In all, a dozen Apollo astronauts would trek across the Moon's terrain by the close of 1972. The space race, heated up by Cold War rivalry, ended with the United States as victor.

Many years would pass before it became public that Soviet space engineers had suffered successive failures of a giant Moon booster in the time period of 1969–72, short-circuiting their hopes of also landing cosmonauts on the Moon. In lieu of human explorers, Soviet

The Challenger Disaster

Space shuttle *Challenger* lifted off from the Kennedy Space Center on Jan. 28, 1986, climbing through the chilly but clear Florida skies. Its ascent to orbit appeared normal, similar to the 24 previous shuttle flights that had been launched since 1981, when the program began.

Just 73 seconds after liftoff, at some 50,000 feet (1,524 meter) altitude, an explosion engulfed the vehicle. From the ground, a Mission Control commentator responded to the fireball of exploding fuel and a rain of debris, along with two solid-rocket motors that separately twisted through the air. "Flight controllers here looking very carefully at the situation. Obviously a major malfunction," he spoke.

Challenger had been ripped apart. The seven members of the crew of the ill-fated mission—Francis Scobee, Michael Smith, Judith Resnik, Ronald McNair, Ellison Onizuka, Gregory Jarvis, and Christa McAuliffe—were killed. A traumatized nation mourned the loss of the *Challenger* crew. The seven individuals were a cross section of the U.S. population in terms of race, gender, geography, background, and religion. Arguably, the sense of tragedy was made even more painful by the death of teacher Christa McAuliffe, selected from 11,000 applicants to orbit the Earth as part of a NASA Teacher-in-Space program.

Tons of space-shuttle debris were retrieved from the ocean during a three-month salvage

operation. Painstaking work ensued to piece together an answer as to why the *Challenger* mission had ended so tragically. Also recovered was *Challenger's* crew module. It had broken away from the fuselage, emerging intact from the explosive fireball. It is likely the crew survived the fireball itself and the

---

space scientists were successful between 1970 and 1973 in launching robotic missions that returned to Earth samples from the Moon and, via automated rovers, carried out various scientific lunar excursions.

Home Away from Home

Soviet attention in the 1970s swung to extensive use of a new piloted spacecraft, the Soyuz, and the operation of the world's first space station, the *Salyut*. During some 15 years, several *Salyut* stations were sent spaceward and put to use by multiple crews to live and work in space for prolonged periods of time.

From leftover Apollo hardware, the first U.S. space station was crafted. Modifying a huge Saturn V upper stage, an orbiting workshop—named *Skylab*—was outfitted to maintain a three-person astronaut crew. *Skylab* was rocketed into orbit in 1973. Once it was in space, Apollo spacecraft were launched to the Earth-circling complex. From May into November of 1973, three separate Apollo spacecraft, each one carrying a three-person crew, were lobbed to the *Skylab* outpost. In total, the three crews inhabited the space station for 171 days and 13 hours.

breakup of the orbiter. Loss of crew-module pressure may have put the astronauts in an unconscious state. However, it could not be discounted that the crew members may have been aware of their situation as the compartment plunged toward the ocean. Falling through the sky for nearly three minutes after the breakup of *Challenger*, the crew would not have survived the 200-mile-per-hour (580-kilometer-per-hour) ocean impact.

The accident led to numerous investigations, including a presidentially mandated blue-ribbon commission chaired by former Secretary of State William Rogers, as well as numerous NASA and aerospace-industry reviews. Identified as the cause of the *Challenger* accident was the failure of a pressure seal in the aft field joint of the shuttle's right solid-rocket motor. An O-ring used to seal joints in the solid-rocket booster, it was revealed, was susceptible to failure at low temperatures. Shuttle hardware had been exposed to cold weather the night before and early morning of the launch. This compromised the O-ring material.

During *Challenger*'s takeoff, hot gases bypassed the cold-hardened O-ring, acting as a blowtorch. The heat weakened a strut holding the solid-rocket motor, letting it torque out of place, thus rupturing and collapsing the shuttle's external tank, which holds 145,000 gallons (548,883 liters) of liquid oxygen and 390,000 gallons (1,476,306 liters) of liquid hydrogen. Within milliseconds, hundreds of tons of propellant ignited in the air, destroying the entire space-shuttle system, including the *Challenger*.

Along with the technical reasons for the *Challenger* disaster, it was found that the accident also implicated NASA's organizational, managerial, and technical oversight abilities. The catastrophic failure led to an O-ring and joint redesign within the solid-rocket booster, implementation of new safety measures, and changes in decision-making procedures. In September 1988, following a 32-month hiatus, space-shuttle orbiters were flying again. NASA was funded to replace the destroyed *Challenger* with orbiter *Endeavour*.

Leonard David

Yet another space project was designed from former Apollo hardware. The Apollo-Soyuz Test Project signaled a true end of the space race between the Soviet Union and the United States. High above Earth, a two-person cosmonaut crew linked a Soyuz spacecraft with the three-seater Apollo. The linkup of Apollo and Soyuz spacecraft on July 17, 1975, constituted the first international meeting in orbit of the former space competitors. A new era had begun.

The 1970s also saw the exploration of Mercury, Venus, Mars, and Jupiter by various U.S. Mariner- and Pioneer-class spacecraft. A Soviet Venera 7 probe made the first transmission from the surface of another planet, Venus, in December 1970. Robotic exploration of the solar system reached a major milestone in 1976 with the landing of two American Viking spacecraft on Mars, equipped to begin the first on-the-spot search for signs of life on the Red Planet. A little more than a year later, two U.S. Voyager missions began a sojourn to more distant locales, uncovering the secrets of Jupiter, Saturn, Uranus, and Neptune.

It took a $10 billion investment to establish the U.S. space-shuttle program, resulting in an initial fleet of orbiters: *Enterprise* (used for airdrop tests only), *Columbia*, *Discovery*, *Atlantis*, and *Challenger*. Following the *Challenger* disaster and the loss of its crew in 1986 (*see* page 300), *Endeavour* was built as a replacement vehicle. The space-shuttle fleet was geared to ferry crews to and from space; haul cargo; resupply, repair, recover, and deploy satellites; and act as a winged laboratory in space. These goals have been accomplished successfully, with the program nearing 100 flights since it began operating in 1981.

A shuttle mission in 1989, for example, dispatched the U.S. Magellan probe to Venus, while another shuttle flight in 1990 deployed the Hubble Space Telescope into orbit. Astronauts later repaired the observatory after it was discovered the telescope was impaired by an improperly configured mirror. Since that time, the Hubble Space Telescope has become an active, on-duty orbiting observatory that grants astronomers the ability to capture glimpses of new galaxies, view the formation of faraway solar systems, and seek answers as to how the universe itself began.

Human space exploration for the Soviet Union (later Russia) since 1986 and throughout the 1990s focused on broad use of its *Mir* space station. Built in orbit, module by module, *Mir* provides its inhabitants with the capability of conducting a myriad of scientific and physiological experiments. One cosmonaut, Valery Polyakov, lived aboard the home-away-from-home complex for more than 14 months, an exposure to microgravity conditions similar to flight to and from Mars.

Soviet robotic space ventures, however, were far less successful, underscored by the failure of two Mars probes in 1988–89, followed by yet another Mars spacecraft loss in 1996. A similar fate had occurred earlier for the United States: NASA lost contact with the Mars Observer probe just before it reached Mars in 1993.

Blueprinting the Future

A three-year, nine-flight program saw space-shuttle orbiter dockings with Russia's *Mir* space station, a cooperative effort that concluded in June 1998. The shuttle-*Mir* dockings permitted American astronauts to reside on the Russian complex and accumulate nearly 980 days of space experience. More importantly, the missions were billed as a prelude to the future. Specifically, the joint work was geared to the construction of an International Space Station. This world-class orbiting laboratory was being orchestrated by a confab of 16 countries that included the United States and Russia. Set to eventually house a seven-person crew, the 407-ton facility is to be assembled fully in 2004. Russia,

The year 1997 was a difficult one for "Mir," as the Russian space station encountered an onboard fire and decompression of a key station module, as well as repeated computer breakdowns. Astronaut Vasily Tsibliyev, below, conducted a space walk during his stressful six months on board the craft.

On Feb. 20, 1962, John Glenn became the first American to orbit the Earth (inset). Thirty-six years later the former Marine, now 77 and completing his fourth term in the U.S. Senate, returned to space on board the space shuttle "Discovery" with an international crew, above. He became the oldest human to travel in outer space. During the shuttle mission, tests were conducted to gauge the effects of space travel on older people.

cash-strapped and rife with political turmoil, has labored to sustain its participation in the international project, much to the chagrin of U.S. lawmakers.

As the 20th century ends, an increasing number of men and women have become space travelers. Robotic spacecraft were en route to Saturn and were reaching out to individual asteroids and comets. The Moon was being resource mapped, pole to pole, by the U.S. Lunar Prospector. Various spacecraft monitored the Sun, helping humans to appreciate how this energetic powerhouse influences the Earth's climate and biosphere. Mars Global Surveyor was circuiting the Red Planet armed with a suite of scientific sensors. Following NASA's Mars Pathfinder and Sojourner mini-rover that explored Mars in July 1997, a virtual armada of robotic orbiters and landers were to continue the search for life on that world.

Dispatched from a space shuttle in 1989, the Galileo spacecraft continued on an extended mission to scrutinize Jupiter's ice-covered moon Europa, and that Jovian hot spot of a world, volcanic Io. Earth-orbiting observatories belonging to the United States, Europe, and Japan studied the surrounding universe in various wavelengths, from radio frequencies to the visible and infrared, from the X ray and gamma ray. Even-more-powerful spaceborne telescopes were being blueprinted to detect Earth-like worlds elsewhere.

Space exploration of today was built upon the dreams and dedication of countless individuals and the fortitude of nations to pursue a new frontier. Given the remarkable achievements of the last 100 years, one only can surmise that the 21st century portends even bolder and more mind-boggling accomplishments.

Leonard David

COMPUTERS

In 1943, Thomas Watson, chairman of IBM, stated: "I think there is a world market for maybe five computers." Not the most prescient of comments, but then it is doubtful than anyone in the early 1940s could have predicted that, before the century ended, there would be close to 500 million computers in operation around the world—used not only for mathematical calculations but also for writing reports, tracking inventory, analyzing blood, chatting with friends, guiding spacecraft, orchestrating music, designing automobiles, teaching reading, transacting business, playing games, and performing thousands of other activities.

Nor could anyone have expected that the work of small groups of engineers, dreamers, and tinkerers in scattered laboratories would explode into a dominant industry in which dramatic advances occur almost daily. No other technology in history has matched the speed of computer development, or the speed with which computer uses have evolved to create demand. The machines are truly ubiquitous—more so than most people realize, for what we commonly call computers are but a tiny fraction of all the computers in our lives. There are special-purpose computers embedded in our cars, thermostats, ovens, televisions, watches, toys, and

telephones, where they replace less-reliable mechanical parts and provide added features.

The Computer Revolution

Computers have transformed the world in fundamental ways. Governments no longer can prevent their citizens from hearing facts and opinions that contradict the party line; physicians no longer are forced to perform invasive procedures to study or correct a host of medical problems; people in the remotest parts of the world no longer are unable to communicate instantly with anyone anywhere. Furthermore, computers are making possible feats previously relegated to dreams—landing people on the Moon, sending probes to distant planets, speeding drug development through simulations, mapping all human DNA.

Computers even have changed and expanded our vocabularies. The words "mouse," "bug," "disk," "piracy," "laptop," and "server" have taken on new meanings. "E-mail," "hard drives," "floppies," "RAM," "cyberspace," "virtual reality," "on-line shopping," and "user-friendly" have become terms that are part of everyday conversations. Companies such as Microsoft, Nintendo, and Apple have become household names. Entrepreneurs such as Bill Gates and Steve Jobs have become legendary.

And yet computers are still babies, not much more than a half century old. Though their impact already has been enormous, it is clear that we are only at the beginning of the computer age, and that these marvelous tools will be a major force in defining our future in the 21st century.

Early Development

The idea that machines could perform intellectual work is an ancient one. Thousands of years ago, people began inventing various counting systems and adding devices. But it was not until the 20th century—following the development of electricity—that creative minds could turn ancient dreams into modern reality.

In 1930, Vannevar Bush built the first large-scale analog computer, called a differential analyzer, at the Massachusetts Institute of Technology. It had six computing elements, six electric motors, and a system of shafts that relayed calculations to an output unit. But an analog device represents data as continuous quantities rather than as discrete entities. It is rather like an old-fashioned watch with hands that move smoothly around the face; one easily can see when an hour has passed, but cannot determine accurately when half a second has passed. This lack of precision meant that analog computers had limited value. The future lay with digital devices.

In a digital computer, there are only two possibilities: An electric current either is

flowing or not flowing. These two states can be represented by the digits 0, for off; and 1, for on. Modern computers use the binary numbering system, in which all numbers, as well as letters and symbols, are expressed as combinations of 0s and 1s.

John Atanasoff and Clifford Berry built the first computer based on the binary numbering system in 1939 at Iowa State University. The onset of World War II spurred developments in the United States and England, as these nations looked for ways to calculate artillery firing tables, scramble messages, and crack an enemy's coded messages. In England highly secret Colossus computers enabled the British to read German messages during the final years of the war. In the United States work began at the University of Pennsylvania on the groundbreaking Electronic Numerical Integrator and Calculator (ENIAC), *photo, pages 304–05.*

Although ENIAC was not completed until 1946, after World War II ended, many people consider its introduction as marking the start of the computer age. "Faster than thought," enthused one reporter. And bigger than many homes: ENIAC was 8 feet (2.4 meters) high, 80 feet (24 meters) long, and weighed 30 tons. It had more than 100,000 electronic components, including 17,468 vacuum tubes, and consumed enough energy in one second to meet the needs of a typical home for ten days. It had a memory capacity of 20 words. To program ENIAC, some 6,000 switches had to be set manually, and hundreds of cables had to be plugged into three walls of plugboards. But when the machine was turned on, it could add 5,000 ten-digit numbers or multiply 333 of them in one second. Suddenly, the public began to sense the vast potential of computers.

Even as ENIAC was introduced, engineers were progressing to the next level. The first stored program—operating instructions that are part of a computer's internal memory—

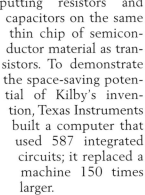

" I REMEMBER WHEN I WAS THE BRAINS OF THE OUTFIT."

was run on the Manchester Mark I in Manchester, England, in 1948. This computer had six memory tubes, each capable of storing 1 to 2 kilobytes (KB) of information.

Smaller and Smaller

Meanwhile, at Bell Telephone Laboratories, a team headed by physicist William Shockley announced that it had invented a device called the transistor. It could do everything a vacuum tube could do, but was only 1/200th the size, used much less energy, generated less heat, and was much faster and more reliable. It took awhile for the significance of this invention to be appreciated. IBM did not introduce its first completely transistorized computers until 1959. By that time, Jack Kilby, an engineer at Texas Instruments, had made the world's first integrated circuit, putting resistors and capacitors on the same thin chip of semiconductor material as transistors. To demonstrate the space-saving potential of Kilby's invention, Texas Instruments built a computer that used 587 integrated circuits; it replaced a machine 150 times larger.

As engineers discovered how to shrink the size of components on a chip, they were able to cram more and more components into the same space. For example, a chip 0.1 inch (0.25 centimeter) square made in 1964 had a total of ten transistors and other components. By 1970 the same-sized chip held 1,000 components, yet cost about the same as the 1964 chip.

In the early 1960s, Digital Equipment Corporation introduced the first minicomputers, which were about the size of home refrigerators; the first computerized airline-reservation system was up and running at American Airlines; and General Motors produced the first computer-designed auto part. Magnetic tape and removable disks were being used as storage devices.

Some 18,200 computers were in operation in the United States by 1964. At Dart-

(Continued on page 310.)

Personal Computers

Early in 1975 a young electrical engineer named Edward Roberts, owner of a small electronics company in Albuquerque, NM, introduced the Altair, a build-your-own computer kit. Assembled, the $397 computer contained 0.25 kilobyte (KB) of memory. It had no monitor, screen, or other input and output devices, though the user could plug in circuit cards for attachments and additional memory. The user entered a program and data by flipping toggle switches up or down. When the program was run, the results had to be deciphered from a pattern of flashing lights.

Roberts estimated he could sell 800 of the kits. His bankers thought 200 was a more realistic number. Three months after the Altair was introduced, however, Roberts had a backlog of 4,000 orders.

The unexpected success of the Altair spurred hobbyists to design their own personal computers (PCs). Steve Jobs and Stephen Wozniak started building their first Apple computer in a California garage. Others looked for ways to expand the Altair's capabilities. In Boston, Paul Allen and Bill Gates wrote a version of the BASIC computer language for the Altair, then went on to found Microsoft.

Established computer companies watched from the sidelines. "There is no reason anyone would want a computer in their home," said Ken Olson, president and founder of Digital Equipment Corporation, in 1977. That was the year Apple, Commodore, and Radio Shack introduced machines that would dominate the early PC market. At first, software for these machines consisted mainly of games. But in 1978, VisiCalc introduced the first electronic spreadsheet, and in 1979, MicroPro International released a sophisticated word-processing program called WordStar. These programs changed the image of PCs, convincing people to buy them for business applications. Dozens of additional manufacturers entered the fray; the number of programmers also swelled, as everyone hoped to create the next big software hit.

IBM introduced its first PC in 1981, using the DOS operating system and an open architecture that allowed other companies to make IBM PC-compatible computers, or "clones," as well as peripherals and software that worked on both IBM machines and clones. Consumers rushed to buy the machines, and computer stores sprang up in even the smallest towns. The number of PCs in use jumped from 2 million in 1981 to 5.5 million in 1982, leading *Time* magazine to name the computer "Machine of the Year" in 1982.

During the 1980s, PCs became familiar fixtures in offices, homes, and schools; they became seemingly indispensable in the 1990s. With the introduction of laptop and notebook computers, PCs took to the road, becoming requisite accessories for traveling salesmen, real-estate agents, and students en route to class. Handheld "palmtops" and mini-notebooks introduced during the late 1990s continued the trend toward smaller, more versatile machines.

In 1998 worldwide shipments of PCs surpassed 90 million. In a quarter century, PCs were transformed from instruments that could appeal only to technical wizards to ones that presented few obstacles to a 5-year-old. They evolved from a hobbyist's dream to devices taken for granted by people in all walks of life.

Jenny Tesar

The Internet is, quite simply, the world's largest group of cooperating computer networks. All the computers on the many thousands of networks that comprise the Internet voluntarily use the same technical standards for their network data, so that any of the computers on any of the networks can exchange messages with any other. Each message sent is broken up into small chunks of roughly uniform size, called packets; each packet is sent along to its destination. If a packet's destination is on a different network from its origin, the packet is switched from network to network until it reaches its destination, often traversing 15 or 20 networks along the way. The destination computer reassembles incoming packets into the desired message. This packet-switched design has let the Internet grow from its original two networks to its current size and beyond, without any fundamental changes in the way that it works.

The Internet's origins date from the late 1960s, when the U.S. Defense Department's Advanced Research Projects Agency (ARPA) funded computer network research to build an experimental packet-switched network called the Arpanet. The Arpanet project started in 1967, and by the end of 1969 a working network connected four computers in California and Utah. By the mid-1970s it was clear that the Arpanet was a success, so much so that it was becoming impractical to connect all of the computers that desired to communicate to a single network. As a result, a new Internet Protocol (known as IP) was devised that lets computers on many networks exchange data packets, as well as a Transmission Control Protocol (TCP, the combination being TCP/IP), which manages conversations between computers using IP. (Incidentally, the Internet is named after IP, not the other way around.) By 1983 all computers on the Arpanet were using TCP/IP, and the military's computers were split off onto a separate network known as Milnet.

During the 1980s, many new networks connected to the growing Internet—including both academic networks funded by the National Science Foundation and commercial networks—and in 1989 the original Arpanet was shut down, since all its functions were being done better by the new networks. The design of the Internet makes it possible to add new user-level facilities at any time on top of the existing TCP/IP framework. For the Net's first decade, the primary applications were Telnet (remote terminal access), File Transfer Protocol (FTP—copying data files from one computer to another), and electronic mail (E-mail).

In the late 1980s, as more academic institutions joined the Net, easier-to-use facilities appeared, notably Archie, from McGill University, which provides an index to the files available by FTP; Gopher, from the University of Minnesota, which provides a menu system making it easier to find and use resources; and WAIS, a text-searching system from Thinking Machines, Inc. These facilities led the way toward an easier-to-use Internet.

In 1991, English researcher Tim Berners-Lee, who was working at CERN, the international physics-research lab near Geneva, Switzerland, wrote the first version of the World Wide Web. The Web provides a unifying model of pages connected by links, based on hypertext work by Douglas Englebart and Ted Nelson as far back as the 1960s. The Web's first application was to present the masses of data from CERN's physics experiments, but its wide applicability was immediately apparent. Student programmers at the University of Illinois soon developed Mosaic, a Web browser that added pictures to the Web, which became extremely popular throughout the Net. Many corporations created Web browsers based directly or indirectly on Mosaic; the most notable of these companies was Netscape Communications, cofounded by Mosaic programmer Marc Andreesen. Netscape's Navigator rapidly became the most popular program used for access to the Web, although Microsoft's Explorer later presented a serious challenge.

Most Internet growth since 1994 has been centered around the Web, which has subsumed or made obsolete most of the older services other than E-mail. The Web is far easier to use than previous Net services, since it combines graphics with text and requires little typing; most actions are clicks of the mouse. Remarkably, since the departure of the original military funders, the Internet has had no central administration other than some volunteer organizations that develop and maintain technical standards and address registries that assign names and numbers used to identify hosts (computers) on the Net. The U.S. address registry, for which the federal government had been responsible, began to be privatized in late 1998.

The World Wide Web organizes all of its information into pages of data. Each page consists of text that is intermixed with codes written in Hypertext Markup Language (HTML). The HTML codes describe the structure of the page, with elements such as headings, colors, italics, tables, columns, and links to other pages. HTML codes also can call for pictures, sounds, and other media to be inserted into pages and combined on user screens. Every Web page has a Universal Resource Locator (URL) that identifies it, along with the type of page and the server on which it resides.

To give an example of this system, the URL http://publishing.grolier.com/publishing.html refers to a page accessible via the Web's Hypertext Transfer Protocol (HTTP), on the server publishing.grolier.com, with the page name of publishing.html. User programs known as browsers send the URL to the appropriate server, which returns the page to be displayed. Each link on the page refers to a URL. When a user clicks on a link, the browser fetches that new URL. The Web is designed to handle any kind of information, not just HTML pages. Each page retrieved is identified with a media type, such as text, image, or sound. If a page is not of a type that the browser can handle, it runs a separate program known as a helper or plug-in to display the page.

John R. Levine

The Internet has become a ubiquitous presence, thanks to Web browsers like Netscape's Navigator, symbol, facing page. The Net is a necessity for students doing research, facing page, top; "cybercafes" make Web surfing convenient, above.

(Continued from page 306.)

mouth College, John Kemeny and Thomas Kurtz demonstrated the first general-purpose computer language, BASIC. IBM introduced System/360, the first family of compatible computers. These were replaced in the early 1970s with the System/370, based entirely on integrated circuits.

In 1970, Intel introduced a memory chip that could store 1K of data—the equivalent of about 25 five-letter words. Smaller than a fingernail, it replaced 1,024 magnetic cores that took up some 80 square inches (516 square centimeters) of space. And in 1971, Intel announced the first "computer on a chip"—a microprocessor, the 4004, that contained all the functions of a computer's central processing unit. Only 25 years after ENIAC, a device no bigger than a postage stamp had replaced that behemoth's innards.

The advances in miniaturization made it possible to build computers small enough to sit on a desk. In 1975 the first personal computer (PC) was introduced by Edward Roberts (*see* page 307).

The Advent of Networking

Another trend was gathering momentum, too. People were linking together, or networking, computers, via either direct wiring (called a Local Area Network, or LAN) or telephone lines. This enabled users to share data, software, and memory space, and to communicate with one another. Eventually it made possible the development of the Internet (*see* page 308).

By the end of the century, millions of people were "surfing the Net" to gather data, find jobs, buy and sell products, play games, chat with friends and strangers, and follow news and sports. A U.S. Department of Commerce report noted that radio existed for 38 years before it had 50 million listeners, and television needed 13 years to reach 50 million viewers, but the Internet needed only four years to gain 50 million users.

As the computer industry grew and expanded into new areas, there were winners and losers. Fortunes were made and sometimes lost. Businesses sprang up seemingly overnight and sometimes disappeared just as quickly. Investors giddily ran up the value of stocks, including those of start-up companies where profits were but gleams in the eyes of dreamers. Silicon Valley—the area around San Jose, CA, where much of the industry was concentrated—became the new "Wild West." Adding machines in banks, card catalogs in libraries, typewriters in newsrooms, and slide rules in engineers' pockets all became relics of a bygone age.

Convergence and Other Trends

As the century draws to a close, computers have become appliances to be bought, used, replaced, and thrown away. The rapid pace of innovation means that one year's state-of-the-art model is a closeout special 12 months later. Machines only three or four years old seem hopelessly outdated, as manufacturers introduce ever-more-powerful, faster, and smaller models. By 1999 a typical laptop computer weighed no more than a bag of groceries, was thousands of times faster than ENIAC, could switch quickly from one large stored program to another, and sold for a price affordable for most Americans.

It is expected that PCs will continue to become smaller, lighter, more powerful, and less expensive. At the other end of the scale are supercomputers such as the IBM RS/6000 SP—much smaller than ENIAC, but with 1,000 processors that together can do 4 trillion calculations per second.

There is growing convergence among once disparate tools such as PCs, telephones, and televisions. For example, "smart phones" combine the capabilities of a wireless phone and a palmtop computer, offering data transmission, word processing, Internet access, and organizational aids such as an electronic calendar, address book, and calculator. From devices such as these will evolve a pocket-sized device that not only will serve as a computer, phone, and fax machine, but also will hold digital money, be able to understand English (or any other language), pinpoint one's location in the world, monitor local or distant weather and traffic reports, and electronically register one at a hospital emergency room.

The number of Internet users is growing exponentially; more than 200 million people around the world were using the Internet in 1999. And thanks to computers, people are communicating with one another as never before: In 1998 some 2.7 trillion E-mail messages were sent—five times the number of pieces of paper mail delivered worldwide.

Jenny Tesar

ARTS AND ENTERTAINMENT

Jackson Pollock's "Going West"

OVERVIEW

The story of the arts in the 20th century may be divided conveniently into two distinct periods. The first, which began with the world at peace in the years preceding World War I, came to a violent end on the battlefields of World War II. This was a period in which artistic developments in Europe dominated the international cultural scene. In the second, which has extended from the aftermath of World War II in the late 1940s to the present day, the United States became an influential power in the arts. In the first, Paris was regarded universally as the art capital of the Western world—the place where ideas about the arts were most advanced, where the greatest reputations were likely to be made, and where the most ambitious new talent was likely to flourish. In the second half of the century, New York emerged as the successor to Paris in this leadership role.

What set the course for the arts in both periods, however, was a modernist movement that challenged traditional artistic practice with innovations that were perceived to be so radical that they often baffled and even outraged respectable opinion. The history of the arts in the 20th century is thus, in large part, a chronicle of modernism and the challenges it posed to established taste. Yet it is the principal irony of the arts in the modern era that almost every innovation that met with public resistance in the first half of the century has been elevated to classic status in the second. As a consequence of this reversal of taste, the closing decades of the 20th century have witnessed not only an unprecedented tolerance and support for new and outrageous ideas in the arts but also what amounts at times to a mania for novelty and shock.

It was in Europe, in the early decades of the century, that the major modernist styles in painting and sculpture were created. Fauvism, cubism, and surrealism in France; expressionism and Dada in Germany; futurism in Italy; constructivism and suprematism

The construction of Lincoln Center, above—which includes the Metropolitan Opera House, the Vivian Beaumont Theater, the New York State Theater, Avery Fisher Hall, and other edifices—in the 1960s was in part responsible for New York City succeeding Paris, France, as the cultural capital of the world.

in Russia; and the first examples of abstract art in Germany, the Netherlands, and Russia—these were the radical styles that set the agenda for modern art for the remainder of the century. Parallel developments in the other arts—including expressionism in the theater, atonalism in music, and glass-box design in architecture—set similar agendas, but with more variable success. For example, while glass-box architecture, which in the 1930s came to be called the International Style, reshaped the look of cities the world over, atonal music remained the cult interest of a small intellectual elite.

Unfortunately, it was also in Europe that these modernist developments in the arts met with the most severe political repression. First in Russia, under the Soviet regime of Joseph Stalin in the 1920s, and then in Germany, under the Nazi regime of Adolf Hitler in the 1930s, all forms of modernist art—not only painting and sculpture but also architecture, music, theater, and literature—were prohibited by the state. Under Communism in the Soviet Union, modernism was condemned as counterrevolutionary "bourgeois formalism." Under Nazism in Germany, it was criminalized as "degenerate." Paintings were removed from the museums, experimental theaters were closed, and modern music and dance were banned from the repertory. As a result of this totalitarian crackdown, the geographic scope of modernist art suffered a severe constriction.

Until the early 1920s, the map of modernist movements in the arts had extended from Moscow and St. Petersburg in the east to New York City and Chicago in

the west, with lively centers of activity in Vienna, Munich, Berlin, Brussels, Amsterdam, Barcelona, and London, as well as Paris. By the time the Nazi army occupied Paris in 1940, however, many of the leading artists in those cities had been forced to seek refuge in safe havens abroad. Although some of these exiled modernists fled to Britain and Latin America, the largest number of them went to the United States. There they were joined by even larger numbers of European art historians, instructors, dealers, collectors, and museum curators, as well as writers, composers, musicians,

Pianist Vladimir Horowitz, above, and composer-conductor Igor Stravinsky, left, were among the Russian-born cultural greats who performed extensively in the United States.

Trumpeter, singer, and ensemble leader Louis Armstrong (1900–71), above, helped develop jazz, an improvisational style of music that was born and evolved in the United States in the early 1900s.

émigrés often brought a level of sophistication to such works that Americans still tended to lack.

This is not to say that the arts in America could not boast of significant achievements prior to this period. In several fields, ranging from pioneering accomplishments in skyscraper architecture (see page 321) to the stunning originality of jazz music, the work of American artists had begun to exert an influence on European cultural life long before World War II. In architecture, no talent was admired more universally than that of Frank Lloyd Wright. In the theater, the plays of Eugene O'Neill quickly became part of the European repertory. American popular culture, especially Hollywood movies, enjoyed even wider acclaim abroad. Yet in the realms of classical music, painting, and sculpture, American artists (as well as the American public) continued to derive their standards and their ideas from Europe in the early decades of the 20th century. This situation was just as true of traditionalists in the arts as it was of the modernists. However much the traditionalists and the modernists might disagree on fundamental matters of style and value—and their disagreements were particularly fierce in the early decades of the century—both factions looked to Europe for aesthetic

theater and film directors, playwrights, and novelists. Thus, another of the ironies that shaped the course of the arts in the modern era was that the repressive policies of Stalin and Hitler had the unintended effect of establishing the United States as a citadel of advanced artistic ideas in the later decades of the century.

This massive influx of European talent effected a profound change in the cultural life of the United States. So did the arrival of large numbers of educated European refugees who were not themselves professionals in the arts but had been enlightened patrons of the arts in their home countries. Especially in the field of classical music, but also in the visual arts and in university departments devoted to the arts, this sizable influx of European émigrés contributed a great deal to raising the intellectual level of American audiences. Much of the music that was played in American concert halls, much of the art that was exhibited in American museums, and many of the plays that were performed in American theaters were, after all, of European origin, and these European

Nobel Prize winner Eugene O'Neill (1888–1953), inset, was the first American dramatist to earn international distinction. His "Long Day's Journey into Night" (1940–41), right, received a Pulitzer Prize.

The Broadway Musical

By the beginning of the 20th century, all three major musical theater genres—the operetta (romantic, often set in the past, with arioso music), the musical comedy (brash, contemporary, with lighter melodies), and the revue (skits and light music)—had been established. Victor Herbert (*Naughty Marietta*) excelled in the first; George M. Cohan (*Little Johnny Jones*) in the second; and Florenz Ziegfeld (famous for his long-lived *Follies*) in the third. About the time of World War I, a remarkable band of American composers came to the fore. Jerome Kern and Irving Berlin were followed by Cole Porter, George Gershwin, Vincent Youmans, and Richard Rodgers. They wrote primarily musical comedies, and their work often displayed jazz influences. Two immigrants, Sigmund Romberg and Rudolf Friml, emerged alongside the Americans to revitalize operetta. Meanwhile, several brilliant lyricists and librettists—including P.G. Wodehouse, Oscar Hammerstein, Ira Gershwin, Lorenz Hart, Dorothy Fields, and composer Porter—appeared. The stories they wrote were lighthearted and later came to be perceived as frivolous. Friml and Hammerstein's *Rose Marie* (1924) was by far the biggest worldwide hit of the era, with Youmans' *No, No, Nanette* (1924) the leading musical-comedy success. But Kern and Hammerstein's *Show Boat* pioneered the truly all-American operetta in 1927, and in 1940, Rodgers and Hart's *Pal Joey* launched the seemingly light, contemporary musical comedy—newly marked by a darker subtext.

During World War II, Rodgers and Hammerstein's *Oklahoma!* (1943), *photo above*, reviving the *Show Boat* school, firmly set the standard of American operetta for decades to come. Some publicists, including Hammerstein himself, attempted to hail it as a new genre—the musical play—but in its romantic nature, settings in the past, and arioso songs, it clearly represented operetta's inevitable American evolution. In fact, many older operettas had been advertised as musical plays. Similar post–World War II gems included Rodgers and Hammerstein's *Carousel* (1945), *South Pacific* (1948), and *The King and*

I (1951); Leonard Bernstein and Stephen Sondheim's *West Side Story* (1957); and Jerry Bock and Sheldon Harnick's *Fiddler on the Roof* (1964). *Pal Joey*–type musical comedies included Burton Lane and E.Y. Harburg's *Finian's Rainbow* (1947), with a political subtext; Frank Loesser's *Guys and Dolls*, (1950), with a sociological subtext; Jule Styne and Sondheim's *Gypsy* (1959), with a psychological subtext; and Porter's old-fashioned but brilliantly literate *Kiss Me, Kate* (1948). By the 1950s, revues had disappeared from the scene.

The postwar renaissance faded perceptibly after the mid-1960s. The most original—and controversial—American works to follow were those by Stephen Sondheim, with their often curiously fractured or difficult melodies and soured-on-life lyrics. Although he has earned a determined and vocal coterie of admirers, his works—apart from *A Funny Thing Happened on the Way to the Forum* (1962), *A Little Night Music* (1973), and *Sweeney Todd* (1979)—have not enjoyed huge success. Since the 1980s, starting with *Cats*, sung-through, spectacle-heavy musicals from England (and sometimes France) have pushed newer American works into the background.

Gerald Bordman

Various museums devoted to modernist art, including New York City's Solomon R. Guggenheim Museum, above, were established in the United States. Marian Anderson (1897–1993), below, was the first African-American singer to perform at the Metropolitan Opera. The contralto made her Met debut in 1955.

guidance. They simply looked to different elements of European culture for their touchstones of excellence.

Where the United States did score a significant advance over Europe was in the creation of independent institutions devoted to expanding the public's appreciation of modernist art. When the Museum of Modern Art was founded in New York in 1929, it soon became the most important museum of its kind in the world, for no institution of comparable scope and ambition yet existed in Europe. In New York, MoMA (as it came to be called) was joined promptly by the Whitney Museum of American Art, which concentrated its collection and exhibition program on 20th-century American art, and the Museum of Non-Objective Art (now the Solomon R. Guggenheim Museum), which originally was devoted to abstract art. Even earlier, Dr. Albert C. Barnes had established the Barnes Foundation, a collection and

school focused on modern art, in Merion, PA, a suburb of Philadelphia; and Duncan Phillips had founded still another museum devoted to modern art and its antecedents, the Phillips Memorial Collection in Washington, DC.

These institutions, like the majority of American art museums, opera companies, symphony orchestras, and the like, differed from their European counterparts in that they were endowed and run privately. In Europe virtually all such arts institutions were the property of the state, which gave them the advantage of huge state subsidies. The downside, however, was that the official status of these state-run institutions obliged them to avoid the kind of art that was likely to be unfamiliar, controversial, or otherwise offensive to public taste. This reticence proved to be a considerable handicap when it came to acquiring significant examples of modernist art. American cultural philanthropy, on the other hand, was answerable only to itself, and under that dispensation provided American art museums, especially the new ones devoted to modern and contemporary art, with a measure of intellectual autonomy their European counterparts did not come to enjoy until the later decades of the century.

This freedom was one of the main reasons why American museums were able to acquire significant collections of European modernist art well before European museums. In the United States controversial modernist art did not have to win the approval of cumbersome and often backward-looking state bureaucracies before it could be accepted for a museum collection; such art usually was acquired privately by a knowledgeable patron who then donated the work to a museum on whose board the donor or some associate might be a member. This system favors independent judgment over established opinion, although it also entails the risk of indulging what may turn out to be merely faddish taste. In the later decades of the century, European governments attempted to solve the problem of having

missed out on acquiring important works of art by imposing massive death duties on the estates of recognized masters, thereby garnering sizable quantities of their art in lieu of inheritance taxes. It is mainly owing to such practices that museums in France, for example, lately have acquired a large number of works by Pablo Picasso and Henri Matisse,

(Continued on page 320.)

French painter Henri Matisse (1869–1954), shown drawing with charcoal attached to a long pole, below, is known for his daring use of color. He painted a portrait of Madame Matisse, right, in 1905.

Maria Callas (1923–77), a beautiful, brilliant, and temperamental coloratura soprano, left a lasting impression on the world of opera. The Greek-American singer's masterful performances in the 19th-century bel canto operas of Verdi, Bellini, and Donizetti in the 1940s and 1950s revived the genre. Her voice sometimes was criticized for being too heavy, wobbly, and harsh, but her dynamic stage presence and passionate acting more than made up for any technical imperfections. Her musicianship, expressive phrasing, and intelligence were admired widely.

But at the same time, Callas epitomized the difficult, egotistical *artiste*, constantly quarreling with directors, managers, costars, and rivals. Her growing unpopularity among her colleagues, as well as her many vocal problems, cut her career short. However, she was dominant for about a decade, and she continued to set the standard for opera performance for years afterward.

Maria Callas

Charlie Chaplin (1889–1977), a British comedian, is associated most closely with the image of his beloved "little tramp" character. For most of the 20th century, that incarnation of Chaplin was the most recognizable sight throughout the world. Considered to be the first movie superstar, he was unique in the amount of creative control he wielded. Chaplin produced, directed, wrote, and starred in most of his films, and he also sometimes composed the music and did the editing as well.

In his most famous movies, including *The Gold Rush* (1925), *City Lights* (1931), *Modern Times* (1936), *The Great Dictator* (1940), *Monsieur Verdoux* (1947), and *Limelight* (1952), Chaplin's defining quality was his ability to combine superb physical comedy with emotional resonance. He has been credited with raising film comedy to an art.

Ella Fitzgerald (1917–96) personified jazz throughout her career, which lasted more than 60 years. She was dubbed "the first lady of song" for her pure, clear, nimble voice, as well as her gift for improvisation and interpretation. She had her first hit, "A-Tisket, A-Tasket," in 1938. A few years later, inspired by the bebop jazz of Dizzy Gillespie and Charlie Parker, she invented the wordless improvisational singing known as "scat," which became her signature.

But Fitzgerald's talent was not limited to jazz; her sophisticated versions of standards by Cole Porter, Irving Berlin, Duke Ellington, and George and Ira Gershwin catapulted her to mainstream stardom. She recorded more than 200 albums, including a series of "songbook" albums in the 1950s, and received a total of 13 Grammy Awards.

George Gershwin (1898–1937) was the preeminent American songwriter of his generation. In collaboration with his lyricist brother, Ira, Gershwin penned such classic songs as "Summertime," "Someone to Watch Over Me," and "They Can't Take That Away from Me." The Gershwin brothers wrote several hit Broadway musicals during the 1920s and early 1930s, including *Of Thee I Sing*—the first musical comedy to win the Pulitzer Prize.

Ella Fitzgerald

Although George Gershwin lacked conservatory training, he studied music and composition privately for most of his life, and he composed several well-regarded serious pieces. *Rhapsody in Blue* (1924), a symphony written for piano and jazz band, remains one of his best-loved creations. And *Porgy and Bess* (1935), the opera he cowrote with Ira, has become a standard and the most famous American opera of all time.

Katharine Hepburn (1907–) deserves to be called a legend. She has won a record four Academy Awards for best actress—for *Morning Glory* (1933), *Guess Who's Coming to Dinner?* (1967), *The Lion in Winter* (1968), and *On Golden Pond* (1981). She has starred on Broadway in such works as *The Philadelphia Story*, *As You Like It*, *Coco*, and *The West Side Waltz*. She also has been featured in various television productions, including *The Glass Menagerie* and *The Corn Is Green*.

Hepburn established a distinctive stage and screen presence thanks to her beauty, aristocratic manner, and crisp New England accent. A feminist icon before feminism was fashionable, she played independent-minded women in such film classics as *The Philadelphia Story* (1940) and *The African Queen* (1951). Hepburn did some of her best work in the movies she made with Spencer Tracy, including *Woman of the Year* (1942), *Adam's Rib* (1949), *Pat and Mike* (1952), and *Guess Who's Coming to Dinner?*.

George Bernard Shaw (1856–1950) wrote many plays that are considered classics of Western literature. The British playwright took theater in a new direction, regarding it as a vehicle for exploring human nature. For example, *Arms and the Man* (1894), his first successful play, satirized the tendency to romanticize war; and *Pygmalion* (1912), the inspiration for the musical *My Fair Lady*, mercilessly attacked the British class system.

The erudite, opinionated Shaw had no reticence about speaking his mind, even when it courted controversy. A longtime socialist, he openly admired Hitler, Stalin, and Mussolini. And when awarded the Nobel Prize for literature in 1925, he dismissed it as "a lifebelt thrown to a swimmer who has already reached the shore in safety." This willingness to express his ambitious ideas regardless of public opinion contributed to his influence.

Frank Sinatra (1915–98), nicknamed "The Voice" and "Ol' Blue Eyes," will be remembered mainly for his music. His phrasing and timing, his skill at expressing lyrics, and his

Frank Sinatra

Katharine Hepburn

connection with audiences contributed to his artistry. His numerous hits included "I've Got You Under My Skin," "It Was a Very Good Year," "The Lady Is a Tramp," "My Way," "Strangers in the Night," and "New York, New York." After performing at New York's Paramount Theater in 1942, the crooner became a teen idol almost overnight. In the 1950s he cut a series of concept albums that sparked a major trend in the recording industry. Although Sinatra stopped performing in concert in 1995, he continued to sell about 1 million records per year—a concrete indication of his popularity and enduring legacy.

In addition, Sinatra was featured in various type roles in 58 movies, winning an Oscar for playing the gutsy soldier Maggio in *From Here to Eternity* (1953).

(Continued from page 317.)

whose art—although created, for the most part, in France—had not been very well represented in French museums, especially compared to museum collections in the United States.

Some of the most important accomplishments in the arts in this century have been the work of independent visionaries who, whether or not they were artists themselves, undertook to promote new artistic ideas and win them significant public attention and influence. In Europe one of the most remarkable of these figures was the Russian impresario Sergei Diaghilev, who, in creating the Ballets Russes in 1909, transformed the somewhat moribund European tradition of ballet dancing into a modernist theatrical art of enormous originality and scope. Diaghilev's Ballets Russes, in fact, became one of the great artistic legends of the century. It brought together the leading composers, choreographers, dancers, painters, and writers of the period in a collaborative enterprise that was as revolutionary as anything to be found in their separate artistic disciplines. Although it originated in Russia in the years preceding the Revolution of 1917, the Ballets Russes achieved its greatest fame and influence in Western Europe in the dozen or so years prior to Diaghilev's death in 1929, and its influence was such that it effectively established ballet itself as one of the major modernist arts of the 20th century.

Diaghilev's principal successor in the ballet field was an American visionary—Lincoln Kirstein, a poet, art historian, and balletomane who, in collaboration with the Russian-born dancer and great choreographer George Balanchine, whom Kirstein brought to America in the 1930s, founded the New York City Ballet.

It was this company that, by the 1960s, had established New York as the dance capital of the Western world—largely owing to Balanchine's artistic genius. Balanchine proved to be an even more radical innovator than Diaghilev by introducing plotless, more or less abstract ballets in which traditional dance narrative was abandoned to concentrate on an art of pure movement and musicality. It was in such abstract choreography that Balanchine created one of the most quintessentially American modernist styles of its time.

More or less contemporaneous with the emergence of the New York City Ballet as a world-class dance company, there also emerged the movement in abstract-expressionist painting that came to be called the New York School, whose most celebrated talents were Jackson Pollock, Willem de Kooning, Mark Rothko, and Robert Motherwell. It was the first movement in American modernist art to win widespread influence and acclaim abroad—first in Europe, and then throughout the world. Although closely based on European precedents in modernist painting, the art of the New York School tended to be larger in its physical scale and less inhibited by the conventions of tradi-

George Balanchine (1904–83), left, cofounder of the New York City Ballet, choreographed ten ballets for Sergei Diaghilev's famed Ballets Russes early in his career. The Ballets Russes, program, above, revitalized ballet early in the 20th century.

Skyscrapers

Very tall buildings, commonly known as skyscrapers by the end of the second millennium, were a uniquely American invention. Most were created during the 20th century after the invention of structural-steel framing that made them possible. Peoples elsewhere had aspired to building skyward much earlier, but they lacked the means, usually because the technology was not available. Tales of humans attempting to erect buildings that would reach up to the heavens go back as far as the story of the Tower of Babel in the Old Testament.

Only in the final years of the 20th century did the U.S. drive to build ever-taller buildings falter. Occupancy rates of these predominantly commercial buildings were fluctuating, corporate ambitions were being modified, and loftier buildings began to spring up elsewhere. In 1997 the Petronas Towers in Kuala Lumpur, Malaysia, at 1,476 feet (450 meters) high, became the world's tallest building, supplanting the 1,454-foot (443-meter) Sears Tower (*photo above*) in Chicago. And even taller buildings than the Petronas Towers were planned or under construction in other Asian countries.

Despite competition from the rest of the world, America is the home of the skyscraper, and many people still regard New York City as the paramount site of soaring towers. The many tall buildings there include the height-record holder for more than 40 years, the 1931 Empire State Building (1,250 feet/381 meters). A New York City upstart, the twin-towered World Trade Center, built in 1972 at a height of 1,368 feet (417 meters), seized the record briefly, but only two years later the completion of the Sears Tower sent the title back to Chicago, where the skyscraper began.

In 1885 architect William Le Baron Jenney built the 15-story Home Insurance Building in Chicago, often cited as the first high-rise with a steel structural frame. The new frame eliminated the need for masonry supporting walls that had become ever thicker with buildings' growing heights. But its bolted steel connections moved with the wind, the greatest enemy of very tall buildings. A later development to solve that problem was the rigid steel frame, in which all the elements, including internal floor supports, were joined to prevent movement. But this too presented height limitations, as it could not accommodate the limited movement that occurs naturally, thus jeopardizing structural integrity on upper stories. The invention of internal full-building-height shear trusses allowed limited movement by bracing columns against wind forces; this innovation was employed in record-setting skyscrapers from New York City's 612-foot (187-meter) Singer Building in 1908 to the Empire State Building. Later skyscrapers used a poured-concrete core for additional bracing or a composite of steel-framing techniques such as diagonal bracing to make the whole frame a series of trusses.

While Asia promised the greatest height records for the near future, Europe also showed signs of picking up on the skyscraper trend. The 790-foot (241-meter) Palace of Culture and Science in Warsaw, Poland, had been the tallest building in Europe since 1955. But its position was usurped in 1990 with the completion of the 850-foot (259-meter) Messeturm in Frankfurt, Germany. In 1998 the 984-foot (299-meter) Commerzbank, also in Frankfurt, broke the record as Europe's tallest building.

Charles King Hoyt

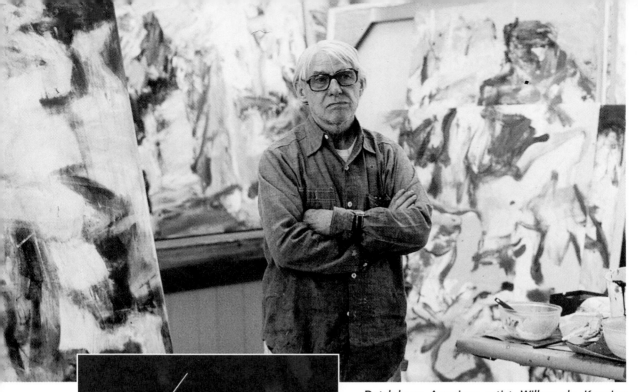

Dutch-born American artist Willem de Kooning (1904–97), above, was one of the originators of abstract expressionism, the New York School. American conductor Leonard Bernstein (1918–90), left, was an accomplished pianist and composer for the concert hall, musical theater, ballet, and film. His Broadway hits included "West Side Story."

tional easel painting than the European art from which it derived. Both its physical amplitude and its daring indifference to European standards of artistic "finish" gave the art of the New York School the look of something genuinely new and audacious. The very size of its mural-scale paintings and the unapologetic subjectivism of its abstract imagery were taken to represent an American idea of bigness, on the one hand, and the American preoccupation with the self, on the other.

The success of the New York School played an important role in establishing New York as the art capital of the Western world in the post–World War II period. Nowhere else—certainly not in a demoralized postwar Paris—did a new art movement display any comparable energy, audacity, and ambition.

The New York School also had the historic distinction of being the last of the modernist movements in 20th-century art to be controversial, for initially it had met with a good deal of public resistance both at home and abroad. Yet by the late 1950s, as European critical taste adjusted to the novelty of an American avant-garde, and American critical taste embraced what it initially had hesitated to approve, abstract-expressionist painting was heralded by the art establishments on both sides of the Atlantic as a major development in 20th-century art. It was only then, too, that abstract-expressionist paintings began to be traded on the international art market as blue-chip holdings—the successors, in that respect, to the now classic works of early 20th-century European modernism.

This fast-paced reversal of taste in the 1950s also proved to be very beneficial to the art movements that succeeded abstract expressionism in the 1960s, especially the pop-art and minimalism movements. In the wake of the New York School's success, it now was considered bad taste and even something worse—a sign of being behind the

(Continued on page 327.)

The Greatest Novels of the 20th Century

John Steinbeck

Virginia Woolf

Ernest Hemingway

William Faulkner

In recognition of the end of the 20th century, the editorial board of Modern Library, a division of Random House, assembled a list of the century's 100 finest English-language novels. The first 50 titles on the list, included with the permission of Modern Library, are:

1. *Ulysses*, James Joyce
2. *The Great Gatsby*, F. Scott Fitzgerald
3. *A Portrait of the Artist as a Young Man*, James Joyce
4. *Lolita*, Vladimir Nabokov
5. *Brave New World*, Aldous Huxley
6. *The Sound and the Fury*, William Faulkner
7. *Catch-22*, Joseph Heller
8. *Darkness at Noon*, Arthur Koestler
9. *Sons and Lovers*, D.H. Lawrence
10. *The Grapes of Wrath*, John Steinbeck
11. *Under the Volcano*, Malcolm Lowry
12. *The Way of All Flesh*, Samuel Butler
13. *1984*, George Orwell
14. *I, Claudius*, Robert Graves
15. *To the Lighthouse*, Virginia Woolf
16. *An American Tragedy*, Theodore Dreiser
17. *The Heart Is a Lonely Hunter*, Carson McCullers
18. *Slaughterhouse Five*, Kurt Vonnegut
19. *Invisible Man*, Ralph Ellison
20. *Native Son*, Richard Wright
21. *Henderson the Rain King*, Saul Bellow
22. *Appointment in Samarra*, John O'Hara
23. *U.S.A.* (trilogy), John Dos Passos
24. *Winesburg, Ohio*, Sherwood Anderson
25. *A Passage to India*, E.M. Forster
26. *The Wings of the Dove*, Henry James
27. *The Ambassadors*, Henry James
28. *Tender Is the Night*, F. Scott Fitzgerald
29. *The Studs Lonigan Trilogy*, James T. Farrell
30. *The Good Soldier*, Ford Madox Ford
31. *Animal Farm*, George Orwell
32. *The Golden Bowl*, Henry James
33. *Sister Carrie*, Theodore Dreiser
34. *A Handful of Dust*, Evelyn Waugh
35. *As I Lay Dying*, William Faulkner
36. *All the King's Men*, Robert Penn Warren
37. *The Bridge of San Luis Rey*, Thornton Wilder
38. *Howards End*, E.M. Forster
39. *Go Tell It on the Mountain*, James Baldwin
40. *The Heart of the Matter*, Graham Greene
41. *Lord of the Flies*, William Golding
42. *Deliverance*, James Dickey
43. *A Dance to the Music of Time* (series), Anthony Powell
44. *Point Counter Point*, Aldous Huxley
45. *The Sun Also Rises*, Ernest Hemingway
46. *The Secret Agent*, Joseph Conrad
47. *Nostromo*, Joseph Conrad
48. *The Rainbow*, D.H. Lawrence
49. *Women in Love*, D.H. Lawrence
50. *Tropic of Cancer*, Henry Miller

The history of popular music in the United States during the 20th century saw the development of many influential styles, including blues, jazz, gospel, country, bluegrass, rhythm and blues (R&B), and rap. Then there is the music that made the biggest cultural noise of all—rock 'n' roll. Musical genres are naturally porous, but rock 'n' roll proved to be a veritable sponge, combining blues, pop, country, and R&B into a big-beat sound that influenced popular music and culture worldwide.

Music critics try in vain to identify the very first rock 'n' roll record. Many point to Elvis Presley's first recordings for Sun Records in 1954, or Bill Haley and His Comets' "Rock Around the Clock" in the same year; others vote for 1951's "Rocket '88" by Jackie Brenston with His Delta Cats, or 1955's "Maybellene," the first of a string of classic rock 'n' roll records by Chuck Berry.

Taking a longer view, however, evidence of the beginnings of rock 'n' roll can be heard in the 1920s Texas blues of Blind Lemon Jefferson, and, during the 1930s, in the northern blues of Big Bill Broonzy and the hard-driving sound of the Count Basie band. Electric-guitar innovators like Charlie Christian in jazz and T-Bone Walker in electric blues—not to mention pioneering electric-guitar builders like Leo Fender and Les Paul—anticipated a time when the guitar would be the dominant instrument in popular music. The roots of rock also can be heard in the boogie-woogie piano popular in the 1940s, the jazz-country hybrid called western swing, the jump blues of singer and bandleader Louis Jordan, and the plainspoken country songs of Hank Williams.

The development of rock 'n' roll is tied inextricably to race, for while it is easy to spot the influence of white country, pop, and folk music in rock, it is impossible to imagine the music without the underpinning of black music, especially the blues. Musical historian Robert Palmer cut to the quick when he wrote, "Rock might not have developed out of a self-contained Afro-American tradition, but it certainly would not have developed had there been no Afro-Americans."

The giants of 1950s rock 'n' roll established a stylistic vocabulary that influenced succeeding generations of pop musicians. Elvis Presley might have been declared "king," but other artists were just as influential. Chuck Berry put a bluesy beat to country melodies and topped it off with an infectious guitar style and bouncy teen-oriented lyrics about cars, girls, and hamburgers sizzling on an open grill. Little Richard's pounding piano, falsetto whoops, and general outrageousness set a standard embraced in later decades by the brilliant guitarist Jimi Hendrix and the artist formerly known as Prince. Buddy Holly showed how a rock 'n' roller could write all sorts of songs, an example that later would inspire John Lennon and Paul McCartney of the Beatles—a name chosen to echo that of Holly's band, the Crickets. Meanwhile, R&B artists like Ray Charles and Sam Cooke played to largely black audiences while laying the groundwork for the 1960s explosion of soul music.

The early music of the two giants of British rock, the Beatles and the Rolling Stones, drew clear inspiration from 1950s rock, with both bands recording songs by Berry and Holly. The Stones also dipped into the influential Chicago blues of Muddy Waters (one of his songs gave the band its name) and Howlin' Wolf. Bob Dylan turned folk music on its ear, first with his sophisticated lyrics, and later by trading his acoustic guitar for a rock band. The British trio Cream and Chicago's Butterfield Blues Band introduced rock audiences to the

Among the greats of rock 'n' roll were the 1950s rockers Bill Haley and His Comets, page 324, top, and Chuck Berry, page 324, bottom. The Beatles, below, and Janis Joplin, right, furthered rock's development in the 1960s.

music of such blues artists as B.B. King and Willie Dixon, as well as such Depression-era legends as Robert Johnson and Skip James.

Black pop music in the 1960s shared the Top 40 playlist with white rock 'n' roll, with the soul-pop of such Motown acts as the Supremes, the Four Tops, Marvin Gaye, Stevie Wonder, and the Temptations creating the era's definitive dance music. James Brown, meanwhile, developed a hard-edged brand of R&B that became known as "funk," a style that dominated black music in the 1970s and anticipated the rise of rap in the 1980s and 1990s.

Rock 'n' roll in the 1960s also was defined

Rock 'n' roll evolved as the decades passed, continually developing and changing. Influential musicians included the Rolling Stones, above, whose wild lifestyle and high-energy concerts made them a legend. Michael Jackson, right, added a dance groove to rock with his hugely popular albums of the 1980s. The forever-changing styles of singer Madonna, below, right, kept her in the spotlight through the 1990s.

by the emergence of a massive teenage consumer market—the "baby boomers" growing up in the prosperity of postwar America. The cultural sway of this market was so significant that the Beatles became not just a hit group but a symbol of what became known as the counterculture. Long hair, recreational drugs, political protests—all became emblematic of the decade's rock culture, as did the

crowd of a half million drawn to the August 1969 music festival near Woodstock, NY.

The early history of rock involved small independent record labels; the 1960s saw major labels struggling to exploit this new mass market. By the 1970s, music businesspeople knew what they were doing. Concerts now took place in major arenas, and records sold in the millions. Significant trends continued to emerge, ranging from punk and disco to rap and alternative rock, and performers like Bruce Springsteen, Prince, Madonna, U2, and Nirvana became major stars. Popular music became a pervasive presence in movies and advertisements and on television, but in a way, the more effectively it was marketed, the less impact the music seemed to wield. Few would argue, for example, that the two biggest-selling albums in history—Michael Jackson's *Thriller* and the Eagles' *Greatest Hits*—impacted the culture as much as the Beatles' *Sgt. Pepper's Lonely Hearts Club Band*.

Rock 'n' roll originated as youth music, but it is now a term that can be applied to music that could appeal to anyone from cradle to grave. These days, the music fan has access to virtually all the music that went into the creation of the genre. These historical connections add depth to rock's enduring legacy—the establishment of a pop-culture business built to market music to young people and to older generations who no longer feel the need to hang up their rock 'n' roll shoes.

John Milward

(Continued from page 322.)

times—to resist new ideas in the arts, no matter what their character or quality. It was in this new cultural atmosphere of easy acceptance and a refusal to be shocked (and maybe at times a desire to be shocked) that the figure of Andy Warhol emerged as the art world's new darling in the 1960s. In his legendary paintings of Campbell's soup cans and his "sculptures" that replicated commercial Brillo boxes, Warhol turned the gravity of modernist art into a public joke, and the newly emancipated art public responded to this repudiation of its own seriousness by making him the most famous and influential artist of his time. It is in this respect that Warhol—or what sometimes came to be called Warholism—set the moral tone of the visual arts for the remainder of the century.

In retrospect, the modernist movement that had ushered in the early decades of the century on a note of high artistic seriousness with cubism and abstract art was ending the century with a celebration of Warholian facetiousness and farce. It is hardly any wonder, then, that in the last decade of the century there was much talk in high places about "the end of art history," and a chorus of praise for the emergence of a "postmodern" sensibility that repudiates new ideas in favor of parodying past achievement—a development that has been accompanied by a mode of arts criticism whose mission it is to "deconstruct" what the modernist movements in the early decades of the century so painstakingly had created.

Yet, while a great many artists in all fields of creative endeavor were engaged in this postmodern mission of derision and deconstruction, the mainstream public for the arts grew enormously in the last decades of the century, and it was a public largely indifferent to the gamesmanship of the deconstruction-

The Andy Warhol Museum, above, left, featuring more than 500 works, opened in Pittsburgh, PA, in May 1994. Lines were long at the 1998 Van Gogh blockbuster exhibition at Washington's National Gallery.

ists and postmodernists. This newly expanded public was particularly responsive to so-called blockbuster exhibitions—exhibitions of great size devoted to the work of individual masters, or to artistic movements, that are well-known to the public because of the immense attention they have received in the media. This phenomenon produced such star attractions as the 19th-century French impressionist master Claude Monet, the postimpressionist masters Vincent van Gogh and Paul Gauguin, and the 20th-century modernists Picasso and Matisse.

To meet the needs of the new public, museums expanded their facilities and staffs—and not least, their museum shops, which bring in huge revenues. This may be the most remarkable paradox of all in the story of the arts in the 20th century: that the century was ending with the contemporary-art scene in considerable intellectual disarray, while the art museums were enjoying the greatest public success in their history.

Hilton Kramer

MOTION PICTURES

Introduced to the world near the end of the 19th century, motion pictures developed into the exciting, far-reaching new art form of the 20th century, taking their place beside the long-established art forms of painting, sculpture, literature, music, and theater. Movies swept to global popularity and kept pace with the century's dramatic technological advances. When television arrived, movies were shown on the tube as well as in theaters. Videocassettes added a new venue, and the computer revolution brought yet another outlet.

As the year 2000 approached, the art form stood entrenched as a universal phenomenon both culturally and economically. Throughout the world, greater numbers of people than ever shared common ground by watch-

"Gold Rush" (1925), considered by many to be Charlie Chaplin's greatest performance, above, and "The Wizard of Oz" (1939)—featuring, right, left to right, Ray Bolger, Jack Haley, Judy Garland, and Bert Lahr—are film classics. Early moviegoers were captivated by Greta Garbo; she appeared with John Gilbert, above, right, in "Love" (1927), an adaptation of Tolstoy's "Anna Karenina."

ing the same films. Billions of dollars were at stake as film distributors competed for international markets. In some respects the history of film reflected what had been happening in the world during the turbulent 1900s.

At first the newfangled entertainment was regarded as more oddity than art. The early experiments by Thomas Edison in the United States and innovators like George Méliès and Louis Lumière in France hardly foretold the possibilities that were to be realized. By the second half of the century, film courses were proliferating in universities and high schools, and aspiring filmmakers could enroll in special college programs devoted to turning out professionals. Increasingly, film critics gained prominence in newspapers and magazines, and on radio and television.

Jimmy Stewart and Donna Reed, above, left, starred in "It's a Wonderful Life." The 1946 Frank Capra film has become a Christmastime favorite for television viewers. Julie Andrews, above, portrayed a young postulant who leaves the convent to care for the Von Trapp children in the Academy Award– winning "The Sound of Music" (1965). Steven Spielberg's "Saving Private Ryan," left, which was released in 1998 and featured Tom Hanks in the leading role, was acclaimed for its realism.

The Silent Days

The discovery that making images move could be entertaining led to showings in small theaters called nickelodeons. Perceptive entrepreneurs, many of them immigrants, built upon this nucleus and made one- and two-reelers that were shown in larger theaters. In the United States the East Coast was the prime location, until the possibility of better weather and warring over patents led the industry to shift to California. It was in 1911 that the Nestor Film Company of Bayonne, NJ, established the first studio in Hollywood.

The buildup of the film business in Hollywood achieved such great success that—although France was at first the major player—in the post–World War I period, Hollywood became the international center of filmmaking. A galaxy of silent-film superstars enthralled the general public. Charlie Chaplin attracted throngs of fans wherever he traveled. Mary Pickford, Theda Bara, Clara Bow, Lillian and Dorothy Gish, and Gloria Swanson became international favorites. Douglas Fairbanks was the swashbuckling hero. Rudolph Valentino made hearts throb.

In 1915 an astonishing, lengthy, and controversial film demonstrated that the motion picture could be more than just entertainment. Director D.W. Griffith's patently racist Civil War epic *The Birth of a Nation*, more than three hours long, broke ground in terms of elaborate filming and editing. It also proved that film could trigger passionate reactions. African-Americans picketed in opposition to its glorification of the Ku Klux Klan and denigration of blacks. Griffith always insisted he really had been trying to make an antiwar film. Developments in the 1920s cemented the realization that film, still silent, could rise to the level of art. Robert Flaherty's *Nanook of the North*

(1922) showed how the documentary form could be used to reveal a way of life. The Soviet Union emerged as another center of artistic advance. Director Sergei Eisenstein's highly charged, pro-revolutionary *Battleship Potemkin* (1925) demonstrated sophisticated editing that still is studied, and reinforced the power of film to stir emotion and mold opinion. The scholarly writings of Eisenstein and other Soviet contemporaries contributed to film theory.

Other important strides were being made in pre-Hitler Germany through what came to be called German Expressionism—films that utilized offbeat scenic design and special effects to explore unusual subjects—such as Robert Wiene's *The Cabinet of Dr. Caligari* (1919), F. W. Murnau's *Nosferatu* (1922), and Fritz Lang's *Metropolis* (1926). The latter, with effects remarkable for the time, imagined and implicitly questioned a futuristic society in which industrialization had turned humans into little more than automatons. Such films inspired directors in various countries to expand their concepts of what was possible in cinema. Lang and many other artists fled after the Nazis came to power, and German film was reduced largely to propaganda; a renaissance would occur in the second half of the century.

New heights of silent-film creativity were achieved, for example, by the remarkably accomplished *The General* (1926), starring the great comic actor-director Buster Keaton. Others among the century's giants of cinema, such as Alfred Hitchcock and Jean Renoir, already were working in silents, and Walt Disney, who was to have a profound influence on animation and family

Alfred Hitchcock's "Psycho" (1960), with Anthony Perkins and Janet Leigh, is believed to be one of the most terrifying films ever made.

Academy Award Winners for Best Picture (1929–99)*

1929 *Wings*
1930 *Broadway Melody*
1931 *All Quiet on the Western Front*
1932 *Cimarron*
1933 *Grand Hotel*
1934 *Cavalcade*
1935 *It Happened One Night*
1936 *Mutiny on the Bounty*
1937 *The Great Ziegfeld*
1938 *The Life of Emile Zola*
1939 *You Can't Take It with You*
1940 *Gone With the Wind*
1941 *Rebecca*
1942 *How Green Was My Valley*

Steven Spielberg's "Schindler's List" took 1994 Oscars for best film and best director.

1943 *Mrs. Miniver*
1944 *Casablanca*
1945 *Going My Way*
1946 *The Lost Weekend*
1947 *The Best Years of Our Lives*
1948 *Gentleman's Agreement*
1949 *Hamlet*
1950 *All the King's Men*
1951 *All About Eve*
1952 *An American in Paris*
1953 *The Greatest Show on Earth*
1954 *From Here to Eternity*
1955 *On the Waterfront*
1956 *Marty*
1957 *Around the World in 80 Days*
1958 *The Bridge on the River Kwai*
1959 *Gigi*
1960 *Ben Hur*
1961 *The Apartment*
1962 *West Side Story*
1963 *Lawrence of Arabia*
1964 *Tom Jones*
1965 *My Fair Lady*
1966 *The Sound of Music*
1967 *A Man for All Seasons*
1968 *In the Heat of the Night*
1969 *Oliver!*
1970 *Midnight Cowboy*
1971 *Patton*

1972 *The French Connection*
1973 *The Godfather*
1974 *The Sting*
1975 *The Godfather Part II*
1976 *One Flew over the Cuckoo's Nest*
1977 *Rocky*
1978 *Annie Hall*
1979 *The Deer Hunter*
1980 *Kramer vs. Kramer*
1981 *Ordinary People*
1982 *Chariots of Fire*
1983 *Gandhi*
1984 *Terms of Endearment*
1985 *Amadeus*
1986 *Out of Africa*
1987 *Platoon*
1988 *The Last Emperor*
1989 *Rain Man*
1990 *Driving Miss Daisy*
1991 *Dances With Wolves*
1992 *The Silence of the Lambs*
1993 *Unforgiven*
1994 *Schindler's List*
1995 *Forrest Gump*
1996 *Braveheart*
1997 *The English Patient*
1998 *Titanic*
1999 *Shakespeare in Love*

*Year award was presented.

Orson Welles directed and starred in the 1941 masterpiece "Citizen Kane," the tale of a newspaper tycoon. The 1931 German film "M," with Peter Lorre, below, was praised for its excellent cinematography.

entertainment in general, launched Mickey Mouse in silents.

Movies Talk

After Al Jolson interrupted the mostly silent *The Jazz Singer* (1927) to speak, film never would be the same. The industry was compelled to retool for the new age of "talkies." There were problems; films had to be dubbed or subtitled for showing worldwide, and some stars had voices unfit for the new demands. Hollywood lured Broadway playwrights with lucrative pay on the assumption they knew how to write good dialogue. The first Academy Awards were given in 1929. By 1931 the nickname "Oscar" was coined.

In the 1930s the Depression that wracked the United States ironically provided new opportunities for the cinema. It was an inexpensive form of entertainment as well as an escapist outlet giving audiences the opportunity to lose themselves in romantic dramas, fast-action gangster films, Westerns, comedies, and lavish musicals. A new generation of stars emerged in the 1930s and 1940s, including Mae West, Katharine Hepburn, Jean Harlow, Bette Davis, Irene Dunne, Clark Gable, Cary Grant, James Stewart,

John Wayne, Shirley Temple, the Marx Brothers, Edward G. Robinson, Henry Fonda, Fred Astaire and Ginger Rogers, Gene Kelly, Judy Garland, Frank Sinatra, Humphrey Bogart, and Ingrid Bergman. In ensuing years they were to be followed by yet another constellation, including such luminaries as Marilyn Monroe, Elizabeth Taylor, Paul Newman, Robert Redford, Clint Eastwood, Jack Nicholson, Dustin Hoffman, Al Pacino, Robert De Niro, and Meryl Streep, and, in Europe, Marcello Mastroianni, Sophia Loren, and Catherine Deneuve. More recently, such performers as Tom Hanks, Meg Ryan, Tom Cruise, Leonardo DiCaprio, and Sean Penn have come into their own.

During the period when Hollywood studios reigned supreme, Paramount, Warner Brothers, Twentieth-Century Fox, Columbia, MGM, and others kept actors under contract to churn out a steady flow of product. Moguls like Louis B. Mayer, Jack Warner, Darryl Zanuck, and Harry Cohn wielded their power and influence. Hollywood became famous for its genre pictures—musicals like *Singin' in the Rain* (1952), Westerns like *Stagecoach* (1939), and film noir such as John Huston's *The Maltese Falcon* (1941). Those films and others—*Casablanca* (1942), for example—achieved classic status.

The most popular and durable film to emerge from the Hollywood heyday was the four-hour Technicolor extravaganza *Gone With the Wind* (1939), the adaptation of Margaret Mitchell's best-seller that represented the apex of Hollywood talent and ballyhoo (*see* page 333). Its success guaranteed that color films eventually would become routine. *The Wizard of Oz*, appearing the same year, was another durable hit. An

Gone With the Wind

What accounts for the durable popularity of *Gone With the Wind*, one of the most renowned films of the 20th century? The nearly four-hour 1939 film set during the Civil War and its aftermath was the epic of an epoch, epitomizing Hollywood at its peak. At the outset, producer David O. Selznick set the stage for catapulting the filming of Margaret Mitchell's immensely popular best-seller into a legend by wooing the public with a barrage of hype.

Clark Gable was clearly the choice to play Rhett Butler. But to cast Scarlett O'Hara, Selznick launched a publicity-oriented talent hunt that lured thousands of hopefuls to compete futilely against existing stars coveting the role. Among the noted and popular actresses considered were Paulette Goddard, Tallulah Bankhead, Norma Shearer, Bette Davis, Joan Crawford, Loretta Young, Miriam Hopkins, Lucille Ball, Katharine Hepburn, Lana Turner, Joan Bennett, Joan Fontaine, Susan Hayward, and Jean Arthur. Selznick's decision to choose British actress Vivien Leigh triggered controversy because many in the South were affronted by the casting of a foreigner instead of a southern belle. During the much-discussed, lavish production, Selznick promoted the burning-of-Atlanta sequence. He put new fronts on old studio sets to represent 1864 Atlanta and, with great fanfare, set fire to them.

Writers and directors came and went. Sidney Howard wrote the screenplay, but numerous others worked on it. George Cukor started as director, but Victor Fleming took over; Sam Wood and the film's production designer, William Cameron Menzies, also directed parts. It is hard to believe at the century's end, but a censorship battle raged before Clark Gable could be permitted to use a word forbidden by the stringent Production Code and say to Scarlett, "Frankly, my dear, I don't give a damn." In fact, Selznick had the scene shot again with alternative dialogue just in case the original had to be replaced.

After all the ballyhoo, the completed film—with its ultimate overbudget cost a then-whopping $4 million—was accorded a glittering premiere in Atlanta. Hattie McDaniel, who played Mammy and for this supporting role would become the first African-American to win an Oscar, was excluded, as was Butterfly McQueen, who excelled as Scarlet's African-American servant Prissy. The film itself drew protests for depicting slave owners and their way of life sympathetically and for stereotyping the slaves as content to serve their masters.

Ten Academy Awards, including one for best picture and one to Leigh as best actress, were presented the film. Although its all-time U.S. gross of $198.6 million only ranks it 25th among top moneymakers, *Gone With the Wind*'s popularity is not reflected accurately, because ticket prices have risen substantially over the years. The film, available on video, remains a fascinating slice of Hollywood Americana, and many scenes—such as the classic one showing wounded and dying soldiers at the railway station—continue to be moving. But the driving factor behind the film's lasting appeal is, as originally, the intensely romantic story and the charisma of its stars. Gable and Leigh, *photo*, still light up the screen. So do Olivia de Havilland as Melanie, Leslie Howard as Ashley Wilkes, McDaniel, McQueen, and other supporting performers.

Will there be a sequel to *Gone With the Wind*? The chances of ever capturing the movie magic to equal the original remain hopelessly slim.

William Wolf

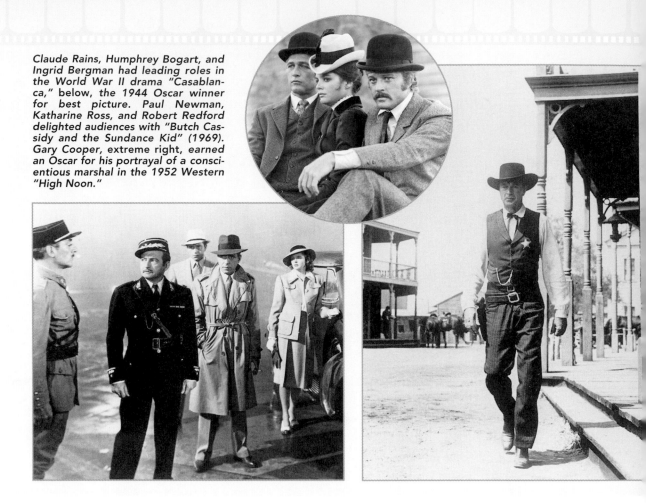

Claude Rains, Humphrey Bogart, and Ingrid Bergman had leading roles in the World War II drama "Casablanca," below, the 1944 Oscar winner for best picture. Paul Newman, Katharine Ross, and Robert Redford delighted audiences with "Butch Cassidy and the Sundance Kid" (1969). Gary Cooper, extreme right, earned an Oscar for his portrayal of a conscientious marshal in the 1952 Western "High Noon."

achievement of a different sort came when a brash young man headed west from New York after his documentary-style radio broadcast "The War of the Worlds" caused a panic among people who really thought Martians had landed in New Jersey. Orson Welles' masterpiece, *Citizen Kane* (1941), brilliantly set new standards for visuals, editing, and sound in telling a controversial story of a newspaper tycoon perceived to be a fictional version of William Randolph Hearst. Efforts to suppress *Citizen Kane* failed, and it became probably the most studied and influential film of the century. In general, the Hollywood pattern throughout the 1930s and 1940s was to shun controversial subject matter. But there were exceptions, the most notable of which was John Ford's *The Grapes of Wrath* (1940), an adaptation of John Steinbeck's searing account of dust-bowl poverty and the exploitation of migrant workers in California.

Postwar Upheaval

During the World War II years, a spate of patriotic films fed the need to boost public support for the war effort. Betty Grable became the leading pinup girl among the troops. Stars helped the war-bond drives and entertained soldiers on the front. Many changes occurred in the war's aftermath. In the late 1940s, efforts were made to spotlight racial problems, a heretofore taboo subject, with films such as Elia Kazan's *Pinky* (1949) and Stanley Kramer's *Home of the Brave* (1949). A measure of the extent to which African-Americans were frozen out was the casting of white actress Jeanne Crain as a black woman trying to pass for white in *Pinky*. The subsequent success of Sidney Poitier as America's first African-American male superstar stimulated public awareness, but it was not until the 1970s that African-Americans began to play a more significant role, and at the century's end, complaints of

Debbie Reynolds and Donald O'Connor joined Gene Kelly, left, in singing and dancing in the 1952 hit "Singin' in the Rain," judged by some as the best musical film ever made. The drama was high in "The Bridge on the River Kwai," with Alec Guinness, William Holden, and Jack Hawkins. It won Oscars in 1958 for best film, actor (Guinness), and director (David Lean).

inequity still were rampant despite the impact of such directors as Spike Lee and stars such as Denzel Washington, Oprah Winfrey, Whoopi Goldberg, and Wesley Snipes.

The late 1940s also marked the start of the infamous Hollywood blacklist. During the anti-Communist Cold War fervor, many were called upon by the U.S. House of Representatives Un-American Activities Committee to confess their political pasts and to name others believed to be Communists or sympathizers, or lose their jobs. Some went to prison in defiance. The blacklist extended into television and continued into the 1960s. Many lives were ruined, and numerous directors left the country to work abroad.

Among the vital changes in the aftermath of World War II was the advent of Italian neorealism. Roberto Rossellini's *Open City* (1945) depicted the Italian resistance. Vittorio De Sica's *The Bicycle Thief* (1948) drama-tized postwar poverty and despair. Such gritty movies, made on low budgets and shot in the streets and other realistic locations, startled audiences and were the antithesis of old-fashioned studio films. Other filmmakers soon strove for the new realism in their own countries. The great Indian director Satyajit Ray cited *The Bicycle Thief* as his inspiration. American director Jules Dassin credited *Open City* with pointing the way to his use of realistic New York locations for his *Naked City* (1948), influential in its turn. U.S. filmmakers sought realistic locations outside the United States, partly for artistic reasons but also to escape rising costs of labor and other aspects of production.

Pressure began to build for more candor and fewer taboos in Hollywood films. Ever since the 1930s, Hollywood had been governed by the restrictive Motion Picture Production Code, whose seal of approval was given only to films that did not flout its rules on sex, language, and content deemed offensive. Many of the nation's cities also had censor boards. Legal challenges increased, and key court decisions led to more freedom and to the abolition of the boards. A 1952 U.S. Supreme Court decision held films to be protected by the 1st Amendment, reversing a 1915 decision that motion pictures were unprotected entertainment. By 1968 the less restrictive but still criticized rating system of the Motion Picture Association of America was adopted.

The more adventurous and mature films made independently of the studios or imported from abroad often had trouble finding theaters, most of which were owned and operated by the major studios. However, in 1948 an antitrust decree that movie companies divest themselves of theater ownership opened the way to greater access.

The next arena of artistic progress was France. By the mid-1950s there were the beginnings of France's New Wave, a designation given to a cluster of low-budget, personal films. Directors determined to create films different from those of the establishment made strides with camera and editing technique, broke rules, and created films that pulsated with life as they saw it. François Truffaut's poignant *The Four Hundred Blows* (1959) and Jean-Luc Godard's cynical *Breathless* (1960) were prime examples. The New Wave reverberated internationally to help spark more independent filmmaking and elevate expectations of serious filmgoers. The French phenomenon also had an impor-

Special Effects

By the end of the 20th century, special effects, fascinating since the early days of motion pictures, had reached a level of sophistication unforeseen when French filmmaker Georges Méliès experimented with them in his 1902 film *A Trip to the Moon*. Since that time, the public's delight with fanciful images beyond the reality the camera normally records has driven filmmakers to experiment with ever-expanding and diverse techniques. By 1999 computer technology and digital know-how offered the ability to create whole environments, including convincingly simulated people and man-made or natural disasters.

Fritz Lang's 1920s silent classic *Metropolis* was a key point along the way. In envisioning a future industrial society, Lang used models and camera technique to depict a city with airplanes flying among skyscrapers, overhead-train transport, and gigantic, ominous factory machinery operated by men who lived and worked underground. He dazzled audiences by seemingly converting a woman leader of the employees into a robot.

In the 1930s similar laboratory hocus-pocus surrounded the creation of the renowned monster in *Frankenstein*. Another milestone was *King Kong* (1933), with its simulation of a giant ape clinging to the top of New York's Empire State Building and batting away attacking airplanes. The methods were primitive measured against Stanley Kubrick's much later *2001: A Space Odyssey* (1968), portraying time-space travel through the universe. But the major escalation of special effects can be traced to George Lucas' *Star Wars* (1977), a huge hit that launched a tremendous public appetite for more of its laser-like weaponry, amusing robots, and space-age battle. Credit also should be given to television's *Star Trek* for advancing the cause. Ensuing films in the Star Wars trilogy and a plethora of other action movies resulted in filmmakers vying to outdo one another onscreen and in the marketing of spin-off toys.

Lucas' landmark Industrial Light & Magic Company, founded in 1975 to provide the wiz-

tant intellectual thrust. The magazine *Cahiers du Cinéma* expounded the auteur theory—the belief that the director is the prime creative force behind a motion picture. New Wave theorists held that some directors could be considered authors of their films despite the collaborative nature of the art. Directors like Howard Hawks, John Ford, Ernst Lubitsch, and Alfred Hitchcock—all of whom had worked within the studio system—were studied, as was the great French director Jean Renoir, creator of such classics as *Grand Illusion* (1937) and *Rules of the Game* (1939). The concept had much to do with advancing theoretical discussion of film in university classes everywhere, as well as with the proliferation of books probing film as art.

Heightened Perceptions

A major influential force providing evidence of the depth films could achieve was Swedish director Ingmar Bergman, who gained international recognition with *The Seventh Seal* (1957). Through his masterly succession of films he explored such weighty issues as the existence of God, the meaning of life, the human psyche, turbulent relationships, war, and matters of conscience. The international scope of the art was evidenced further by Western recognition of the Japanese director Akira Kurosawa, whose *Rashomon* (1950) won first prize at the Venice Film Festival and led to the focus, not only on Kurosawa's films, but on other works from the Far East. In the 1960s, Britain became a key player with films that reflected

The 1931 film "Frankenstein," featuring Boris Karloff, page 336, was an early demonstration of the influence of special effects. The 1977 space-age adventure "Star Wars," above, left, opened new doors in imaginative and complex special effects. Following the movie's success, George Lucas expanded his company devoted to the technology. "Titanic" stunned audiences by re-creating the famous cruise ship and its tragic sinking. The hit film was awarded numerous Oscars, including one for visual effects.

ardry he wanted, was hired by other producers and directors and emulated by about a dozen other such companies. Computer animation, robotics, digital creation of scenery, the technique of placing live actors in the midst of artificial settings, the ability to fake such weather phenomena as a tornado or a hurricane, the creation of lifelike dinosaurs for Steven Spielberg's 1993 *Jurassic Park*, and other remarkable achievements demonstrated that it was possible to do almost anything onscreen. The hullabaloo reached its zenith with the costly filming of the effects-laden *Titanic* (1997), the highest-grossing film in history.

Will the craze continue into the 21st century? There were no serious signs of abatement. On the contrary, George Lucas had created a prequel to *Star Wars* with *Episode I: The Phantom Menace* for release in 1999, and he planned to release Episode II in 2002 and Episode III in 2005.

William Wolf

Lauren Bacall, Betty Grable, and Marilyn Monroe, above left, left to right, sought romance in "How to Marry a Millionaire" (1953). The 1967 film "Guess Who's Coming to Dinner" offered Spencer Tracy and Katharine Hepburn as the parents of Katharine Houghton, who has returned home from a trip with a new fiancé—Sidney Poitier. Marlon Brando gave an Academy Award–winning performance as "The Godfather," below.

the "swinging London" boom that developed along with the new music of the Beatles. One country drew inspiration from another. More attention was paid to films from Germany and Eastern Europe. Offbeat, individualistic films broke new ground in the United States. Films such as *Easy Rider* (1969) epitomized an ongoing effort to shatter the Hollywood mold.

Whereas actors were once the primary focus, the spotlight turned to directors. Film buffs enjoyed and argued about the work of Bergman, Federico Fellini, Rainer Werner Fassbinder, Woody Allen, Orson Welles, Robert Altman, Stanley Kubrick, Sam Peckinpah, Billy Wilder, Lina Wertmuller, and others. Francis Ford Coppola's *The Godfather* (1972) fired up a new generation of buffs, as did Martin Scorsese's *Taxi Driver* (1976).

The Blockbuster Era

Changes were taking place in the way people viewed movies. In the 1950s, Hollywood had experimented with wide-screen projection in larger theaters to lure the public away from television. But the old movie palaces, expensive to run and rarely filled, began to give way to the multiplexes—many in shopping malls. Movie theaters also discovered they could make as much or more money on popcorn and soft drinks as on admissions.

In the mid-1970s, Steven Spielberg's *Jaws* (1975) and George Lucas' *Star Wars* (1977) led to volcanic change. Spielberg went on to become a powerful mogul in the new Hollywood, making such significant films as *Schindler's List* (1993), his Holocaust epic, and *Saving Private Ryan* (1998), his war epic. The enormous international success of *Jaws*, with its worldwide box-office gross of $470.6 million, triggered a hunger for more huge grosses. In an era when the power of agents had grown, stars had become independent of the studios, and movies were put together with deal-making far removed from the way studios with contract players had functioned in earlier days, more-expensive productions and less interest in films with modest expectations became the norm.

Star Wars not only contributed to this blockbuster mentality but ushered in an era of fantastic special effects, the opportunities for which were enhanced by rapidly growing technologies (*see* page 336). Computers could create virtual environments or forces of nature, and a filmmaker could use a panoply of explosions, chases, disasters, and combat previously impossible on such a grand scale.

By 1999, *Titanic* (1997), with its elaborate effects, led the field as the highest-grossing film of all time, with more than $1.8 billion worldwide. Others in the top ten, in ranking order, were *Jurassic Park* (1993), $919.7 million; *Independence Day* (1996), $810.4 million; *Star Wars* (1977), $780 million; *The Lion King* (1994), $766.7 million; *E.T., the Extra-Terrestrial* (1982), $704.8 million; *Forrest Gump* (1994), $679.4 million; *The Lost World: Jurassic Park* (1997), $614.3 million; *Men in Black* (1997), $586.2 million; and *The Empire Strikes Back* (1980), $533.8 million.

The struggle to make films not pegged to such expectations became increasingly difficult, but a rising independent movement yielded films that sometimes could break through and gain public attention and acclaim. Ready forums were offered by the proliferation of film festivals. Such standbys as the major festivals in Cannes, Berlin, Venice, New York, Toronto, Montreal, Sundance, Telluride, San Francisco, and Chicago were targeted by fledgling filmmakers in hope of international recognition. More attention was paid to films spanning the international spectrum—films from Africa, Iran, China, and Taiwan.

Two special developments stressed the recognition of film as a vital art form. The awareness that early films were lost through deterioration prompted major institutions to institute preservation programs, and the Library of Congress began designating lists of classic films to be preserved in their original state and requiring the public labeling of any tampering with them by exhibitors, whether through editing or colorizing.

William Wolf

By 1999, "Titanic," which opened in late 1997 and starred Leonardo DiCaprio and Kate Winslet, left, had become the highest-grossing film in history. Other financial blockbusters included Steven Spielberg's "E.T., the Extra-Terrestrial" (1982), above; "The Lost World: Jurassic Park" (1997), bottom; and Roland Emmerich's "Independence Day" (1996), below.

TELEVISION

Although television dazzled the millions who lined up for its first public demonstrations at the 1939 New York World's Fair, there was no rush to buy the receivers when they came on the market. The public's initial verdict was that television was an interesting novelty with an uncertain future and was too expensive for the home. Commentators in the press doubted that it ever could be a mass medium because the sets were difficult to operate and the programs too expensive to produce on a consistent basis. One prominent critic declared that television never could replace radio in the home because one had to sit down and watch it, and nobody had the time to do that.

The "Golden Age"

After World War II, however, with the technology significantly improved and the United States at last enjoying a degree of pros-

perity, the new medium was seen in a different light—an electronic marvel to enrich home life, a window on the world, a peace dividend. Crowds standing outside the windows of appliance stores to watch the black-and-white images on the small screen were familiar sights in the cities during the late 1940s, and when the prices of TV sets dropped to where they were widely affordable around 1950, the medium's proliferation was swift. In a scant few years, television supplanted radio as the dominant form of broadcasting and siphoned off most of its most popular programs and stars. By the end of the 1950s, the TV set was an appliance few households could do without.

Unlike most other countries, the United States entrusted the new medium to private industry. The two leading radio networks—CBS and NBC—made the transition handily and flourished, while two lesser players—

from Hollywood. But the staple of prime time in those early years was the studio drama, for which the era came to be remembered as "The Golden Age of Television."

Early network programs emanated mainly from New York, because the advertising industry was centered there, and most programs were overseen by their sponsors. Drawing from the Broadway-talent pool was opportune, since programs had to be presented live, and for those trained to perform onstage, the transition to the studio was a simple matter. In some seasons as many as a dozen original plays were presented each week in such anthology series as *Studio One*, *Playhouse 90*, *Kraft Television Theatre*, and *The U.S. Steel Hour*. Television was beginning to produce a significant body of literature with poignant dramas like *Marty*, *Twelve Angry Men*, *Patterns*, *The Miracle Worker*, and *The Days of Wine and Roses*. These shows launched the careers of dozens of actors— including Paul Newman, Sidney Poitier, Grace Kelly, Jack Lemmon, Eva Marie Saint, Lee Remick, James Dean, Peter Falk, and George C. Scott—who went on to star in other media. Also, such dramatists as Paddy Chayevsky, Rod Serling, Gore Vidal, Reginald Rose, and Horton Foote, along with noted directors—such as Sidney Lumet, Arthur Penn, Delbert Mann, George Roy Hill, and John Frankenheimer—began their careers through television. This era began in 1947 and ended some ten years later, when the networks shifted primarily to filmed entertainment produced in Hollywood.

Mainstream of Popular Culture

An impetus to that shift came from the quiz-show scandal, which broke in 1959 with the discovery that producers of the popular big-money quiz-downs had rigged them for the sake of ratings by providing certain charismatic contestants with answers in advance. A serious breach of the public trust, the episode—which involved such shows as *Twenty-One*, *The $64,000 Question*, and *The $64,000 Challenge*—led to congressional hearings and a reshaping of network policies. In acting to assume greater control over their

ABC and DuMont—struggled to survive in what was characterized as a two-and-one-half-network TV economy. When ABC was acquired by United Paramount Theaters in 1953 and received an infusion of sorely needed capital, DuMont had no choice but to fold its tent. Thus began what now is looked back upon as "the network era," the three decades in which three networks ruled television and, on any given night, held more than half the nation in their thrall.

Programming in the 1950s was a rich smorgasbord of poor man's theater: variety shows ranging from the low comedy of Milton Berle to the brilliant satire of Sid Caesar's *Your Show of Shows*; engaging game shows like *I've Got a Secret*, *What's My Line?*, and Groucho Marx's *You Bet Your Life*; light family sitcoms typified by *I Love Lucy* and *Father Knows Best*; and, in mid-decade, a flood of filmed low-budget Western series

programming and keep sponsors at a distance except to advertise, the networks came to favor filmed programs over live, because these could be edited prior to broadcast, if necessary.

By then the networks had become the mainstream of popular culture and the national glue. Each evening provided Americans of every region, ethnicity, and age group a shared cultural or informational experience. TV also proved itself the greatest advertising medium ever and was a boon to the economy. Yet there was considerable public ambivalence toward the medium for mesmerizing viewers with its glut of shallow and often moronic programs, earning it the nickname the "idiot box." Of widening concern, too, was commercial television's influence on children—its exploitation of them as a market and its interference with their education, particularly in limiting attention spans. In the view of many, television contributed to moral pollution and promoted materialistic values. TV even was blamed for the rising crime rate, because it caused the streets to be deserted at night. Yet for all this,

and though television was criticized incessantly for excesses of sex and violence, people could not resist its essential appeal, especially after all programs began to be beamed in color in 1965.

The social effects of the medium became more pronounced when, by the late 1960s, most households had multiple sets, and families stopped watching together. Cultural separation on such a vast scale unquestionably contributed to the generation gap that troubled the society in the 1970s. By then advertisers had become obsessed with demographics, paying substantially more to reach young adults than people over 50, and the networks and stations responded by concentrating on programs that fed the interests and attitudes of the 18–35 age group. Thus the centuries-old pattern of the elders passing down culture to the young was inverted.

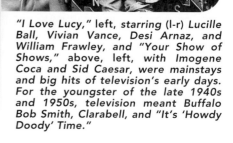

"I Love Lucy," left, starring (l-r) Lucille Ball, Vivian Vance, Desi Arnaz, and William Frawley, and "Your Show of Shows," above, left, with Imogene Coca and Sid Caesar, were mainstays and big hits of television's early days. For the youngster of the late 1940s and 1950s, television meant Buffalo Bob Smith, Clarabell, and "It's 'Howdy Doody' Time."

Though it was the primary system for most other countries, public television came late to the United States, and it has remained from the first an underfinanced service with a modest audience base and a considerable dependency on programs from Britain. But it has been mainly where cultural programs, social documentaries, educational children's programs—including the award-winning *Sesame Street* (*photo*)—current-affairs discussion, and serious dramas are consistently to be found on the American television landscape.

Its progenitor was the frail noncommercial ETV service that began in 1953 with a handful of local stations dedicated to educational and informational programming. Expansion came in the 1960s when the government, amid widespread concern over the plethora of escapist programs on the networks, acted to put new ETV stations on the air. The Ford Foundation provided them with equipment grants and established National Educational Television (NET) to facilitate a program exchange, and the Carnegie Corporation appointed a commission to study long-range funding for the system.

Congress passed the Public Broadcasting Act in 1967, which reorganized the system and incorporated the ideals articulated by the Carnegie commission. A new nongovernmental entity, the Corporation for Public Broadcasting (CPB), whose 15 members would be appointed by the president, would be the central force responsible for disseminating the federal funds and insulating the system from government interference. CPB then created the Public Broadcasting Service (PBS) to replace NET as the provider of national programs.

PBS began operating in 1970 and immediately became a target of President Richard Nixon, who was convinced that the organization was politically liberal and hostile toward him. Through a White House official, he warned the industry to decentralize or risk losing the annual federal appropriation. The broadcasters responded in 1973 by reasserting local-station autonomy, creating a cooperative market for programming, and reducing PBS to little more than a distributor of programs. After the Nixon years, PBS gained a stronger voice in program decisions and, in the 1990s, a budget for program production.

With regard to building an audience, the system was harmed by decentralization, because there could be no strategic planning of a schedule to compete with those of commercial television. Moreover, it was difficult to promote programs on a national scale when they were not carried uniformly by the stations in the same time periods, if at all. The U.S. system is an odd patchwork of stations with differing agendas. With the federal money flowing directly to the stations rather than to a central organization, the system was limited in what it could produce without financing from private business, called underwriting, which was akin to program sponsorship. And since it costs much less to import programs than to produce original ones, the system became all but a satellite of British television. Yet American public television developed a loyal constituency, and it introduced several program forms, including the miniseries and the serialized novel, that were adopted by the commercial networks.

Les Brown

During the "Golden Age of Television" in the 1950s, future big-name playwrights and stars made their debuts on live studio dramas, such as "Twelve Angry Men," above, left. In 1959 television viewers were shocked to learn that quiz shows, including "The $64,000 Question," were rigged. Reruns and tapes of the 39 episodes of "The Honeymooners," starring Jackie Gleason and Art Carney, below, still produce many laughs.

A Witness to History

This captive audience, which over the years shared the enjoyment of programs and series like *The Ed Sullivan Show*, *All In the Family*, *M*A*S*H*, *Cheers*, *Friends*, *Seinfeld*, and *E.R.*, also joined in bearing witness to the tumultuous events that shaped the history of the last half of the 20th century. Even with the fragmenting of audiences by cable in the 1980s and the arrival of new terrestrial networks in the 1990s—Fox, the WB, UPN, and PAX-TV—the United States came together over a variety of channels through coverage of such events as national election campaigns, the Persian Gulf war, the collapse of communism, the O.J. Simpson murder trial, the death of Princess Diana, the baseball home-run race between Mark McGwire and Sammy Sosa in 1998, and the travails of President Bill Clinton resulting from his extramarital affair with a young White House intern.

From the time Edward R. Murrow courageously exposed the ruthless tactics of Sen. Joseph McCarthy in his hunt for commu-

nists during the early 1950s, television's most redeeming service, by far—and its most consequential influence on 20th-century life—has been its journalistic involvement with critical news events. As television's premier journalist who set the standard for all who followed, Murrow was as much a part of the Golden Age as were the actors and dramatists. So was his producer, Fred W. Friendly. The 1954 programs that brought McCarthy's injustices to national attention aired on their popular prime-time CBS series, *See It Now*, but the telecasts that actually brought down the Wisconsin senator a few months later were those of the Army-McCarthy hearings held before Congress, carried live for 35 days on both ABC and DuMont, neither of which had a significant daytime-program schedule. The hearings resulted in McCarthy's censure by the Senate, but it was the camera's revelation of the senator's callousness and malevolence that caused him to lose virtually all public sympathy and ended his political career.

More than a mere window on history in the making, television became the electronic

The excitement generated by ABC's telecast of *Roots* (*photos, below*) on eight consecutive nights in January 1977 was nothing short of phenomenal. The 12-hour miniseries, based on Alex Haley's best-selling novel of that title, scored the highest average ratings ever for a series and broke all individual records with the final episode, which drew an audience of 80 million. An estimated 130 million people—representing 85% of households with televisions—watched all or part of the series, which traced the history of an African-American family from the cruel abduction of a young West African by American slave traders to contemporary times. The immense popularity of the series was remarkable, given that the cast was predominantly black and most of the villains were white. Times indeed had changed.

Twenty years earlier, when NBC created a variety show for the great pop singer Nat (King) Cole, no advertiser would sponsor the series—ostensibly for fear of a boycott in the South. Many artists rallied to the show's support and offered to perform at union scale, but their efforts were unavailing; Cole was canceled before the 1957–58 season ended. For the next ten years, when an African-American appeared on television (other than in sports), it was usually as servant, sidekick, or guest entertainer. An exception was Bill Cosby, who received costar billing in the espionage series *I Spy*, which premiered on NBC in 1965.

Amos 'n' Andy, a carryover from radio with an all-black cast, had been a successful comedy series in the early 1950s, but it was driven off CBS by black citizens' groups who found the show patronizing and an embarrassment to their race. However, the series continued in syndication until the mid-1960s.

Not only were African-Americans true minorities on the TV screen prior to the civil-rights movement, they scarcely existed at all in the executive suites or news divisions of the networks or TV stations. The real turning point came in 1969, after a court ruled that WLBT in Jackson, MS, should lose its license when citizens' groups brought proof, from having monitored the station, that it actively promoted segregationist views while denying any airtime to civil-rights proponents. This was both a violation of the regulation known as the Fairness Doctrine and of the licensee's pledge to serve the needs and interests of its community, 40% of which was African-American. The court's decision sent shock waves through the industry, and soon after, all stations and networks were featuring black journalists on camera and training black executives.

There was another breakthrough in 1968, when NBC scheduled *Julia*, a situation comedy starring Diahann Carroll that proved a surprise hit and was to have a three-year run. But it was criticized widely for its unrealistic portrayal of black life in America. Nevertheless, its success opened the way for other shows with black principals. In the 1970s, programs with black casts gracefully entered the mainstream, and since then many series with black casts—notably *The Flip Wilson Show*, *Sanford and Son*, *The Jeffersons*, *Good Times*, and *The Cosby Show*—have enjoyed enormous success.

Les Brown

The Beatles made their U.S. debut on "The Ed Sullivan Show," above. "The Mary Tyler Moore Show," above right, and "All in the Family" became TV fixtures in the 1970s. "Carnac the Magnificent," below, was a regular on "The Tonight Show Starring Johnny Carson."

stage on which historical events occurred—the Vietnam war and the demonstrations protesting the war; the civil-rights movement, including the march from Selma, AL, to Montgomery, AL, led by Dr. Martin Luther King; the assassinations and funerals of President John Kennedy, Sen. Robert Kennedy, and King; Neil A. Armstrong's and Col. Edwin E. Aldrin's walk on the Moon on July 20, 1969; the Watergate hearings and President Richard M. Nixon's resignation; the assassination attempts on Gov. George Wallace, President Gerald Ford, and President Ronald Reagan; the Los Angeles race riots; and the Persian Gulf war. The medium, by its existence, changed the conduct of American politics, raised the blinds on governance, and arguably made for a better-informed electorate. In becoming the proscenium for national politics, capable of creating new political stars overnight, television ended the old practice of party power brokers meeting in smoke-filled rooms to select candidates.

A Lightning Rod for Public Opinion

Moreover, television also became the lightning rod for public opinion. Certainly, 20th-century history would have unfolded differently had TV not become a mass medium. The plague of the McCarthyist witch-hunts might have continued for many years more, with a damaging effect on the 1st Amendment; the United States might have prosecuted the Vietnam war many years longer than it did; and there probably would

"M*A*S*H," top, and "Seinfeld," left, set new standards for TV comedy. The CBS newsmagazine series "60 Minutes," above, celebrated its 30th anniversary in 1998. Mike Wallace (second from left) has been a correspondent on the show since its debut.

not have been civil-rights or women's-rights movements on the scale experienced.

The power of the image proved itself repeatedly in the turbulent 1960s. The nightmarish pictures from Vietnam—napalmed villages and burnt children fleeing—that came into American homes nightly on the news in time caused the public to switch from supporting the war to opposing it. And when the esteemed CBS correspondent Walter Cronkite returned from a tour of the battle zone and, to his audience of millions, pronounced the war "unwinnable," the end had begun. With the civil-rights movement, it was largely the images of segregationist cruelty, including the unleashing of attack dogs on peaceful demonstrators and the turning of powerful water hoses on them, that seared the national conscience and illuminated the immorality of race prejudice and segregation preached so eloquently by Dr. King.

Not by design but simply by virtue of the image, television affected the order of the national leadership in the second half of the century. Had there been only radio in 1952, Richard Nixon's so-called "Checkers Speech," which served to secure his place on the Republican national ticket as Dwight D. Eisenhower's running mate, might not have produced the extraordinary write-in response that saved his political career. On radio it would have missed the audience involvement with Nixon's visual emotionality that was such an effective distraction from the sidestepped issue of whether he had misused campaign funds. Television was to harm Nixon eight years later, however, in the first of the "great presidential debates" ever staged for the networks. Though as vice-president he should have scored an easy victory over the relatively unknown Sen. John F. Kennedy in the 1960

Cable Television

Cable television became a mass medium almost by accident. Rare among technologies, it was not developed in a laboratory and has no known inventor. It was created in the early 1950s by enterprising appliance-store owners frustrated by their inability to sell TV sets because they were in low-lying areas where television signals could not travel. The problem was solved by erecting an antenna on high ground to catch the transmissions, and then delivering them to the local households by means of broadband wires. These early installations became known as Community Antenna Television, or CATV, and were welcomed by TV stations for extending their reception. But that was before the discovery that, with a set-top converter, cable could expand the channel capacity of the TV set and offer original program services to compete with broadcasters for viewers.

With multiple channels, cable became a medium in its own right and expanded gradually to small towns and suburbs during the 1960s and early 1970s. But it was stymied in the cities by the high costs of construction and consumer indifference to what cable had to offer beyond better reception of the over-the-air stations. The great boost came during 1975, when Home Box Office (HBO), then a New York–based pay cable channel, took the bold step of hitching itself to a satellite—a $7 million gamble—and demonstrated that national networks could be created overnight at far lower costs than by terrestrial means. In less than three years, virtually every cable system throughout the United States had installed a dish to receive the satellite transmissions, and HBO was in the black.

Other existing and prospective operators of cable channels moved swiftly to secure satellite transponders. One of them was Ted Turner, who arranged to uplink his obscure Atlanta UHF station, thus establishing the first "superstation." Building on the success of WTBS, Turner created other cable channels—including the Cable News Network (CNN), the

presidential election, he lost his advantage completely in the first of the four TV encounters. Nixon came across the tube looking pale, tired, and shifty, while his youthful, suntanned opponent projected vitality and self-confidence. Reportedly, a majority of those who heard the debate on radio, where the focus was on the issues rather than the images, found Nixon the clear winner. But that initial debate, watched by 75 million people—the largest audience ever, at the time—gave Kennedy the boost that carried him to the White House.

Some three decades later, television similarly saved Bill Clinton in his first campaign for the presidency, when he and his wife, Hillary Rodham Clinton, appeared in a *60 Minutes* interview on which they denied allegations that he, while governor of Arkansas, had had an extramarital affair with state employee Gennifer Flowers. The piece, scheduled immediately after a Super Bowl game, drew a huge audience and won the couple sympathy for their candid admission of having had marital problems in the past. Then, in 1998, with his presidency in possible ruins as the result of a sex scandal with intern Monica Lewinsky, Clinton's high standing in the public-opinion polls helped his cause. A strong economy

first of its kind. Turner's channels—along with HBO, ESPN, USA, MTV, Lifetime, A&E, BET, Nickelodeon, Showtime, and C-SPAN—were responsible for cable's phenomenal growth in the 1980s as the wiring of the major cities progressed. By the end of the decade, more than 60% of U.S. households subscribed to cable, exceeding the industry's own expectations. That percentage eventually would grow to 65%, the virtual saturation point in light of families too poor to subscribe and homes too remote to be wired.

Though the audience ratings for most cable channels were minuscule by the general standards of broadcasting, these "narrowcast" services flourished because they were supported by two distinct revenue streams—advertising and a share of the subscriber fees from the cable systems, initially a few cents per household each month. Meanwhile, the operators of cable systems derived incremental revenues from pay services and pay-per-view movie channels. Continual refinements in set-top technology made for ever-greater channel capacity, and the number of national and regional program services continued to grow. By the end of the 1990s, there were more than 70 services on the satellites, including Discovery, The Weather Channel, The Disney Channel, The History Channel, E! Entertainment, FX, CNBC, and The Nashville Network. The two largest cable-system operators, Time-Warner and TCI, were among the seven companies that owned or controlled 85% of the program channels.

Cable was responsible for most of the steady audience erosion that reduced the TV networks' prime-time audience share from 90% to 58% over a period of 20 years. In 1998 the cable channels collectively sold some $7 billion worth of advertising, about half the combined revenues of the broadcast networks. More than a dozen cable channels were handsomely profitable. The TV networks were hardly profitable at all.

Les Brown

---

contributed to his high standing in the polls. So too, did the release of the four-hour, televised tape of his grand-jury testimony, during which he could be seen as a victim. The entire Lewinsky episode, with its frequently broadcast references to sexual topics that previously were taboo, had the effect of lowering the barriers of what could be said in the American public media, including television, and in polite society.

By the late 1990s, about 70% of American households were receiving a multitude of TV channels through cable and direct-to-home satellite services, even as all the electronic media were equipping for the digital age, which promised even greater channel expansion. The networks were experiencing continual audience erosion, and television was becoming demassified in the inexorable audience drift to channels providing entertainment and news for specific interests. Yet, as the 1990s demonstrated, important national and world events remain a shared experience regardless of where the images are received by a dispersed audience, leaving no doubt that television, in whatever forms it may take, always will be part of the fabric of history.

Les Brown

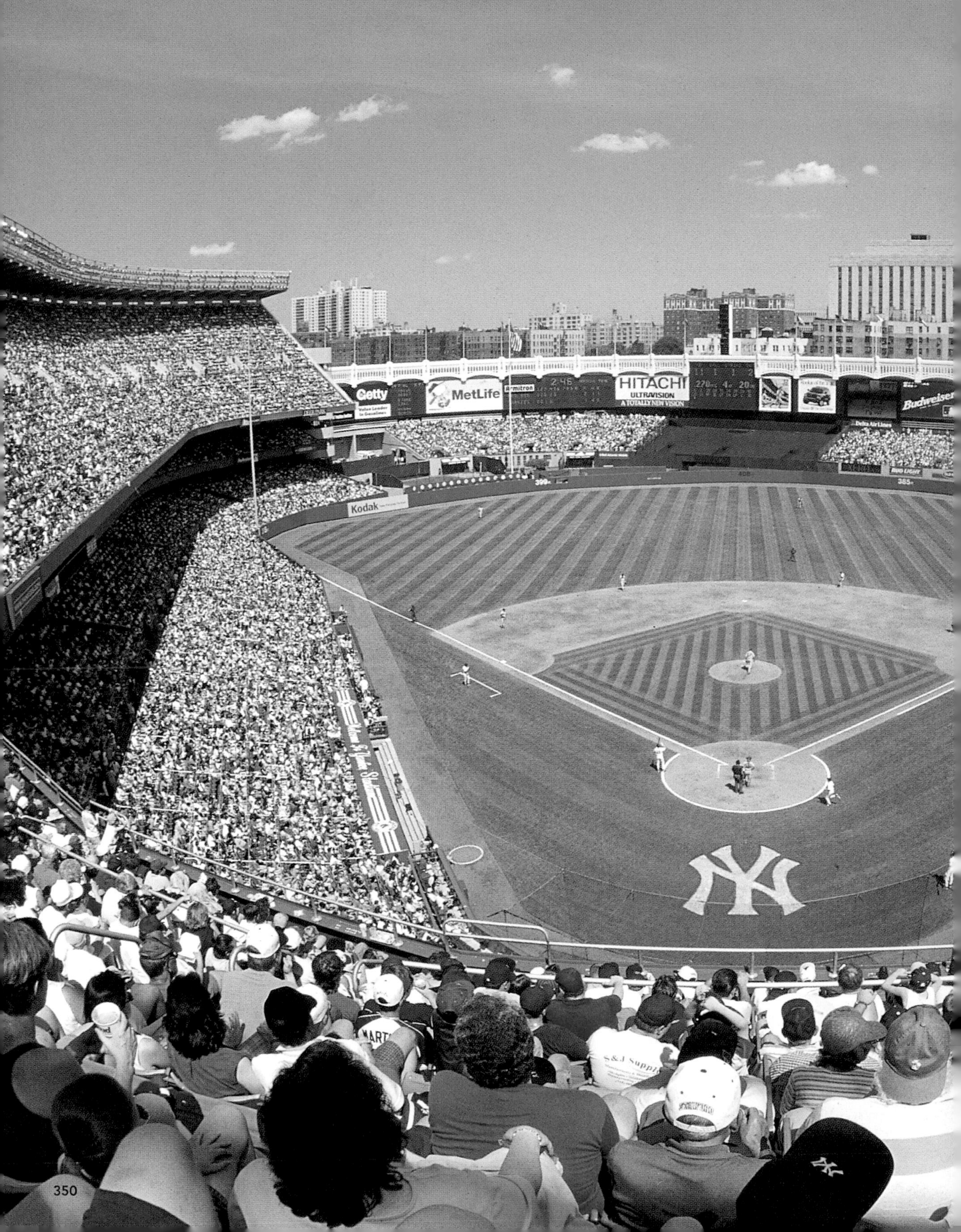
Getty
MetLife
HITACHI
ULTRAVISION
Kodak
Budweiser

Very simply, the story of the American century in sports is told by iconic athletes who burst from the boundaries of their games to become both reflections and definers of their times. One enters the sports world of the 20th century with Jim Thorpe, who was raised on an Oklahoma Indian reservation to run howling with the hunting dogs, and exits with Michael Jordan, who was raised in rural North Carolina in a spirit of hopeful integration.

Through the century, as sports commentary cycled between idolatry and cynicism, these thrilling men and women were called heroes or symbols or commodities or pampered jock entertainers. But the roles they modeled always were real, based on the American ethics of hard work, equal opportunity, upward mobility, and fair play. Some icons got closer to the ideal than others; almost all were objectified by mainstream values and by marketing; yet they all inspired their fans to try harder, to dream bigger, to at least fight to survive until the buzzer.

Jim Thorpe

Jim Thorpe, for example, part Irish but mostly Native American, kept running away from his father's harsh discipline and from the repression of Indian schools until his amazing athletic gifts won him privileges

A sunny day at the ballpark became the essence of pleasure for sports fans everywhere. Jim Thorpe, above, was one of the century's greatest athletes.

and spending money. When he carried the football for little Carlisle Institute, a government-operated school for Native Americans in Pennsylvania, through the Harvard line, the press celebrated him as "a host in himself—as powerful as a turbine engine." Meanwhile, that other new national craze, the motion picture, was building an audience on movies about heroic cowboys whipping drunken, foolish, rapacious "redskins."

It was not so paradoxical. Thorpe won two gold medals—in the decathlon and the pentathlon—in the 1912 Stockholm Olympics and became a major-league-baseball outfielder. He justifiably was known as "the greatest all-round athlete in the world." As he edged toward middle age, he became a player-founder of what eventually would become the National Football League (NFL). But he also was regarded as symbolic of a native people who had been tamed and

taught European Christian ways. What better proof than athletic excellence—not only did he follow the rules of the white man's game, he used his natural savagery to entertain his "masters." It was a theme that, with variations, would run through the century as various immigrant groups, African-Americans, and then women took their turns in the arena.

Thorpe's coach in football and in track and field, Pop Warner, just was starting his own illustrious career; his genius for innovation on the field and for rule-bending off would become staples of college sport for the rest of the century. One of the men Thorpe defeated in the Olympics was Avery Brundage, who would go on to become a leading force in the rise of those Games. Neither would be much help when Thorpe's Olympic medals were taken away after it was discovered that he had spent summers

Jackie Robinson's Legacy

Jackie Robinson broke baseball's long-standing "color line" when the Brooklyn Dodgers promoted him to the majors from the Montreal Royals in 1947.

Specially recruited for the task by Brooklyn president Branch Rickey, Robinson had agreed in advance to turn a deaf ear to the considerable racial abuse he endured early in his career. Rickey had told the future star that he needed a ballplayer "with guts enough not to fight back." Robinson kept his cool and his word despite a torrent of racial insults that included death threats. That was not easy for the former UCLA standout, who had arrived in the majors with a reputation as a fierce competitor. He persevered with the support of his teammates and by letting his considerable baseball talent speak for him. In all, he played under more pressure than any other modern-day athlete.

On the eve of Robinson's first season, Brooklyn manager Leo Durocher held a midnight meeting to stop Dodger players from circulating a petition against playing with Robinson. It was Harold (Pee Wee) Reese, a Southerner, who diffused a potential anti-Robinson revolt among the Dodgers in 1947. Together, Robinson as the second baseman and Reese as the shortstop would form a Hall of Fame double-play combination. The racism of the time forced Robinson to accept separate, often inferior, accommodations on the road and during spring training. In fact, his presence was one of the reasons the Dodgers built their massive Dodgertown spring-training complex in Vero Beach, FL. Rumored strikes by Dodger opponents never materialized, but race-baiting was a fact of life for the new Brooklyn star. Most Americans sympathized with Robinson, how-

playing minor-league baseball. "Poor Jim," sympathized those cheerleaders of democracy, the sporting press; the cult of amateurism—sports for love, not money—was a British upper-class concept too complex for an Indian. If only he had been smart enough to have played under an assumed name, as did the white college boys.

The Two Babes

Despite their lip service to amateurism, Americans always have appreciated the spirit of professionalism—an honest day's work by people who know what they are doing, take pride in their craft, and enjoy it. Few athletes embodied that spirit as fully as did the two Babes—George Herman Ruth and Mildred Didrikson—two vulgar, rambunctious, loud, talented symbols of fun, excess, and sexuality.

In an age of consumption, Babe Ruth, a Baltimore saloon keeper's throwaway kid, ate more hot dogs, smoked more cigars, had more women friends, and hit more home runs than anyone else, and he did so without apology. His fans saw him as a natural man-child; his teammates saw him as their meal ticket; and his owners and managers saw him as enough of a box-office draw to finance building Yankee Stadium. Ruth made baseball the national pastime again after the Chicago White Sox conspired to fix the 1919 World Series. Along with Charles "Lucky Lindy" Lindbergh and Al "Scarface" Capone, Ruth gave the Jazz Age larger-than-life characters. But only the Babe, the "Bambino," remained beloved. There could be no ambiguity or evil in pounding a baseball over a fence. He existed only to delight himself and the public. He became the prototype of the cocky male athlete whose irresponsibility, total self-absorption, and commercial greed could be excused as necessary parts of

ever, and a postseason popularity poll placed him second only to crooner Bing Crosby.

Jackie Robinson was not only baseball's first black player of the 20th century but the first African-American to win a rookie-of-the-year award, most-valuable-player trophy, and a plaque in the Baseball Hall of Fame. He also was the first to be honored with a U.S. postal stamp. Though he spent most of his career as a second baseman, Robinson also served extensive terms at first and third during his ten-year career, spent entirely with the Dodgers. His .311 lifetime batting average included one batting title (.342 in 1949) and helped him win two stolen-base crowns.

Jack Roosevelt Robinson was born in Cairo, GA, on Jan. 31, 1919. The grandson of a Georgia sharecropper, Robinson spent his youth in southern California and eventually enrolled at UCLA, where he became the first player in that school's history to letter in four sports. He left UCLA just short of his degree because of family financial pressures. He played professional football for the Los Angeles Bulldogs before enlisting in the U.S. Army as a second lieutenant in 1942. A year later, he refused to sit in the "colored" section of a military bus and was court-martialed. After winning acquittal, he received an honorable discharge and began his pro-baseball career in the all-black Negro Leagues.

Robinson was playing shortstop for the Kansas City Monarchs when a Dodger scout, on a mission from Rickey, spotted him. He joined organized baseball in 1946 with the Montreal Royals, top farm club of the Brooklyn Dodgers, and immediately led the Triple-A International League in batting and runs scored. A year later, he broke into the Brooklyn lineup at first base. He hit his first home run in his third game, but none of his teammates shook his hand when he returned to the dugout.

Many historians believe the end of the color line marked the real beginning of major-league baseball. Thanks to Robinson's pioneering efforts, many bastions of segregation collapsed. Numerous contributions by Robinson and other African-Americans have made a major impact on the national pastime. In addition, Robinson's success was an inspiration to African-Americans in other sports as well.

Dan Schlossberg

the winning whole. He was, according to a teammate, "the kind of bad boy it's easy to forgive."

His female counterpart, probably the greatest woman athlete of the century, was the daughter of Norwegian immigrants. Her father, a carpenter, built his children a backyard gym. Mildred was nicknamed for the Babe because she could hit the ball farther than the boys in her hometown of Beaumont, TX. She was as cocky as the boy Babe, but never as easily loved or forgiven. Because she could whip most men at most games, her femininity was constantly suspect. She was called "tomboy" with a wink. This was less important in the beginning, as a basketball star in high school and then in the amateur leagues sponsored by factories and corporations. She was the belle of the 1932 Los Angeles Olympics, winning two gold medals and palling around with movie stars and sportswriters.

It was as an amateur and professional golfer, however, that Didrikson totally dominated and reshaped a sport. In creating what is now the Ladies Professional Golf Association (LPGA), she turned a dilettante recreation for country-club wives into a fiercely competitive business. She gave women permission to sweat to win, to enjoy the power of their bodies, to promote themselves, and to demand money for their performances. Tough and courageous, she won her third U.S. Open tournament and an unprecedented sixth Associated Press Woman Athlete of the Year Award while enduring an eventually fatal bout with cancer. However, Babe Didrikson paid a price. To sell herself and her sport, she had to reinvent herself as an acceptable female. She "dolled up" to comfort those who would be put off by her

Babe Ruth, above, was famous not only as a great home-run hitter but also for his colorful personality. His ability to draw a capacity crowd caused Yankee Stadium to be known as "the House That Ruth Built."

ambiguous sexuality. She had married George Zaharias, a professional wrestler.

Joe Louis

Sports stardom frequently has required the suppression of self; athletes must pretend to be what the world wants them to be. A striking example was Joseph Louis Barrow, who was born in Alabama to sharecroppers and was brought to Detroit in the great migration of southern blacks to the northern factories. It was Joe Louis' speed, strength, and natural ability that made him a local amateur boxing champion, but it was careful schooling by his black managers and trainers that made him the world heavyweight champion. A savage textbook fighter whose public image was laconic and nonthreatening, he told reporters, "I do my talking in the ring." Sportswriters and promoters called Joe the "Brown Bomber," the "Sepia Slugger," and the "Dark Destroyer"—names that in a sense denied his humanity. He had been taught never to gloat over a fallen white fighter or to be seen with a white woman. It was the only way a "Negro" would get a chance at the heavyweight title in pre–World War II America. After Jack Johnson had won the crown in 1908, novelist Jack London wrote, "The White Man must be rescued." It took seven years for a Great White Hope to beat Jackson, and for 22 years after that, blacks systematically were denied a chance to be the "King of Men." Louis finally got his chance, on June 22, 1937, because America needed to be rescued. The logical challenger had been Max Schmeling of Germany, who had beaten Louis the year before. But as the world teetered on the brink of war, Adolf Hitler was touting Schmeling as an Aryan hero. Joe Louis, African-American, suddenly became all-American because his country did not want to risk having a Nazi boxing champ.

Louis' dominating championship reign, which included a one-round knockout of

Schmeling in 1938, was of enormous social importance—empowering blacks, educating whites, ennobling Americans. As a ceremonial soldier, Louis not only aided the war effort by raising morale and selling bonds, he used his influence to keep a hotheaded young officer, Jackie Robinson, from going to military prison after a racist army-camp incident. Without Joe, there would have been no Jackie. Robinson's integration of major-league baseball in 1947 (*see* page 352) was even more spectacular than Louis' breakthrough, because beating up men of a different skin color never has been as difficult as working with them successfully. Robinson's team was the storied Brooklyn Dodgers; his sport was baseball, the moral classroom.

"Arnie's Army," Cassius Clay, TV, Billie Jean

By the 1950s—afternoon in America—the country was ready for a hero to reflect the new leisure. Arnold Palmer, a Pennsylvania groundskeeper's son with a sunny smile and a charging style, led "Arnie's Army" across the new frontier, the suburban golf course. He democratized the ancient Scottish game, which had been a signifier to Americans of the upper-class life. Once television began broadcasting major tournaments, Palmer also led the first wave of matinee-idol athletes that would include Mickey Mantle of the New York Yankees, who succeeded Joe DiMaggio in center field; Joe Namath, who put the Super Bowl on the map (*see* page 356); and football's great running back O.J. Simpson. At least as important as any athlete was Roone Arledge of ABC, who created *Wide World of Sports* and *Monday Night Football*, and put Howard Cosell on the air.

It was the combination of television and the 1960s' explosion of civil rights, Vietnam, and rock 'n' roll that produced arguably the most exciting, and the most controversial, idol of our arenas. So long as Cassius Clay

At New York City's Yankee Stadium on June 22, 1938, Joe Louis knocked out Germany's Max Schmeling in the first round to retain his world heavyweight-boxing title, above. During the 1950s and 1960s, Arnold Palmer was personally responsible for golf's newly found popularity. "Arnie's Army" followed Palmer around the links, left.

Football's Super Bowl—Sports' Biggest Extravaganza

When the National Football League (NFL) and the American Football League (AFL) agreed in the late 1960s to end their football war and merge, they also agreed to start playing a season-ending game between the champions of their respective leagues. Little did they understand the impact this game would have on sports in America.

What began as a highly anticipated event that stirred football fans but certainly did not overwhelm them has grown into the biggest sports extravaganza in U.S. history, bigger than the World Series or the Olympics. Now known as the Super Bowl, the initial contest was called the "AFL-NFL World Championship Game." It first was played on Jan. 15, 1967, in the Los Angeles Coliseum between the Green Bay Packers, champions of the NFL, and the Kansas City Chiefs, champions of the AFL. Only 61,946 fans showed up in the 100,000-seat facility. Tickets went for a top price of $12; two rival networks televised the game, with commercials selling for up to $85,000 a minute. A small media contingent covered the event.

On the suggestion of Chiefs owner Lamar Hunt, the game began being called the "Super Bowl." Hunt heard his daughter talking one day about playing with a "Super Ball" and decided it would be great to make the football championship the "Super Bowl."

Certainly, the game has become super in every aspect. The turning point in the game's history came with Super Bowl III, between the Baltimore Colts of the NFL and the New York Jets of the AFL. Jets quarterback Joe Namath (*photo, below*), a flamboyant playboy off the field, predicted his team would win, and it did. His boldness, coupled with the upset victory, catapulted the popularity of the game, which has grown ever since.

Now the Super Bowl has taken on an identity of its own. For one Sunday afternoon every January, the nation all but shuts down. The game annually is one of the highest, if not the highest, rated television events of the year. Commercials now sell for more than $1 million for 30 seconds; tickets sell for up to $475 a seat and are scalped for thousands of dollars on the open market. Networks pay the league millions of dollars for the right to televise the game.

The media contingent at a Super Bowl now numbers in the thousands, and the contest is shown throughout the world, mostly on a live basis, to countries that do not even play football. The game has become an excuse for day-long Super Bowl parties throughout the United States and the object of extensive gambling, including everything from legalized betting in Las Vegas to office pools everywhere.

Paul Attner

used his 1960 Olympic gold-medal platform to harangue Soviet journalists about American superiority, the establishment could tolerate his doggerel ("Meeee, wheeeee!"), his boasts ("I am the Greatest!"), and his predictions ("This is no jive/Moore goes in five"). He was on the cover of *Time* magazine before he whipped Sonny Liston to become heavyweight champion in 1964.

But the establishment was never comfortable with the champ after he became Muhammad Ali. The day after he won the title, he declared: "I don't have to be who you want me to be, I'm free to be who I want." He joined the separatist Nation of Islam and became a critic of integration ("I don't want to go where I'm not wanted") and of the Vietnam war ("I ain't got nothing against them Vietcong"). He was stripped of his title just as soon as he refused—on Muslim religious principles—to be drafted into the army.

Eventually, in 1971, the Supreme Court upheld Ali's right to refuse to be drafted, but not before he was denied a license to fight for three years and lost millions in purses and endorsements. In that time of exile from the ring, he was educated by the give and take of the college speakers' circuit, and his popularity soared. Even Americans who were disgusted by his politics and religion respected his willingness to sacrifice for his principles. Antiwar Americans made him their saint. And then, incredibly, he went on to win and lose the title two more times, including his stunning victory against George Foreman in Kinshasa, Zaire, in 1974.

The final role in Ali's operatic life—as a shuffling but unself-conscious Parkinson's-disease patient, a nearly mute speaker for love and tolerance who lit the flame at the 1996 Olympics Games in Atlanta—made him something of a worldwide holy man. Yet despite Ali's almost-universal acclaim, no other athlete ever has taken such principled stands; Ali's victory has seemed Pyrrhic in a time when money earned became the most important sports statistic.

Only Billie Jean King was in his league as a social activist. She may have had even more impact. She was a stereotypical 1950s tomboy who wanted to play baseball and football but had to settle for tennis. The amateur rules routinely were circumvented by under-the-table payments that assured officials control over athletes. Billie Jean's aggressive playing style and shameless self-promotion were matched by her outrage at the so-called "shamateurism" and the sexism. In 1967, when she was the Number 1 woman player in the world, she said she earned about $4,000 in secret payments, far less than the top-ten

men. A year later, she was the engine for so-called Open tennis, in which players could choose to play in tournaments as pros or amateurs. When men took over the professional game and created a double standard of prize money, King helped organize the women's pro tour. Only a cigarette company was willing to sponsor it. In 1973, King, then 29, beat 55-year-old Tennis Hall of Famer Bobby Riggs in a $100,000 winner-take-all tennis match in Houston's Astrodome. The so-called "Battle of the Sexes" was the emblematic event of the women's movement in sport.

But the 1981 disclosure of King's lesbian relationship closed the door on major endorsements for her, although she went on to develop pro- and recreational-tennis leagues, among other ventures. She learned that, while corporations wanted athletes as salespeople, they wanted ones who carried only sports equipment in their baggage.

Michael Jordan

It was not surprising that by the late 1980s the world's most expensive supermodel (not necessarily role model) was a handsome bas-

(Continued on page 361.)

Billie Jean King, who won 12 major singles titles in tennis—including six Wimbledons, top—promoted the women's sports movement. Muhammad Ali, above, was stripped of his heavyweight-boxing title for refusing to be drafted into U.S. military service. He later was allowed to return to the ring.

The 20th-century sports world was filled with memorable moments and especially gifted athletes. In 1997, Ukraine's legendary pole vaulter Sergei Bubka, left, became the first person to win gold medals at six World Track and Field Championships. In 1973, Secretariat, the Horse of the Year for 1972, captured the Kentucky Derby, above, the Preakness, and the Belmont Stakes. He thereby became the ninth winner of horse racing's Triple Crown, and the first since Citation in 1948. Ron Turcotte was the jockey. Seattle Slew and Affirmed took the Triple Crown subsequently—in 1977 and 1978, respectively. At the 1936 Summer Olympics in Berlin, Jesse Owens of the United States, below, won four gold medals—the 100-meter and 200-meter dashes, the long jump, and the 400-meter relay. Owens' performances stunned Germany's Chancellor Adolf Hitler, who saw the Games as a means to showcase Aryan superiority.

Wayne Gretzky, left, became the all-time leading scorer of the National Hockey League (NHL). In the 1980s he led the Edmonton Oilers to four Stanley Cups and was awarded the Hart Trophy as the NHL's most valuable player eight consecutive times. The rebounding abilities of two of professional basketball's outstanding centers—Bill Russell (above, number 6) of the Boston Celtics and Wilt Chamberlain (above, number 13), who played for the Philadelphia 76ers and other teams—delighted fans. American swimmer Mark Spitz, below, left, won seven gold medals at the 1972 Summer Olympics in Munich, West Germany. Baseball-record books, meanwhile, have a special page for Don Larsen, below, who pitched a perfect game for the New York Yankees in the 1956 World Series.

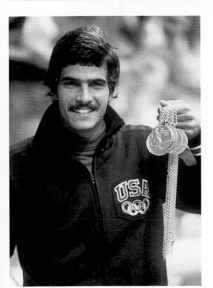

Politics and the Olympics

Perhaps it was inevitable that the modern Olympic Games—envisioned by their founder, Pierre de Coubertin, as the purest of all athletic competitions—could not avoid the ravages of political interference. After all, the Games do not exist in a vacuum; rather, they function amid the ongoing intricacies of the complex everyday world. This became very apparent prior to the 1980 Summer Games in Moscow, when a U.S.-led boycott over political differences with the Soviet Union severely diminished the importance and impact of the event and mixed politics and international sport in a way that never could be reversed. But that defining moment served only as a climax to a long-simmering cauldron involving the Olympics and the political world.

The 1936 Games in Berlin were scarred by the specter of Adolf Hitler, with his Nazi philosophies, extolling white supremacy and grimacing at the accomplishments of Jesse Owens, the fabulous black American sprinter who won four gold medals. World War II forced the cancellation of the 1940 and 1944 Games, but the Olympics managed to function smoothly again from 1948 until 1972, when the Summer extravaganza in Munich was marred by a terrorist attack by Palestinian guerrillas on Israel's team in the Olympic Village. Eleven athletes, five terrorists, and one policeman were killed before the kidnapping was aborted.

That tragedy opened the floodgates to political interference. In 1976 the Summer Games in Montreal were boycotted by 32 nations, including more than 20 black African countries. Those African countries stayed home in protest over New Zealand's participation, since New Zealand's rugby team had played in apartheid South Africa. Then, in 1980 the Americans led a boycott stemming from the 1979 Soviet invasion of Afghanistan, which Western nations vehemently opposed. Some countries that did travel to Moscow (*photo, left*) used the Games to register their own protest; some carried the Olympic flag during the opening ceremonies instead of their national flag. With only 81 countries represented at those Games—and without such powers as the United States, West Germany, and Japan—the event lost much of its impact.

Likewise, the 1984 Summer Games at Los Angeles suffered mightily from the absence of the Soviet bloc. Those countries claimed they did not go to Los Angeles due to concerns about security, but their refusal was an obvious retaliation for the U.S. boycott of the Moscow Games. Fortunately, calmer political developments helped restore continuity to the Olympic movement in time for the 1988 Games in Seoul. Only five nations, notably Cuba and Ethiopia, sat out these Games. Still, they were not without tension. North Korea, the staunch enemy of South Korea, did not participate, and the threat of some terrorist attack by the North Koreans during the Games hung over the event. By 1992 the Soviet bloc was disintegrating, and the Games at Barcelona welcomed a record number of countries.

Paul Attner

Major League Baseball returned to its glory days during 1998, as Mark McGwire of the St. Louis Cardinals, above, and Sammy Sosa of the Chicago Cubs were engaged in a dramatic home-run race.

(Continued from page 357.)

ketball wizard who kept his politics and private life to himself. Michael Jordan was not only the greatest basketball player of all time but one of the greatest athletes, period. "Air Jordan" was also the quintessential athletic commodity. His agents and producers packaged him brilliantly as performer, peddler, and entrepreneur. Post-Ali, he grew up in a time when blacks were being channeled into sports, with high schools scouting elementary schools, colleges outbidding each other, and professional teams hiring doctors and psychologists to vet the blue-chip prizes. Drugs were rampant as training aids.

Jordan did it the old-fashioned way. He drove himself and his teammates mercilessly. He actually was cut from his high-school squad in his sophomore year, yet elbowed back to play high-school ball and to become a University of North Carolina star in the early 1980s under coach Dean Smith. He carried the Chicago Bulls to six National Basketball Association titles. In the 1992 Barcelona Olympics, he led the so-called Dream Team, the first American professional-basketball players in the hitherto "amateur" games, on a triumphant march to the gold medal. His first retirement, to play baseball, was endearing; even the world's greatest athlete had a sports dream beyond his grasp. But his second retire-

ment, after the triumphant 1997–98 season, left pro basketball in disarray. There was no backup star of Jordan's appeal.

By the final year of the century, the Olympics were reeling after it was revealed that International Olympic Committee members had accepted payoffs to vote for host cities. Of the major sports, only baseball seemed to resonate with some of that old-time feeling. That sport still was glowing from the 1998 season, in which Mark McGwire hit 70 home runs, while being chased by Sammy Sosa, who hit 66.

That sense of innocent enthusiasm, of sports as a muscular meritocracy in which character would be forged, seemed to have been overwhelmed by a century of sport as a stage for characters who could push product. Jim, the Babes, Joe, Billie Jean, and even Ali had their huckstering moments, but selling had seemed like a sideline, not a goal. Post–Air Jordan, the lessons of the arena were less clear; there was no doubt of Michael's passion for his game, but he seemed to work just as hard scoring with sneakers, soft drinks, cologne, and telephone services. Maybe the fans' ultimate triumph would be in seeing past the jingle of the golden rings to the original lure of sports, the joyous pleasures of spirit and flesh.

Robert Lipsyte

TRENDS AND FADS

Poet Ralph Waldo Emerson wrote, "Each age has its own follies, as its majority is made up of foolish young people." The 20th century, which has been called "the American Century," was no different. After Americans threw off the constraints of Victorianism and other things European at the start of the century, they went on a century-long binge of establishing a uniquely American culture, some aspects of which were so zany that they defy explanation.

They kept pet rocks, yet swallowed goldfish. They wore string bikinis and granny dresses. They played with Silly Putty and wore happy-face buttons. They danced the mashed potato and then became couch potatoes.

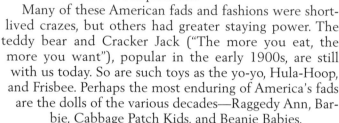

Many of these American fads and fashions were short-lived crazes, but others had greater staying power. The teddy bear and Cracker Jack ("The more you eat, the more you want"), popular in the early 1900s, are still with us today. So are such toys as the yo-yo, Hula-Hoop, and Frisbee. Perhaps the most enduring of America's fads are the dolls of the various decades—Raggedy Ann, Barbie, Cabbage Patch Kids, and Beanie Babies.

Music and dance, from the jitterbug to the twist and disco, kept Americans on the dance floors during the 20th century. Will any of these dances be revived? Do not be surprised if they are. In the late 1990s the big-band sound of the 1930s returned—and Americans eagerly took to the dance floors to hear the music and dance the dances their parents and grandparents loved. That is the power of nostalgia. For more nostalgia, we offer you some of the frivolous fads and fabulous fashions of the past century.

1900–1909

The Teddy Bear The Teddy Bear is named for one of the most popular U.S. presidents—Theodore "Teddy" Roosevelt. In 1902, when Roosevelt was on a hunting trip in Mississippi, some friends captured an old bear, tied it to a tree, and invited Roosevelt to "take aim." He refused, saying he would not shoot a defenseless animal. Newspapers across the country reported the story, but got the facts wrong. *The Washington Post*, for example, published a cartoon that showed Roosevelt refusing to shoot a bear cub. That cartoon gave one New York shopkeeper an idea. He created some stuffed toy bears and sent one to Roosevelt, asking permission to call the toys "Teddy Bears." The president agreed—and the teddy bear was born. It was as popular in the late 1990s as it had been nearly 100 years earlier.

Cracker Jack "Take me out to the ball game,
Take me out to the park,
Buy me some peanuts and Cracker Jack,
I don't care if I never get back."

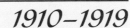

This still-popular 1908 baseball song ensured Cracker Jack's place in American pop culture. But F.W. Rueckheim's popcorn, peanut, and molasses confection was a popular treat before that. Concocted in the 1870s and sold by the barrelful to retailers, it was a big hit at the 1893 World Columbian Exposition in Chicago. When a Rueckheim salesman tasted it, he shouted, "That's crackerjack!"—using a phrase of the time that meant "fantastic." Rueckheim soon put his confection into boxes to sell directly to the public and called the treat Cracker Jack. The box featured a boy, Sailor Jack, and his dog, Bingo. Sailor Jack was modeled after Rueckheim's grandson—and Bingo stood for the prize in every box. The prizes, which mirror 20th-century American culture, have included everything from tin whistles to warplane cards.

1910–1919

Construction Toys As factory workers were building everything from cars to warplanes during the 20th century's teen years, youngsters were building too—with their Erector Sets, Tinker Toys, and Lincoln Logs. Using the metal sheets, girders, nuts, bolts, wheels, and gears of their Erector Sets, they turned out windmills, bridges, and other structures. The Erector Set was introduced in 1913 by A.C. Gilbert, a physician and accomplished magician. Charles Pajeau, a tombstone cutter, developed another construction toy—the Tinker Toy. Its wooden dowels and wooden spools with holes drilled in them could be assembled into structures as elaborate as windmills and carousels. The simplest of the construction toys was Lincoln Logs. Its creator, John L. Wright, son of architect Frank Lloyd Wright, hit the jackpot by tapping into the patriotic image of President Abraham Lincoln and the log cabin in which he was born. Soon, youngsters everywhere were busy constructing their own log cabins, forts, and other frontier buildings.

Cuddly Dolls The 20th century's teen years also saw the introduction of Raggedy Ann and Kewpie dolls. With her red-yarn hair, black-button eyes, triangular red nose, and ear-to-ear smile, Raggedy Ann was the brainchild of John and Myrtle Gruelle. They created the doll for their daughter, Marcella—who, sadly, died in 1916. But Marcella's father, a book illustrator, went on to write and illustrate the Raggedy Ann stories. In the 1920s he gave Raggedy Ann a brother named Raggedy Andy. While Raggedy Ann started out as a doll and ended up in print, the Kewpie appeared in print before it became a doll. Kewpies, so-called because they had the cherubic look of a Cupid, were created by Rose O'Neill to illustrate stories that she wrote for *Women's Home Companion*. Almost all Kewpie dolls were male, and their pudgy-cheeked, wide-eyed look made them wildly popular.

1920–1929

Flappers They were young and rebellious. They wore bobbed hair, thigh-high skirts, rolled-down stockings, and lots of makeup. They smoked and drank in public. And when they were not on the road in fast cars, they were on the dance floor doing wild dances like the Charleston and Black Bottom. Known as "flappers," these young women and their boyfriends—their "sheikhs"—were the "flaming youth" of the Roaring 20s, a period of prosperity in America. The flappers symbolized the restlessness of an America that was reexamining its social structure and its values.

The flapper style first appeared on college campuses, then was picked up by young working women. They copied the dress and lifestyle shown in magazines and onscreen by such movie "vamps" as Theda Bara and Clara Bow, and they sought thrills and pleasure. But when the stock market crashed in 1929, bringing about the Great Depression, the flappers' pursuit of pleasure ended as suddenly as did American prosperity.

Flagpole Sitting Dance marathons, rocking-chair derbies, and transcontinental marathon races were among the other fads of the 1920s, but none was zanier than flagpole sitting. For days and weeks at a time, men and women would sit on flagpoles or high up in trees, attracting crowds of curiosity seekers and surviving on food that they hauled up by rope. The fad was started in 1924 by a former boxer named Alvin "Shipwreck" Kelly, when he was paid to draw attention to a Hollywood movie theater by sitting on a flagpole. Before long, copycat pole sitters appeared, and flagpole sitting became a nationwide craze. When the stock market crashed in 1929, flagpole sitting followed the flappers into obscurity.

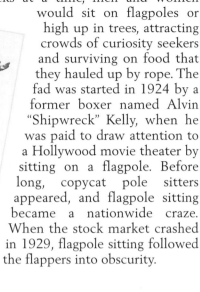

1930–1939

The Jukebox They had names like "Singing Tower," "Throne of Music," and "Luxury Light-Up"; they featured brilliantly colored molded plastics and bubble tubes; they glowed and bubbled and flashed. And if you put a nickel in the slot, they played jazz, blues, and big-band music. These were the magnificent jukeboxes of the 1930s and 1940s, which came about as the result of the invention of sound amplification and the automatic record changer. When jukeboxes were installed in soda fountains, diners, bars, and hotels, people got up to dance to their favorite tunes.

When the machines were introduced, dance halls already were being called "juke joints" by African-Americans—"juke" is an adaptation of an African word that means "dance"—so the new machines were called jukeboxes. The high-tech CD jukeboxes of the 1990s could play many more songs—up to 1,500 of them—but for sheer beauty, they could not compare to the old-timers. As one individual put it, the jukeboxes so popular in the 1930s and 1940s were a "feast for the eyes as well as an enchantment for the ears."

The Yo-Yo Rock the baby; walk the dog; milk the cow. These are not chores for someone to do—they are some of the fancy tricks you can perform with the yo-yo, one of the most popular toys of all time. Children played with toys similar to yo-yos 3,000 years ago in China. But the modern version originated in the Philippines several hundred years ago, as a weapon. Filipinos used a large yo-yo–like weapon to hunt animals, much as the aborigines of Australia used the boomerang. They called it a *yo-yo*, which in their language meant "come back." Soon, Filipino children were using a small version as a toy. In the late 1920s, Pedro Flores, a Filipino living in the United States, began making the toy. He sold the rights to Donald F. Duncan, who began manufacturing O-Boy Yo-Yo Tops, kicking off the yo-yo fad of the 1930s.

1940–1949

The Jitterbug At the start of the 20th century, dance enthusiasts loved the elegant but slow-paced waltz and two-step. But dances soon became more lively, with the Charleston and Black Bottom of the Roaring 20s and the Lindy and Big Apple of the Depression years. For sheer exuberance, however, nothing equaled the frenetic quality of the jitterbug. Born in the 1930s in Harlem, the jitterbug swept the nation during the World War II years. Jitterbuggers loved swinging their bobby-sox partners between their legs and over their heads. Older Americans called the jitterbug "shocking" and "immodest," but teenagers loved the shuffling back-and-forth movements, combined with the high-flying gymnastics.

The Zoot Suit In ballrooms and jazz clubs, the zoot suit was a common sight in the early 1940s. It was named by Harold Fox, a clothier and trumpet player. His creation included a very long jacket with big, padded shoulders and wide lapels, and high-waisted pants that ballooned out at the top and tapered abruptly to a narrow cuff. "Zoot suiters," such as bandleader Cab Calloway (*photo, left*), added to the look by wearing a wide-brimmed hat and a long, looping watch chain. But this fashion fad was short-lived. These were the war years, and the government needed fabric for military uniforms, so zoot suits and other clothing that wasted material soon were prohibited.

1950–1959

Drive-In Movies Americans love cars—by the late 1950s there were 50 million of them on the road. And they love movies—every week during the late 1950s, 40 million people flocked to the nation's 20,000 movie houses, of which 4,000 were drive-ins. It was Richard M. Hollingshead, an inventor, who first thought of combining America's two greatest loves. In 1933 he opened the world's first drive-in movie theater, in Camden, NJ. People loved the idea. By the 1950s, there was a speaker for each car, so people could watch movies on giant screens without getting out of their cars. Teenagers could turn an evening at the movies into a date, and parents could take their children, so they did not have to get baby-sitters. At century's end, there were only a few hundred drive-ins left, but nostalgic filmgoers could look back with fondness at the 1950s—the golden age of the drive-in movie.

The Hula-Hoop In 1958 a toy company named Wham-O handed out some colorful plastic hoops, 3 feet (1 meter) in diameter, to a bunch of young people in California. Soon the youngsters were rotating their hips to make the hoops whirl around their waists. When their antics were shown on television, the Hula-Hoop fad was born. Wham-O called the hoops "Hula-Hoops" because the movements used to make the hoops twirl around the waist were similar to the movements used in the Hawaiian hula dance. The Hula-Hoop became such a craze that other companies copied Wham-O's hoops, giving their products such names as Spin-A-Hoops, Hoop Zings, Hooper-Doopers, and Whoop-de-dos. "The biggest fad in history" soon ended, but not before more than 100 million hoops had been sold in the United States alone. The hoops retained some popularity and still were sold at the dawn of the 21st century.

1960–1969

Barbie Dolls When Barbie, the "anatomically perfect" fashion doll, was introduced in 1959, many people said it would not sell. "Fashion dolls are dead," said one critic. "Too sexy," said another. How wrong they were! More than 500 million Barbies have been sold since then. What accounted for the immediate popularity of this 11 3/4-inch (29.8-centimeter) doll? Was it her big blue eyes and mascaraed eyelashes? Her smiling red lips and painted fingernails and toenails? As time went on, perhaps it was the fact that she was presented as a modern woman with many careers—from model to nurse to Olympic athlete—and many more wardrobe changes. In the 1990s, Barbie was most popular with girls between the ages of 4 and 9, who loved to dress her up. But there were Barbie fan clubs and magazines for adults, and serious collectors would pay $2,000 for an original 1959 Barbie that sold then for $3. Some people have said that the long-legged Barbie is a role model for anorexia, or that she is too materialistic. But as the 20th century ended, she remained the most popular doll ever made.

Miniskirts While little girls were dressing their Barbies in a variety of outfits, big girls were dressing themselves in miniskirts—the fashion fad of the 1960s. Credit for this fad belongs to Mary Quant, an English fashion pioneer who became known as the "mother of the miniskirt." Miniskirts were tight—and, as the name suggests, short. Modest minis ended 4 inches (10 centimeters) above the knee, but the most daring ones climbed to 10 inches (25 centimeters) above the knee. Parents, like those who witnessed their daughters dressed flap-

per-style in the Roaring 20s, were aghast. But young women loved the mini, and they loved the go-go boots and other accessories that went with it. The mini gave them freedom, they said—freedom to dance the twist, the frug, and other dances of the 1960s, and freedom to express their distinct individuality.

Disco Dancing Disco clubs, disco music, disco dancing, disco fashions— the 1970s were the Disco Decade. The word "disco" came from France—where, years earlier, jitterbuggers and swing enthusiasts had taken to the dance floors at clubs known as *discothèques*. But when disco reached the United States in the 1970s, it took on a whole different beat. The jitterbug and swing were out, and at such hot nightspots as New York's Peppermint Lounge and Studio 54, the pulsating, rocking Hustle and Bump were in. TV star John Travolta's dazzling portrayal of a disco dancer in the 1977 film *Saturday Night Fever* lured millions of fans to discos to gyrate to such popular songs as Donna Summer's "Love to Love You Baby" and the Bee Gees' "Stayin' Alive," which was on the sound track of *Saturday Night Fever*.

Mood Rings and Pet Rocks Are you blissful or depressed? Angry or contented? To find out, during the 1970s all you had to do was slip a mood ring on one of your fingers. According to its creators—and masterful marketers—the ring's stone, which was a heat-sensitive crystal, would change color according to the wearer's mood. As one columnist quipped, it was a "thermometer of the mind." Mood rings went for anywhere from $2 to $250, and tens of millions of them were sold in the mid-1970s.

Gary Dahl's mood ring probably showed that he was in a state of euphoria—because in 1975 he came up with the idea of the pet rock. Rocks, he said, were cleaner, better behaved, and less expensive than dogs, cats, birds, fish, or other pets. The American public bought it—but probably just for the fun of it. And Gary Dahl became an instant millionaire.

Rubik's Cube What could be moved into more than 43 quintillion different positions—and could drive people crazy? It was Rubik's Cube, the frustratingly fabulous fad of 1980–81. Invented by Hungarian architecture professor Erno Rubik, it was a six-sided plastic cube with three rows of three colored squares on each side. To solve the puzzle, one had to rotate the rows of colored squares until all nine squares of the same color were on one side of the cube. Some bright people did it in less than a minute; others, frustrated, smashed the puzzle to smithereens. Frustrating or not, millions of the puzzles were sold.

Smurfs and Cabbage Patch Kids Much more soothing than Rubik's Cube were Smurfs and Cabbage Patch Kids, the must-have fad characters of the 1980s. Smurfs, invented as cartoon characters in Belgium in the late 1950s, were 2-inch (5-cm)-high statuettes that looked like blue gnomes and featured such names as Brainy, Greedy, Clumsy, Grumpy, and Jokey—and, of course, Papa Smurf. All were males except for one female "Smurfette." The Smurfs became a craze in 1982 after NBC began a Saturday-morning Smurf cartoon television series. A year after Smurfs hit the big time, the cuddly, funny-looking Cabbage Patch Kids came on the scene. Chubby and soft, each doll came with its own name, birth certificate, and "adoption papers." While the craze for Smurfs and Cabbage Patch Kids faded, they still were sold in the late 1990s—and many were collector's items.

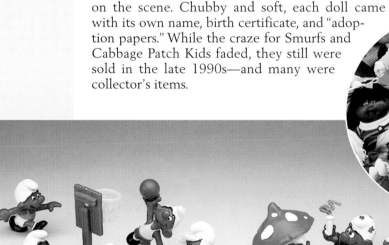

Beanie Babies Humphrey the camel; Fortune the panda; Chocolate the Moose; Fleece the lamb; Spike the rhinoceros; Peanut the elephant. Is this the start of an inventory of the San Diego Zoo? No! These are Beanie Babies, the tiny, squishy beanbag animals that have sold in the hundreds of millions; they were introduced in 1994 by Ty Inc. Some Beanie Babies that originally sold for $5 were going for $1,000 or more by 1999. What is the appeal? Beanie Babies are cuddly; their bodies, which are filled with plastic pellets, not real beans, can be posed. Kids love them, and children and adults collect them. When would the fad for Beanie Babies end? It looked as though they would be around into the 21st century.

1990–1999

Cyberpets Tamagotchis, Dino Pets, Nano Pets, and Giga Pets are not as cuddly as Beanie Babies, but these cyberpets were another craze of the 1990s. The small electronic devices beep their owners to alert them, with demands such as "Pet me!" and "Feed me!" displayed on a tiny screen. When the cyberpet owners—mostly kids—respond by pressing buttons on the device, their screen "pets" flourish and grow. If they do not respond, the cyberpets disappear into cyberspace. Does this worry youngsters? No—all they have to do is hit the reset button, and their cyberpet reappears. Cyberpets became so popular after they were introduced in 1997 that some teachers banned them from classrooms.

William E. Shapiro

ADVISERS AND CONTRIBUTORS

Advisers

The World Scene
ARTHUR CAMPBELL TURNER
Professor Emeritus of Political Science,
University of California, Riverside

The U.S. Scene
ROBERT SHOGAN
National Political Correspondent, Washington Bureau,
The Los Angeles Times

Business and Industry
DAVID R. FRANCIS
Senior Economics Correspondent,
The Christian Science Monitor

Science and Technology
LOUIS LEVINE
Professor of Biology,
The City College of New York

Contributors

THOMAS B. ALLEN, Freelance Writer, Bethesda, MD; Coauthor, *America at War 1941–45, CNN: War in the Gulf*: **Instability and a Second World War; Atomic Bomb; Korean War**

PAUL ATTNER, Senior Writer, *The Sporting News*: **Michael Jordan; Football's Super Bowl—Sports' Biggest Extravaganza; Politics and the Olympics**

ADRIEL BETTELHEIM, Medical and Science Writer, *CQ Researcher*: **The Environmental Movement; Medicine and Health; AIDS**

GERALD BORDMAN, Author, *Oxford Companion to American Theatre*: **The Broadway Musical**

BARBARA J. BRAASCH, Freelance Travel Writer, Palo Alto, CA: **Travel**

LES BROWN, Author, *The New York Times Encyclopedia of Television, Keeping Your Eye on Television*: **Television; Public Television; African-Americans on Television; Cable Television**

JANUSZ BUGAJSKI, Director of East European Studies, Center for Strategic and International Studies, Washington, DC; Author, *Ethnic Politics in Eastern Europe: A Guide to Nationality Policies, Organizations and Parties*: **The Breakup of Yugoslavia**

ARDATH W. BURKS, Professor Emeritus, Asian Studies, Rutgers University; Author, *Third Order of the Rising Sun*: **Japan's Post–World War II Economic Rise**

BETTY BOYD CAROLI, Author, *First Ladies, The Roosevelt Women*: **Eleanor Roosevelt**

DAVID C. CASSIDY, Professor, Natural Science Program, Hofstra University; Author, *Einstein and Our World*: **Albert Einstein**

SUSAN E. CAYLEFF, Chair, Department of Women's Studies, San Diego State University; Author, *The Life and Legend of Babe Didrikson Zaharias*: **Babe Didrikson Zaharias**

MITCHELL L. COHEN, M.D., Director, Division of Bacterial and Mycotic Diseases, National Center for Infectious Diseases, Centers for Disease Control and Prevention, Atlanta, Georgia: **The Wonder Drugs**

DAVID P. CONRADT, Professor of Political Science, East Carolina University; Author, *The German Polity, West European Politics*: **Adolf Hitler**

MARY H. COOPER, Staff Writer, *CQ Researcher*; Author, *The Business of Drugs*: **OPEC; Women's Liberation Movement; Business and Industry—Overview; Smoking**

JOHN CUNNIFF, Business News Analyst, The Associated Press; Author, *How to Stretch Your Dollar*: **The Conglomerate**

CHET CURRIER, Financial Writer, The Associated Press; Author, *The Investor's Encyclopedia, The 15-Minute Investor*: **The Great Stock-Market Crash of 1929**

ROBERT DALLEK, Professor of History, Boston University; Author, *Franklin D. Roosevelt and American Foreign Policy, 1932–1945*: **Franklin Delano Roosevelt**

LEONARD DAVID, Director, Space Data Resources and Information: **Space Exploration; "One Giant Leap for Mankind"; The Challenger Disaster**

GEORGE ESENWEIN, Associate Professor of History, University of Florida; Coauthor, *Spain at War: The Spanish Civil War in Historical Perspective*: **The Spanish Civil War**

LENORA FOERSTEL, Author, *Confronting the Margaret Mead Legacy: Scholarships, Empire, and the South Pacific*: **Margaret Mead**

DAVID R. FRANCIS, Senior Economics Correspondent, *The Christian Science Monitor*: **Banking; The Steel Industry**

RICHARD M. FRIED, Professor of History, University of Illinois at Chicago; Author, *Men Against McCarthy, Nightmare in Red: The McCarthy Era in Perspective*: **McCarthyism**

MAYNARD M. GORDON, Senior Editor, *Ward's Dealer Business* magazine; Author, *The Iacocca Management Technique*: **Henry Ford; The Automobile Industry**

LAWRENCE GROSSMAN, Director of Publications, The American Jewish Committee: **The Holocaust**

ALEXANDER J. GROTH, Professor Emeritus of Political Science, University of California, Davis; Author, *People's Poland, Contemporary Politics: Europe*: **Solidarity**

NATHAN HALE, Jr., Author, *The Rise and Crisis of Psychoanalysis in the United States; Freud and the Americans, 1917–1985, Vol. 2*: **Sigmund Freud**

JONATHAN E. HELMREICH, Professor of History Emeritus, Allegheny College; Author, *Belgium and Europe: A Study in Small Power Diplomacy*; Coauthor, *Rebirth: A History of Europe Since World War II*: **The Search for a New Stability**

CHARLES K. HOYT, Fellow, American Institute of Architects; Author, *More Places for People, Building for Commerce and Industry*: **Frank Lloyd Wright; Skyscrapers**

PEPE KARMEL, Adjunct Assistant Curator, Department of Painting and Sculpture, The Museum of Modern Art, New York, NY; Coauthor, *Jackson Pollock*: **Pablo Picasso**

HILTON KRAMER, Art Critic; Editor and Publisher, *The New Criterion*: **Arts and Entertainment—Overview**

MARC LEEPSON, Freelance Writer: **Prohibition; Social Security; The Assassination of John F. Kennedy; The Woodstock Generation**

JOHN R. LEVINE, Freelance Writer, Lecturer, Consultant on Computers; Author, *Internet for Dummies*: **The Internet**

LOUIS LEVINE, Professor, Department of Biology, City College of New York; Author, *Biology of the Gene, Biology for a Modern Society*: **DNA: The Molecule of the Century; Cloning: A Worldwide Issue**

ROBERT LIPSYTE, Sports Columnist, *The New York Times*; Author, *Sports World: An American Dreamland*: **Sports**

EDWARD MALONEY, Professor of English, Ohio State University; Cocreator, James Joyce Resource Center on the Web: **James Joyce**

ROBERT MENDEZ, M.D., Professor of Urology and Surgery, USC School of Medicine; Director, Multi-Organ Transplant Program: **Organ Transplantation**

ARUNA NAYYAR MICHIE, Department of Political Science, Kansas State University: **Mohandas Gandhi**

RANDALL M. MILLER, Department of History, St. Joseph's University; Author, *Shades of the Sunbelt: Essays on Ethnicity, Race and the Urban South*: **Martin Luther King, Jr.; Brown v. Board of Education of Topeka, KS; The 1963 March on Washington**

JOHN MILWARD, Freelance Writer and Critic: **Elvis Presley; Rock 'n' Roll**

THE REV. RICHARD JOHN NEUHAUS, Editor in Chief, *First Things*; President, Institute on Religion and Public Life, New York, NY: **John Paul II; The Second Vatican Council**

A. MICHAEL NOLL, Professor of Communication, Annenberg School for Communication, University of Southern California, Los Angeles, California: **Communications**

PATRICK O'MEARA, Dean of International Programs, Indiana University; Coeditor, *Africa, International Politics in Southern Africa, Southern Africa, The Continuing Crisis*: **Nelson Rolihlahla Mandela**

DON PERETZ, Professor Emeritus of Political Science, State University of New York at Binghamton; Author, *The West Bank—History, Politics, Society and Economy, Government and Politics of Israel, The Middle East Today*: **The Birth of Israel; Egypt-Israel Rapprochement**

ERIC QUIÑONES, Freelance Writer; Former Writer, *The Associated Press*: **William Henry Gates III**

WILLIAM L. RICHTER, Associate Provost for International Programs, Kansas State University: **Confrontation and Détente**

MICHAEL RIORDAN, Physicist and Science Historian, Stanford Linear Accelerator Center, Stanford University; Coauthor, *Crystal Fire: The Invention of the Transistor and the Birth of the Information Age*: **The Transistor**

J. MARTIN ROCHESTER, Professor, Department of Political Science, University of Missouri—St. Louis; Author, *Waiting for the Millennium: The United Nations and the Future of World Order*: **The United Nations**

DARRELL SALK, M.D., Vice-President, Clinical Affairs, Targeted Genetics Corporation, Seattle, WA: **Jonas Salk**

DAN SCHLOSSBERG, Author, *The Baseball IQ Challenge, The Baseball Book of Why, Cooperstown: Baseball's Hall of Fame Players*: **Babe Ruth; Jackie Robinson's Legacy**

WILLIAM E. SHAPIRO, Freelance Writer and Editor, New York City: **20th-Century Time Line 1900–1999; Trends and Fads**

ROBERT SHARLET, Chauncey Winters Professor of Political Science, Union College; Author, *Soviet Constitutional Crisis*: **Joseph Stalin; The Russian Revolution; The Fall of the Soviet Empire and a New Era**

ROBERT SHOGAN, National Political Correspondent, Washington Bureau, *The Los Angeles Times*; Author, *A Question of Judgment, Promises to Keep*: **A New Century, A World War, and the 1920s; Depression, New Deal, Second World War; Truman, the Cold War, and Ike; The New Frontier, Great Society, Civil Rights, and Vietnam; The Cuban Missile Crisis; Richard Nixon, Watergate, and the Aftermath; The Watergate Scandal; The Reagan Revolution and the New Era; Bill Clinton and the Perils of the Presidency**

KATHRYN SPINK, Author, *Mother Teresa: A Complete Authorized Biography*: **Mother Teresa**

JOHN BRYAN STARR, Managing Director, Annenberg Institute for School Reform, Brown University; Author, *Continuing the Revolution: The Political Thought of Mao*; Editor, *The Future of U.S.-China Relations*: **Mao Zedong**

LANA STEIN, Associate Professor of Political Science, University of Missouri–St. Louis: **The Postwar Housing Shortage**

JACK STIEBER, Professor Emeritus, School of Labor and Industrial Relations, Michigan State University; Author, *Manpower Adjustments to Automation and Technological Change in Western Europe*; Editor, *Employment Problems of Automation and Advanced Technology: An International Perspective*: **Automation**

JENNY TESAR, Science Writer; Author, *The New Webster's Computer Handbook*: **Computers; Personal Computers**

ARTHUR CAMPBELL TURNER, Professor Emeritus of Political Science, University of California, Riverside; Author, *The Unique Partnership: Britain and the United States*; Coauthor, *Tension Areas in World Affairs, Ideology and Power in the Middle East*: **Winston Churchill; A New Century, World War, the Search for Peace; North Atlantic Treaty Organization; End of Colonialism in Africa; The Persian Gulf War**

F. ROY WILLIS, Professor of History, University of California, Davis; Author, *France, Germany and the New Europe, 1945–1968, Italy Chooses Europe, The French Paradox*: **Marshall Plan; Steps toward a United Europe**

ROBERT N. WISNER, Professor, Iowa State University; Coeditor, *Marketing for Farmers*; Author, *World Food Trade and U.S. Agriculture*: **Agriculture**

WILLIAM WOLF, New York University; Author, *The Marx Brothers, Landmark Films, The Cinema and Our Century*: **Walt Disney; Motion Pictures; Gone With the Wind; Special Effects**

JOHN WOLFE, Senior Vice-President, American Association of Advertising Agencies: **Advertising**

MICHAEL J. WOODS, Science Editor, Washington Bureau, *The Toledo Blade* and *The Pittsburgh Post Gazette*; Weekly Health Columnist, *The Medical Journal*; Author, *What's Happening in Chemistry*: **Science and Technology—Overview**

MEL J. ZELENAK, Professor of Consumer and Family Economics, University of Missouri-Columbia; Author, *Consumer Economics: The Consumer in Our Society*: **Retailing; The Credit Card**

INDEX

378